THE : SILVER

LIBRARY

ENTRANCE TO THE BAY OF RIO.

THE

CRUISE OF THE "FALCON"

A VOYAGE TO SOUTH AMERICA IN A 30-TON YACHT

BY

E. F. KNIGHT

AUTHOR OF "THE 'FALCON' ON THE BALTIC"
"WHERE THREE EMPIRES MEET," ETC., ETC.

WITH MAPS AND NUMEROUS ILLUSTRATIONS

NEW EDITION

LONGMANS, GREEN, AND CO.
39 PATERNOSTER ROW, LONDON
NEW YORK AND BOMBAY
1904

PREFACE.

In this volume I have told the story of the voyage, extending over a period of twenty months, of my yawl the *Falcon* (eighteen tons register, thirty tons RTM), in South American and West Indian waters.

We left Southampton on the 20th of August, 1880, the crew being composed of four amateurs, three of whom were barristers, and a cabin-boy.

The narrative includes the description of a five months' cruise in the yacht up the Rivers Parana and Paraguay, and of a ride across the Pampas to Tucuman.

The number of miles travelled over by land and sea was roughly 22,000.

THE AUTHOR.

NOTE TO FOURTH EDITION.

~~~~~~~

CIRCUMSTANCES prevented me from resuming my cruise as intended, so I sold the *Falcon* two years ago to a gentleman in St. Vincent.

I was yachting in the West Indies this spring, and borrowed the old boat for a day's sail. She was very dilapidated and quite unfit for any more ocean cruising.

A report has this day reached me that she was destroyed by the terrible hurricane which devastated St. Vincent last month.

THE AUTHOR

September 16th, 1886.

CONTENTS.

~~~~~~~~

LIST OF ILLUSTRATIONS.

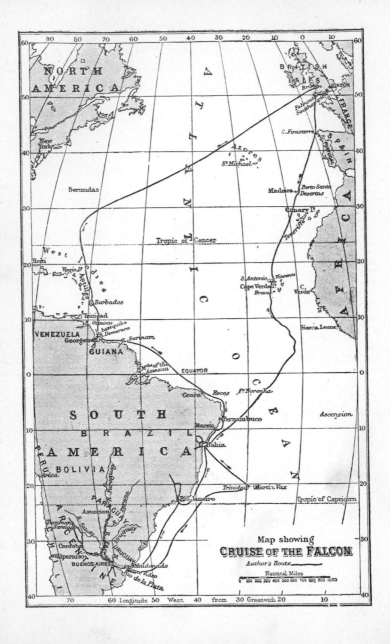

Map showing
CRUISE OF THE FALCON
Author's Route
Nautical Miles
0 100 200 300 400 500 600 700 800 900 1000

THE CRUISE OF THE FALCON.

~~~~~~~

CHAPTER I.

IT was one of those beautiful lazy July days that even London is occasionally blessed with, and which tend to inspire busy man with profound misgivings as to the truth of that trite old lesson, that unremitting toil is his destiny and sole object here below.

My friend Arthur Jerdein and myself, urged by the glory of the weather, concluded that a holiday would be to our moral, physical, and mental advantage, and thereupon acting up to our laudable determination, walked away from the narrow city streets, and took boat at the Temple stairs for the ancient port of Greenwich—a favourite trip of both of us this, but one that never wearied and seemed ever new.

To come out of the confined city, and to steam through the fresh breeze down the grand old river, among the big ocean-going ships, by the stately storehouses, and quaint water-side wharves and slips, has a peculiar fascination of its own, with its manifold suggestions of enterprise in many a strange land and sea. We enjoyed the orthodox fish dinner, had another stroll through the models of antique ships of war and relics of many victories in the hospital, and then lingered, lazily smoking, on the sea platform of the palace, as we waited for the boat to take us back to the unquiet town.

It was indeed a lovely evening—a Thames-side evening as Turner loved to paint, with just that suspicion of haze in the golden atmosphere to tone down all hardness of outline and crudity of colour, and glorify all.

We looked over the waters, saw the barges dropping down with the tide, their tanned sails gleaming like red gold in the western light.

A big vessel passed us—an Australian clipper, crowded with emigrants, who raised a farewell cheer as the last shore-boats left her side. A smart yawl yacht of some sixty tons lay at anchor close in front of us. We looked on all this, silent for a time, but our thoughts were very similar, the surroundings influenced us in like manner.

In all the restless air moved the spirit of travel and adventure. Each sound of chain rattling through hawse-pipe, each smell of tar and odorous foreign wood, each sight was full of reminiscence of far lands, warm seas, and islands of spice. All seemed to say, "Go out on the free seas."

We were both vagabonds, I fear, in disposition, with nomadic blood in our veins, and our previous wanderings had not been few. So far, this summer, various causes had kept me in London, so I was more than usually thirsting after change from city-life—and lo! already there was an autumnal beauty in the sky; it would soon be too late—a summer wasted; all these months of glorious sunshine and breeze—winter was near.

The weariness of the city, the sigh of the autumn wind, the surroundings of travel, all combined to wake a rest-lessness and a regret in me; so too was it with my friend, for when one of us awoke from the reverie and spoke, the conversation was on that of which our hearts were full.

We admired the beautiful yacht riding at anchor. "How well," one said, "to set to work now and fit out with all stores a vessel like that, and with a few good friends sail right away from the coming northern winter – right away for a year or two into summer seas!"

In five minutes—though before leaving London the faintest shadow of such a plan had not fallen on our minds —we decided to follow this impulse, and at the very idea of what we were about to do, all our discontent vanished like a smoke, and a most joyous enthusiasm succeeded it.

As is the custom under such circumstances we retired to the "Ship," with solemn ceremony uncorked a bottle and poured out a libation to propitiate the sea-god, and Æolus of the winds; then we returned to London, light-hearted and full of our plan, to commence preliminary work that very evening.

Thus it was that the cruise of the *Falcon* came about.

My friend Jerdein, I must tell you, has been a sailor, an ex-officer of the Royal Mail and P. and O. Companies. I myself am an amateur mariner, having had many years' experience of fore-and-afters. As skipper, cook, steward, mate, and crew of my little yawl, the *Ripple* of Southampton, in which I used to make periodical descents on the coast of France, I had gained a fair knowledge of practical seamanship. Now what we proposed to do, was to find two or three friends to join us in a lengthened cruise in a small yacht, say of twenty tons burden. The idea was that we should sail her ourselves, and dispense altogether with a professional crew—an advantage in a small vessel.

On our return to town we exposed ourselves to some chaff when we revealed our grand scheme. Those who did not doubt our sincerity were dubious of our sanity, and unhesitatingly expressed their opinion that both the boat and the crew would be found at about the Greek Kalends.

But before many days had passed we found the vessel ; and very lucky we were in her ; had we searched all round the British Isles we could have discovered nothing so perfectly adapted for our purpose.

I had written to Mr. Pickett, of Stockham and Pickett, Southampton, who had built the *Ripple* for me, asking him if he knew of any vessel that would suit us. He wrote back and told me that there was the very thing for us laid up for sale in his yard, alongside the *Ripple*.

So Jerdein and myself took the next train to Southampton to inspect her.

We found the *Falcon* to be a yawl of eighteen tons register ; thirty tons yacht measurement, a boat of exceptionally strong construction, for she had been built in Penzance for a fishing-lugger, and the Penzance luggers have the reputation of being the strongest and best sea boats of their size.

She had a square stern, which did not perhaps improve her beauty, but gave her a character of her own, and pole masts. Her length was forty-two feet, her beam thirteen, and her draught about seven feet and a half.

She was a most solid vessel, looking as if she meant business, perfectly sound and possessing a fair inventory, so it was not long before I had arranged matters with her owners, and became the proud possessor of the gallant little craft that was to be my home for nearly two years.

Jerdein and myself left London, and at once commenced to fit her out, for we were anxious to sail away into calm seas before the autumnal equinox was on us with its gales.

There was plenty to do; we had her coppered well above the water-line, fitted her with water-tanks and biscuit-lockers, reduced her canvas, and ordered spare and storm-sails. Beside her main, jib-headed mizen, fore-staysail, and jib, she carried a sliding gunter gaff-topsail, and a spinnaker.

We procured all the necessary charts, directories, nautical instruments, stored away some nine months' provisions, decorated the main cabin walls with arms for defence and sport—Martini-Henry rifles, cutlasses, and revolvers, and purchased a small brass swivel gun with grape and canister.

No one who has not undertaken to fit out even so small a vessel for a cruise of years over tens of thousands of miles of ocean, can conceive how much there is to think of and provide for.

The report of our proceedings spread in Southampton.

Long-shore loafers, yachting-men, and others took an interest in the curious expedition of an amateur crew in so small a craft, and there was generally a small crowd watching the preparations that made Pickett's yard noisy with sound of hammering, sawing, and caulking. Jerdein and myself were employed for three days in unpacking and storing away bales of tinned meats and other stores.

Hearing that we did not intend to take professionals with us, many affected to disbelieve in us, jeered at our plans and prophesied we should weary of the trip before we got out of the chops of the Channel, put into Cherbourg, stay there a week or so, and then return.

By some ill-omened soothsayers we were advised to paint the vessel's name conspicuously on her keel, so that she would be easily recognized when found floating upside down on some sea or other.

West Quay, however, believed in us, and Pickett was enthusiastic on the subject and sanguine as to our success; but he and others too would often inquire, "Here are you and Mr. Jerdein, but where's the rest of the crew? We have not seen them yet."

With great difficulty we found two gentlemen to join us, Mr. Andrews and Mr. Arnaud, but unfortunately neither of these had the slightest idea of sailing a boat. They knew nothing whatever of nautical matters.

At last they turned up in Southampton, and Pickett's yard came out to study them. The yacht sailors looked on with interest as one of these bold would-be circumnavigators in top hat and kid gloves, with gingerly steps carefully ascended the ladder which lay against the *Falcon's* side, reached the deck, and, looking round, remarked with quite a nautical air, as he hitched up his trousers, "What a lot of strings there are about this boat! I shall never know the use of them all."

West Quay likewise studied bold circumnavigator Number Two, smiled, and shrugged its shoulders.

This was certainly not a promising crew to take across the Atlantic, and no one knew this better than Jerdein and myself.

Thus were we bound to add another member to our crew, who was of much more use, though small in volume.

This was a small boy, a very small boy of about fifteen, homeless and characterless, who was loafing about West Quay in search of odd jobs, a half-starved, melancholy, silent little wretch, who had been the recipient of more kicks than halfpence during his short existence. On questioning him, we found he had been two years on board a North Sea fishing boat—no gentle school.

When we offered him a berth on the *Falcon* he gladly accepted it.

He never smiled then, that boy—he does now. When we first engaged him, Jerdein catechized him thus :—"What is your name?" "Arthur." "Can you steer by compass?" "Yes." "Can you make a bowline-knot on this piece of string?" He satisfactorily accomplished this feat. "Do you ever get drunk?" "Ain't often got the chance, sir." "Do you ever smile?" "Yes, sir." This response came out doubtfully, and forthwith he tried to screw something like a smile out of his despondent features. It was a ghastly failure ; his muscles were unaccustomed to the necessary movements, and worked rustily and with effort. Perhaps it was well for him that he could not smile during the early stages of our voyage, for there *were* things to smile at ; deeds of eccentric seamanship on the part of some of the crew, at the which, were he to have smiled, a box on the ears might have brought him back to his normal melancholy.

Others now volunteered to join the *Falcon ;* stewards and French cooks, reading of a proposed lengthy cruise in the papers, came for engagements, beheld the vessel and her crew, shook their heads, and vanished.

As far as the provisions were concerned, the *Falcon* was well supplied. We had stores sufficient for five men for nine months, consisting, among other things, of 400 lbs. of biscuits and nearly 1000 tins of preserved meats, vegetables, &c. A supply of lime juice was, of course, not forgotten, and an ample cask of rum was securely screwed down in the main cabin. We carried about 250 gallons of water, which we reckoned would last us three months with proper precautions. On our long passages, as across the Atlantic, all washing with fresh water was of course forbidden. We did not omit to take with us some tinned plum-puddings wherewith to keep up in orthodox form the Christmas days which we should spend on the *Falcon.*

We shipped yet another hand before we sailed. Mrs. Pickett presented us with a little kitten to take with us. Poor little thing ! it purred merrily and romped about when it first came on board, little knowing what was before it.

Before starting, the discipline of the ship had to be arranged, and the duties of each apportioned out. Jerdein was officer of the port, I of the starboard watch ; Andrews was on Jerdein's watch, Arnaud on mine. The boy, Arthur, was on no watch, as he had a good deal of lamp-cleaning, &c., in the day. He used to turn in for the night, only steering now and then in the day-time, especially at meal-times in fine weather, when he was left in charge, while we four sat down to table together.

We used to keep four-hour watches, watch and watch, in the usual way, with dog-watches from four p.m. to eight p.m.

The plan of our cruise was as follows : To sail by easy

stages to Buenos Ayres, and then navigate the great tributaries of the River Plate, the Parana and Paraguay, as high
as we could in the yacht. We had heard much of the
glories of those huge streams, and of the abundant sport to
be found on their wild banks. No yacht had ever ascended
the Paraguay before, and we anticipated a good deal of
novelty and excitement in those fair regions, should we, as
we little doubted, effect our purpose.

CHAPTER II.

WE appointed four p.m., on the 20th of August, 1880—a
Friday, too—for our departure.

That morning the *Falcon*, ready from truck to keel, lay at
anchor off West Quay. The Blue Peter was at the mast-
head, indicating to all friends that we were off at last. West
Quay took a holiday, and a crowd of small boats rowed
round us all the morning, filled with many who wished to
inspect the craft.

At two p.m. we stretched the awning on deck, and a lunch
was spread out for a few friends—a boisterous lunch, in
which many toasts were drunk, and our success warmly
wished. At 3.30 p.m. the bell was rung, the main-sail
hoisted, and as the last shore-boat left our side, up came the
anchor, and, with cheers from the spectators, we dropped
down the river on the top of a good ebb.

Almost all the yachts we passed knew us, and their crews
cheered us lustily. We still had a large company on board,
who insisted on seeing us safe to the chops of the Channel
—two friends from town, Captain Forbes, who had rubbed
up our navigation at Southampton, and a pilot.

At midnight we were outside the Needles, and commenced
to feel the swell of the Channel. The weather was very
favourable for the voyage, a light north-east wind was
blowing, which continued until we dropped our anchor in
Falmouth Harbour on the following midnight, that is,
thirty-two hours after leaving Southampton.

We were now enabled to judge more or less of what stuff
our crew were made during our trial trip. The philosophic

calm which distinguished Arnaud commenced to declare itself. He reclined in his cabin smoking and thinking during the greater part of this voyage; turning out only at meal-times, and evincing no inclination to undertake his due share of the work. On the afternoon after leaving South-ampton, while we were passing the Eddystone lighthouse, he did crawl slowly on to the deck, to our great surprise, with a blanket over his arm. He rubbed his sleepy eyes, looked round with a lazy smile at the smooth sea and cloudless sky, stretched his blanket on the deck, lay down on it, lit a cigarette, and with a half yawn, half sigh of extreme content, said, " I could go round the world like this ! " and resigned himself once more to his beloved *dolce far niente*.

Andrews, though more active and willing than Arnaud, was equally incapable of mastering the very elements of fore-and-aft seamanship, and caused Jerdein, the officer of his watch, as much trouble as Arnaud did me. There was a good deal of hard language to be heard occasionally on board the *Falcon*, sounding above winds and waves, when such an incident as the following, for instance, would occur :—Time, two a.m. Dark and squally night. Knight steering. Arnaud smoking and pondering (supposed to be looking out). Knight, observing squall coming up, *loquitur :*—" Arnaud, just run forward and scandalize the mainsail, will you ; begin by tricing up the tack."

Arnaud creeps deliberately forward, and disappears in the darkness. Five minutes elapse. Knight, impatiently, " Now, then, have not you finished that yet ? "

Arnaud : " In a minute ; in a minute."

Another five minutes elapse ; we are now in the middle of the squall, which does not prove so violent as was anticipated. Knight, very impatient, " You are a nice, useful fellow on board a yacht ! Ten minutes, and you have not triced up that tack ; if that had been a serious squall, we might have gone to the devil while you were fiddling about there."

Arnaud, very indignant, " I do not care. I will leave the beastly thing alone. I will not be sworn at. In the daytime I can find the strings ; in the night I cannot, and I shall no longer try."

Follows a prolonged and very noisy discussion, whereon the face of Jerdein appears above the hatch. " How the blank do you think we can get a wink of sleep down here when you are kicking up such an infernal row ? &c., &c., blank, &c."

This little episode occurred months after leaving England, so the reader will perceive that the education of my friend progressed but slowly. So, too, was it when Jerdein and Andrews were on deck. I was awakened one night by a tremendous row, a banging about of ropes ; and, far louder than all, the stentorian exclamations of the wrathful Jerdein. On coming on deck I found that, on being ordered to let fly the jib sheet, that the ship might go about, Andrews had got rather mixed up among the "strings," and had let go in succession the jib haulyards, the bowsprit shrouds, and the peak haulyards. A very nice crew, this, to cross the Atlantic with !

And here is another little adventure of Arnaud's. On one fine day, the wind being steady, light, and right aft, and our spinnaker and top-sail set, he was left alone on deck for a few minutes to steer. Suddenly I heard a great flapping of canvas, and on hurrying on deck, perceived that all our sails had been taken aback. The main-sail, top-sail, and spinnaker were bellying out the wrong way, and the vessel was slowly travelling stern first. The booms, being guyed, had not swung aft. I looked at the compass, and perceived that Arnaud had steered the vessel right round, so that she was heading away from her course ; then I looked at the culprit. He was sitting, with his legs crossed Turkish fashion, on the locker aft—placid, calm as a Hindoo idol. He was deliberately rolling himself another cigarette, the while professing to be steering with his elbow, and evidently unconscious of having done aught wrong.

"Well, Arnaud ? " I said.

" I think," he remarked in a weary, careless voice, looking at the burgee at the mast-head; " I think the wind has changed."

We passed two days in the quaint old Cornish seaport. Some yachting men called on us, and were somewhat surprised to behold our arrangements. " Where does your crew live ? " they asked after going all over the vessel, for we were at the time in our shore-going " togs," and not to be recognized as the four seamen our friends had perceived in the morning swabbing decks. " Where do your men live ? there seems to be only room for yourselves on board."

We pointed to the solemn small boy sitting in the fore castle, with his perpetual huge quid of tobacco in his cheek, and his chum the kitten on his lap. " That is our crew."

" But the others ? "

" There are no others."

I think these gentlemen looked upon the *Falcon*, with its amateur crew, as being one of the most eccentric craft that ever wandered about the oceans. We lay in a quantity of oft tack, bottled bee r, and vegetables at Falmouth, so that

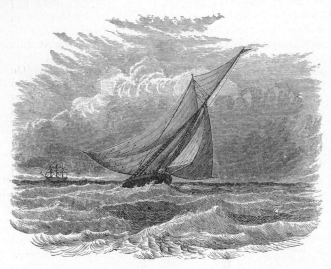

OFF AT LAST.

we might enjoy the wonted luxuries of the shore for some few days of our first voyage.

On the evening of the 24th of August we bid adieu to the friends who had accompanied us down from Southampton. The anchor was weighed and catted. The last link between us and home was broken, and under all plain canvas the *Falcon* glided out of the bay, bound for Madeira.

Well off, at last, we four, the boy, and the kitten ; and it was with a curious mixture of sensations that we sailed out into the dark cloudy night on the choppy waters of the

Channel. The last we saw of old England was the Lizard lights gleaming from the darkness. From these we "took our departure," and steered a course straight across the Bay of Biscay for Finisterre. At eight o'clock we lost sight of the light, and from that moment the routine of shipboard commenced. Eight bells was sounded; the patent log, one of Walker's taffrail logs, was dropped overboard; and the watches set; for from now our life was no longer to be divided out into days and nights, but into spells of four hours up and four hours down—rather trying, at first.

There was usually a strong contrast between the expression of the faces of the watch coming down to turn in and of that about to turn out. To the latter the jovial and noisy way with which the former would rouse it from its slumbers was disgusting in the extreme. Arnaud's face, for instance, when he was turned out at midnight wore anything but a happy expression. He did not seem to see any fun in Jerdein's boisterous " Now, then, you sleepers ! Now, then, starboard watch ; up you get !"

We met splendid weather all the way to Madeira; too splendid indeed, for we were becalmed for two days in the Bay of Biscay, rolling helplessly in the long swell; the redoubtable gulf treating us kindly, and sparing us all its terrors. We were also becalmed for nearly three days in the neighbourhood of Madeira. Notwithstanding these five days of enforced idleness, we accomplished the voyage of 1200 nautical miles in fourteen days, for the wind was right aft all the way. It is off the south coast of Portugal that the mariner may expect to fall in with the north-east trade-wind ; but we carried the wind from that quarter all the way from Southampton, a great piece of luck.

It would be tedious, I think, for my readers were I to give the narrative of these voyages in log form ; I will therefore but briefly jot down the particular events of each, especially such as may prove of interest or of service to yachting-men. The little *Falcon* gave great satisfaction on this her trial trip, and we got a much higher speed out of her than we anticipated—on some occasions she has logged as much as nine and a half knots an hour, running before a heavy sea. We were enabled to carry our spinnaker and gaff-topsail throughout this voyage, two days excepted.

On approaching Finisterre we got into a confused and nasty

sea, in which the vessel rolled heavily—and these lively Penzance luggers do know how to roll.

Jerdein and myself had now to take all the steering through our watches, as Arnaud and Andrews could as yet only be trusted at the helm in fine weather.

On the evening of the 29th of August we sighted the lofty cliffs of the Spanish coast; and at dusk made out the light on Cape Finisterre.

This day we spoke the *Maria*, a Spanish barque bound for Coruna. In the night we lost a hand overboard ; we could not recover him, as it was very dark, and there was a heavy sea running.

The sad event occurred in the middle watch. I was steering, with Arnaud standing by my side, when we perceived the kitten crawl out of his lodging under the dinghy, which lay upturned on the deck. The poor thing had been pining ever since we sailed. The terrible liveliness of the little craft had made him very sea-sick—and perhaps tinned meat and preserved milk did not agree with him ; anyhow, he was a melancholy object, becoming thinner and sadder every day, as his chum the boy grew fatter and more contented-looking.

This particular afternoon the kitten had sighted the smiling downs of Spain, had smelt the land ; so he plucked up a bit, tried to purr, and evidently entertained hopes of soon setting foot on *terra firma* again. But now that he saw us bearing away once more, and the Finisterre light fading away behind us, despair seized him. He climbed on to the bulwarks, and stretching out his neck, looked yearningly out towards the receding land. Now he gazed down shrinkingly at the black water, now back at the deck, evidently in doubt ; and just as the light became quite invisible, with a piteous mew and one last reproachful look at the cruel *Falcon*, and her crueller crew, resolutely leapt overboard— a deliberate suicide ; death, he thought, was to be preferred to this life of misery on the ever-heaving seas.

On the 1st of September, being in about latitude 38° N., and longitude 14° 12′ W., off the mouth of the Mediterranean Sea, we encountered our strongest breeze—a moderate gale from the N.E., before which we ran nearly 100 miles in twelve hours. On the 29th of August, we ran 142 miles ; on the 30th of August, 118; on the 31st of August, 108 ;

on the 1st of September, 180 ; on the 2nd of September, 150—dead before the wind, so we had no reason to complain.

We were, on the 2nd of September, only 168 miles from the Madeira islands, but we did not drop our anchor in Funchal roads until the 7th of September; for we now encountered calm and light baffling winds, progressing but slowly under a leaden sky, across a long, smooth-swelling, leaden sea. Tepid, uncomfortable weather it was, with the thermometer standing at 85° in the shade.

Early in the morning of the 6th of September we sighted a rugged, rocky coast right ahead of us, which we soon made out to be the island of Porto Santo, the northernmost of the Madeiras. It appeared to be a wild spot; a small isle not six miles long, with an iron-bound coast, on which the Atlantic seas perpetually broke with a thunderous roar. It seemed to be barren in the extreme, merely a tumbled mass of rugged black mountains, in some places running sheer into the foaming sea, in others fringed at the foot by beautiful beaches of golden sands. Strange did these lofty mountainous islands of mid-ocean appear to us, after the low verdant shores of old England.

There was but a light wind blowing, and it was not till midnight that we sailed between the group of barren rocky islets known as the Desertas (only distinguishable this dark night by the roar of the surf on them) and the east coast of Madeira. Then we bore away to the westward until we were abreast of the lights of Funchal, some four miles from the anchorage, and hauling the fore-sheet to windward, hove-to till morning.

The next day was cloudless, sultry, and with scarcely a breath of wind to fill our sails, but with the assistance of the sweeps we brought the *Falcon*, by about mid-day, to the roadstead of Funchal, and came to an anchor within hailing distance of the shore under the walls of the Loo Rock Fort.

And now, indeed, we could perceive that we had come to a summer land. On the shore in front of us was the white Portuguese city, and behind it the island rose in swelling domes of luxuriant vegetation and dark forests, up to the barren rocky mountain-tops, 6000 feet above the sea. It was pretty hot too; the Leste was blowing, the hot wind from the African Sahara, which brought the thermometer up to 90° in the shade.

As soon as the Customs' and the health boat had come off and we were free to hold intercourse with the natives, a bum-boat came off to us from the shore—the regular old traditional bum-boat of Marryat's novels—laden with oranges, bananas, figs, mangoes, fresh butter, fish, soft tack, and other unwonted luxuries. But the bum-boat woman, the sweet little musical Buttercup, was wanting. In her place was a shifty-eyed, grave, dark man of unprepossessing countenance, one Marco, who undertook to supply us with water, stores, look after our washing, and so on. He could speak some English, and was laden with certificates from all the English yachts that had visited Madeira for years. There are no ship-chandlers here, so one is left to the mercy of these irregular land-sharks. Marco is perhaps no worse than the rest.

Jerdein said, " He may prove to be an honest man, for he did not wince when swallowing the very strong tot of whisky I gave him." I have some doubts myself as to the general efficacy of this ordeal.

The town of Funchal we found to be very dull and uninteresting ; but like all who visit this island of perpetual summer, we were astonished at the beauty of the surrounding country. From the steep, paved, narrow streets of the suburbs, over whose every wall hung large bunches of purple grapes, to the tops of the swelling hills, the land overflowed with an exuberant and lovely vegetation. Myrtles, large trees of grand geraniums in full flower, roses, vines, oleanders, bananas, covered the hill sides, while every lane was shaded with festoons of vines.

Mr. Falconer, our host of the excellent English hotel known as Mile's Hotel, a beautifully situated place built in the centre of a lovely tropical garden, made arrangements for us to visit the world-renowned view of the Gran Corral. He procured good horses for us. The Gran Corral deserves its reputation, and we had a most pleasant ride to the sublime gorge, by a road which winds along the sides of mountains, sometimes precipitous and barren, but generally covered with verdure and flowers and noble forests of chestnut. The broad, blue Atlantic was always a feature in the scene ; so high were we above it that we could see the light clouds skimming over it below us like phantom ships.

On our return to the city we went to the circus, for dull Funchal just now boasted this excitement—a Yankee circus that was travelling among the Canary Islands and up and down the West Coast of Africa. We were already provided with tickets for the performance, for the shrewd American had already pounced down on us as likely people to be looking out for entertainment. We had made the acquaintance of some of this queer crowd of light-hearted wanderers in the following wise.

We were sitting in a café, indulging in glasses of strong red wine in which cream ices had been stirred up, a pleasant combination in vogue here. At another table was sitting a man who eyed us silently for some time, mentally taking our measure. He was a shortish man, with close-shaved head and keen Yankee features, with an eye ever twinkling with good-natured fun, and a mobile, nervous mouth. After, no doubt, having pretty well gauged the character of the *Falcons*, and having detected some freemasonry of Bohemianism in the appearance of those great navigators, he came boldly up to us and with Yankee twang burst at once *in medias res.*

"Wall, strangers, and so ye've come all the way from England in that little craft in the harbour, eh? Proud to make your acquaintance. I'm the fi-nance man of Feely's circus, that's who I am. Now I guess you'll want a dash of moral recreation to-night after all those days of hauling and heaving, eh? Here you are (producing an envelope), just four places left—four box-tickets for to-night's grand representation of Feely's American Circus—right. Yes, I'll take a little *aqua pura* with whisky. *Evviva, senores.*"

We visited the circus and enjoyed it too, for the little company was clever. We all lost our hearts to a pretty and merry-eyed little Yankee girl, who gracefully did *la haute école* on a fine bay horse. I think our friend, the finance man, saw this, for he considerately spared us any further wounding of these too susceptible hearts.

He came off in a boat to call on us the next morning, and brought with him his "boss," Mr. Feely, and the Neapolitan clown, but none of the "fair artistes." "They are liable to sea-sickness," he diplomatically explained. This trio stayed to lunch, and we turned them out our best curry and minced collops, stimulating their appetites first with the world-renowned *Falcon* fog-cutter, a terrible beverage of the cock-tail species, invented by Jerdein in the early days of the cruise, but much improved by further research and experiment, as we progressed. It contains manifold in-gredients, of which whisky and Angostura bitters form the base. What comes on the top of these depends much on the products of the clime the *Falcon* happens to be in, thus a detailed recipe is impossible. If you ask a denizen of British Guiana what a " swizzle " is, his reply will be " a Demerara tipple." He will not condescend to analyze further for you that delicate pink foaming draught. So be it with the *Falcon* fog-cutter—it is a " *Falcon* tipple."

For two years this company had owned a small schooner-yacht, in which they travelled with all their paraphernalia from island to island of the West Indies, and up the Spanish Main. Then they were wrecked. Many a curious yarn these three Bohemians spun us of their roaming life on the warm Western seas among the pleasure-loving people of the Spanish Main. Mr. Feely was the gravest of the three, as became his responsible position ; circus proprietors always are more or less solemn. It must indeed be hard and delicate work to keep in order the curious little world of a travelling circus, with its artistic jealousies and squabbles.

CHAPTER III.

In the afternoon of the 13th of September, having got a clean bill of health for St. Vincent, and laid in a good stock of vegetables and Colares wine, we weighed anchor, and sailed out of Funchal Bay before a light breeze. We did not get out into the strength of the fresh trade-wind until past midnight, as is generally the case on the lee-side of this island, with its lofty mountains.

Our next port was to be Porto Grande, in the island of St. Vincent, Cape Verde Islands, a distance of 1026 nautical miles. This voyage we accomplished in seven days and twenty hours, notwithstanding that we had in all about forty hours of light winds and calms, and twelve hours of head-wind. But during the rest of the voyage we had strong north-east trade-winds. In three consecutive days we made the following runs : 169, 166, and 183 nautical miles, which is not bad work for a tubby, jury-rigged craft like ours.

We were now sailing over a lovely sea. The old Spanish discoverers named this vast region of the north-east trade-wind, that extends almost from 36° N. to the Equator, the Ladies' Gulf. Well named it is too. A tropic sea where storms are very rare, where there is a perpetual summer, tempered by the fresh, strong trades.

In these warm latitudes the four a.m. to eight a.m. watch is the pleasantest of the day. There is first the matutinal coffee and pipe—for on the *Falcon* smoking on duty is not absolutely forbidden. You steer the gallant little vessel as she reels off her eight knots an hour before the steady breeze, rolling and heaving gently as the great green seas pass under her, sometimes playfully dropping a bucketful of salt water over the bulwark. You watch the gradual approach of dawn : there comes a pale flush with bright emerald streaks in the eastern sky ; and far quicker than in our northern climes, the sable night is driven back, and the stars put out ; and gloriously the tropical sun rises from a throne of rainbow clouds over burning Africa.

During our voyage to St. Vincent, the thermometer ranged from 80° to 85° in our cabin. On September the 14th it rained for the first time since we left Southampton, but not for long.

On the evening of September the 16th, four full-rigged ships were in sight of us astern.

The following morning the wind freshened from the south-east quarter. We held our own against three of the four ships, still keeping them astern of us. Only one could gain on us, and at two p.m. she was alongside. She was a magnificent British ship with all sail set. We were in company with her for some hours, during which we kept up a conversation with her by means of the international code of signals. She hoisted her number, H.F.S.R., and we found she was the well-known fast London clipper, the *Paramata*, of 1521 tons, bound from Plymouth to Sydney.

Her passengers crowded her decks to look at us, the sight of so small a craft as the *Falcon* in mid-ocean evidently sur-

2

prising them. The flag conversation went on in an animated manner, until we bade each other farewell, dipped our ensigns and separated, she taking a course considerably to the westward of ours. This pleasant little encounter was in latitude 26° 24′ N., longitude 20° 30′ W. The other three ships did not overtake us.

On September the 18th we boomed along merrily before a fresh breeze. It was Saturday, so at eight p m. as is the old sea rule, we drank to sweethearts and wives, and even found occasion for another toast, so merry were we at our luck and prospect of a smart run. This was to the tropics, for it was this evening we entered the torrid zone, crossing the Cancer at sunset. This night the wind freshened considerably, but blew steadily.

At daybreak, as I was steering, it being my watch, the spinnaker outhaul carried away, so I had to call up the watch below to muzzle the sail and repair the damage. A curious and undignified spectacle the port watch presented as they hurried up _en déshabille._ Andrews was arrayed in a blanket and a pair of hideous blue spectacles which he considered to be necessary for his eyes when in tropic seas.

On the 19th, we had reeled off another 166 knots. And now the gallant north-east wind blew fresher and fresher still; at times we made eight and a half knots an hour, driving showers of spray from our bows as we plunged "like a frighted steed" from one great sea to another.

Top-sail and spinnaker were stowed in the afternoon; by evening the wind had increased to the force of a gale, and we close-reefed the main-sail and shifted the jib.

Jerdein and myself had now to do all the steering, as was usual when the tiller required delicate handling. The old boat behaved splendidly, and in twenty-four hours we had made another 190 miles on our course. On the morning of the 20th, we sighted a brig steering W.S.W., with topgallant mast gone.

Nearly every morning about this time we had a little fresh fish for breakfast, for many flying fish would jump over our low bulwarks by night, attracted by the glare of the bull's eye and side lights (when we carried them).

On the night of September the 20th, we knew that we were in the close vicinity of the Cape Verdes. As the weather was very thick, we first shortened canvas, and later on, during the middle watch, hove to, so as to keep off the land till daybreak. At four a.m. I relieved Jerdein on deck, made sail and proceeded on our course. We were unfortunate in having an exceedingly unfavourable morning for making a landfall. It was squally, drizzly, thick weather, in which it would be impossible to distinguish the highest land at the distance of two miles; a not uncommon state of things to encounter off these lofty, cloud-collecting islands. At seven a.m. we perceived through the drizzle a dark, undefined mass on the port bow that might be a lofty coast, so we bore down towards it.

Then a violent squall came down on us, which compelled us to lower the main-sail. At eight p.m., of a sudden, a great rift opened out in the thick atmosphere, and lo! right ahead, for a moment only appeared a mass of inky rock filling up the rift, its edges and extent not yet discernible. Then the rift in the mist closed, and we were left again in uncertainty for a while. But soon, with the strengthening sun, the thickness cleared once more, and we perceived before us, not three miles off, a dark threatening mass of mountains which we recognized as the island of San Antonio.

This is the most northward of the Cape Verde Islands and one of the most fertile of the group, though it looks barren and inhospitable enough from the sea. These islands lie at the southern limit of the north-east trade-winds, and are about 200 miles distant from Senegambia on the West Coast of Africa. They belong to Portugal, and are for the most part inhabited by a fine-looking race of negroes, giants of their kind, who are good sailors and farmers. The whole group is volcanic—a congregation of curiously-serrated, dark mountains, that look as if vomited out from hell itself, so weird some of them appear.

The island of San Antonio presents a fine appearance from the sea. It is a grand volcanic mass of dark rock, whose peaks rise above the clouds (it attains an elevation of 7100 feet), and at whose feet is a perpetual white line of heavy surf. Bleak and uninhabited as it appears to be, this island has a considerable negro population, and they say contains fertile vales, between its precipices, where vines, cocoa-plantains, indigo, and cotton, are cultivated by a mild and industrious coloured people.

The island of San Vincente is separated from that of San Antonio by a channel seven miles wide.

After close-hauling the *Falcon* on the port tack so as to double the north-east Cape of San Antonio, we then bore away down the channel for Porto Grande—the harbour of St. Vincent.

This is the most important island of the Cape Verde Archipelago, having been selected as a coaling station and place of call for several lines of ocean mail-steamers. But of all the group, none I imagine is so barren and burnt-up a desert as is this little islet. As we approached it we could easily distinguish its volcanic origin. It is merely a burnt-out volcano. From the golden sands that divide it from the blue tropic sea it rises a confused mass of utterly bare, fantastic mountain-peaks. Steep and profound ravines descend to the sea in places, black and lifeless some of them as if they had been cloven but yesterday with a great pickaxe out of a mountain of coal. This arid African crag is not a cheerful-looking place.

At midday we dropped our anchor in Porto Grande Bay, close to the wretched little Portuguese town. This is a splendid and well-sheltered harbour, capable of holding at least 300 sail. The entrance, which looks out toward the island of San Antonio, is about two miles wide. Once within the bay one finds himself in clear, smooth water, surrounded on all sides by shores of beautiful yellow sands and coral rocks, from which rises the amphitheatre of barren, tooth-shaped mountains. The only objection to this land-locked basin is the almost daily occurrence of furious squalls, which sweep down on it from the ravines. Twice during our stay here we dragged our anchor in consequence of these.

The little town on the beach, with its whitewashed houses and bright red roofs, looked cheerful against the dreary background ; for from the domed mountain-tops to the shore sloped down the *couloirs* of black lava and *débris* of old volcanoes. Travellers have likened this aspect to that of a raked-out coal fire of giants—a Titanic heap of cinders—and this exactly describes it. One could almost imagine that the fire still smoulders below, so intensely hot is it in this land-locked bay ; an atmosphere of a furnace at times envelops the town. On the desolate land there is no green to relieve the eye, no trees to keep off the burning rays of the tropic sun.

The health-officer came off in a boat rowed by sturdy negroes clad in white, and gave us pratique; then in his turn came off the Marco of St. Vincent in his bumboat—a merry little Portuguese, with a ne'er-do-weel twinkle of eye and cock of hat, José by name ; he spoke English fluently, and offered to find all we wanted in the way of provisions during our stay. Very well he did it too ; and, to our surprise, without swindling us in the least. Let me recommend little José to future callers at this port.

It is easy to procure any quantity of bananas, mangoes, cocoanuts, and other fruits here. They are brought over from the other more fertile islands in small craft by the negroes. These same islanders appear to be a merry, prosperous people, perpetually jabbering and grinning like so many monkeys. Some of these islands, they tell me, are very negro and half-caste Utopias. Each man owns his little plot of land, which produces more than suffices for his needs. Coffee, papias, sugar, bananas, &c., are cultivated in the fertile vales beneath the volcanic crags. Yankee schooners carry on a brisk trade among these people, bartering cheap and gaudy cottons, knives, and such goods, for agricultural produce. San Vincente is not self-supporting even in the way of water, of this necessary there is very little, if any. Some is brought over from San Antonio in schooners, but the shipping is chiefly supplied by Miller the coal-king, who condenses large quantities of sea-water in giant tanks.

San Vincente is one of the stations of the Anglo-Brazilian Telegraph Company, so there are about fifteen young Englishmen in the company's employ, resident here. It was chiefly owing to the companionship and hospitality of these gentlemen that we lay at anchor off this cinder-heap for so long as nine days. Every naval and royal mail officer knows the telegraph station and the telegraph men of St. Vincent. These all live together in one large building, by far the most luxurious place on the island, with a spacious verandah surrounding it, libraries, reading-rooms, billiard-rooms, and all the other luxuries of a club. Were it not for the number of the company's *employés*, and this pleasant system of half-club, half-college fellowship, I should imagine their life in such a hole as Porto Grande would be intolerable, so utterly destitute of all society or amusement is it. As it is they live jollily enough. They give their little dances to the officers and passengers of passing mail steamers; play at cricket on the blazing sands; keep their four-oared boat, and so on. The arrival of a steamer with a good supply of first-class passengers of the fair sex, is generally the signal for a ball, for St. Vincent can turn out little in the feminine line—save negresses and mulattoes. Sadly were the telegraph men, and we mariners of the *Falcon* too, for the matter of that, disappointed, when the SS. *Cotopaxi* called here on her way to Australia, with a full complement of passengers. We had eagerly looked forward to her arrival. There would be English papers, the faces of English girls again, a jolly ball. But, alas! there was a case of scarlatina on board, so she was put into quarantine during her stay. A great disappointment for all parties—the passengers perhaps not least; the emigrants hung over the bulwarks all day, gazing sadly at the forbidden *terra firma*.

One fine morning Arnaud and myself started off in our Berthon collapsible boat to explore the other side of the bay under Washington Head, where the sands, piled up in huge dunes, glittered like pale gold under the vertical sun. The outward journey in the little ten-foot canvas boat was smooth enough, but on nearing the land we found, what we could not perceive from the *Falcon's* deck, a heavy surf breaking on the shore. The edge, too, of the beach was thick with sharp, ugly-looking, coral rocks.

Anyhow, here we were, and land we must to explore those great slopes of glaring sand. As soon as we had reached the breakers, and were, as we imagined, in sufficiently shallow water, I gave the order to jump overboard, so that we might lift the boat safely on shore without running a hole in her bottom. To Arnaud's astonishment the water was well over our heads; so when we had at last successfully landed and carried the boat out of reach of the breakers, he upbraided me sadly. "You told me we were in shallow water—do you call that shallow water?"

We sat down on the burning sands under the sun to dry, and forthwith entered into a fierce discussion as to whether ten feet was shallow water or the reverse; I holding the former, Arnaud the latter view. Shallow, I said, was a purely relative adjective, and in these circumstances ten feet was shallow. Arnaud held that water could not be shallow for walking and fording purposes, when there were three or four feet of it above your head.

In five minutes the tropical sun had dried us, so we postponed the discussion, and wandered about collecting shells and specimens of coral, enjoying this amusement, I verily believe, as much as we used to do when we were small imps with spade and bucket in the olden times.

The trade-wind blows all the refuse of Porto Grande across the bay to this beach, and so stalking about on the sands, greedily gobbling, were the ugliest and most mangy-looking vultures I have ever cast eyes upon. They were quite tame, and allowed us to approach them within a yard or so. These useful scavengers are protected by law, and a heavy fine is inflicted on any one who kills one of them—hence their tameness. They are evidently quite aware of this law, and insult you with impunity. They are most insolent beasts, worse than Barbados niggers.

Arnaud and myself now proceeded to re-embark—no easy matter, for the surf had increased considerably. Our naked feet suffered a good deal during the process, for the shore was covered with sea-urchins, whose hedgehog-like bristles pierced and broke off in them. We waded in quickly after a returning wave, carrying the boat with us, jumped nimbly in and paddled out ; but, alas ! we were not sharp enough, for before we had got beyond the second line of breakers a roller caught us, slued the boat round, capsized her, rolled us out, and we had to draw her up on shore, bale out, and start again. Five times in succession we were thus capsized, but always managed to save the boat and keep her off the coral. We knew that there were ground sharks in this part of the bay—not a pleasant matter to think of. The sixth time we altered our tactics and succeeded. We followed a breaker, carrying the boat with us ; Arnaud jumped in, seized the paddles ; I held on to the stern and managed to guide her safely over the next breaker ; then he rowed with all his energy till he was well outside the surf in deep water. It was now my turn. I swam out till I came to the boat, put a hand on either side of the stern, and jumped in between my hands. My weight pulled her under, and half-filled her with water, but she did not capsize, and we soon baled her out.

I have mentioned this to show what can be done with a Berthon's boat; no wooden dinghy could have got off from that shore then; she would have most certainly been stove in. But two men with practice and a little activity can carry this little light canvas tub through the broken water and safely embark as we did on this occasion, without scratching a particle of paint off her fragile sides.

Sunday, the 26th of September, was a hot day, a day of oppression and irritability, which found vent, as far as the *Falcons* were concerned, in two fashions. The morning was too sultry to do anything; we lay about the cabin lazy and sulky, sleeping and wrangling alternately. First we entered into a most fierce discussion on some subject of dynamics, in which all parties waxed savage; as a matter of fact, none of us knew anything about the question in point. Then came lunch—curry and Collares wine; this mollified us somewhat, and the talk veered round to a more gentle discussion as to the comparative beauty of the fair sex of different nations, over our pipes. But, alas! from that we go on to some profound metaphysical question, which stirred up all our latent irritability again. At last, unable to convince each other, we went to sleep.

In the evening we were engaged to dine with the telegraph men. Arthur put us on shore, then pulled back to the *Falcon.* When we reached the verandah of the telegraph station, just as the sun was setting, Jerdein's sharp eye detected a suspicious circumstance—a boat with three men in it was rowing off to the *Falcon.* Yes! there could be no mistake; they were now alongside; now they had boarded her. Then the rapid night of the tropics fell, and all was obscure. Jerdein and myself ran down to the beach, found a boat with two negroes, and engaged them to row us off. We told them to go off quickly, but noiselessly, explaining our plans to them. They greatly enjoyed the situation.

We found a boat made fast to the *Falcon,* but no one suspected our arrival; our foemen were all in the forecastle, where we heard them laughing boisterously. Jerdein and myself jumped down the companion, passed through the main-cabin, and so into the forecastle, where we surprised three Portuguese sailors. Without parley we proceeded to belabour these fellows; there was a fine scrimmage. They were driven on deck; one fell into the boat they had come

in, and alone managed to escape with her; the other two we
knocked overboard, to find their way to their vessel as well as
they could through the sharks; the latter, by the way, are
too delicate in their tastes to feed on Portuguese mulattoes
unless very hard pressed for a meal, so I suppose they returned
safely to whence they came.

Arthur told us that he was below when they came on
board; they paid no attention to his remonstrances at their
uninvited appearance, but seized him, prevented him from
going on deck, and commenced to inspect the vessel for grog,
and anything else, I suppose, that might come in handy.
After our victory, which proved a fine safety-valve for the
irritability caused by the sultriness of the day, we handed
over a loaded six-shooter to Arthur, in the presence of our
two grinning negro boatmen, with injunctions to challenge
once, and then shoot, any other visitors who might come off
that night.   The boy was proud of his post, he took the
revolver with a grin and meaning gesture that made the
niggers shudder.   I did not think that we should be troubled
any more after this.

He is a bloodthirsty boy, this Arthur.   He has, I think,
fed his youthful mind with literature of the " penny dreadful "
class.   At every port he would ask such questions as, " Be
there savages here, sir ?"   " Be there Indians in these parts ?"
He used to appear very disappointed on receiving an answer
in the negative, but used to solace himself with dreams of
future bloody encounters.   " With all these guns and
cannons we ought to do for them when we do see them—eh,
sir ?" he would say.   He used to look at our little brass
cannon with great respect and admiration, as being a wonderful piece of ordnance; was very fond of it, indeed, save
when he was set to polish it.   When, later on, we did come
across his long-looked-for Indians and savages, I fear one of
the cherished illusions of his life vanished, a fragment of his
youth was gone; for lo! they were not cannibals; neither
did they scalp him; neither were they, as a rule, even naked
—simply a drunken, dirty, very ugly set of uninteresting
ragamuffins.

The morrow after this night of wrath was a busy day for
all hands; we were employed in oiling spars, taking in stores
and water—in short, preparing all for sea.   But after all this
work we did not sail on the following day after all, but

indulged in a holiday; for the SS. *Thales* was in the harbour, with the latest English papers on board, so we went in for a grand read at the telegraph station. The same steamer had also landed in St. Vincent a small quantity of that unwonted luxury, ice. One of the storekeepers near the beach had obtained a supply of the precious article, so most of the white population were in and out of that store a good deal during that day.

CHAPTER IV.

OUR first long run was now before us; Bahia dos Todos os Santos in Brazil, across the broad Atlantic, was to be our next port. The time this voyage might occupy was rather uncertain, for we were now towards the southern limit of the north-east trade-winds. We had to traverse the region of the south-west African monsoon, which blew in our teeth, and that broad belt of equatorial calm, so terrible to sailors—the sultry doldrums, where a ship may lie for weeks on the hot, smooth water under a cloudless sky, with the pitch oozing from her decks; a region of unbearable calm, broken occasionally by violent squalls, torrential rain, and fearful lightning and thunder. All these difficulties conquered, we should be in the pleasant realm of the strong south-east trade-wind—the trade-wind of the southern hemisphere— which blows fresher and steadier than the north-east trade, and under whose favouring breath we should be able to reel off the knots right merrily.

We steered so as to cross the equator in longitude 24° W., which Jerdein considered to be the best route at this time of the year.

As this voyage will be of some interest to yachting men, I shall, contrary to my usual custom, narrate it in the form of a diary. It will be observed that we were thirteen days reaching the equator; that for the greater part of that time we encountered calms and south-westerly monsoons, so that sailing as we generally did, close-hauled on the starboard tack, we were driven considerably to the eastward of our course, on the tenth day being as far east as 21° 30′ W. Not till we were on the equator did we fall in with the south-east trade, which then stood by us pretty steadily till we reached Bahia.

Throughout the voyage the thermometer ranged between 85° to 90° in the shade. In the following diary I divide time in the civil fashion for convenience, but the positions and distances are extracted from the log, and given at midday, nautical fashion.

October 1st.—Weighed anchor at midday. Light N.E. wind. Ran down the San Antonio channel under all canvas. On our left were the bare volcanic masses, the forbidding gorges of San Vincente ; a thundering line of breakers dashing against the shore everywhere : on our right the more smiling mountains of the isle of San Antonio. The lofty summits of both islands were hidden in the clouds. At night wind dropped ; calm, and vivid lightnings.

October 2nd.—Dead calm ; nasty drizzle ; hot, debilitating weather; vessel rolling uncomfortably in the swell. Through the haze perceived the lofty mountains of Brava, the southernmost and most beautiful of the Cape Verde Archipelago. Towards evening an E.S.E. wind sprung up, which enabled us to average six and a half knots an hour during the night.

October 3rd.—Glorious sunny weather; wind E.S.E. Eleven a.m.—one of the crew was caught in a serious breach of discipline ; man at the helm, too, at the time He was sitting down to his work ; was wearing blue spectacles, and, worst of all, was reading a play of Sophocles in the original. Fancy a man at the wheel reading Sophocles ! He was seriously rebuked by the officer of his watch, Jerdein, who is a martinet in his way, and who gazed at him for fully five minutes, speechless with dismay, ere he could find voice for vituperation.

October 4th.—Wind E.S.E. At midday in longitude 25° 1' W., latitude 10° 32' N. ; distance made this day 152 miles. During the day the wind came round, till it was quite aft. The glass fell rather suddenly—more than a tenth in a few hours. In the evening there was a wild appearance in the sky, slight squalls of wind and rain, and signs of worse weather coming ; then followed a magnificent sunset, ominous of storm, and a calm for a while.

So threatening was the appearance of the heavens to windward, that all hands stayed on deck, to see what was coming. Right aft we perceived an inky mass of cloud rising from the horizon. It had huge, rugged, black streaks diverging from it in all directions, like the claws or arms of some great monster crab or polypus. Bigger and bigger the threatening mass swelled, and the evil-looking arms stretched half round the horizon and to the zenith, as if the monster was about to inclose the whole world in its grasp—a wonderful and awful appearance. Our sails flapped as we rolled in the calm ; we lowered the main-sail, made all snug, and waited. First constant and vivid sheet and forked lightning of a blue colour came out of the cloud, and then down burst the squall on us, and such a squall. The cloud had enveloped all the sky, had blotted out all the stars ; never have I experienced so complete a darkness on the seas. The wind blew with great fury ; and we could not turn our faces to the stinging rain, so smartly it struck. We scudded on before the heavy gusts. As I steered I had to keep the vessel right before them, judging the direction by the feel of the wind on my neck, for the binnacle-light was blown out. The roar of wind and rain rendered even our loudest shouts inaudible to each other across the decks.

It was, as I said, pitch-dark. As I steered I could only see two whirling masses of foam on either side of our bow like two great wings, thrown up by our speed. Our side-lights were lit. On the foaming mass on our port side fell the red, on that on our starboard side fell the green light, lending a spectral horror to the scene. With this exception, the occasional lightnings alone threw a fitful light on the noisy darkness around. Above the roar of wind and water but one sound was heard—our bell pealed forth loudly, with each exceptional pitch of the vessel, a deep funereal tone that added to the solemnity. This squall lasted nearly an hour ; others succeeded it throughout the night from various quarters, but none coming nearly up to it in fury.

October 5th.—Cloudy, warm, no wind. We were in that most uncomfortable position for a vessel, becalmed in a heavy sea ; for last night's weather had raised a confused tumult of choppy waves, in the trough of which we rolled and pitched horribly with all sail stowed. It was a lazy day for all, our chief employment being eating bananas and vainly attempting to catch a large shark who was prowling round us, a wary old ruffian who refused the most tempting bait. The calm continued throughout the day. As usual, ill-temper resulted.

Two of the crew entered into a fierce discussion as to whether the plantains which were to serve as one of the courses for dinner should be cooked and eaten with salt like potatoes, or be treated with sugar like fruit.

At eight p.m. there were signs of squally weather in the sky, so the crew waxed hopeful and good-tempered again. During the night we had occasional showers and light squalls from S. to S.S.W., at which we put the vessel close-hauled on the starboard tack. Then came the calm again. We were now having an experience of that tantalizing, wearisome region where the doldrums and south-west African monsoons fight for mastery over the equatorial sea.

All this time we were being drifted a considerable distance daily out of our course to the eastward, for we were now in the Guinea current, an equatorial stream of hot water (its temperature is about 84°) setting into the Gulfs of Benin and Biafra. So warm is the water that the morning douse with the bucket, which took the place of the tub, was no longer refreshing as it used to be, for the temperature of the sea was of course higher than that of the night and morning air. When a sea came on board in the night it felt like hot water to our faces and bare feet.

October 6th.—Again a dead calm; 88° in the shade; a high sea running; a fearful rolling, creaking, and groaning of ship; all our canvas was stowed; a barque in sight in the same situation; for forty hours we did not lose sight of her, though we were bound in different directions; lat. 9° 14′ N., long. 24° 30′ W. As no sharks seemed to be near, I jumped overboard for a short mid-ocean swim. At midday there came on us a slight squall with rain. We hoisted the canvas, but in half an hour it was as calm as ever.

October 7th.—A light northerly air and very heavy equatorial rain. We stripped and enjoyed a freshwater shower-bath; also blocked up the scuppers and collected enough water to refill some of our empty breakers. We only made seventeen miles this day, so light was the wind.

October 8th.—Calms and light northerly airs. There was a haze to the S.E. as if portending our entrance into the region of the trades. This day we made seventy-two miles on our course.

October 9th.—Tacking very slowly against head variable winds, divided from each other by hours of dead calm. In the afternoon we came to a disturbed sea, where it had evidently been recently blowing: 87° in the shade. Spoke an English barque homeward bound. At night passed very close to another vessel. Neither of us were carrying side-lights, and the night was dark, but we showed them our bull's-eye, to which signal they responded by showing another. A night of calm with occasional squalls from every point of the compass.

October 10*th.*—A strong and squally S.W. monsoon sprang up. We sailed close-hauled on the starboard tack. The vessel was very lively but not wet. At noon the wind freshened to a half-gale from the S.W., with heavy squalls at intervals. We sailed under close-reefed main-sail, fore-sail, and storm-jib. In the night it was blowing a moderate gale of wind in our teeth. The *Falcon* was livelier than ever; the way she jumped, first her head and then her stern into a sea, was a thing to experience. At midnight the vessel was labouring so heavily that we hove her to, for it was a shame to tax too much the endurance of the brave old boat.

October 11*th.*—At dawn the great seas looked most im-posing, with the fiery sunrise lending a weird colour to them, as they charged on towards us. At eight a.m., as the wind was moderating, we proceeded on our voyage. We put the vessel on the port tack, for the wind was S. by W., and we had been driven considerably to the eastward of our course. At midday our position was lat. 4° 58′ N., long. 21° 49′ W. All hands were now well weary of this S.W. monsoon blowing in our teeth, with its heavy, confused seas and squalls.

October 12*th.*—Fine, sunny, but disagreeable day; for the wind, though still as a rule from the S.W. quarter, seems to come at times from everywhere and anywhere, hence a troublesome sea. There was a curious hazy appearance to-day to the S.E., which cheered us somewhat as indicative of change. We had now reached a locality between the S.W. monsoon and the S.E. trade, where these winds contend continually for the mastery. They certainly have ploughed up their battle-field with their rival artillery into short, choppy furrows, very nasty for small vessels like ours that have to cross them.

At midday we were in lat. 3° 56′ N., long. 22° 50′ W.

October 13*th.*—A marvellous sunrise; on the eastern

horizon lay a bar of bright gold, with a mass of fiery red above, like a coast of golden sand lit by an intense light, and backed by mountains of half-molten iron. The wind blew fresh to-day from S. by W., to S. by E. At noon our position was lat. 1° 47' N., long. 23° 8' W.; distance made in the twenty-four hours, 146 miles.

During the night, of a sudden, with a squall, the trade-wind burst down on us at last, then settled down strong and steady : so we rejoiced exceedingly.

October 14th.—A glorious morning, no cloud in the sky, and a fresh trade-wind. At seven a.m. we crossed the line. At midday we had reeled off a hundred and sixty miles on our course, and at lunch were glad over our last two bottles of Collares wine from Madeira, which we had reserved for our arrival at the equator. Our luck had changed as we entered the southern hemisphere, after thirteen days of calms, squalls, and head-winds.

Jerdein reported a most curious phenomenon in his morning watch. The sea about a mile from us became suddenly disturbed, boiling up violently, as from a subterranean spring. This lasted for about two minutes. He said he thought it would have been dangerous had we happened to be over the spot. Throughout the day we observed great patches of discoloured water, having exactly the appearance of shoal water. These and similar phenomena are frequently observed in this part of the ocean. Often a ship reports that here-abouts she has experienced a violent shock, similar to that which is felt when a rock is struck. Sometimes a great rumbling is heard like that of a heavy chain running through the hawse-pipes, and the vessel quivers like a leaf in the wind. Another time in smooth water a vessel has been known to heel right over suddenly, as if she had run on a sand-bank, for this is a region full of most uncanny appari-tions for the mariner—a sort of haunted corner of the sea.

Before this ocean had been as thoroughly sounded and surveyed as it is now, these phenomena were attributed to the presence of unmarked sand-banks and rocky shoals, and are thus put down as *vigias* in the old charts. But it must have astonished the mariner somewhat to find that he got no soundings with his deep-sea lead, immediately after ex-periencing one of these shocks ! It is now known that there is no less depth than 2000 fathoms anywhere in this neigh-

bourhood, and submarine earthquakes are acknowledged as
the true cause of these convulsions. So frequent are these
manifestations of suboceanic disturbance, that this is now
termed "the volcanic region of the Atlantic." Fearful indeed must be the forces that can transmit such violent action
upwards through three miles of water.

This afternoon we noticed that the sea changed to a light
green colour, and the thermometer suddenly fell six degrees.
These, I believe, are also usual phenomena on this mysterious
tract of ocean.

October 15th.—We sailed to-day through an enormous
fleet of Portuguese men-of-war (Nautilus), under full canvas.
Pretty these little creatures (I don't suppose I can call them
fish, and creature is a safe term) appeared, with their delicate
pink fairy sails spread to the favouring wind. This day we
logged 160 miles. Position at midday, lat. 3° 15′ S., long.
24° 39′ W.

October 16th.—Day's run, 175 miles ; lat. 5° 45′ S., long.
25° 55′ W. Spoke a full-rigged ship bound for the Cape of
Good Hope.

October 17th.—We generally hold our own against the
trading-vessels we come across, and on many occasions have
shown some barque or ship a clean pair of heels ; but this
day we were ignominiously beaten, but by so beautiful a
vessel that we forgive her. She was a clean, bright Yankee
barque, the *Golden Cross*. Her sails were as well cut as a
yacht's, and as snowy. By noon we had added another 169
miles to our score.

October 18th.—The wind was now so much to the E. of
S.E., that we were enabled to hoist our spinnaker with
advantage. A very hot day. The wind was lighter, so our
day's work was only 141 miles.

October 19th.—Wind still lighter ; day's work, 118 miles ;
passed a jackass-rigged craft.

October 20th.—Thermometer 90° in cabin, 125° on deck ;
·vind light and variable ; day's work, 89 miles.

October 21st.—A light breeze from S.E. ; barometer fell a
tenth. We observed three interesting phenomena this day.
The first was a huge waterspout, which crossed our bows at
about two miles' distance ; the second phenomenon was
America ; the third a bottle of Collares wine.

I was at the tiller ; Arnaud was sadly contemplating a

small whale, which was floundering about near us; Arthur was, as was his wont, at the mast-head, looking out for passing vessels—this and fishing for flying-fish with a bull's-eye at night being his chief diversions on board.   Suddenly the boy cried "Land right ahead, sir!"   I was incredulous, for I did not expect to sight the coast for some hours.

On going aloft with the glasses I saw that the boy was right; there was no mistake about it at all.   There before us lay a long line of low sandy dunes, fringed with cocoanut-trees.   I rather surprised Jerdein, who was sleeping below, when I touched him on the shoulder and remarked quietly, "Here is America."

It was a dreary coast—and so it is all the way from Bahia to Pernambuco, low and monotonous, but strange and of the tropics to one coming from the northern lands for the first time.   A treble belt of striking colour clove the vast blue spread of sea and sky.   First was a band of bright white, the foam of the perpetual breakers on the coast; then a long strip of golden sand, and above, a broader green belt of waving cocoa-palms, dark against the pale blue sky.

The third phenomenon I spoke of was a bottle of Collares wine.   Having had a good look at the American coast, our storekeeper took a dive below, and soon reappeared on deck with a smile and this same bottle.   He was greeted with a shout of surprise.   The existence of such a treasure on board had not been in the least suspected by the rest of us; but this wary member of the crew had secreted this last bottle of our Madeira cellar, in order to produce it on our first sighting the New World.   It was formally uncorked, and with its assistance we saluted the Western Continent.   We had made the land about 100 miles to the northward of Bahia.

October 22nd.—A hot sun and a light breeze.   We slowly followed the coast, at a distance of about two miles from it. A line of sand fringed with cocoa-nuts, and—visible from the mast-head only—dense black masses of forest behind, unrolled themselves before us in monotonous panorama as we sailed by.   We perceived no signs of human life on the shore, save here and there what appeared to be a negro hut.

At last we sighted the lighthouse of San Antonio, and the scenery changed; gently sloping hills came down to the shore, covered with all manner of tropical forest and garden, among which nestled the villas and palaces of the wealthy merchants of Bahia. A wonderful sight this brilliant tropical verdure to us fresh from the barren seas : a luxuriant growth pouring right down to the narrow merge of sand, where stretched the long line of graceful cocoanut-palms, casting dark shadows on the clear water. We rounded the point of San Antonio with its picturesque fort, and sailed into the smooth waters of the beautiful bay of Bahia. At seven p.m. our chain once more rattled out through the hawse-pipe, and we came to an anchor off the city.

We were twenty-one days and seven hours out from San Vincente, a much shorter voyage than we had anticipated. The distance by the route we had taken is 2538 nautical miles.

As soon as we had stowed our canvas, we brought out from hidden places, white shirts, neckties, clothes, boots, and other articles of civilization,—for our sea costume was barbaric in the extreme,—and awaited the authorities.

Two boats soon came off; first, the patrique boat. The doctor was satisfied with our hygiene and gave us permission to land, as far as his department was concerned. Then came off the steam-launch of the captain of the port. The officer informed us that we were anchored in a prohibited spot, and must move farther in.

And now for the first time we experienced that universal courtesy which so pleased us in all the authorities we had dealings with in Brazilian and indeed in all other South American ports.

As we were flying the blue ensign, man-of-war rights were granted to us ; the captain of the port gave us permission to anchor in the man-of-war ground, and to land with our boats at the naval landing-stage at the arsenal.

As the wind had now dropped, he very kindly towed us up to our anchorage with his launch, and offered to give us every assistance in his power. The above privileges are of the greatest value in a Brazilian port, where the custom regulations for merchant-vessels are so strict. One cannot go off or on one's vessel, if she be a merchantman, after eight p.m., without a special permit from the custom-house. Now, we had the privilege of rowing to and fro at any hour ; we could leave our boat alone and in safety at the arsenal steps. All we had to do when coming off late at night was to call the sentry at the arsenal gates to open them for us, telling him the name of our vessel. Again, an insolent negro guard is put on board every merchantman by the custom-house. There he has to be fed, lodged, bribed, and made much of generally, during the vessel's stay in the port—a horrible nuisance which we were also excused, by virtue of our blue ensign.

Ours was a nice snug anchorage in four fathoms, under the antique fortress of Fort la Mar, a round, grey mass built on a rocky islet. We were close to the beach and could see all the busy life of the Praya from our decks.

Bahia is a picturesque place viewed from the sea. First along the shore is the Citade Baxa, or lower town, the more ancient portion of the city. Here are the lofty stone houses of the old colonists, with antique churches of massive and quaint architecture. For Bahia is one of the most antique cities of South America. It was founded in 1511, and is now the second city of Brazil.

The lower city is built on a narrow strip of land along the water, at the foot of a steep, black cliff some 240 feet high. One great street stretches along the beach, known as the Praya—it is four miles long, with a tramway running down its length. This Praya presents a very animated appearance. For here are the huge stores, magazines, and warehouses, and along the quays are moored the native craft, the queerest imaginable, with their gaudy paint, lofty sterns, strange rig, and semi-nude negro crews. Here are to be seen the giant blacks with glistening ebon skin, rolling down the bales of cotton, coffee, and sugar, and other produce of this rich province. At first sight, this is evidently one of the busy marts of the world. Along the front of the Praya is a fruit, vegetable, and odds-and-ends market, where at their stalls sit the fattest and most voluble of negresses, with the gaudiest and most voluminous of turbans on their heads, and a rather liberal display of their large charms.

This Praya is a hot place, and somewhat malodorous at times, for the fresh breezes are kept off by the steep cliff. Here the English sailor, too, rolls about red and sweating, drinking the vilest of new white rum, and eating half-rotten fruit under the tropic sun, till of a sudden a sickness and a dizziness comes upon him, and in a terribly short time he falls, another victim of the invisible fiend Yellow Jack.

Behind this Praya, as I said, rises a cliff, but not a smooth, bare cliff, but rugged, with quaint houses let into it, and rich vegetation filling each crevice. The contrast between the two is most striking. For the houses are antique with gloomy arches, dingy, many of them, as if they had stood through centuries of London smoke, whereas the vegetation —who can describe its freshness, its marvellous exuberance of youth! its fairy-like beauty! Graceful palms, luscious-leaved bananas, wonderful creepers of rainbow colours, over-flow the cliff, forming a luxuriant curtain of tropical verdure, flower and fruit, depending from the upper to the lower city.

On the summit of this cliff is a plain on which is built the Citade Alta, or upper city, with its crowded narrow streets (nearly each with its tramway line), its broad squares, and the cathedral.

On either side of the town, on the hill-sides overlooking the bay, are the most beautiful suburbs imaginable, with palatial villas nestling in gardens of such colour and aroma as intoxicate the senses. No wonder if the Brazilian is voluptuous and lazy, living as he does in such a Paradise as this.

A steep road winds from the Praya to the upper city, but there is also another means of ascent prepared for an indolent population that will not walk ten yards if such exertion can be avoided. From the sea an imposing-looking tower is observable, built from the lower town to the upper, along the cliff-side, and terminating in a broad platform on the summit. This is the elevator, or *parafusa* as it is here called, being merely one of our now common hydraulic hotel-lifts on a large scale. A smart Yankee hit upon this speculation, and it has proved successful. Any invention that can save a Bahian a ten-minutes' walk must pay well. The network of tramways in every Brazilian city is almost incredible ; even small villages inland, like S. Amaro, have their tramcars; and fine dividends the directors show too.

There is in Bahia another means of locomotion which I have never seen elsewhere. Nothing less than the good old-fashioned sedan-chair of Queen Anne's day, carried by two stout negroes. The model is exactly that of the queer box in which our great grandmothers were wont to be carried to rout and ball. Such is Bahia, a city of about 230,000 inhabitants, of whom nearly three-quarters are mulattoes, native negroes, and Africans, the remainder Brazilians, Portuguese, and foreigners. On the morning after our arrival we prepared to go on shore to stretch our legs after our long confinement.

So here we were at last on shore in South America, with plenty to see and wonder at. I am afraid the first thing we did was to enter Freitas and Wilson's store, and indulge in the unwonted luxury of English beer. And now that I am on the subject, let me strongly recommend this firm of ship-chandlers to any yachts that may come into Bahia. I shall not soon forget the courtesy and kindness they showed us.

A ship-chandler's store in a foreign port offers no small opportunity for the study of character, for it is the loafing-place of the merchant captains. Here they sit, drink, and gossip through half the tropic day. Quite at home, sitting astride his chair, is the Yankee skipper of the smart schooner, with broad Panama hat and long cigar. That bluff gentleman, who sports a white helmet, is the captain of the fine English barque that came in yesterday. The jovial German in the straw hat is the master of the ship *Fräulein* from Hamburg. Somewhat savouring of shop is their talk as a rule. Freights are discussed ; the best longitude to cross the equator in ; and the law is laid down with a thump of a horny hand on the counter. Then crews are disparagingly overhauled, somewhat in the manner of women talking over the much-vexed subject of domestic servants.

We were introduced to an old American skipper with a snowy goatee, who hailed from Virginia, a tough old sea-dog of the Spanish Main and the Southern Seas. He had been a whaler in the great South Pacific, and was full of strange yarns of islands where one white lives alone—a king of savages. He was a walking pilot directory, and gave us a long string of directions as to where we should go and what we should do. Said he, " I guess you should go to the Solomons ; they *are* fine. If you dew, don't land at such or such an island, for they air a queer people thar ; they'd treat you just as you would a fat bullock as walked on board your vessel. No ! you visit the little bit of an island just south of that, so-and-so isle. Now ! you mind me ; keep the big hut in the east bay in one with a tall palm you'll see all by itself on a hill, east by south, and steer bold in and bring up in four fathoms, two cables off the shore. There you land ; tell the people you want the white man—say Jake. They'll know then that you've smelt him out, and they'll fetch him for you ; for he is shy, is Jake. Rather queer ; can't abear a white man ; ain't accustomed to him. When you see him, say you know me, and he'll show you round that thar island, I bet. You'll have high old times. Shouldn't wonder as you'll stay there altogether, you'll like it so much. I guess you'll take half-a-dozen wives each and fix ; and they air fine women, young men. For that there island is a paradise ; what with the fruit and the flowers and—the women ; whitish, too, whiter than I am, with long black hair. Why, Lord ! see Jake sitting under his palm-tree smoking all day, while his wives do all the work there is to do—do it willingly too, singing all the time, not like them darned sailors we were talking of just now."

We start for an expedition to the upper town. We take our tickets for the elevator, and enter a half-dark sort of wild-beast cage, where we sit down beside several of the gorgeous fat negresses, for the production of which Bahia is celebrated, and a few dark gentlemen smoking huge Bahia cigars. A strong and not delectable aroma pervades the cage, which strikes me as being somehow familiar, and seems in some strange way to call up reminiscences of my innocent childhood long ago. I have it—it is castor oil ! The machinery of the elevator is evidently lubricated with this horror of my youth. The pretty tree from whose berries this useful drug is extracted grows in great profusion in Brazil ; and this oil is here the cheapest of all lubricators, and is therefore extensively used for this purpose.

At last our smooth, well-castor-oiled journey is completed, and the cage stops suddenly. We effect our exit, and find ourselves on a platform on the summit of the cliff, an extensive square open on the sea side, and surrounded by lofty hotels and houses on the other three sides. We pause awhile by the railing on the edge of the precipice to admire the marvellous scene that stretches before us. The cliff with its curtain of tropic verdure falls perpendicularly from our feet. Below are the roof-tops, the narrow streets of the lower town, the busy Praya, the shipping ; and then beyond, a great, blue inland sea, with islands of waving palms and dense mangoes scattered over it, a sea indented with many a beautiful sandy bay, and with many a forest-clad promontory jutting out, noisy with the cry of parrots, and bright with many jewel-winged birds. On the further side stretch ranges of great purple mountains, scarce visible even in this clear air, for the distance of them.

And many a great river is seen pouring in from the inner lands, and many towns and picturesque whaling villages are scattered here and there round the wonderful coast, which is one ever-changing tropic garden. For this is the world-renowned Reconcava of Bahia, surely one of the wonders of the world. A bay seven miles broad at its mouth, then opening out into this land-locked sea of more than one hundred miles in circumference, where all the fleets of the world could find safe anchorage, free from any danger, and opening out with its many tributary rivers one of the richest regions of Brazil, that wonderful country of tropical prodigality—a gulf which seems as if formed by nature to be the emporium of the universe. All these shores are famous for the production of tobacco; for Bahia is the great tobacco port of Brazil, just as Rio Janeiro is the coffee, and Pernambuco the sugar port.

Interesting it is for a stranger from the old world to stroll for the first time through the Citade Alta of Bahia; the streets are narrow, some of the houses are of antique architecture, built of solid stone, the gloomy mansions of the old merchant-princes of the land. The more modern are plastered, gaudily painted, pseudo-classic and Byzantine gingerbread—which, however, harmonize well with the brilliant air and vegetation. Most of the buildings here are five stories high, thus utterly differing from the *patio'd*, one-storied, flat-roofed houses in the cities of the Spanish people to the South.

A busy life, too, throngs these narrow streets, tramways rattle down the principal thoroughfares, a mongrel crowd of black and white and yellow jostles and jabbers. Towards evening, it is the custom for the women to come out on the balconies to enjoy the fresh breeze that then springs up. Up and down a long street, at every balcony, up to the fifth story, they hang over—mulatto and negro belles, in orange, green, white, scarlet, every gaudy colour, fanning, flirting, laughing, chattering vigorously. Above the shrill scream of the tram-whistle rises their shriller Babel; a bewildering pandemonium of extreme light and sound and colour and motion, mellowed slightly as a rule by an all-pervading, mysterious, heavy odour.

On the morrow Arnaud and myself took tram to a certain ancient convent, whose nuns are famous for their skill in the manufacture of feather flowers. All manner of precautions are taken to keep the male sex from intruding on these gentle recluses. We were not admitted within the precincts at all, but had to stand outside a stoutly-grated window, and hold parley through it with the caged inmates. Indeed, one grating was not deemed a sufficient barrier between them and the outer world. The wall was about seven feet thick, and there was a double grating in the recess, one at each side, so that a partition seven feet deep was between us—an unnecessary precaution, a biting sarcasm, I should imagine, to the poor nuns, for in carnal attractions they were sadly, hopelessly deficient. They passed the flowers through the gratings to us in long-handled ladles. Very beautiful some of these flowers were, of metallic-lustred, rainbow-hued feathers of humming-bird and parrot. Very keen at a bargain were the ladies; they jabbered and wrangled and pushed each other aside in the excitement of their rivalry. It was an unpleasing sight, so we purchased a few flowers and departed.

CHAPTER V.

DURING our stay in this port we organized several pleasant expeditions up country; but to describe all these would swell this work to a size far greater than I mean to trouble my readers with. I should like to tell you of the pretty village of Rio Vermilio, where the fresh trade-wind blows full on the shore, driving the great Atlantic seas till they break grandly on the rocky beach, scattering showers of spray over the bending cocoanut-palms, whose leaves glisten like diamonds with the salt crystals.

I should like to narrate, too, a five-days' trip of Arnaud and myself, when we crossed the bay, steamed up a river through jungle and forest, then progressed higher still in a negro dug-out to the little town of St. Amaro; how on the muddy banks the pink cray-fish gambolled; and how the branches of the mangroves were thick with oysters hanging like fruit; and how from St. Amaro we rode across fifty miles of roadless country to Faira St. Anna, now by the palatial mansion of some rich sugar-planter, surrounded by its slave village and sloping hills of waving cane, and now through virgin forest, where the tall palms rose high above the lesser growth of trees, linked by intricate creepers, lianas, and convolvuli. I should like to linger over the description of the wonderfully-plumaged birds—parrot, humming-bird, canary, and a hundred others; of the fruits growing wild and in profusion in the woods pine-apples,

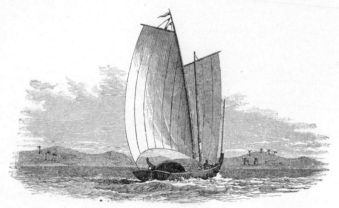

A BAHIAN TRADER.

bananas, mango, jachas, bread-fruit, and the rest. I should like to tell you of the people we met, the half-naked slaves, standing outside their huts, with their curious little, pot-bellied, wholly-naked children; of the proud planter, with poncho and massive silver spurs, galloping across his lands: how we journeyed on from Faira St. Anna to Cachoeira by train through plantations of sago and coffee, and thence by steamer again down a broad river to the Reconcava. But all this would fill a volume by itself.

Having been now a fortnight in port, we once more prepared for sea. We refilled our rum barrel with white rum, laid in a stock of pine-apples, yams, and other vegetables;

and on the 6th of November weighed our anchor and sailed
out of the Reconcava. Salvoes of crackers and rockets, and
the tolling of manifold bells from all parts of the city,
seemed to be bidding us a farewell as we dropped slowly
down the smooth bay.

In Bahia every day of the year seems to be a *fiesta*, and
dedicated to some saint or other; keeping a saint's day here
implies a terrible waste of fireworks, and clanging of church
bells. All day long, for they do not even await the shades
of night, the rockets ascend. There is no place in the
world like Bahia for these amusements. Far out to sea you
know when you are approaching this port by the sound and
the blaze of the worship of its inhabitants. It is called
Bahia dos Todos os Santos—the bay of All Saints—of all
of them with a vengeance. It is the most religious and
most vicious city of religious and vicious Brazil.

The eve of our departure there stood forth an omen in
the sky, which, said the sailors on shore, is but rarely seen,
and only when some terrible hurricane is imminent. Inside
the thin crescent of the moon was one solitary, bright star,
the only one in the heavens. It was a curious appearance;
but it seemed to me not likely to be connected with terres-
trial storm.

Our next port was to be Rio de Janeiro, the beautiful
capital of this empire. We had fresh winds from the E. to
N.E., and so completed the voyage in four days and twenty
hours. We carried our spinnaker and gaff-topsail nearly all
the time. At 5.30 p.m., the 6th of November, we were
outside the Reconcava, off Point San Antonio. By midday,
the 7th of November, we had logged 116 miles; the 8th of
November we made 174 miles; the 9th of November 152
miles; the 10th of November 167 miles; the 11th of
November 164 miles. It was glorious, sunny weather, and
bracing and pleasant was the fresh Atlantic breeze, after the
rather debilitating climate of Bahia.

The second night out would have seemed to some pilot of
old as full of alarming portents. The mariner at times does
encounter such nights, weird and awe-inspiring, that fill his
breast with vague, superstitious terror as he keeps his midnight watches. It was an exceedingly dark night and still;
the long ocean swell rolled on smoothly, only at rare intervals breaking into phosphorescent spray. The air was hot

and stifling as before storm. The clouds that passed overhead were utterly black and assumed fantastic shapes.
Arnaud recognized Gambetta's head, and a fiend riding
across the heavens on a black horse, in the slowly-floating
masses of vapour. It seemed at times as if the whole sky
was full of uneasy spirits, fixing up everything ready for a
good old hurricane. The moon only appeared at intervals
through rifts in the cloud. It was surrounded by a beautiful
triple halo of green, yellow, and pink circles. In the middle
watch the sky cleared somewhat, and Arnaud and myself
became the amazed spectators of several most remarkable
phenomena, meteoric or electric—I cannot be certain which.
We saw first in the midst of a cloud an appearance like that
of a great shell bursting. It illuminated the whole cloud
and the sea for a moment, and its explosion was accompanied with a dull thud. Again we observed several
meteors that sailed across the sky like rockets, with bright
tails of fire, and then burst. A mysterious night this on
the warm tropic sea, and ominous of tempest, which, however, did not overtake us.

On the fourth night out, we kept a sharp look-out for
Cape Frio, in whose neighbourhood we knew ourselves to be.
There is a lighthouse on this point with a powerful light;
we made it out about two a.m. As we neared the cape the
thermometer fell rapidly, till we really felt quite cold for
the first time since we had left England. This sudden fall
of the temperature is always experienced near Cape Frio,
hence its name, the Cold Cape. I believe the phenomenon
is attributed to the presence of some oceanic current of cold
water which comes to the surface hereabouts. This cape is
also famous for the furious squalls that sweep down from it
seawards.

When daylight came we discerned land once more on the
starboard bow—a distant range of blue mountains, which
we recognized from their sharp spire-like peaks to be the
Organ Mountains, which lie to the back of the Bay of Rio.
On approaching the entrance of the gulf the water shallowed
and became light-green in colour ; the sea, as is not uncommon on this bar, was coming in in heavy breaking rollers,
which would have proved dangerous to many a yacht of the
Falcon's tonnage, that I know of. We heard that a heavy
pampero had been blowing for three or four days to the

south of Rio, hence the exceptionally disturbed condition of
the sea when we arrived.

Who can describe the grandeur of the gates of the Bay of
Rio, and the wonderful beauty of the bay itself? I thought
nothing could be so beautiful as the Reconcava of Bahia;
and lo! here is a gulf that transcends all one's wildest dreams
of the magnificence of tropical scenery. Not here are the
gently sloping hills of the Reconcava. The entrance of this
bay is between stupendous and fantastically-serrated mountains. Steep and forbidding domes of granite fall sheer into
the boiling surf. The aspect of this coast from the sea is
grand and terrible in the extreme; but once within the bay,
all changes. One moment we were running before a cool,
strong breeze, rolling heavily in the steep seas, the next
moment we had passed between two walls of rock—we had
entered the inland sea. Immediately the water fell smooth
as glass—the wind died away, and the bracing sea-breeze
was changed for the sultry atmosphere of the tropic harbour.
We came to an anchor inside the island and fortress of
Villegagnon.

What a scene was there round us, what a variety of beautiful form and colour! To give any adequate description
of this bay is quite impossible. It is as extensive as the
Reconcava of Bahia, and is studded with the most beautiful
islands, whose beaches are lined with cocoanuts and stately
palms. All round the bay rise the stupendous mountains;
some covered with gorgeous-coloured forests, others of barren
crags and lowering precipice. And there stretching far along
the shore is the empire-city, Rio Janeiro—the queen of South
America, lying at the foot of an amphitheatre of great mountains. There is the huge granite crag of the Sugar-loaf,
seeming ready to fall down on the suburbs at any moment.
There is the Gavia, a square-headed mass of rock with a flat
top like Table Mountain; there the Tajuca and the forest-
covered Cocovado, with its springs of sweet water. And all
round the inland sea are little sheltered bays, the most beautiful imaginable, with beaches of silver-sand, and wonderful
tropical forests covering the mountain sides, where the guava
and mango grow in wild profusion, and there are islands in
these bays too, like little gardens of Eden.

Our first stroll through the city gave us a very favourable
impression of it; we were evidently in a civilized and luxu-

rious capital, where we could recreate and relax very pleasantly for a few days.

Rio Janeiro is a fine city of about 500,000 inhabitants, and is thus much larger than Bahia; it is also much "whiter" than Bahia; the negroes here are not in so overwhelming a majority as in the former city.

Tramways of course are everywhere; gas and tramways are the specialities of Rio; no town in the world is so well lit. Far beyond the city, up to the mountain-tops, through country lanes, are the tram-metals laid. and the lamps planted. Far out to sea is the city visible at night by the great glare of it.

Five minutes after landing, instinct led us to the establishment of Jimmy Graham, the well-known Yankee barman. A smart man is Graham; as you enter his place the first thing in the morning, uncertain as to what your eye-opener shall be, do not, if you be a wise man, tax your brains on the subject. Jimmy knows what will fix you up better than you do; simply say,—

"Graham, I want you to prescribe for me."

"Take a seat," he will reply. He will look at your face for a moment or so with his shrewd eye, then a gleam of intelligence will flit over his expressive face. He has diagnosed your case.

"Wall, I guess I can fix you up what you want," and forthwith he will arrange for you some iced delectable poison, long or short as the case may be, which you find will exactly suit your disease and make a new man of you. But if you are that rare bird a wise man, you will forswear strong drinks in this climate, and patronize Jimmy only for the prawn curries he knows how to prepare, and the delicate rock oysters from the bay.

This first evening we went up to dine at the Hotel Vista Allegre, which is out of the close city, on the healthy hillside. Thither we travelled partly by train and partly up a very steep, inclined plane in a car which is hoisted by a chain, just like the railway from Lyons to the Croix Rousse.

It was now night, and the aspect of the city and the bay from the elevation at which we were, was very strange and beautiful. Steep ravines and hill-sides sloped from our feet to the city, mountains were around us, and all were lit by myriads of gas-jets. The crags were covered with the rich vegetation of the tropics. Tall palms towered above the houses. A most fairy-like view, a wonderful contrast of city-streets and nature at her grandest.

Rio is a lively town enough after dull Bahia, for here we have theatres, an opera-house, an alcazar, concert-gardens like those of Paris, and other dissipations. The Rua Ovidor is the Bond Street of Rio. Carriages are prohibited from traversing it after dark; for it is then that the Brazilian ladies promenade this narrow thoroughfare to do their shopping. Ten p.m. is the fashionable hour.

The niggers here live a very out-of-door life, and one thus acquires a very fair insight into the habits of their private life, or rather what would be the private life in the case of a white man. The negro barber carries on his profession in the middle of the street; when a customer comes, he simply sets him down on the pavement, if no other seat be at hand, and lathers his chin and shaves away, undisturbed by the crowd of little niggers that generally admiringly surround the artist.

Here sitting in a long string on the kerb-stone of a crowded street are negro slaves weaving straw hats; listen to them; that barbaric tongue cannot be Portuguese; no, it is an African dialect. For these are not creoles of Brazil, like most of the slaves here, but Africans, men who have once known freedom.

I had noticed that one of these half-naked hat-weavers was always treated with great respect by his fellows. He was a giant in size and had evidently been a man of uncommon strength, but he was now of great age, his back was bent, and his curly wool was white as snow. I was informed that he had once been one of the greatest kings of Africa, and that all Africans from his part of that continent, even over here in America, after years of slavery, observe the same form of etiquette when approaching him as they perforce did in the old times, when he was every inch a king, and the life and death of his subjects were in his hands. Barbarous indeed these savage courtiers must be thus to still revere their prince and be loyal to him, knowing well that there is not the slightest chance of his ever again recovering his freedom and his kingdom, and being in a position to reward them for their fidelity. For it is not only by mere courtesy that they show their devotion, it is customary for them to

PAQUETA.

quarrel among themselves as to who shall complete the aged
sovereign's daily hat-weaving task, when their younger and
nimbler fingers have completed their own. You can observe
this amiable squabble among the poor fellows every afternoon,
the old king, sitting the while blinking sleepily, taking no
interest in the proceedings, apathetic beneath the burdens of
his many years, and now, I should imagine, hardly remem-
bering and regretting those days when—

> "At furious speed he rode
> Along the Niger's bank."

Two days after our arrival at Rio, we got up anchor and
sailed up the bay to the island of Paqueta, a distance of about
ten miles. This is a pretty little, wooded, hilly island, with
a population of about 1700. A friend of Jerdein, an ex-
royal-mail officer, and now superintendent of that company
in Brazil, was living here with his family, so we came to an
anchor off his house, and remained there until we sailed for
the River Plate. A beautiful spot it was, nestling among
the stately palms and bamboos, tamarinds and almonds.
And very pleasant it was for us after our semi-savage life to
see once more in Mr. May's hospitable home the faces of
English ladies and English children.

This islet of Paqueta is a lovely little corner of earth to
pass a lazy time in. Here we are, for instance, in the evening
sitting in Mr. May's verandah, puffing at our post-prandial
cigars. The too short tropic dusk has passed, and it is night;
all round us is the tropic garden of rare fruits and palms and
creepers. The garden terminates on a sandy beach, on which
break, with gentle plashes, the small waves of the sheltered
bay; along the sand is a fringe of cocoanut-trees, waving
their great leaves gently in the evening breeze. A promontory of round boulders projects, a dark mass, into the water
gleaming in silver arrows under the moon. Beyond the
rocky islets and palmed promontories, across the broad bay
is seen, looming dark against the sky, the opposite coast,
with the mountains of the interior still further back, vague
and misty.

The faint lights of the charcoal-burners' fires are seen here
and there on the far-off hill-sides, where the virgin forests
are; and to return once more to the foreground, there within
a stone's throw rides the stately old *Falcon* at anchor. Now
add to this the still, warm night-air, heavy with the odour of

4

flowers and fruits and spices, the flight of bats, the perpetual shrill cries of cicadas, the sad splash of the waves on the rocks, and you have the very surroundings for an indolent man who loves to ponder silently over his cigar and coffee, or rather not even to ponder at all, but sink into that *rêverie qui ne pense à rien*, his mind intoxicated with the beauty of all that fervid yet lazy nature around him.

But after all there are few lotos-eaters at Paqueta. Certain perspiring black savages, with a rag round the waist as their sole clothing, here pass anything but a life of *dolce far niente*. Above the cry of cicada, and the moaning of sea, and the rustling of palm-leaves, all through the long night, from the time that the sun sinks into the fiery crimson clouds that crown the Organ Mountains to when he rises again from the Atlantic—you can hear a strange and melancholy song rising in wild bursts on the night-air; a barbaric, monotonous and sad chorus, such as Israelite bondsmen might have sung long ago in Egypt. And this too is a chorus of bondsmen, of African slaves. For there are lime-works on Paqueta Island, and by night and day, unceasingly, the native blacks toil on in batches. The night-watchers are obliged to sing this chorus at intervals, so that their master in his bed, if he chance to awake, may know that they are toiling and watching, and not falling to sleep with weariness.

This lime is made from the shells of the oysters that so thickly cover every rock in the Gulf of Rio. About Paqueta can be seen daily a regular squadron of quaint native craft, manned by naked slaves, dredging for the bivalves.

The process is a very primitive one, involving a great deal of labour and very little proportionate results. The slave has a long bamboo with a small cradle fitted to one end ; this he scrapes along the rocky bottom, raising each time only a handful or so of shells, I should imagine.

I will not inflict on my readers a description of the lions of Rio and its neighbourhood, which of course we *did :* and what city on earth has such marvellous scenery in its immediate neighbourhood ? Why, even in the narrow streets of the city itself you come suddenly on the most lovely little oases of tropic vegetation. Here, for instance, is a gloomy and ugly old mansion in a squalid lane. It has some pretensions to architecture, and it is the palace of some merchant-prince, maybe, but it is as dingy and uninteresting-looking as are the houses near Fitzroy Square. You are passing it, when suddenly the portal of it is opened, and there is revealed a glimpse of Paradise itself. Under that dark door as a frame is seen a bit of bright azure sky above, and below, a garden; but what a garden, what colour, what form! among the dazzling creepers and bushes, stone fauns and nymphs disport themselves, and fountains splash on cool marble and tesselated pavements. And down the great garden is a drive through an avenue of immense palms, smooth and straight as columns, with their leaves joining overhead like the aisle of a cathedral of giants. It is a glimpse into fairyland; then the portal closes, and we might almost be in dingy London, save for the sky above and the niggers around.

So pleasant was found our stay here that it was not till forty days had passed unnoticed by, that we sailed from Rio. We came in on November 11th, and left on December 21st. It was the midsummer here south of the line, but the heat on the Brazilian coast is rarely oppressive. Our thermometer in the cabin only once, as far as I remember, registered more than 95°. We found lots to do. Sometimes in the city, sometimes making pleasant excursions into the interior, sometimes organizing cruises and picnics with the *Falcon* in the bay, and, best of all to my mind, sailing about in the dinghy among the beautiful islands near Paqueta. Those little exploring expeditions were most delightful. There is a little archipelago of islands near Paqueta, all beautiful; some large, with pleasant villages of peaceable mulatto folk; others uninhabited, but overflowing with a glorious vegetation; others bare, mere boulders rising from the clear water with, maybe, a solitary cactus growing on the summit. Nowhere on earth is there an inland water so adapted for a cruise in a small boat. One could travel on for months, and anchor each night off some new picturesque island, or in some new bay, so extensive is this great winding gulf.

Here is the log of one of these little cruises:—One glorious morning I put the mast and sail in the dinghy, provisioned her with a keg of water, a bottle of wine, bread, oranges, pipe, tobacco, matches, and sketching materials, and started for a solitary sail. First I circumnavigated Paqueta, keeping close to the shore, where the palms overhang the water, steering among great boulders. These boulders that rise out of the Gulf of Rio are of interest to the geologist ; they are smoothly rounded, by the action of water, into a dome shape, and nearly all of them are split down the middle as by a wedge, so that they present the appearance of so many episcopal mitres.   Then passing several islets, I reached one—an uninhabited little paradise which I named Cocoanut Island, from the multitude of those graceful trees that lined its shores—and beached the dinghy in a little sandy cove.   If that island could be transported as it is to Kew Gardens, it would be one of the sights of Europe.   It was hilly, and about a mile or rather more in circumference, and covered with a dense vegetation. Mangoes and tamarinds, and the most gorgeous flowers grew on its slopes, all bound together by intricate network of lianas and purple-flowered convolvuli.   Brilliant-plumaged humming-birds, and rainbow-hued butterflies seemed to be the sole inhabitants.   From the summit of the islet one looked over the broad many-islanded bay and the far moun-tains, glowing under the blue tropic vault.   In order to acquire an appetite for my picnic, I treated myself to a plentiful feast of oysters.   All the rocks were covered with these up to high-water mark ; small and delicate they were too ; so I waded about in the tepid water, cutting them off in clusters with my knife.   Then came lunch, for which the mangoes on the island provided a dessert.   Then off again to explore further islets, all uninhabited, till I felt like a sort of Robinson Crusoe of half-a-dozen isles instead of one ; and the sun was low and it was time to beat back against the fresh sea-breeze to where the *Falcon* lay at anchor by the stately row of palms.

One of the things to be *done* by the visitor to Rio is Petropolis, a model highland village founded by the Emperor of the Brazils, and in the midst of which he has built to himself a summer pleasure-palace.   Thither one fine morning we proceeded, and a pleasant journey it was.   First, a steamer took us across the bay to a point where a train awaited us.   After but a short voyage on the line, we again changed our mode of conveyance, and entered one of the six coaches that were intended to carry the passengers across the mountains to the imperial village.   In single file they slowly ascended the pass—a fine road in sharp zigzags, reminding one of " Les Échelles " of the Mont Cenis—but the view around was somewhat different; not the grey crags and the snows and sombre pines of the Alps on this tropical mountain-pass. On either side of us were palms, tree-ferns, lianas, and all manner of unknown plants and flowers, with colours such as no orthodox plants should have, stolen from the minerals. Great leaves of burnished copper strewed the ground, and the green, and silvers, and yellows, and reds of the twining creepers and flowers were as of molten and incandescent metals. The parrots, humming-birds, butterflies, and beetles, gaudy-hued as they were, were not more so than this glorious vegetation they inhabited. From the summit of the pass the view was grand in the extreme. A vast expanse of country lay beneath us like a plan. The mountains sloped down from our feet to a dark, wooded plain; beyond that was all the Bay of Rio, with its islands and mountains, the Sugar-loaf guarding the entrance; and then still farther the Atlantic horizon-line.

Descending again, we soon reached our destination, the luxurious village nestling in a hollow of the forest-clad hills. We rattled down the main street by which flows a babbling river shaded by avenues of willows, and dismounting, introduced ourselves to Mr. Mills, of the comfortable English hotel, who forthwith proposed to mix for us the refreshing cocktail of the New World, the while dinner was preparing.

Petropolis is built in the centre of a large imperial estate, the emperor, who is, as every one knows, not only one of the most hard-working monarchs in the world, but one of the most active in every scheme of benevolence, is, if nowhere else, popular in Petropolis. Some years ago, some pseudo-philanthropist sent over to Rio a large batch of German colonists. When the unfortunates landed, they found they were not wanted, there was nothing for them to do; they lay about the quays, living on garbage, till yellow fever thinned their ranks woefully. They would probably all have perished had not the emperor taken up the matter. He transported them *en masse* to his highland estate, where the cooler climate permits the white man to work without danger in the fields, and founded Petropolis. And now it stands a model village in which there is no sordid house, no poverty, all is clean, tidy, and prosperous-looking. For some miles round where the forest is cleared, are the little farms of the happy and contented people. And so, as you ride along the well-made roads that traverse the little colony, you perceive about you everywhere comfortable-looking Teutons with blue eyes and yellow hair, and well-dressed children going to school, and comely matrons knitting at cottage-doors, as in Europe, instead of the half-naked negroes and the barbarism of the slave plantations which surround this little oasis of liberty. And now in addition to all this, a further cause of prosperity has come to the village of Dom Pedro Secundo, for a blessing seems to be on the place. The cool and healthy air has induced many of the wealthy citizens of Rio to resort here during the summer months, when the yellow fever is hanging about the hot city. It is rapidly becoming quite a fashionable little place, and several good hotels have sprung up around the imperial summer palace.

We stayed at Mills' two days, visited the virgin forest— another thing we had to *do*—in a downpour of rain ; I think we were *done* more than the forest was, for we did not appreciate its beauties under the depressing circumstances, though we had brought some *cana* with us, wherewith to dilute the rain. Besides, the virgin forest was a fraud, though a beautiful one, for the vegetation of it was in no wise more magnificent than that of most portions of the neighbouring country, though these gave themselves no high-sounding titles. From Petropolis we took coach to Entre Rios, a drive of about fifty miles, along a very well-kept road. The coach-mules were splendid animals, and carried us on in grand style, past the coffee plantations and the uncleared forests. From Entre Rios, we travelled about on the Dom Pedro Railway in rather an unmeaning way, from one uninteresting place to another.

On the 15th of December we sailed from delightful Paqueta to our old berth off Rio, under Fort Villegagnon. The weather was now becoming oppressive—ninety-five in the shade, with no cool nights as a relief. The calm water in the harbour began to stink horribly ; and far from odorous was the vegetable refuse that lay about the markets—so yellow Jack found his opportunity, and there were five vessels in the harbour, with the ominous yellow flag flying at their main.

While we were at anchor here the emperor came off to the

Falcon in the *Wanderer's* launch; he was interested in our cruise, and, as I understand, intended to honour us with a visit. Unfortunately we were all on shore at the time, so he merely steamed round us, and remarked that we must be very uncomfortable and very foolish to wander about the oceans in such a cockleshell. If I were an emperor I think I should be of the same opinion, and prefer something a good deal bigger if I cruised at all; but after all, would it be half so enjoyable?—maybe not.

For several days in succession, during our stay, a violent squall arose every afternoon in the bay. The weather would wax sultrier and sultrier from sunrise till about three p.m., when suddenly a mass of black cloud would sweep over the sky, pouring down rain in such torrents as only tropical clouds can, accompanied by thunder and lightning. These squalls blew with very great force, lashing the bay into a mass of foam. On two occasions we had to put down two anchors, with fifty fathoms on each, to prevent driving. One day during the squall two large vessels near us fouled each other in consequence of the anchors of one dragging. Signals of distress were hoisted, and two men-of-war's boats' crews were sent to their assistance. After considerable damage had been incurred by both they were cleared. This is the old-fashioned Rio weather. Once this daily storm was so regular in its coming, that it was customary when one made an appointment with another to say, " I will meet you after or before the storm," as the case might be. But of late years the climate of Rio has changed considerably, as has that of every part of the world it seems, more or less; and the three p.m. storm is not as punctual as was his wont of old.

One of our crew here left us—Andrews—so we were now rather under-manned, and determined to pick up some one else in the Plate.

It was now about time for us to leave Rio; two of us were down with slight attacks of fever, and we all felt as if the fresh winds of the Atlantic would be beneficial as a change.

We had made the acquaintance of the officers of the SS. *Norseman* in Rio, the telegraph-vessel of the Anglo-Brazilian Telegraph Company. She was bound about this time for Maldonado, in Uruguay, and the captain kindly offered, if he met us out at sea, to give us a tow if we were in want of one.　Maldonado Bay, he told us was a pleasant spot, with lots of sport on shore, and in every way preferable to Flores Island as a place to spend our quarantine in; for into quarantine we were certain to be thrust as soon as we touched at any Uruguayan or Argentine port after leaving Rio.　The River Plate people have the greatest dread of yellow fever, their countries lie outside of the usual limits of this pest, but they have a vivid reminiscence of the fearful epidemic at Buenos Ayres ten years ago, when the whole city was put into rigid quarantine, all business was at a standstill, and the horrors of a mediæval plague, such as that of Florence, were experienced to the full in the crowded South American city; no less than a thousand people perishing a day, for several weeks.

CHAPTER VI.

WE sailed out of the harbour on December the 21st the city looking very beautiful from the sea in the early morning.

There was but little wind, and we progressed but slowly. It happened that the *Norseman* steamed out the same day, so ten hours after our departure she came up with us.　The captain stopped his vessel and repeated his invitation as to the tow; adding, as a further inducement, that we should thus reach Maldonado by Christmas Day, and we could all pass that festive season together.　We gladly accepted his offer, so the *Norseman* lowered a boat, and we soon got a tow-line to each of her quarters.　It was as well that we did get this tow, for now that Andrews had left us we were only four on board.　Of these Jerdein was laid up below with slight fever; I was far from well recovering from the same; and the boy had also been suffering from a sort of bilious fever for some days.

Under these circumstances Captain Lacy sent on board of us one of his black sailors to lend a hand at steering.　He and the boy took one watch during Jerdein's illness, Arnaud and myself the other.　Steering a small vessel when towing fast requires some care, so, as usual under similar circumstances, I had to do all the steering in my watches. Arnaud, however, was not allowed to be idle. He was kept very constantly at the pumps, for we were towing so fast through the short seas—ten knots an hour at times—that much water came on board, and found its way below through the hatch of the sail-room.

We had not been towing long before we parted one of the warps : the steamer stopped and lowered a boat with another. This boat was manned by Krumen, who kept time to their oars as they came off with a queer dirge-like song. The words of this song were delightfully simple, consisting of a constant repetition of the monosyllable Bo.

Some of my readers may not know what Krumen are. Well, they are a superior race of black men who inhabit a certain strip along the West Coast of Africa. They are all boatmen by profession, and are engaged by European vessels for service in the unhealthy oil-rivers, and other parts where work in the sun is perilous for the white man. Excellent fellows they are, with a far more intellectual cast of countenance than any of the West Indian or Brazilian blacks. These they despise, and will hold no communion with, for the Kruman boasts that he is not only a freeman, but the descendant of freemen. He is certainly a superior being to the ordinary negro, faithful and honest.

Curious names these jolly blacks take to themselves. On the *Norseman* we had Silver, Maintop, Ropeyarn, Jibboom, and Zulu ; this latter was so called because he was taken to London to impersonate one of the Zulus exhibited at the Aquarium. He there enjoyed himself amazingly, and still receives letters from an Aquarium barmaid. Zulu was the man sent on board of us by Captain Lacy. Rather funny that we should ship an Aquarium Farini-Zulu as a hand on the *Falcon!*

As the sea increased a good deal on our second day out, it became necessary for the *Norseman* to diminish her speed to eight knots, so as to avoid straining the yacht, which towed very heavily. We had now crossed Capricorn, and were once more out of the tropics. The difference of latitude soon made itself apparent. The wind blew from the south, cold and bracing after its passage from Antarctic seas. It was a very great change after sultry Rio, and we found pea-jackets necessary for the first time.

The distance that the *Norseman* proposed to tow us was above 900 miles. The experiences of the voyage were such as to make me resolve never under any circumstances to undertake anything of the kind again. The *Norseman* had been compelled to go easy, and stop so often in order to enable us to put fresh chafing-gear on the hawsers, and to get a new tow-line on board when one was carried away, an incident which occurred thrice, so violent were the sudden jerks at times, that on the 24th of December, Christmas Eve, we were still so far from Maldonado, as to render all chance of eating our Christmas dinner in port very remote.

This day a nasty short sea was running, that was continually filling our deck fore and aft. The vessel pitched about with extraordinary quickness, showers of spray came over the bows constantly, half-drowning the man at the tiller, who alone stayed on deck. Everybody and everything was wet through. Poor Zulu, unaccustomed to the cold and wet, looked very miserable indeed when his turn used to come round to steer. No doubt he regretted his native wilds in the well-warmed London Aquarium, where he was wont to raise his terrific Farini war-cry, and hurl his assegai into the targets, surrounded by admiring pale-face damsels. The poor fellow was laid up for three days after his experience of *Falcon* life.

About two p.m. I was at the tiller: a confused sea was running at the time, so that it was very difficult to steer the vessel. And now a serious accident that I had for a long time foreseen as probable occurred. I must explain that the *Falcon's* bowsprit runs straight over the top of her stem amidships, and that the forestay leads to the bowsprit gammoning-iron—an exceptionally strong one of course—instead of to the stem, as is the usual method. I do not know whose idea this arrangement was, but it is obviously a very bad one; not only is that most important support to the mast, the forestay, fitted in an insecure fashion, but the bowsprit cannot be taken wholly on board, as the mainmast is in the way of so doing. Thus we had a good many feet of bowsprit overboard when the heel of it was jammed up against the mast. The result was, after one heavier pitch than usual, and a shower of water that half-blinded me and took away my breath for a moment, I saw with consternation that all the main rigging and shrouds were flying about

quite slack. I knew in a moment what had occurred—
one of the hawsers had got under the bowsprit close to the
bow, and wrenched the gammoning-iron and stout iron band
right out of the stem, thus carrying away our forestay as
well. I called all hands on deck, and hailed the *Norseman*,
which at once stopped and lowered a boat to lend us assistance. We found that a large piece had been wrenched off
our stem in addition to other damage: so we were in a fine
pickle. The bowsprit itself was not broken.

But a more serious mishap was now to follow, which all
but put a termination to the *Falcon's* cruise altogether, by
sending her to the bottom of the South Atlantic. The
Norseman had stopped. Being to windward we drifted on
to her. Seeing that we were getting too near, we shouted
to the officer in charge to take a few revolutions ahead
occasionally so as to keep clear of us. As soon as he attempted to do so it was found that one of the tow-lines had
got round her screw, so that she could not move, but lay
helplessly rolling about in the seas. In a few moments we
had drifted right down on her, and we were foul of each
other. Our rigging then got entangled in the stock of her
anchor, and thus having secured us, she locked us in her
embrace, and, like a great sea-monster as she is, deliberately
proceeded to crush us to pieces. She was rolling heavily at
the time, and with every roll the stock of her great anchor
and her iron sides came down on us with pitiless weight.
First our main-mast was nearly wrenched out of us. Then
the great black mass of the ocean steamer leaned over us,
bending in our davits, and crushing our beautiful dinghy
into matchwood. Then another great lurch, and the stock
of her starboard anchor coming down between our port-
shrouds carried away all the ratlines, about ten feet of bulwark, and threatened to stave in our decks. Then our
bowsprit went. We were now right across her bows, a most
perilous situation; for over the bows of a telegraph-vessel
hangs an enormous iron machine, weighing many tons, used
I believe, for winding in the electric cable. This rose and
fell above us like a battering-ram, as the steamer pitched in
the great seas. It was indeed a " bad quarter of an hour "
for us that; not a merry way of passing Christmas Eve.
We tried our best to disentangle our rigging from her
anchors, and shove clear of her, a difficult and even dan-

gerous undertaking. One plucky Kruman was very nearly crushed while helping us.

At last, almost miraculously, we fell clear of her, and setting a bit of sail drifted some half-mile away to leeward, where the poor old *Falcon* lay a dismal and dishevelled wreck upon the waters. The remains of our dinghy oars and other articles were floating away, visible at times on the summit of the waves, a pitiable sight. But it was no time for lamentation; it was important to repair the damage as far as possible without delay. On inspection we rejoiced to find that to all appearance only our upper works had suffered, the body of the vessel was as sound as ever. We passed our chain through the two hawse-pipes, set up our forestay to it as well as we could, and got everything shipshape again.

In the meantime the *Norseman* managed to get the hawser clear of her screw, so steaming down to us she took us once more in tow.

We had a most uncomfortable time of it this Christmas Eve. The wind and sea had risen considerably, and it was very dark. I remember well what curious work it was steering that night by the rising and falling stern-light of the heavily-pitching steamer. The motion of the *Falcon* was at the time the most violently quick I have ever experienced. We were constantly jumped off our feet while steering. At regular intervals the vessel would take five or six terribly rapid rolls in succession, rolling her gunwales under, and filling her decks right up with water, heeling to such an angle as made even capsizing seem quite a possible contingency at times; then she would pitch as violently as she had rolled, and we expected to see the main-mast chucked out over her bow at any moment. Water-breakers and other articles broke adrift, floated on deck, and flew about wildly with the frantic leaps of the little craft. Down in the cabin the water was a foot over the flooring, and washing over the bunks, drenching everything, notwithstanding that some one was always at the pump. Every one was wet, cold, and miserable, and bruised, too, with the banging about, against which no sea-legs availed. It was rather an anxious time, for had the weather been a little worse the steamer would have been obliged to slip us, no agreeable prospect in our half-wrecked state. So passed our merry Christmas Eve.

But when Christmas Day broke there came a change. It was a lovely morning, bright and bracing; the wind had moderated considerably; the sea, too, had gone down; so the *Norseman* increased her speed to make up for lost time.

Towards dinner-time the steamer stopped, and Captain Lacy sent a boat with a fresh hawser to us, and an invitation to partake of the orthodox roast beef and plum-pudding on board of his vessel. He lent us two Madagascar negroes to steer the *Falcon* in the meanwhile. After the wet and cold of the last few days we thoroughly enjoyed our Christmas dinner in the comfortable saloon of the steamer. In the evening we returned to the *Falcon* once more to renew our duties. Throughout the night the sea was smooth, and all went well.

On the morning of the 26th of December we perceived the loom of land on our starboard side, the coast of Uruguay. On nearing it we were enabled to discern what manner of country this was that we had now reached. The climate, the colour of the clear sky, and the aspect of the vegetation showed us that we had indeed left the tropics. Very different all appeared after torrid Rio, one thousand miles to the northward. It was a low shore with sandy dunes and hills of no great altitude in the background; a desert-looking country where thistles and aloes seemed especially to thrive. Of ill-repute too is all this wild coast from here to the Brazilian frontier, and a terror to mariners. The currents of the ocean hereabouts are powerful and inconstant. There are few landmarks, and disasters to vessels are frequent. On the shore among the surf one can perceive the skeletons of many ill-fated ships, as one coasts along the dreary sand-banks. And woe betide the mariners who are wrecked on this inhospitable land; for the only inhabitants of it are wild gauchos, professional and skilful wreckers when not employed in the almost as lucrative pursuit of pillaging and ravaging all over their native country under the banner of one or the other of those rival guerilla chieftains who are ever contesting who shall next be the chief magistrate and arch-robber of poor revolutionary Uruguay.

These land sharks are bold in the extreme in their malpractices, and of course commit all sorts of atrocities with absolute impunity, for the Government cannot be troubled with inquiry into such little peccadilloes as wrecking and piracy. These brave gauchos must be humoured, or they will join the other side in politics, and lend their lances to a rival cut-throat.

At about sunset we were in sight of our port. As we approached the land, the whole vessel was enveloped in a dense cloud of dragon-flies, which completely covered our rigging.

That very common phenomenon in the River Plate, a mirage, was observable along the whole coast. All the inland hills seemed to have turned upside down; and these floated at some height above the plain, midway in a band of lovely pink sky.

We rounded Pt. Este, and sailing inside Lobos Island, famous for its many seals, entered Maldonado Bay. This little harbour seemed but little protected, should the wind choose to blow hard from seaward. It is but a shallow bay surrounded by sand-banks, with one little island called Goriti, overgrown with wild asparagus, and inhabited by rabbits alone, in the centre of it. It was here that H.M.S. *Agamemnon*, Nelson's old vessel, was lost. The town or village of Maldonado is situated a few miles from the shore and is hidden from it by the sand-hills. Only a few little houses are to be seen on the beach at the extremity of the bay. Not a very prepossessing spot, but Captain Lacy promised us plenty of sport on shore by the lagunas which lie beyond the sand-hills.

" Partridges, snipes, teat, geese, &c., are to be found here in amazing numbers, *at times*," he said.

Just before sunset we perceived a dismasted vessel far out to sea, a derelict evidently, for she had no signals flying. Unfortunately a mist came on just then, or the *Norseman* would have steamed after her and brought her in. A wind arose in the night that carried her far away before morning.

The *Norseman* put to sea again the day after our arrival, and proceeded towards Chuy, as the submarine cable required repairing somewhere thereabouts. She did not return for two days. This time we spent in repairing as much as possible the damage the collision had inflicted on us. We naturally were desirous of going on shore and having a look at the country, but of course could not do so until we had received pratique. We waited twelve hours, and no one came off to us. There was no sign of life anywhere : there were two small craft anchored in the bay, but no one was on board of them ; the shore might be a bit of the central Sahara for loneliness. Twenty-four hours passed, and still no one. At last a solitary horseman appeared on the summit of a sand-hill and looked at us. Hope revived in our breasts ; but after remaining a few seconds only, he galloped away again. Forty-eight hours passed away, and we waxed impatient. We hoisted all manner of signals, but no one paid the slightest attention to them. Where were all the Maldonadans ? Had they gone away revolutionizing ? or seeing from afar that imposing brass gun of ours, had they taken the peaceable *Falcon* for a pirate, and betaken themselves in terror to the inner wilds ? These two days a south-west wind blew fresh and squally right into the bay, and brought into it a sea that made us far from comfortable at our anchorage.

Waxing impatient, I took the collapsible dinghy, and went off to the desert islet of Goriti to shoot rabbits. Here I made the acquaintance of the only inhabitant, a sociable horse, who followed me about everywhere ; walked on when I walked on, sat down when I sat down, and standing on the beach gave me a plaintive farewell neigh when I ultimately rowed off. Of rabbits I saw no traces save their habitations. They too, I suppose, had gone revolutionizing. There were several old iron cannons lying about on the island, for it was strongly fortified in the days of the Spanish, when there was a viceroyalty of Buenos Ayres.

On the third day the *Norseman* came in again ; and at last the inhabitants took notice of us, for a boat came off with a gentleman most gorgeously uniformed and much sabred, who politely told us that he was the captain of the port. Hearing we had come from Rio, he gave us two days' quarantine.

" But," I suggested, " we have already been two days here."

" Ah ! indeed ! " he replied ; " then it is well ; your quarantine is over."

We went on shore, scampered up the sand-hills, and were surprised, on reaching their summit, to behold on the other side a wild but pleasant-looking country ; an undulating Pampas of grass and thistles, aloes and cactus, lay between us and the distant hills, diversified with little lakes, bogs, and sandy wastes. In the foreground was Maldonado town, a small congregation of white-washed, flat-roofed houses, with a street or two, in which it seemed as if no man ever walked. We were introduced to the aristocracy of the place. First to a store-keeper, who is also a commandant, or something of the kind; next to a portly major-general in the Uruguayan army, who is also a butcher; and to an ex-high-admiral of the Uruguayan fleet, who is willing to pilot us to Montevideo in consideration of a small gratuity. Truly a republican country! The latter grandee is an ex-admiral at present because his politics are not those of the party now in power. For with a change in the Government of a South American republic every one goes out of office—admirals, generals, telegraph clerks, policemen, crossing-sweepers—to make room for the friends of the new presidents, and the friends of those friends, and the friends of all their sisters, their cousins, and their aunts, and so on. One rises and falls pretty rapidly out here—admiral to-day, ordinary pilot to-morrow.

We stayed two days more in Maldonado Bay, and had some pleasant rides over the country with the officers of the *Norseman :* but I cannot say that we shot quite so many partridges, snipes, &c., as we anticipated. However, we had a very good time of it, thanks to our friends on the *Norseman* and on shore.

On December the 31st we got up anchor, and sailed for Montevideo, which is about seventy miles from Maldonado. We took the ex-admiral with us as pilot; not that a pilot was really necessary, but the old gentleman seemed anxious to come with us, and was very companionable and jovial in disposition.

We were now in the estuary of the Rio de la Plata, for the limit of the river and the ocean is held to be a line drawn between Maldonado and the Cabo San Antonio, 150 miles across. At Montevideo the river is sixty-four miles wide. At Buenos Ayres, 210 miles higher up than Maldonado, it is thirty-four miles wide. All this gigantic estuary is obstructed by shoals and sand-banks ; the depth of water is hardly anywhere upwards of three fathoms. Luckily the bottom is generally of soft mud : hence there is little risk to a vessel that runs ashore unless the weather be bad. But, unfortunately, bad weather is very common indeed off the River Plate. It is a region of storms and extraordinary electric disturbance. The pampero, the storm-wind from the Pampas, is frequent, and blows with great violence ; often being, indeed, a true hurricane in its fury. The ocean tides do not affect to any great extent the waters of the River Plate, but strong sea-winds cause it to rise con-siderably. The water is fresh almost as far as Montevideo, where, indeed, it is occasionally drunk on the vessels in the roads, so slightly brackish it is. A desolate waste of choppy, muddy waves, flowing between dark mud-banks, with here and there little floating islands of lilies, and trees drifting seawards from the great rivers of the interior ; such is the mouth of the La Plata, the widest river of the world ; and the one which, with the exception of the Amazon, discharges the greatest volume of water into the ocean.

At daybreak on the 1st of January we were in sight of Montevideo. From afar off we observed that there were many men-of-war of different nations and sizes in the har-bour and in the roads—some twenty, at least. Furthest to seaward of all we perceived a British squadron of five huge vessels at anchor. These we soon recognized as the *Bacchante* and the four other men-of-war composing the flying squadron, now bound on a voyage round the world with the two sons of the Prince of Wales. Montevideo presents a very pleasing appearance from the sea, looking very much like an Eastern city with its whitewashed, low, flat-roofed houses. Like an Eastern city, it looked very clean and bright from a distance. We afterwards found that, unlike an Eastern city, it proved as clean and bright on closer inspection.

We came to an anchor well up the little bay which answers as an apology for a harbour here—a very poor harbour in bad weather, as we afterwards found—and hoisted the yellow flag for the health officer. When that functionary came off, he expressed great dissatisfaction at the conduct of his colleague in Maldonado.

"Two days' quarantine is insufficient for a vessel coming from Rio ; you must sail to Flores, and pass three more days off that island before I can permit you to land here."

But now a steam launch, with some other gorgeous officer, came off ; and hearing how matters stood, took our part, and argued that in the case of so small a vessel, with so few men

5

on board, it was hardly necessary to inflict the full allowance of quarantine. After some parley the first doctor gave in, and we were granted pratique, to our great delight, for three days off Flores was not a pleasant prospect. Montevideo was having a good time of it with all these men-of-war in the roads, no fewer than nine of which were British. Bull-fights, masked-balls, hells, and other dissipations were not wanting to relieve the mariner of his hard-earned cash. They told me that there were frequently 5000 men-of-war's men and marines on shore at a time.

A walk through the streets and squares of the capital of Uruguay soon showed us how very different were these people that we were now among from the Brazilians in every respect. No two cities could be less alike than these two capitals of neighbouring states. Not here the lofty houses of Rio, but clean streets of one-storied glaring white houses, built in the style of a Pompeian dwelling. A square, flat-roofed building, with an open courtyard, or *patio*, in the centre, on to which all the rooms open ; a fountain and a flower-garden in the *patio ;* towards the street the windows, if any, small and heavily barred with iron—such is the residence of a South American Spaniard, a retiring sort of a dwelling, shutting itself jealously from the outer world with a Mussulman-like love of seclusion. The populace, too, how different from that of a Brazilian city ! No negroes here, and no ugly-looking Portuguese ; but handsome and dignified Spaniards, with a good deal of Indian blood in the veins of the lower orders of them. Cleanest of cities is Montevideo, with straight streets cutting each other at right angles in the American chess-board fashion.

In the evening of New Year's Day we visited the fine Plaza de l'Independençia, where an excellent military band was playing. Here we were enabled to study the different orders of the populace. The ladies floated by with stately Spanish walk, looking well in their black silk dresses and mantillas ; but why will every South American lady so besmear her face with powder, however good her complexion be ? Officers of the army strutted by in gorgeous uniforms, and with the clash of sabres on the pavement ; a motley crowd of the lower orders loafed about—Basques, Italians, Greeks, and the native gauchos in their barbaric but becoming costume. Here was a group of British blue-jackets slightly overcome by cãna. The native soldiers were everywhere, dressed in their hideous parody of Zouave uniforms. And here were two of the Spanish bull-fighters in their picturesque off-duty dress and pigtails ; smart, wiry, neat-cut fellows they were, and rather foppish in their general get up. The young native swells hung round them admiringly, were proud of their acquaintance, were delighted when allowed to sit at the same table as the matador at a café and treat him to champagne—in short, courted them and made much of them, much in the same way as English gentlemen did prize-fighters not so long back, and the young Roman patrician the crack gladiators of his day when he wanted to be considered as a fast man about town.

CHAPTER VII.

THE climate of the River Plate is exceedingly changeable and trying. The day we came in it was quite cold. The day before the thermometer registered 102° in the shade. When the south wind blows from over the cold Antarctic seas the weather is bracing and cool. But with the north wind coming as it does from over thousands of leagues of parched Pampas and tropical jungles, the atmosphere is hot, dry, and oppressive as that of North Africa when the khamsin blows.

All skippers that have been unfortunately compelled to put into Montevideo for repairs to their vessels, anathematize it ; we were not exceptions to this rule. A wretched German, who called himself a ship's carpenter, undertook to repair the damages to our stem and bulwarks. He not only made a miserable job of it, but detained us seventeen days, and finally presented us with a most exorbitant bill.

Never having been a witness of a bull-fight, curiosity led me to visit the arena one Sunday. It was a glorious day— true River Plate weather—that is, with a cloudless, pale blue and peculiarly clear sky overhead. The clearness of the atmosphere in this land of the Pampas is very remarkable, and it causes the vault of the heavens to appear to be much farther off and vaster than in other lands. The stars, too, at night shine with an exceeding brightness. They seem to be at a far greater distance off than those over our hemisphere, and one can see more of them, further up into the heaven as it were, so pure is the sky; stars behind stars, archipelago behind archipelago of them, to infinity.

On this day a great slaughter of bulls and horses had been promised to the populace; so the glaring white streets that led out of the town to the amphitheatre were thronged with the thousands of pleasure-seekers who were on their way to the cruel games. It was like the road to the Derby without the rowdyism. In carriages, trams, and on foot the crowds poured on, while over the balconies of the houses leaned the pretty Montevidean girls, fanning, and laughing, and flirting as they looked down on the human flood. We entered a tram-car—for of course, being a South American city, Montevideo has scarce a street down which the tram-way-rails are not laid—and drove some miles through the pretty suburbs of the town, where nestling in lovely gardens are gaudy villas of *pseudo*-classic and Italian style, generally painted outside in delicate tints of pink, yellow, and blue, which suits the climate well enough. At last we reached the amphitheatre, gay with the flags of Uruguay and Spain.

We paid our dollar and a half for a *sombra* seat—that is, one on the shady side—and entered the huge structure. It was just the Roman amphitheatre over again. Uncovered to the blue sky was the great circus, with the flights of bare stone steps sloping down to the arena, on which the common spectators sat. And there, too, was one scarlet-draped box, in the which sat a bloated grandee in bright uniform and much be-medalled—president or great minister, I know not which, with his sycophants around him; just as bloated emperor or consul sat in his purple-draped box long ago, under as blue Italian skies, while beneath him the gladiators fought to the death, or Christians fed famishing lions. And no wit less brutally savage was the spectacle, and no less cruel and ready with the " *pollice verso* " were the spectators on this fine Sunday afternoon, in this civilized city of Monte-video, in the year of grace 1880, than in the Roman circus of 2000 years ago. There was a very full house, and there was no small number of our ruddy blue-jackets and marines among the sallow Spaniards. I was pleased to see that, contrary to my expectations, only two women were present, and these were foreigners, and evidently members of the *demi-monde.* Constant communion with strangers has possibly softened the manners of the women of this branch of the Spanish race; for it is certainly not *the thing* in Montevideo for a lady to assist at a bull-fight. But on the other hand, there were a great many young children of both sexes present that had been brought hither by their fathers, and the bloodthirsty little dears enjoyed themselves amazingly.

I had never seen a bull-fight before, and in my ignorance imagined that there might be something more in it than mere cruel brutality—some good sport or display of skill. I do not know that such may not be the case in Spain, but in Montevideo this amusement is merely the ordinary business of an *abattoir* glorified by music and gay costumes, and a strong spice of unnecessary cruelty. Danger to those engaged in the fight is reduced to a minimum. After waiting about half an hour there arose a martial fanfare of trumpets, a door opened, and there galloped forth a picturesque procession. First rode the proprietor in his black velvet dress, mounted on a fine coal-black horse, then came the toreadors, picadors, and matadors in the gaudy and beautiful costumes peculiar to their respective duties; and lastly came four horses drawing a yoke : this to drag out the carcases of bulls and horses that were to be massacred during the games.

Three times, to the lively strains of the band, this procession galloped round the arena, and then went out again; the door closed, and there were left alone in the centre two picadors on their horses, each with his long lance, and a group of footmen with scarlet cloaks over their arms, and the cruel little darts in their hands. Then came a suspense and a pause in the chatter from the stone steps for a few moments, and quickly another door opened, and out rushed, head down, a savage little bull of the Pampas, who made it pretty lively for every one for a short time. But between his wild rushing hither and thither, the being dazed by the scarlet cloaks that were thrown across his head, the loss of blood from lance wounds, and the eight little darts that were sticking in his flanks, the poor beast after a few minutes became weak and showed disinclination to continue the unequal combat. But this was not what was intended by his cowardly foes—he must kill a horse or two ere he be permitted to gasp out his life on the blood-stained sand of the arena and be at peace—the people wanted the smell of more gore, and the pleasant spectacle of prolonged dying agonies before they could let him go. It was now the duty of the picador to place the horse on which he was riding across the path of the bull as much as possible, and no longer to avoid him. It was a disgusting spectacle. The picador himself, with his legs thickly padded with lead and cloth, could suffer no injury from the animal's horns—while his wretched horse had bandages over his eyes, that he might not perceive the infuriated bull that charged him, take alarm and run away. Neither horse nor bull were quite up to the scratch, for the former heard and trembled though he could not see, and the latter was now weak and faint. So we enjoyed the elevating spectacle of attendants whipping up the poor horse, and others stabbing and torturing the dying bull into one last infuriated charge. Maddened by his tormentors, at last he did charge ; the picador kept his horse broadside on to the attack, and loud cheers of *bravo, toro!* saluted the bull as he ran his horns into the belly of the poor animal, that then rushed wildly away, almost unseating his rider in his agonized plunges, with his bowels dragging over the ground as he went. The bull had yet the horse of the other picador to disembowel, or blind, or tear asunder in some other way, before his turn came to die. He lay crouching in a corner, with the blood pouring out of his nostrils with every heavy gasp ; still at bay though, and ready to stagger to his feet and defend himself on the approach of an enemy, only to fall again with half his life gone out with the exertion. Then came up the matador, with scarlet cloak on the left arm, and rapier in the right hand. He came deliberately up to the bull, and after a little dodging deftly run the long steel into his brain, and the poor beast was free at last. The work of the matador is the most merciful to the bull, and the most dangerous to the man, of the whole performance ; for when the bull, as often happens, has still a good deal of life left in him, the slightest divergence in the rapier-thrust might be fatal to the unskilful swordsman. Seven bulls were tortured and slain this fine Sunday afternoon, and some fourteen horses, till the white sand was red and reeking with the blood and entrails of the poor beasts. When a horse was not killed outright by a bull—only disembowelled, or with shoulder ripped up, or the like—he was taken out, doctored and patched up, his wounds sewn up and plastered over to stay the flow of blood, and then he was brought on again half an hour afterwards, weak and staggering, to face and be ultimately killed by another bull.

During the course of the afternoon, one incident gave great pleasure to the spectators. A savage little yellow bull charged with such fury that he tossed a horse and picador clear into the air. The man fell, half-stunned, with the horse on the top of his legs. The bull then stood over them and commenced to deliberately gore his prostrate enemies to death. It was splendid sport for the people, and a loud cry of *bravo, toro ! bravo, toro !* went up ; no horror, no sympathy for the wretched man was expressed on any face of that large crowd of Spaniards—merely fiendish delight in the horrible scene. The people stood up and shrieked with frantic joy, and laughed to see the cruel horns bury themselves in the soft flesh. The picador was not killed, for his comrades diverted the bull, and rescued him. I am sure that many of the spectators looked on this as very unfair— they had been defrauded of the best part of their entertainment—how exciting to have seen a man slowly gored into shreds ! Brutal our prize-ring was, no doubt ; but what can be said of this torturing of the noblest of dumb animals, that I have attempted to describe as I saw it myself this day ?

Throughout our stay at Montevideo the weather was abominable. Violent squalls occurred daily, and it blew a gale of wind three days out of four—an exceptional state of things in midsummer. We rolled and pitched so much at our anchorage in this unprotected port, that the carpenter was unable for ten days at a stretch to get his stage alongside, in order to fit on our new stem-post. Indeed, we were occasionally running our bows right under in the short, nasty seas. Nor was he able to effect the repairs on deck during this time, for the wretched fellow got sea-sick as soon as he stepped on board of us. Thus it was not until the 20th of January that we got all straight again.

On the 21st of January we weighed anchor at noon, and proceeded out of the harbour under all plain canvas to sail to Buenos Ayres. It is customary for strangers to take a pilot from Montevideo to Buenos Ayres, but we did not consider this necessary in the case of a small vessel like ours.

There was a fresh E.S.E. wind blowing, so that we were enabled to set our spinnaker, and kept up an average speed of seven knots throughout the voyage. At ten p.m. we made the Chico light-ship, and then, keeping the lead constantly going, sailed over the flats in about three fathoms of water, until, at seven a.m. on the morrow, we reached the guard-ship, which is moored about twelve miles or so from Buenos Ayres. From here we could see the long line of the houses of the city and the vessel in the inner roads.

We hove-to off the guard-ship in order to await the doctor's boat and obtain pratique before sailing into the town. Many large vessels were at anchor around us, rolling heavily in the rough pea-soup-coloured water, for no vessel of considerable draught can approach nearer to the shore than this; indeed, none of our big men-of-war could come anywhere near Argentine Waters. The royal mail steamers have been known to ground even so far out as these outer roads, as they are called. For where the vast plains of the Pampas terminate in the sea, so gradual is the incline that it is really difficult to say where sea begins and land ends. The gnarled mangroves grow far out into the water from the swampy shores. So flat are these alluvial plains that a rise of one foot of water only will overflow the land miles inland in many places.

At ten we received pratique, and proceeded towards the city. As we sailed in, the water very gradually shoaled until we reached the inner roads where lay a large number of vessels whose lighter draught enabled them to come thus far in. We proceeded still further, and came to an anchor in fourteen feet of water off the Catalina Mole in the midst of a crowd of lighters, shallow coasting schooners, river steamers, and other small craft; still, however, a considerable distance from the shore. We got into our dinghy and proceeded to sail towards the end of the pier. So shallow became the water long ere we reached it, that even our little boat bumped continually against the bottom. For half a mile or more we sailed through a large fleet of carts and horses; for in this extraordinary port of Buenos Ayres merchandise has to be transhipped three times between the vessel, fourteen miles out in the outer roads, and the railway trucks on shore— from vessel to lighter, from lighter to carts drawn by amphibious horses, and so to the railway. This port, if it can be called such, of Buenos Ayres, is a very unpleasant place to lay in, whether one be in the outer, inner, or small craft roads. For this coast is quite open to the Atlantic on the south-east, and when the wind blows hard from anywhere near that quarter a very short, dangerous sea soon rises on these shallow waters. The Argentine Republic is very unfortunate in the matter of its ports; save far south, in Patagonia, where there is little if any commerce, there is no harbour worthy of the name. Just to the south of the city of Buenos Ayres a small river runs into the sea—the Riachuelo. This has been dredged sufficiently to admit small craft. It is the head-quarters of the Italian river schooners, which are here built and fitted out. A large town has now sprung up around this port—the Boca, inhabited almost exclusively by Italians and Greeks, a rather cut-throat place by reputation.

North of Buenos Ayres, and some ten miles from it, is another river, the Lujan, one of the many channels of the intricate delta of the River Plate. Near one of its mouths is the little town of San Fernando. Here the Argentine Government has constructed docks, and here are the naval stores and workshops. It is a sort of Argentine Chatham; but unfortunately the entrance of the river is impeded, like all others hereabouts, by a bar, and there are times when the water is so low that a vessel drawing only eight feet has to wait weeks before it can cross it. Once within the river there is plenty of water. To lie off Buenos Ayres was, of course, impossible, so we had to choose between these two harbours for the *Falcon* during our stay here. We decided on the latter, or rather on the River Tigre, which is a branch of the Lujan. On its banks, and close to the Tigre railway-station, is the boat-house of the English rowing club. Our friends recommended us to drop our anchor close to it, as being a quiet spot where we would be unmolested, and where we would have the advantages of trains running into the city at short intervals.

We lay at anchor off the Catalina Mole during the night, tossing about very uncomfortably in the short seas. On the morrow, the 23rd of January, we weighed anchor at one p.m., and proceeded in charge of a pilot to the River Tigre. A fresh wind was blowing from the E. by S., and we sailed rapidly along the low coasts. The pilot kept the lead con-

stantly going. As we approached the mouth of the Lujan
the water gradually shoaled, for here the alluvial matter
brought down by the many rivers of the delta have formed a
great bank known as Las Palmas, that stretches far out to
sea. From two fathoms we shoaled to ten feet, then to nine,
then to eight. The pilot looked anxious.

"How much did you say you were drawing?" he
asked.

"Seven feet six inches," was the reply.

"Well, we may do it. We'll hit the channel soon, and be
in deep water. Besides the mud is soft here, we can drive
her through it."

Another cast of the lead showed us we were in seven
feet of water. Bump, bump the vessel went, as she
sailed over the mud, before half a gale of wind, with all
canvas set.

"We shall be in deep water soon," said the pilot; "but
the river is precious low; there should be more than eight
feet here by rights."

Another cast of the lead indicated a depth of only six feet,
and the *Falcon*, after vainly attempting to force her way a
little further, stuck firmly, to the great disgust of the pilot,
who seemed to be surprised that a vessel drawing nearly
eight feet of water could not sail where there was a depth of
six.

We quickly lowered all the canvas on deck, while Jerdein
who had promised himself a pleasant evening in town with
some old friends, admonished that unhappy pilot with his
usual eloquence. There was no particularly pleasant evening
for any one that night. We got two anchors down, and
proceeded to wait until some sea-wind, or flood, or other
phenomenon, should cause the waters to rise, an event which
might be in an hour or in a month, as far as we could tell,
and the pilot could not enlighten us. The water was still
going down, for in three hours after we struck we found
that there was a depth of only five feet round us. The
wind now freshened considerably, and howled and whistled
through our rigging.

It was a weird and melancholy scene from the *Falcon's*
deck. A few miles to the port hand was the low leaden-
coloured shore of mud, a leaden sky was above, and the
choppy seas of dirty water that were around us were of still

more dismal a shade. Towards evening the rain commenced to fall heavily, and the wind increased till it blew a gale from the south-east. This made matters look rather serious for us, for this coast is a lee-shore to this wind, which blows straight from the Atlantic. The seas became higher and higher, and occasionally washed over us, and had we bumped about throughout the night in the manner we did at first, the *Falcon*, strong though she be, might possibly have broken up. But this south-east wind, blowing straight into the estuary from seawards, is the wind of all others to cause the waters of the Plate to rise rapidly, for it stops the currents from proceeding out to the ocean, and drives them back towards the delta. In about an hour the water had risen upwards of two feet, and we were afloat once more, riding safe to our two anchors, only striking the bottom with our keel at long intervals, after some higher wave than usual had passed by.

We remained at anchor during the night, rolling about very heavily ; but we had good holding ground under us, and good ground tackle to hold on by, else we should have felt more anxious than we did, riding out a gale of wind on this lee-shore. In fact we got off very well considering everything, and much better than some others did, for we afterwards found that two schooners had been driven ashore at Buenos Ayres that night, and broken up. At daybreak the wind moderated and came round from the north-east, while the water commenced to fall again. We weighed anchor, and proceeded to cross the bank towards a buoy that marks the entrance of the channel—not without touching the ground occasionally. At last we found ourselves in deep water once more, and sailed into the Lujan, which we found to be a narrow river, with low banks overgrown with forests of willows. After ascending the stream for about two miles we reached the junction of the Tigre and the Lujan, and proceeded up the former river a few hundred yards till we reached the rowing-club house. We brought up alongside the bank, put out an anchor ahead, and one astern, and took a warp to a tree on shore.

On looking around us we were very contented with our new berth. It was the snuggest that the old *Falcon* had known for a very long time. The banks of the river were thickly grown with graceful willows and other trees, while handsome villas were scattered here and there, with beautiful gardens of sub-tropical shrubs and flowers stretching from them to the water's edge.   The captain of the port of the Tigre came off to us, inspected our papers, and gave us pratique, so we were free to take train into Buenos Ayres.   On landing and looking around us we found that we were in a very different sort of country from any we had yet visited. This delta of the Parana is one vast flat jungle, scarcely raised two feet above the level of the water, and intersected by innumerable creeks and channels, that flow sluggishly between islands of every size, only a few of which are inhabited, or for the matter of that have even ever been trodden by the foot of man.   The richest portion of this mosquito-infested labyrinth, and the most thickly peopled, is in the neighbourhood of the Tigre.   This indeed is a beautiful region, called the Venetia of South America.   Here the many islands are covered with a prodigal natural vegetation and very forests of peach-trees, for the fat alluvial soil is as rich as that of the Nile banks, and the river is continually overflowing it to leave fresh deposits.

French and Italian immigrants possess many of these islands, and cultivate on them millions of peaches and splendid vegetables of all kinds.   Very pleasant little farms these are.   Each family has a little island to itself, surrounded by narrow creeks—a secluded little paradise among the drooping willows.   The house is built invariably on piles, so as to be above the level of the waters in time of flood. The most lovely roses and other flowers grow luxuriantly around the homestead.   The only means of communication is by water, and every morning can be seen canoe after canoe laden with fruit and flowers floating slowly down the willow-shaded canals to market, the light-hearted owner singing merrily as he stands up in the stern propelling his little craft with one long oar, as they do in the Venetian gondolas.

There is a peculiar dream-like beauty about this enchanted region that strikes all visitors to La Plata.   The citizens of Buenos Ayres are very proud and fond of the Tigre.   Its banks are a favourite resort on Sunday, and many a pleasant picnic party and *fête champêtre* enlivens the isles in the summer days.

Before any one decides to purchase land and settle among the channels of the delta, he should first consider one or two rather serious drawbacks. In the first place, the mosquitoes are terrible; in the second place, real property hereabouts is by no means an "immovable." These islands and creeks are ever changing. If you buy an island one year, it may have grown to double its original size by the next, or it may have disappeared altogether; where houses once stood, deep waters now roll; and on the other hand, the peach-trees grow thickly where the river schooners were wont to sail a few years back.

CHAPTER VIII.

AND now, my readers, I am going to take you with me far away from the salt seas, not to return to them again until you have followed me over many thousands of miles of inland travel extending over nine months of time. For the *Falcon* was now to sail up the great fresh-water rivers to the central wildernesses of the continent, where no yacht had ever been before; and again she was to be left for months at anchor, while her crew changed their sailor life for that of the gaucho, and rode across the great Pampas, through the arid *montes* of St. Iago, to the great Cordilleras and tropical forests of Tucuman.

A few months before our arrival, Buenos Ayres had passed through one of these periodical revolutions, without which no South American Republic is long happy. The bumptiousness of the province of Buenos Ayres provoked the contest; for the Portenos, as the Buenos Ayreans term themselves, wished to raise by force their own man to the office of President, in despite of the votes of the other thirteen provinces.

These revolutions are a great nuisance to the *estançieros* (cattle-farmers) in the camps; for while they last the country is overrun by irregular troops and marauding gauchos, who requisition and rob in a most promiscuous fashion. Robbery is after all the whole object of these civil discords; the two parties fight their little game out, and the winner enjoys the monopoly of swindling the nation for the term of the presidential office; bloodshed is avoided as much as possible. This time, however, one serious engagement was fought in Buenos Ayres; for the rival armies met by accident, and about 2000 of the Buenos Ayreans were slain by the wild Indians and half-breeds of the provincial army. This battle, so they say, was entirely due to bad generalship, for all the rival forces desired was to keep apart and plunder in different directions. Unfortunately, it came to pass that the two armies came across each other, and were plundering at the same time in the same locality. It was exceedingly awkward They could not very well wink at each other and continue to plunder on different sides of the street. They could not ignore and cut each other dead, so were obliged, if only as a matter of form, to do a bit of fighting. I suppose they got warmed up when they once commenced, for it was a serious business as long as it lasted, and the butcher's bill was longer than the Government liked to confess afterwards.

We loafed about Buenos Ayres until we were bored; were " welcomed on Change "—Anglo-Portenos will know what that means; visited several *estançias* in the southern camps and elsewhere, acquiring an insight into the unnecessarily brutal way in which horses are broken in and cattle worked in this part of the globe; were interested in the ostrich farms, which promise to be as remunerative here as in South Africa; and then considered whither we should next go.

Our chief object in coming out to this part of the world was to ascend some of the tributaries of the great La Plata, as far as was possible in the yacht; for from all we had heard and read, such a voyage would not fail to repay us with the enjoyment of strange and marvellous scenery and splendid sport; nor were we altogether disappointed in our expectations.

But for the present the river voyage was not to be thought of. It was now midsummer, and even as far south as Buenos Ayres—by the shores, too, of the refreshing sea—the thermometer did not rarely indicate 100° in the shade. Those at Buenos Ayres who knew the Parana and Paraguay, advised us to postpone our cruise till the winter, and drew alarming pictures for us of the intolerable torment of the mosquitoes, that would render our life a misery to us on the inland waters at this season.

We therefore determined to leave the *Falcon* at her safe moorings in the Tigre in charge of the boy, purchase a horse each, and undertake an expedition into the interior of the continent of about two months' duration. Our plans were rather vague when we left the capital, but Cordoba, the ancient Jesuit city in the heart of the Republic, was to be our immediate destination; and Rosario, the second city of this country and 280 miles higher up the river than Buenos Ayres, our starting-point. From Cordoba we would journey either to the tropical provinces to the north, or westward to the Andes, as we might consider best.

Jerdein, Arnaud, and myself met at the Estaçion Centrale one delicious February morning. Our luggage was simple and business-like; each took with him a saddle, saddle-bags containing spare flannel shirts, &c., top-boots, a blanket, a revolver, a poncho, and a wide native belt of carpincho hide; while a broad-brimmed felt hat was on each head. After a three hours' journey in the comfortable American cars of the Campana Railway Company, across treeless, dusty plains of pasture whose monotony the rare agave and cactus alone relieved, we reached Campana, a small port on one of the many channels of the great delta of the La Plata. This is the terminus of the railway, and here we had to embark on David Bruce and Co.'s steamer *Provedor*. These steamers run between Campana and Rosario, a distance of about 200 miles, thus connecting Buenos Ayres with the Central Argentine Trunk Railway, whose southern terminus is at Rosario. We were enabled to form a good idea of what was in store for the good ship *Falcon*, from what we saw on this short voyage up the great Parana. We steamed all that afternoon and throughout the night up a broad stream of muddy water, winding across an alluvial plain flat as a pancake. This stream was broad and deep, as a huge river should be, and yet this was but one minor branch of this tremendous watercourse, which, with its sister the Amazon, drains the huge southern continent; and whose head-waters are in the unexplored tropical forests and savannahs, in close proximity to those of that other mighty river.

The Paraguay, the Parana, the Uruguay, and a dozen other mighty streams pour their waters into the common estuary of the Rio de la Plata, and it is estimated that the volume of water brought down hourly by this river exceeds that of all the rivers in Europe put together. As we steamed up we could perceive the main land on neither side of us, for this was but a comparatively narrow channel between two huge islands. And what a strange country was this intricate network of island and channel. On our starboard hand, for instance, the mainland was thirty miles away ; between us and that were islands numberless, rising not more than two feet or so above the average level of the water—an unknown wilderness of swamp and jungle, uninhabited save in rare spots, by the shores of the more commonly navigated channels. The islands are thickly overgrown with a rank

A GAUCHO'S HOME IN THE SWAMPS.

and ever-verdant vegetation. Willows, great reeds, the gnarled seibo-tree, with its bright green leaves and scarlet blossoms; strange bushes, all interwoven with rich convolvuli, render these wilds impassable save to the Carpincho or river-hog, the tiger, and the lion (as the natives call the jaguar and the puma), and deadly snakes of resplendent colour.

Near Rosario, the islands are frequently inhabited. Enterprising foreigners cultivate rice successfully on some of them, and on others, as I read from the *Buenos Ayres Standard* certain not desirable people are to be found: gauchos, who have given up the horse to take to the canoe—a lawless set, who make frequent raids on the *estançias* of the mainland, fishermen by profession, but pirates and banditti by practice. For those good old-fashioned ruffians, the buccaneers, are by no means extinct on the tributaries of La Plata. There are districts on the banks of the Parana, for instance, near Corrientes, a thousand miles from the sea, that have acquired a very evil reputation; cut-throat crews have often come out in canoes from the secluded *riachos* of the Chaco, seized and plundered the passing Italian trading-schooners, and murdered the men. Most of these trading-schooners now carry a small cannon in addition to their muskets. The *Falcon*, though much smaller than any of these vessels, would, I think, be quite as capable as any of them of resisting the pirates successfully, for we are incomparably better off as regards arms.

On the following morning we found that we had reached the main stream of the Parana. On our port hand was the mainland, on our starboard a string of islands about three miles away. The river itself is still very wide, for the Entro Rios shore is quite forty miles off, an unexplored wilderness of shallow streams and long green isles intervening.

There is now a considerable navigation on the Parana. Vessels from North America and Europe load with hides, bones, and alfalfa (a sort of lucerne) at the quays of Rosario; but the navigation above this is almost exclusively in the hands of the Italians. Their vessels are handsome schooners, of little draught, but great beam, with enormous spread of canvas, and great square top-sails high aloft to catch the wind above the trees. The running-gear is generally of plaited hide, a very excellent substitute for rope. They go up against the stream, laden with wines and European produce, even as far as the centre of the Brazilian province of Matagrosso, about 2400 miles from the sea—the voyage there and back occupying about a year. They return to Buenos Ayres and Montevideo with cargoes of cedar and valuable hard woods from the virgin forests of the Chaco, of oranges from Paraguay and other produce of those rich but little cultivated countries.

At last we came to an anchor off Rosario, the second city of the Republic, stretching along the banks of a river which even here, so many hundreds of miles from the sea, is so broad that from a ship's deck the horizon between the many islands is of water, the further coasts being invisible. Such are the sea-like expanses that stretch between isle and isle. Mr. Keenan, the popular host of the English hotel at Rosario, soon made us at home in his comfortable hotel. He already knew us by reputation, having read about our wanderings in the papers.

If you study any old atlas, and not so very old either, you will not be able to discover such a place as Rosario on the map of South America, yet you will most probably see Santa Fé, its neighbour, marked in prominent letters, though this is but a little village to the first-named large and wealthy city. For Rosario is one of those mushroom cities that rise so rapidly in this new Western world. Its prosperity is of yesterday; it is bran-new—painfully new from an artistic point of view; a money-making, tramwayed, prosperous place, that has doubled its population in ten years, and will, in all probability, double it again in another ten years; for it cannot but always be a most important place, being as it is the terminus of those great railways that will in time open out all the rich regions between the Bolivian forests and the Pampas, the Pacific and the Atlantic. Now that the influx of foreigners into the Argentine Republic is augmenting so amazingly, and revolution is waxing feebler and feebler before it, who can foresee limits to the increase of the commercial enterprise and wealth of these wonderful countries? Even now the produce that lies on the quays of Rosario ready to be put on board ship will give us an insight into what is yet to be. There are the sugars—the valuable cabinet woods of Tucuman—the hides and beef from the estançias of the Pampas—wines from the eastern slopes of the Andes, the vintage of Mendoza and San Juan; minerals, too, from the Cordilleras, and from the Sierras of Cordoba, where gold and silver and copper abound, and only await the adventurous miner.

There is but little to say about these modern Spanish South American cities. They are very uninteresting. In describing one you describe all. The same straight streets drawn at right angles to each other, with the dismal one-storied, flat-roofed houses. Tramways everywhere. A square or two. A cleanly, prosperous look about the whole, inhabitants included. Here you have everything. This chessboard-like, block system of laying out cities produces one effect that eminently strikes the stranger. In any of these long, straight streets one has an uninterrupted view right through the town. At Buenos Ayres, and more especially at Montevideo, the sea terminates the view as a rule. Here it is the Pampas. If you stand in the centre of Rosario where any two streets cross, and look up and down them, you will see that each abruptly terminates far off in a sort of mist, for no straggling suburbs surround the town. At the end of each street is the desert. The mist you perceive is the dust of the immense plain that commences at the verge of the city and stretches unbroken for a thousand leagues. The suddenness of the exit from the thickly thronged street into the roadless wilds is very remarkable in many of these cities, and is doubtless a relic of the old days when Indian raids were frequent, and the first few founders of the *pueblo* crowded their habitations together for mutual protection, and surrounded them with a common stockade. It is indeed a marvellous contrast; a wilderness untilled, inhabited by wild half-breeds clad in a barbaric costume, coming up to the very streets of cities, where every article of European civilization is to be found, and whose citizens are delicate in their lives and fastidiously dressed in the height of the latest Parisian fashion. It is curious to see the gaucho from the Pampas strolling through the busy streets, so out of place with his striped poncho, his laced drawers, ana nis hide belt ornamented with coins. He does not evince any interest or curiosity, but from his looks evidently hates and despises towns and their pale inhabitants. Life in the saddle, on the Pampas or in the Monte (bush), is the only life he knows or cares for. Horse-stealing and cattle-lifting, in his opinion, are the only pursuits worthy of a man.

One more day we pottered about the glaring hot city and its environs. In the morning we visited an ostrich farm on the river-bank; in the evening attended a public ball. For the carnival was approaching, and South Americans only requiring an excuse to commence their favourite pastime, generally open the masked balls weeks before the orthodox time, so as to get into full swing for that fearful Terpsichorean orgie which they celebrate once a year. The Indo-Spanish race, lazy in all else, is certainly indefatigable in dance. For nights in succession these people will tread unwearied their graceful native figures with supple limbs. The head—every limb—indeed the whole being, seems to be entering into the measure, inspired with a species of phrenzy. At three theatres here there were public masked balls this night attended by all classes, from stately white ladies in Parisian costume, to the simple little copper-coloured *chinas* with pink dresses of common stuff and black mantillas, ever-laughing faces, and perpetually shaking fans. There are, by-the-bye, some not uncomely faces among these dusky half-breeds—the Indian blood producing a much handsomer type than the negro, when crossed with the Spanish or Por-tuguese.

Before starting on our expedition we had to exchange the notes we had brought from Buenos Ayres for the money current up country. Every province of this republic has a circulation of its own not current in the other provinces, which accounts for the enormous number of money-changers one comes across in every city. There is a common standard throughout the whole country, called a patacon, which is about the value of four shillings; but this patacon has no real existence, it is a purely imaginary quantity; there is no coin or bank-note which professes to be one or more pata-cones, or any fraction of the same; but I suppose it serves as a standard whereby to compare the variously fluctuating provincial moneys.

In the province of Buenos Ayres gold or silver is unknown, paper money being the only currency. The original paper dollar was intended to represent a Spanish silver dollar or peso; but between revolution and what not this paper peso gradually depreciated till it reached its present value of about twopence. This seeming somewhat unsatisfactory to the sage rulers of the country, they issued another superior sort of paper dollar which they called the *peso fuerte*, or hard dollar, to be of the full value of the original four and twopenny silver coin before mentioned. This is now current in Buenos Ayres by the side of the twopenny paper dollar, or *peso corriente*. But, alas ! the *peso fuerte* has also terribly depre-ciated by this time; whether the Government will issue an *extra-fuerte*, and then when that goes down a *fuertissimo*, and so on, is beyond my power to say.

The Government of Santa Fé, the province in which we

now are, issues a paper dollar of the value of about three shillings. The Cordoban paper dollar is worth a little more, and does represent some fixed value—the silver dollar of Bolivia. In the remoter and poorer provinces there is no paper money; but quaint old silver Bolivian coins, Peruvian and Chilian dollars, and the like foreign money are the sole currency. I have said enough to show how confusing this system is, and how the unfortunate traveller must lose in the frequent exchanges while travelling through this republic. It is rather a curious fact that in the wealthier republics of South America metallic currency is quite unknown, while the poorer countries like Paraguay and Bolivia have nothing else. I suppose the fact is that no one would have anything to do with the paper of these untrustworthy states, had they the impudence to issue any.

About seven leagues from Rosario, on the Central Argentine Railway, is the small town—I must not risk offence by calling it a village—of Carcarañal. Hearing that this was a likely place to purchase horses in, we took train thither on the second morning after our landing at Rosario. This railway is carried in a perfectly straight line, without curve or gradient, for hundreds of miles across the Pampas—and strange these vast plains seemed to us as viewed to-day for the first time from the windows of the car. We saw an interminable pasture, roadless, treeless, stretching all around; here and there a great cattle farm, either unfenced or surrounded with a wire fence; vast herds of sleek cattle and troops of half-wild horses roamed over the plain. Here and there were partial deserts of burnt-up earth and sand; here muddy lagunas; while at long intervals, like oases in this treeless waste, rose small isolated clumps of eucalypti, marking the sites of the estançias. Under the intense blue sky the horizon seemed to be infinitely far off, trembling and rolling like the waves of a distant sea with the mirage, while the distant eucalypti were raised by it, and seemed to be rooted in mid-air.

At Carcarañal we found a little inn, kept by a hospitable dame from old Gaul, who made us very comfortable. A curious little camp-town this: merely a straight row of clean flat-roofed white one-storied houses; in front a lane of small acacias, and all around and beyond, glaring under the cloudless implacable sky, the arid plain with its short dried-up grass ; a cloud of dust over all, dust of the finest and most penetrating nature, dust that will find its way through all your clothes to your skin in no time, dust that is as bad as an Egyptian plague, irritating, blinding, pore-closing, parching,—stay, let us at least give it justice—it did prepare us to thoroughly enjoy the brimming cups of caña and water, flavoured with some delicate essence of fruit, that our landlady mixed for us. There is use in everything, even in dust.

A funny collection we were in the little hostelry after dinner. At one table was our party playing at euchre in shirt-sleeves; at another several natives in camp garb gambling desperately at monte, with a very greasy pack of cards. In the next room we could perceive through the open door a merry wedding-supper party—*gringos* these, English, German, French, and Italian colonists. We had arrived here very opportunely ; for as soon as these people had dined they cleared the room for a jolly ball, which was energetically kept up all night to the merry music of a three-tuned barrel-organ. As is the free and easy fashion of this country, all strangers were welcome to join them in their merry-making. Wedding garments were by no means *de rigueur*, but it seemed the proper thing to take off one's coat while dancing.

In the middle of the night we heard in a lull in the revelry a shouting of many voices in the distance, and then the tread and lowing of numerous cattle. This turned out to be a vast herd of many hundred head that was being driven down to Rosario from some far northern province, where a long *seca* had been prevailing, and where all beasts were dying for want of water and pasture. As soon as the *peons* had rounded in these cattle outside the town for the night, the head-man and a few others came in to seek hospitality. Attracted by the sound of the *baile* they entered the inn, and were soon dancing away with the best of us, in despite of the fatigue and stiffness of a month in the saddle. They danced in their camp dress, top-boots, silver spurs, chiripas, poncho and all, so that one might almost imagine oneself at a fancy-dress ball at home, such was the variety of costume.

CHAPTER IX.

NOT being able to find what we wanted in the way of horses at Carcarañal, we again took train to Cañada de Gomez, another camp-town a few leagues higher up the line. We found this to be a typical little camp settlement, the mushroom growth of a few years—new and prosperous, with an astonishing amount of civilization, too, considering where it is. We entered the *fonda*, or general store where the camp-man comes down to buy all he wants, groceries, powder, and especially caña, I fear. The proprietor, Schnack, is an old Dutchman, a sailor, whose long service in British ships accounts for his perfect knowledge of our tongue. He put an upper room at our disposal to sleep in. He could not feed us, only lodge and drink us, he said; but there was a restaurant at the railway station opposite, so that mattered little.

A wonderfully cosmopolitan continent this South America is. Having left our Dutchman for the restaurant over the way, we found the proprietor of this was an old French soldier, of the Garde Imperiale, and a *maître d'escrime.* Then we went to the barber to be shaved, and found that he was a citizen of Naples : his razors, I imagine, came out of the torture-chambers of the Inquisition. This is indeed a very civilized little town. We not only have our restaurant and our barber, but also our judge ; also a half-finished church —this the common condition of a camp-town church, for the priests, after squeezing a certain amount of dollars from the pious, start building on an over-ambitious scale, run short of funds, and then comes a standstill in the work, until the little dribblets of offerings enable further progress. There is also a prison here, this being an imposing pair of stocks considerately placed under the shade of the pretty çina-çina trees in front of a grog-shop. The court-house where justice is dispensed, and which is also the residence of the judge, belongs to friend Schnack. The Government is a bad paymaster, and our host tells me that after many vain applications for arrears of rent he has been obliged to evict the poor judge and Mistress Justice to seek a roof elsewhere.

Peaceful and civilized though this little place appears, the untamed Indian tribes are not so far off. It is now but twelve years since the Indians made a raid here, and carried away 10,000 head of cattle, and many women, for the aboriginal has the good taste to prefer the white to the dusky beauties of his own race.   But the camps of the white men have advanced many leagues further into the Indian territory since that time, and Cañada de Gomez has little to fear now.

Schnack's was a type of the regular camp-town store; loafing about the bar, drinking caña, gin, and cocktails, was the usual crowd from the camp.   Natives in their picturesque dress, and English estançieros—these, many of them, in the native costume also, but mostly in shirt-sleeves, top-boots, broad felt sombreros, and hide belts with six-shooters and knives stuck ostentatiously therein.   The Englishman of the province of Santa Fé rather affects this brigand-like get up; but I believe there is good reason for it, as there are no few bad characters about, and the hand of justice being almost impotent hereabouts, each one must look out for himself.

When the men standing at the bar heard of our proposed ride, they of course overwhelmed us with advice.   When in reply to their queries we said that we thought of riding through Cordoba to Tucuman, first one, a Yankee, said,—

"Take train from here to Cordoba, and commence your ride from there.   There is nothing to interest you between here and that city."

Said another, a Britisher,—

"No; ride from here to Cordoba; that will be all very well.   To go beyond that will be madness; you will lose yourselves and die of thirst in the Salinas, salt-deserts where there is no water—salt and cacti and sun, salt and sun and cacti, nothing more."

Said a third, a native,—

"My advice is, don't go at all.   It is too hot to ride this time of the year; what pleasure can you find in galloping through the eternal salt and sun and cacti that my friend here speaks of?"

I tried to persuade this last that we were a scientific expedition, that had been sent hither by the English Government to inspect sun and salt and cacti, and send home returns thereon; but he would not swallow this, and set us down as harmless lunatics.

We were not a little laughed at, too, when we informed our friends that we intended to accomplish our journey with one horse each—taking no remounts. This was pronounced as impossible. In this land of cheap horseflesh it is the universal custom to travel with a *tropilla*—four or even eight horses to each man. A mare, the *madrina*, with bell tinkling at her neck, is also taken, and all the spare horses follow her like sheep do the bell-sheep, as she leads the way. It is only necessary to hobble the madrina when the party encamps for the night; the troop of geldings can be left to graze at will, for these animals will not stray far, but keep near the lady, with an affecting Platonic tenderness. This method of travelling by tropilla is certainly by far the fastest. The fashion here is to go at full gallop, leap from one horse to another, as they in turn weary, and get over about one hundred miles a day—the South American caring little if he lose a few of his animals by the way. We however preferred our own quieter mode of travelling, which our experience in other lands has taught us was certainly possible. One horse well looked after will carry a man for a journey of months ; at a very fair pace too.

The result proved that we were right, for we reached, later on, lands where there was no pasture, and where hard food for our horses had to be purchased at extravagant prices. Had we been travelling with thirty instead of four horses we should have found it rather expensive work.

Many a long yarn was spun this night for our benefit by our revolvered friends on the dangers of our way. They told us of the *monteneros* of Santiago, who would cut our throats and steal our horses ; of the salt-deserts, where we would perish of thirst—deserts in whose midst two tropillas have been known to meet and fight to the death for the little skin of water that was all left to one party ; of the deadly chuchu, or fever, of the northern provinces ; of jiggers that would bring mortification to our toes, and the bicho colorado that would lay eggs in our legs ; and so on.

About thirty miles from here is the estança of Las Rosas, the property of the well-known Mr. Kemiss, whose horned cattle and horses are the pride of the Plate, an enterprising man who has introduced blood from England, and whose horses carry all before them on the race-courses of South America. On the morning after our arrival at Cañada de Gomez we procured a trap and two horses and drove up to this estança. A pleasant drive it was, too, through the clear exhilarating air of the plains; beneath our feet were flowers of every hue, chief among which that commonest flower of the Pampas, the scarlet verbena. The grasses hereabouts were long and of various species. All of them were now capped with plumes of silver seed, so that on the horizon the white stretches of it were exactly like the sands of a distant desert. We followed the tropilla-track to the north, which consisted merely of the ruts made by the huge waggons of the caravans that have for ages wended their slow way by this route. In places which are apt to be swampy in wet weather, the ruts become very deep, so that the waggons have to avoid them and make a slight circuit: thus new tracks are formed parallel to the old, till in some softer parts of the country the road is a band of a thousand ruts, a mile or so in breadth. Such are all the roads of the Pampas—roads to the construction of which man has contributed no labour.

The pastures we crossed to-day were some of the richest of this province. Here you have a typical view of the camp as we saw it when we unharnessed our horses and allowed them a rest and a roll at midday. First, just before us stretched the muddy tropilla-track, a dark line through the bright grasses. Across it lay the huge clumsy walnut wheel of a broken-down waggon; the bones of cattle were frequent, and a little further off we could see a crowd of mangy vultures feeding on the carcass of a horse. At the entrance to the numberless bizcacha holes, among the wild pumpkins, sat, solemnly blinking, the grey owls, generally in twos, sociably. Why, by-the-bye, does the bizcacha always plant pumpkins and owls at his door?

Looking further away we perceived on one side the silver stretch of a laguna a league or so off, with many cattle and horses by it—also numerous plover; the grass by it not yellow and partly burnt as elsewhere, but of a vivid green. Beyond that, afar off, stretched the unbroken horizon of the plains, a long line of smoke rising from it in one place, showing where some leagues of camp were on fire.

Turning round in the other direction we could perceive some shy gama, the deer of the Pampas, playing under the shade of a solitary ombu; beyond that on the horizon the waving sea of the mirage, and two tall columns as of a water-spout dark against the bright sky—two dust-whirls that broke and vanished as suddenly as they had arisen. A strange solemn land this lonely Pampas ; still, too, save for the sound of the dry north wind sighing in the grass.

At last we reached the wire fences and passed through the strong gates on to the lands of the great breeder of horses, and drove up to the hospitable house. A pleasant place this, and possessing what is very rare on the Pampas—a garden of flowers and one of fruit and vegetables. The native estançiero is far too lazy a man to cultivate these ; he breeds his cattle in his rough brutal way ; and yet, though he number them by thousands, butter and milk are unknown luxuries in his house. He is content to eat his perpetual *asado* and *puchero* without vegetables or bread or seasoning ; alfalfa and maize being the sole produce he condescends to raise from his estate.

The locusts had been playing considerable havoc in Mr. Kemiss' gardens of late : the peach-trees stood stripped of all leaf and fruit, the stones alone hanging bare of flesh from the skeleton twigs. The blue gum-trees and the prickly pears, of which the hedge round the garden was composed, had alone resisted the ravages of these destroying swarms. As the sun set we perceived what is a common sight enough on the Pampas in summer. All around the horizon, at five different points, were long bands of ruddy flame. These camp fires sometimes burn and smoulder on for months, devouring league after league of pasture. We had an opportunity of seeing how these fires are extinguished while we were in this neighbourhood. The method is one which will illustrate as much as anything the value of horseflesh in this country. The *peons* of the estate which we were visiting perceived a fresh fire breaking out on the verge of their master's lands : immediately they galloped off to it. There happened to be a troop of mares close by grazing tranquilly. In almost less time than it takes to describe it, two of these were lassoed, thrown on their backs, killed, and their stomachs ripped right up with the long knife every native carries ; lassos were attached to the legs of the animals, and the mounted men dragged the bleeding carcasses across the burning grass—and a very efficacious method it proved to be, for the conflagration was thus got under in a few minutes.

On the morrow we borrowed horses from Mr. Kemiss, and galloped all over the country to see if any neighbouring estançieros had horses fit for our expedition to sell us. We rode to the estançia of Las Tres Lagunas, then to that of Las Lomas, and that of California—where three brothers from Central California were trying their fortunes,—but all in vain ; save one tropilla of unbroken young *riscos* from the Entre Rios camps we could find nothing.

So the next morning we drove back to Cañada de Gomez in our trap. It was a sultry day, heavy with storm. When we had about half-completed our journey the sky became overclouded, and vivid fork lightning flashed in the distance. The horses trembled : their instinct evidently told them what was coming ; for nothing is more terrible than a storm on the Pampas. All animals, and man himself, are struck with terror when they find themselves overtaken on the unsheltered wilderness by these terrific tempests. The blast sweeps over these thousands of leagues of plain with force unchecked, meeting no obstacles of hill and dale to deflect and break its strength. The wind drives all before it, the vast herds of lowing cattle till they fall one on the top of the other into the swollen rivers, and are drowned. Clouds of dust are stirred up that make day as dark as night, and have been known to bury great herds—even as does the dreaded sand-storm of the Sahara—and the hailstones fall so large and with such force that they kill man and horse exposed to their fury, and, as I have myself seen, break through the tiled roofs of houses like so many round shot.

But curiously enough, where there comes but only a little and rare cultivation and civilization, the climate of a country changes. Of old the dust-storm used frequently to rush into Buenos Ayres—now it does so rarely and to a limited extent. And wonderful though it may seem, they tell me that the presence here in the wilds of Santa Fé of a few scattered estançias, with their eucalypti, has greatly contributed to break the fury of the desert tempest, and that to see it in all its horrible majesty one must now go further out into the wilder regions of the Pampas ; for not only the Indians, but drought and the hurricane itself retreat before the advance of the white man. But the storm we experienced this day was quite enough for us. It came on with amazing suddenness ; one moment it was hot, sultry, and calm, the next moment a wind of hurricane strength rushed down on us, and we shivered with cold, so rapidly the temperature fell. The dust rose in clouds, the hurricane threatened to capsize our trap and roll it over the plain before it. We had to turn it to the wind and heave-to as it were, stooping down with our heads buried in our ponchos; then the rain came down sharp and stinging—a rain of mud, for it gathered up all the dust from the skies as it descended—a rain, too, of sticks and stones and grass, and millions of prickly thistle-heads.

This deluge luckily did not last long, and the fury of the short-lived tempest soon subsided; but it left us most miserable objects. We were drenched; an inch of mud covered our clothes, as thickly studded with thistle-heads as a plum-pudding is with plums; and we were not sorry when we found ourselves once more under Schnack's hospitable roof.

Not being able to purchase horses in this neighbourhood, we took train to the camp-town of Fraile Muerto which is in the province of Cordoba.

Before reaching this place we observed that the aspect of the Pampas was gradually changing. For we were nearing the region of the *monte*, or bush, which stretches hence to the tropical forests of the north. The camps, no longer monotonous wastes of grass and thistles, were covered, save in some open patches, with mimosas and thorny bushes; commonest and most imposing among which rose the algarobbas, noble trees of the mimosa species. The algarobba is a tree of great importance in South America. In the first place it is used in the place of coal on the railway engines, and its wood serves for sleepers. In the hot provinces of Santiago del Estero it bears fruit every year; but here, in more temperate Cordoba, but once in four years. This is a large bean-like pod full of saccharine matter. It is excellent food for cattle; and horses, when hard-worked, thrive on it as well as on maize. Even human beings extract nourishment from the algarobba pod. The poor of Santiago almost entirely subsist on cakes made from it, and the children seem to be perpetually chewing the hard sweet seed in its raw state. An enterprising Frenchman attempted to prepare sugar from it, but failed to compete with the cane sugar of Tucuman. However, a very palatable spirit is extracted from it. The algarobba is of the same species as the locust-tree of Cyprus and Asia Minor.

On arriving at Fraile Muerto station, which is some way from the settlement, we found that civilization had progressed so far that there were two coaches to meet us. The driver of one, a sharp Indian, pounced on us first, and claimed the caballeros as his own.

We drove at a gallop across a plain of alternate pasture and brushwood ; then over an iron bridge that spanned the Carcavañal, a typical river of the Pampas, flowing rapid and muddy between two steep forty-feet-high banks of earth, glittering with particles of diamond-like mica—banks that were topped with evergreen mimosas, while the interspaces of the bush were full of lovely flowers, and the lofty pampa grass with its plumes of silver feathers.

Fraile Muerto is a prosperous-looking little camp-town. It for the most part consists of one big square with a double row of trees round it. Whenever a new *pueblo* is founded in South America, the native colonists commence by laying out an immense square. At first it is a mere waste, with only three or four ranchos, maybe, scattered along its lines, while all round is the tiger-haunted jungle. The next thing they do is to cut a race-course through this jungle, and then they sit down and rest—they have done enough—let Providence do the rest. From this nucleus a great city may spring or it may not, *Quien sabe ?* As a rule it does not ; but where there is much of energetic foreign blood about, cities do spring up very rapidly indeed in South America —so is it with Fraile Muerto, which is fast becoming quite a considerable little village.

The Spanish American mind always seems to run in squares. His cities are built in cuadros all of a size ; he even measures length by squares, and speaks of so many cuadros where we should say so many dozen rods. The Portuguese American prefers lines to squares and irregularity to symmetry. The net-work of streets in a Brazilian city is puzzling in the extreme. You do not find there the chess-board arrangement the Argentine people are so fond of. Again, when Brazilians found some new village in the interior, they prefer to make one long irregular street of it, stretching along the high road. They do not understand concentration around a central square. At Faira St. Anna, for instance, there is one street only, with no others branching off it. Yet this town is of considerable size, and the one street it does boast is, I am afraid to say how many miles in length. There is a *café* at either end of it. If you breakfast at one, and walk briskly to the other, you will reach it just in time for dinner—at least, so the natives say ; but the story seems hardly probable. I should like to see the man who performed this pedestrian feat, for there happens to be a tramway running all down this one-streeted town, and what Brazilian would walk ten yards when he could drive, or even when he couldn't ? for in that case he would remain in the end of the town he was born in, and decline to venture to the unknown further end of the street.

We drove into the courtyard of the fonda of Don Pépe. Our host came forth to meet us. Don Pépe is a great character in his way—a Roman of noble family, they say, and an ex-bandit of Calabria ; he is a fine, handsome, white-haired old ruffian, and a terrible swearer. His sister, a most stately Roman dame, assists him in preserving order in his, at times, rather noisy establishment. This lady rolls off the sonorous Spanish and blood-curdling Italian oaths as volubly as her brother.

Fraile Muerto is associated with the fortunes of the ill-fated Henley colony. About twelve years since there came hither from England a strange crew of young English gentlemen with the ostensible object of cattle farming. If energy and skill in caña drinking and horse-racing are the sole requisites for a cattle farmer, then none could be better than these. These young men, unsteady, fresh from school and college and regiment, without any practical knowledge of anything, arrived at Rosario in a batch, and considerably astonished the natives by their manners and customs. The Henleyites came down on the land in the fashion of a hostile army. They had a uniform of which a helmet was not the least conspicuous article ; each was provided with a regulation rifle, revolver, and sabre, not to speak of the very arsenal of wonderful weapons he took on his own account in addition. They were encamped for some time in a village of wooden huts, while lands were being apportioned out to them ; and here they soon showed what manner of colonists they were going to be. Drinking, gambling, and horse-racing was the order of the day. The capital they had brought with them took unto itself wings, for let the

gringo, however knowing in his own land, skin his eyes ere
he match himself on the turf with the simple gaucho of the
Pampas. So things went on, and the natives smiled at the
ways of the *locos Inglesas*, won their money, acquired their
mortgaged lands, while the colonists diminished woefully in
number. Many of these gentlemen ultimately were driven
to take any menial work they could get ; some died of
delirium tremens, others self-despatched with their own
revolvers ; the remainder settled down, after the first wild
burst was over, with diminished means to the business they
had come over to undertake.

This prosperous little town of Fraile Muerto has been
built for the most part on the spoils that have been wrung
from the ill-fated Englishmen by publicans and usurers.

Fiascos in the way of emigration are frequent out
here, and bring discredit on this fine country ; whereas it
is the folly, or worse, of people at home that is really to
blame.

There have been schemes of this nature in South America
that have turned out far more unfortunately than even
this one of poor, well-meaning, but misguided Mr. Henley.
The Paraguayan Lincolnshire farmer scheme, for instance.
During our ride I happened to see a navvy working on a
remote portion of the Tucuman railway line. On my asking
him the way, or some such question, he proved to be a
fellow-countryman. He rested his foot on his spade, and
started a chat with me :—

" Right glad I am to have a chance of talking the old
language now and again," he said. He told me he had been
a jockey in his youth ; then a groom in London.

" And how came you out here ? " I asked.

" Oh, I came here as a Lincolnshire farmer," he replied,
with a humorous twitch about the corners of his mouth.

" As a Lincolnshire farmer ? I don't quite understand."

" Ha ! ha ! Well it do seem rum, don't it now ? But
that's right—a Lincolnshire farmer. Why, you know, I
saw a grand emigration scheme advertised· in the papers,
Lincoln farmers to go out to Paraguay and grow tobacco
on land that had been bought dirt cheap from the Government ; splendid climate, and so on. *Bueno.* I did not know
a rap where Paraguay was, and didn't care ; but I was
main tired of town, and times was bad, so I scraped some

money together, and off I went; and here I am, less of a Lincoln farmer than ever, I guess."

But his case was light enough. The misery that wretched Lincoln farmer scheme brought on hundreds is inconceivable. In the first place these emigrants, who were supposed to be experienced agriculturists from the rich lowlands of East Anglia, were anything but that. Farmers, forsooth! No more so than, and as useless in their way as, the young gentlemen of the Henley colony; roughs from London, the offscourings of the Dials and Whitechapel, rusty acrobats, race-meeting minstrels, and the like, not unaccompanied by a large following of dirty, noisy women and puny children.

Well, this motley crowd was packed off a thousand miles inland to grow tobacco in the tropical climate of Paraguay. They reached the lands assigned to them, an uncleared jungle alternating with swamp. Here, as any one could have foretold, fever fell on the miserable, uncared-for wretches, living as they could amid deadly miasma; so helpless and ignorant that they could not even put their hands to building huts to cover them. So they perished by dozens, the little children, weak with privation and fever, being literally devoured by mosquitoes and jiggers, till they died of putrefying sores. The remnant had to be sent south again by the exertions of private charity; and, would it be believed, the men of this melancholy relic—independent, helpless, surly British workmen as they were proved to be—refused to carry from the bakers the biscuit charity had provided for them and their starving families, unless they were paid for doing so! Some of the specimens of the British working-man one sees in South America are verily strange beasts, and not calculated to do credit to their fatherland. But there was one emigration scheme that I know of that beats all the others. A peculiarly pestilential district, in a state adjoining this one, was the locality chosen. The originators of the scheme were sleek, godly men of the city of London, who richly deserve to be brought out and delivered over to the tender mercies of those that have been deluded by their plausible prospectus.

CHAPTER X.

CARNIVAL was in full swing at Fraile Muerto when we arrived. Buckets of water were being thrown liberally over passers-by, and every one was armed with the inevitable *pomito*, or squirt, of Florida water. The dark-eyed little rogues under the black mantillas made it very hot, or rather, wet and cool, for the Falcons with the aid of these detestable instruments. The night was one of revelry ; the twang of the guitar was heard through many an open door, and at least a dozen *bailes* were under way in different parts of the town ; indeed, there were as many balls as there were houses, for all the estançieros, rancheros, and gauchos for leagues around had flocked into Fraile Muerto for the occasion.

Thoroughly the laughing little camp girls threw themselves into the spirit of the wild and beautiful native dances. Horse-racing, cock-fighting, and dancing are the only amusements of the Pampas, and the last is the only one which the fair sex can share with the sterner. They certainly are not stingy in their preparations for carnival in these parts ; many pretty masquerade dresses were to be seen among the revellers. This afternoon a grand procession of clumsy waggons, drawn by handsome oxen, slowly perambulated the glaring, dusty streets. Waggons and oxen were tastefully decorated with flowers and coloured draperies. In one waggon was a band of musicians clad fantastically in yellow coats, that recalled the penitential dress of the victims of the Inquisition ; while two men worked a huge squirt, or fire-engine, pouring volumes of water right and left—rather too rough carnival play this, but all good-naturedly taken. Another waggon was full of pretty *chiñas*, dressed in a uniform of red and black, laughing and squirting scent.

At the Union Club, for we boast a club in our village, was the grand affair of the evening, the masked ball for the aristocracy. Thither we repaired. The club turned out to be merely a fair-sized room on the ground-floor of a house. This was a particularly select entertainment, yet where the exclusive grandees of Fraile Muerto drew the line I did not exactly perceive. The door of the ball-room was on the street, and was wide open ; all who wished could look in and behold the spectacle, could even, as far as I could see, enter and join the dancers. The commandante was there with his pretty daughters; the storekeeper, too; and the shoemaker, with his lady and family—these exhausted the list of the native aristocracy. Then came people with whom "one did not like to mix," and on whom the daughters of the above swells turned up their little noses—gauchos from the camp, murderers and cattle-lifters many of them—wild fellows in native dress and of savage mien. *Mate* seemed to be the only refreshment provided, and nothing there is that will better pull together the wearied dancer than this invigorating decoction of the Paraguayan yerba.

On the morning after our arrival Pépe insisted on taking us round his establishment. This caravanserai of the Pampas consisted of a large square courtyard, round three sides of which was a low, one-storied building—simply a series of small rooms with doors opening on the said court; on the fourth side were stables and a blacksmith's forge.

"That forge,' said he, "has only recently become my property. It belonged to a Frenchman; poor fellow, he drank it all away in absinthe; got drunk 'on tic,' as you English say, at my bar; so now it is mine."

"And now," said Pépe, "come, and I will show you my museum." He took us into a small room, surrounded with cases of arms and other curiosities.

"These," said he, "are chiefly the spoils of your country-men, taken by me in lieu of bad debts; all represent so much caña drink."

It was a melancholy spectacle—Westley Richards, Cogswell and Harrison, and the like names were to be seen on many a fine arm in this collection. Here were the best shot-guns and rifles out of English and French workshops: Martini-Henrys, Sniders, Winchester repeaters, Colt's and Smith and Weston's six-shooters, swords, sabres, and so on—the relics of the ill-fated Henley colonists. Here, too, were strange-made Italian stilettos, some such as are served out by the secret societies to their initiated,—all pawned for drink.

But do not imagine from all this that Pépe is a sort of Fraile-Muertan Shylock, an unpitying, grasping usurer; on the contrary, he is a very kind-hearted old fellow, who has done many a good turn for our countrymen, as well as his own, who have come to grief here. He is beloved by all, save the authorities, who entertain a wholesome dread of him ; for Pépe holds very strong opinions as to his fonda being his castle, and more than one British ne'er-do-weel or Italian cut-throat has found a harbour of refuge in this hostelry. When the *serenos* come to seize the refugee, old Pépe will stand at his door and swear sonorous oaths, and with a hundred horrid blasphemies, threaten to rip up the *tripos* of any who venture to cross his threshold against his will.

Carnival was now over, so it was possible to promenade the streets with a dry coat ; and the natives once more began to attend to the little business they ever trouble themselves with. We let it be known throughout the village that we were in want of four good horses—five-year-olds that were accustomed to eat maize and other hard food, for the camp-horses will not do this, and a fortnight's starvation, at the least, is necessary before they can be induced to touch it.

A pure-blood Indian offered his services ; he said he knew every horse for ten leagues round, he would gallop over the camps and bring every animal in that he thought would be likely to suit us. A curious old ruffian this was, short, stumpy, with straight, long, black hair, laughing, groggy eyes, bandy legs, and a sort of duck's waddle in the place of a walk—as is that of all horse-Indians. For three days he galloped about and brought horse after horse to us for inspection, while other ragged and wild-looking fellows, who had heard of our wants, came in with tropillas and single animals. We pitted the rival vendors against each other : it was amusing to listen to their voluble lies and denunciations. After inspecting one tropilla of twenty we picked out the best two, and made a bid of thirty Bolivians for them. The owner laughed us to scorn. "Why forty will be dirt cheap for these two splendid thoroughbreds ; the Colorado is the fastest horse over four cuadros in the whole province—besides, you spoil my whole tropilla by taking these two out." And so he argued after the manner of one that sells a horse, in all times and among all peoples. After some haggling we brought him down to thirty-two Bolivians for the two, that is about fifty-five shillings each —quite a fancy price, but they were decent animals, and seemed to have anything but an objection to eating maize when we put some before them. They were five-year-olds, and in addition to their other virtues were provided with papers in proper form, so we purchased them.

In this country the traveller needs no passport, but his horse does. There are title-deeds to horses here as to land, and any transfer has to be made before the judge of the district, and registered in the archives—a new title, or *guia*, stamped with the judicial seal is then delivered to the purchaser, which describes the conditions of sale, and is illustrated with a diagram of the animal's marks. These marks are large characters branded in very conspicuous fashion on the horse's flanks, so that there can be no mistake about them. So it is too with cattle, and the market value of their hides must be somewhat diminished by the custom; but all this is very necessary in this land of horse-stealing and cattle-lifting.

Our old Indian generally got a few reals out of us each time he brought a horse round for inspection. These he used to invest on the replenishing of his caña jar, from which he was wont to sip freely, as he galloped over the plain in search of other animals. This went on for three days : he got drunker and drunker till he could scarcely talk and certainly could not walk ; but his seat on horseback, and his discrimination in choosing, and sharpness in selling horses was not in the least affected. Horse-dealing is a delightful pursuit for such as he ; the gaucho loves to prolong the agony of a bargain. He would rather take less for his horse and linger over the haggling, than be paid the sum he opens the market with straight down. We managed to pick up another decent horse for about thirty shillings, and were now ready to start.

It was a glorious morning in early March that we paid Pépe our bill, drank the stirrup-cup, and rode out of Fraile Muerto in full marching order. Each of us had his saddle-bags under him, and his blanket rolled up behind. A felt sombrero, top-boots, a native hide belt six inches broad, with a six-shooter stuck in it, and a striped poncho over the shoulder, made each man look quite an orthodox roamer of the Pampas.

And now commenced a most delightful journey, concerning the direction of which I will make a few preliminary remarks.

On looking at a good map it will be seen that wild tribes of Indians, for the most part, occupy the centre of South America from north to south, and that the Europeans occupy a band more or less broad along either coast. But in this part of the continent a thin strip of civilization has been carried right across, connecting the eastern country of the white man with that of the west; the Atlantic with the Pacific; the camps of Santa Fé and Buenos Ayres with the Andes and the Chilian territory. This strip is not a broad one, and as yet is but sparsely inhabited by the conquerors; but it is ever and ever broadening. The line of the frontier forts is ever advancing both north and south into the lands of the savages. Here at Fraile Muerto the strip is not very broad. If one travels but a few leagues to the southward, one arrives on the Indian territory of the Pampas—an almost unknown country, on which the white man has no footing—even to the deserts of Patagonia and the cold shores of Magellan's Straits. If one travels to the northward again, one will soon reach another Indian territory, that of the Gran Chaco, an unexplored waste of forest and jungle and swamp that lies between the rivers Parana and Paraguay on the east, and the provinces of Santiago Salta, &c., on the west; and stretches north, through latitudes claimed by Bolivia and Brazil, who knows how far into the steaming tropics. It is down the centre of this strip of civilization that the Central Argentine Railway is carried, a line that is destined to be the trunk line of the whole South American system when these countries are opened out.

We proposed to ride along the line as far as Cordoba, and there leave it to travel by the old tropilla-track to Santiago and Tucuman. It is by this route that of old the caravans used to wend their slow way from Potosi to Buenos Ayres.

From Buenos Ayres to Tucuman by this tropilla-track, which winds a good deal, is 1119 English miles, according to an old Argentine postal road-book which a friend lent me. By following this route we should see a good deal of the country, and also much variety of scenery. It was curious to observe the gradual change in the vegetation as we advanced northward to tropical Tucuman, which is eight degrees nearer the equator than Buenos Ayres is. First comes the green Pampas of Santa Fé, where the rain-fall is considerable and the climate temperate; then gradually drier lands, the camps of Cordoba, where water is scarce, and the sky is cloudless for long months of drought; then the regions of the monté, the bush that forms the northern limit of the Pampas; and then a hotter and drier land, where spinous bushes and giant cacti of many species can alone extract nourishment from the arid sandy soil, encrusted as it is with glittering salt. Finally another change comes, a range of stupendous mountains blocks the horizon, the Sierras of Tucuman and Aconquija, branches of the Andes, whose summits attain the height of 17,000 feet, mothers of many rivers. Under their giant shadows spreads a great plain, a land of streams and much rain, a steaming, hot, unhealthy region, breeding fatal fevers, yet rich withal, with great plantations of sugar-cane waving in the tepid breeze, and brilliant orange-groves ever noisy with parrots and other gorgeous birds of the tropics—for this is the province of Tucuman, known far and wide as the garden of South America.

I must not let the memories of that delightful ride lead me to the occupying of undue space in this book with the story of it, so let us prick our horses into a "little gallop" as they call it here, and speed across the plains alongside the straight line of the railway.

We took it easily at first for sake of selves and horses, and made a six days' ride of it to Cordoba. Our first day's journey was across a parched country of burnt earth, scant and coarse pasture, with here and there a clump of algarrobas. The grass in this part of the Pampas does not cover the earth in a rich velvety carpet as in Santa Fé, but grows in scattered tufts with bare baked earth between—a very grass of the desert, wiry and prickly. Numerous eagles, vultures, owls, and bizcachas, seemed to be the sole inhabitants of this wilderness, a desolate expanse, with a horizon as is usual on the Pampas and most characteristic of these plains —vague, mysterious, immense—seeming to be infinitely off, and melting into a waving mirage, as if into some strange magic-land far beyond. And a strange land it is that does lie beyond, for there is the wilderness of the Indian, a desert of peril and thirst and death, stretching—so immense is it —as Head writes, "from tropic forests of palm in the north to eternal snows in the dreary south."

But there is one sign of civilization about us, and that with its contrast tends only to increase the sense of solemnity and desolation. Only two thin bars of iron running parallel in the very straightest line, till they meet in the far perspective like a wedge, and disappear in the trembling horizon. But this insignificant-looking line of the railway has tended as much to carry progress and justice into dark lands, as even that other thin red line, of which we Englishmen are so justly proud. The thin edge of the wedge of civilization has now been driven deep into the barbarism of the Pampas, notwithstanding the fanatical obstruction of Cordoban priests, and the vain opposition of novelty-hating gauchos, who tried to lasso the engine as it passed, and found that they had something more stubborn than an infuriated bull to deal with.

We rode on in the teeth of the hot north wind, till we came to where a bush-fire was smouldering over some leagues of country. All the grass had been consumed, the algarroba-trees had been all more or less carbonized, and tongues of fire leapt up hungrily here and there. Between the hot sky above, and the baking ashes beneath us, we soon acquired a very respectable thirst, that an old toper would have given much for; but, alas! we had no means of alleviating it, so it was not of much use to us.

Before dusk we reached the station of Ballesteros. We expected to find a little town here, but could perceive nothing but two or three wretched huts, none of which was an inn.

The only decent-looking establishment was the railway station; so we repaired thither, and to our delight found that the station-master was an Englishman, Mr. Coleson. He received us with great hospitality, and we did justice, after our exhilarating ride, to the hearty supper he put before us, as did our horses to their alfalfa and algarroba pods.

We were now gradually leaving the region of the foreigners. But few British *estançieros* are to be found beyond Fraile Muerto, and we were to change the comfortable homesteads and civilized ways of the *gringo* for the at any rate as hospitable, if more primitive, homes and manners of the old Andalusian colonists.

There are several native estanças round Ballesteros, so of

course a *juez*, a *commisario* of police, and a *commandante*
have been put in authority over the rising *pueblo*. There
is some amusing scandal running about concerning these
great men, which is worth repeating, so illustrative is it of
life in these wild camps. What I am about to relate will
seem almost incredible to those who have passed their lives
among the well-ordered communities of Europe; but here,
be it remembered, we are in the midst of a half-barbaric
people, and a people that have never known what justice is,
and whose state of civilization is in many respects far
inferior to that of our recent foes, the Kaffirs of South
Africa.

Each of the three functionaries I mentioned above imagines
himself to be the boss of the place; for their powers are
rather vague, and they are hardly men capable of understanding nice distinctions. Of the three the judge, I believe,
alone can write, and that only to the extent of being able to
sign his name to official documents. This legal luminary
receives no fixed pay, but is supposed to reserve one-half of
all the fees he receives and the fines he exacts, a method
which, of course, leads to unlimited extortion. The poor
old gentleman, who looks more like a gaucho than a judge,
had suffered a run of very bad luck of late. His cattle had
perished of drought, fees and fines did not come in, for people
would not be married or commit crimes as they should, so he
was at last at his wits' end even how to procure a sufficiency
of beef to keep up his judicial proportions. About a week
before our arrival he hit upon the following happy plan. He
procured a few bottles of vile gin on credit from the *pulperia*,
and invited all his friends to a little carnival *baile* at his
house. Several of these abused his hospitality and his gin
to such an extent, that on leaving towards the early hours of
the morning, they commenced to reel about the township in
a boisterous and unbecoming manner, and waxed quarrelsome
to boot. This was duly reported to their host, who summoned
them all to his presence, severely censured them, and then
fined each offender five pesos. He dined sumptuously every
night for a week afterwards.

Another instructive incident recently occurred at Ballesteros. It seems that a certain unfortunate debtor was so
pestered by his importunate creditors that he fled into another
province. It happened that a storekeeper here owed certain

moneys to the fugitive. On learning this our old friend the judge, losing no time, hurried round to attach the debt, with the intention of apportioning it among the creditors, after, of course, deducting a fair percentage for court fees. But, alas! he was too late. It happened that the commissary of police was one of the creditors, and had wisely anticipated all the others. He had visited the storekeeper, and obliged him to deliver the whole sum over to him. A stormy meeting between judge and commissary ensued in the open road before the assembled populace. The judge demanded a restitution of the moneys by the commissary. The latter refused to do anything of the kind, and openly accused the old gentleman of desiring to appropriate all to himself and rob the creditors. Thereupon the judge, gliding over the retort courteous and other intermediate stages of discussion, passed on at once to the countercheck quarrelsome, and said :—" Senor Commisario, you lie;" at the same time striking him across the face with his *rebenque,* or whip of plaited hide. On this the commisario retorted by knocking the judge down with the back of his sword, called assistance, and arrested that high functionary. Next he had him placed on a horse with his feet tied underneath its belly, and marched him off to Fraile Muerto, where he put him in the stocks.

Barbarous enough, too, as a rule, are these camp-town stocks. There is no convenience for sitting down as in our comfortable old English stocks, where Hudibras took his ease. Here the feet are imprisoned at some height from the ground, while the body is left to shift for itself, dangling down often with the head undermost. In this uncomfortable position an unfortunate wretch is often left untended and without food for days, through sun, and rain, and dew.

Another rather good story, and an authentic one, is told of our judge. Some time back he was playing at cards in the baker's house with a *capataz* of railway navvies. The *capataz* was unlucky, and lost considerably. Suspecting the judge of foul play, he refused to pay up. Thereupon the judge determined to sue him, but being so far conversant with law as to know that *nemo in suâ lite potest judicare,* he assigned this debt of honour to the baker, who then hailed the offending *capataz* before him. Our judge solemnly listened to the case, inflicted a fine, and sentenced the defendant

to imprisonment until it was paid. But the *capataz* was a
sharp man, and found means to repay the judge for this
judicial farce. He went off to another, I suppose a superior,
judge, who though he did not think it right to set aside the
decision of his learned brother, at any rate inflicted a heavy
fine on him, for countenancing unlicensed gambling. In this
land of liberty a licence is needful for nearly everything—a
game of cards, a private party, or a ball.

Such are the magistrates who are supposed to administer
justice in the camps; petty tyrants who imagine that their
powers have no limit, whom the fear of assassination alone
keeps in check. The poor people, the friendless widows
whom they can bully and rob with impunity, are of course
quite unaware that there are higher tribunals to which there
is an appeal from the decisions of these ignorant and unjust
judges. Perhaps it is as well after all that they are so
unaware in this land, where, if rumour be true, the highest
as well as the lowest official has his price.

The laws of this republic are excellent in theory, codified
as they are after the schemes of Bentham and the French
jurisconsults, but men capable of administering them are
sadly wanting.

The law as regards murder here is very extraordinary; too
harsh and too lenient at the same time. Accidental and
justifiable homicide is placed more or less on the same footing
as wilful murder. Thus, if an honest man by accident or in
self-defence kills another, he is imprisoned awhile and then
sent into the army to serve on the Indian frontier; no
pleasant and luxurious station that. Again, if a villain stab
an old man in the back to rob him of his little hoard, he
likewise is transformed into a soldier as a punishment, and
like all others has his chance of rising in the ranks. The
late station-master of Ballesteros was brutally murdered by a
peon. He is by no means the only British station-master
that has been assassinated at his post on these railways.
His murderer is now a non-commissioned officer, and was
pointed out to me at the head of an escort of prisoners on
the march.

This night I am writing my notes in a bedroom, with a
candle in front of me on the table. The light has attracted
all the insects of the neighbourhood, who are immolating
themselves wholesale in the tempting flame, a very entomo-

logical museum that only South America could turn out at so short a notice. There are all manner of moths and beetles and strange creatures of all sizes and shapes and numbers of legs—some lean, some fat—of all colours; some very uncanny of appearance; and all humming and buzzing in different notes and keys. Verily, this is the land of *bichos;* every month has *bichos* of its own peculiar to itself, but the omnipresent mosquito flourishes through all the months. Of this plague, too, there are many species; some are enormous fellows, striped like tigers, and capable, I should imagine, of sucking your blood through a thick hide boot; others small and black, but no less irritating.

That word *bicho*, by the way, is a very useful one. I suppose originally it was intended to signify beetle, but it means a good deal more than that now. It is more comprehensive in its meanings than even the Yankee bug. The term *bicho* is used here to signify not only an insect but any strange beast. The gaucho calls the tiger a great *bicho*. If he were to perceive any animal—say an elephant—that were new to him, he would speak of it as that *bicho*. Not only to animals but even to inanimate things is the term applied. I heard a native call a grain unknown to him a *bicho*. Old Pépe, of Fraile Muerto, would call his morning draught his *bicho;* and people talk here of putting spirit in their water to kill the *bicho*, and very careful they are, too, to do this. The water *bicho* has a poor chance indeed with the average South American.

A violent storm of thunder, wind, and rain refreshed the parched soil this night, and was very grateful after the recent heats.

CHAPTER XI.

ON the morrow we saddled betimes and rode through the town, or rather nucleus of a town, consisting as it did of a store, one other house, a pair of stocks, and a race-course.

We galloped over the plain, brighter and more beautiful after the rain. Here by monté of prickly bushes, under whose lee the grass was pressed down, showing where the wild beasts had crouched for shelter during the storm. Here by clumps of feathery pampa grass, and over greenest pastures thickly dotted with the scarlet and purple blossoms of verbenas and polyanthi. A south-west wind blew in our faces, odorous of mint and vanilla and a thousand flowers, and fresh and invigorating after the norte of yesterday, dry and hot as it was from its passage over a thousand leagues of parched steppes.

Who can do justice to these glorious Pampas—to the irresistible fascination of this vast expanse of grass and flowers—to the intoxicating delight of a gallop over them at breezy dawn, and to that peculiar quiet charm and sense of ecstatic calm that subdues even the most unimaginative man, when sitting by the evening encampment he is a spectator of that magnificent appearance—a sunset on these ocean-like solitudes? There is no scenery, not even of the great mountains, that so overwhelms a man with a sense of his littleness, with a consciousness of what an immense unknown there is around him, as that of the South American steppes, where all Nature is so vast and vague.

Just before we entered the township of Villa Maria, which we had chosen as the destination of our second day's journey, we traversed a pretty wilderness of rank weeds, ten feet in height, all new to us, luxuriant, of many scents and flowers, and noisy with song of bird and hum of cicala. Riding through this we suddenly came upon a strange scene worthy of the brush of a Long. Dark between us and the golden sunset, there came towards us through the varied vegetation a troop of some thirty women, walking in slow and solemn procession ; dusky half-breeds and Indians these, with their shoulders and raven hair covered with the black shawl of the country, and barefooted. Before them walked four girls who bore a little gaudily-painted image standing erect on a stretcher. This was a celebrated saint, who was now on his way to pay a visit to a neighbouring saint. Every native likes if possible to have a little wooden saint of his own in his rancho. It is believed that these saints are of sociable disposition and like to meet each other at times. So San Martin, in Lopez's rancho, is carried to visit Santa Rosa, in Gonzalez's rancho ; an excuse for much caña-drinking and gambling. Some of these saints are celebrated for the miraculous cures they perform. Such a one's saint, for instance, is great at the curing of rheumatism. When this is the case, he is often a good thing to his owner, who lets him out to sufferers at so much a day. A man will even pawn his saint sometimes ; but this is looked upon as unlucky, and the saint has been known to lose his virtues after having been thus treated. The priests do not much encourage this system of private saints—they like to have a monopoly in them, I suppose, and to act as go-betweens to saints and sufferers. Far from my intention is it to ridicule any of the rites of the Roman Catholic Church, but the religion of the South American camps is not the Roman Catholic religion— and none deplore this more than the educated dignitaries of the Church at Buenos Ayres—but a superstition of the very grossest kind, encouraged by an ignorant native priesthood, which, as Mr. Bates says in his excellent work on South America, "on everything pertaining to morals and the ordinary decencies of life, has its own opinions and ideas, which are certainly somewhat at variance with those usually entertained in Europe on such matters."

Villa Maria is an important little place, being at the junction of the Cordoba railway and the new and yet unfinished line to Mendoza and the Andes. Here we passed the night in an hotel kept by M. Albert, a Frenchman, who prepared for us a capital dinner that reminded us of Europe, and which was washed down with wines from the slopes of the Cordilleras—the vintages of Mendoza, Rioja, and San Juan —which are by no means despicable.

We were now experiencing for the first time the attacks of that plague of the Pampas, the *bicho colorado*. This minute pest burrows into the lower half of the human leg, and there proceeds to lay its eggs under the skin ; when the young bicho is hatched he works his way out of his cradle to the outer world, a performance that produces the most intolerable itching. These little beasts do not attack one singly but in hundreds, and in some cases produce nasty sores, but *aguardiente*, or other spirit, well rubbed in, generally brings relief.

On our third day we rode to the camp railway station of Chañares, a distance of only twenty-two miles ; but here we had to halt for the night, as a waterless, pastureless wilderness lay between this and the next stage, Laguna Larga, forty miles further on. This day we perceived a broad purple streak along the horizon like a sea of blood. On approaching it this proved to be thickly-growing polyanthi, covering a vast area of plain. Not only a land of bichos is this, but of thorns. As we unsaddled our horses, and lay ourselves under a big mimosa among the ants for our midday halt and siesta, we were made unpleasantly aware of how thorny a land we were approaching. The grass of this arid portion of the Pampas is a very grass of the desert, stiff, hard, sharp as a needle. Every plant and bush and tree is covered with thorns. There are balls of seed, too, studded round with cruel needles, like porcupines ; if you pluck these, your hands are filled with the minute and irritating points. Some of these seed-balls are as big as large plums, and roll along with the wind. When they strike one's coat they anchor themselves there and cling so tenaciously, that in wrenching them away much of the material of the cloth comes away also.

Our poor horses did not seem to appreciate this sort of vegetation in the way of pasture, but the algarrobas were covered with pods, which we plucked and fed them with, to their evident gratification. At Chañares, jovial Mr. O'Donohue, the station-master, and his kind wife received us with true Irish hospitality. After our asado and praties—unwonted luxury—we camped out for the night on the platform, and slept the sleep of the just until midnight, when the train to Cordoba thundered in. " Caramba ! what a lot of passengers for Cordoba," I heard the guard say as he saw our prostrate forms. " Ah, no, it's those yacht fellows ; for I can see Don Arturo's nose peeping above his blanket." The guards of the trains—old English sailors most of them —knew us by this time, and were wont to exchange greetings with us, as we passed each other daily on the line— for the train runs to Cordoba one day, and returns to Rosario the next. That particular nose, by which they recognized us this night, was one of the great features of the *Falcon ;* its owner is very proud of it, and, indeed, once seen, it is not soon to be forgotten, with its noble proportions coloured by the suns of many climes.

Our fourth day's journey was to Laguna Larga, a longer ride than usual. To one travelling over these plains each day brings some new feature in the vegetation. This day we crossed a large space where grew a grass three feet in height, topped with the most lovely feathery seeds ; these, waving in the wind, caused the plain to assume the appearance of a rolling sea of softest wool or down—a most pleasing and curious effect. We noticed how far more numerous the birds were in this region, where the Pampas merged into jungle, than in treeless Santa Fé. Pewits, vultures, eagles, and many other varieties were here, while a vast multitude of green parroquets kept up a perpetual chatter over our heads. An immense cloud of martins too were flying north, doubtless emigrating from the impending winter of bleak Patagonia; a wonderful number of them. Many were resting awhile on the telegraph wires; they crowded on them, sitting close together, fluttering and chattering—living festoons of birds stretching a league away.

We then crossed a very parched district, waterless and treeless, where a strong stink of the skunk was the prevailing odour of the sultry air. Towards midday we sighted right ahead a square, black mass, rising conspicuously over the level plain. This turned out to be a tank in which the scant water of a neighbouring laguna is collected after rainfall in order to supply the railway engines. We called a halt, unsaddled our horses, and indulged in a welcome draught of the water—brackish, muddy, and tepid though it was. A native was in charge of the tank; beside the hut in which he lived there was another wretched mud rancho, into whose roof a stick was thrust, with a white rag flying at its summit, indicating that this was a grog-shop; for even this ungodly, houseless spot in the wilderness must needs have its pulperia.

It is astonishing how far off the thirsty traveller can distinguish that blessed white flag in the clear atmosphere of these level steppes. We lit a fire by the tank, and bringing forth from our saddle-bags some ribs of beef we had brought with us, pierced them with our iron *asador* (spit), which we then stuck into the ground in the midst of the fire. Thus was soon ready for us that national dish of South America, the asado. A luxury it is, too, out in the camps, with the sauce of a healthy appetite; but an asado eaten with knife and fork within doors, is hardly to be recommended. We washed this down with some caña from the pulperia, enjoyed a siesta, and then rode on to the station of Laguna Larga, where Mr. Wynn, the station-master, who was expecting us, had prepared a good square supper for the travellers. This night, like the last, we passed on the platform comfortably enough.

Early in the afternoon of our fifth day's ride we reach the banks of the Rio Segundo, a river that rises in th Sierras of Cordoba, and ultimately flows into the Mar Chiquita, an inland lake whose waters never reach the sea, but are absorbed by the thirsty wilderness. The Rio Segundo is here a broad, rapid stream of clear water flowing over a sandy bed; extensive sand-banks border its edges, backed by banks overgrown with tall grasses and shrubs, a jungle inhabited by many pumas and parrots. We met a native, who gave us instructions where to cross the river so as to avoid the quicksands. The water was low, so we found no difficulty in fording. This is by no means always the case. Many men and cattle are lost at this ford yearly. In a real *crescente* it is, of course, quite impossible to effect a passage. These *crescentes* of the rivers of the Pampas are as terrible and sudden as those of South Africa. A few hours' heavy rain in the far Sierras, and down comes the flood with a thunderous roar—sweeping all before it, bearing down on its swollen waters huge trees and drowned cattle and the wrecks of habitations.

The water of this river is very wholesome, and is strongly impregnated with the sarsaparilla that grows thickly on its banks in places. Having effected a safe passage we gave our horses a rest, while we indulged in the very unwonted luxury of a bath. For this purpose we waded to a pretty, willowy island in the middle of the stream.

The little township and station of Rio Segundo is but a mile distant from the river bank. Here we passed the night. Mr. Mott, the station-master, gave us much information as to the profusion of game in the neighbouring montés. The pumas are almost the only sportsmen who revel in this grand hunting-ground, where are to be found innumerable wood-pigeons, parrots, three varieties of partridges, teal, snipe, duck, geese, chunas, ostriches, jaguars, deer, and many other beasts and birds.

The next, our sixth, day's march was to be our last in the company of the railway line; we were no longer to have the certain hospitality of a British station-master to look forward to at the end of each day's journey, for this night we were to reach the city of Cordoba.

The Sierras now loomed distinctly on the north-west horizon, refreshing indeed to the eye after these hundreds of

leagues of unbroken plain. We greeted the hills once more
with almost as keen a delight as the mariner the loom of
land after a long voyage on the plains of the salt sea.

The country between the Segundo and Cordoba is of a
very pleasing character. We had evidently left the Pampas
proper at last, and were entering the region of the bush that
stretches hence to the tropic forests of the north. We rode
through groves of algarroba and beautiful flowering shrubs,
carpeted with the variegated blossoms of verbena, polyanthus,
and other plants. The land, no longer of a dead level, was
slightly undulating. As we were galloping down the pleasant
glades one of us shouted in delight, " Hurrah ! here is a
peach-tree covered with fruit." We all drew near, but were
doomed to disappointment. It was but some poisonous plum
of the monté, amber of hue, and comely, but acrid in taste,
and not any kin to the familiar old fruit we had mistaken
it for.

At midday we hobbled our horses, plucked some algarrobas for them, and lunched off some sardines, biscuit, and
caña we had brought with us. As I was sitting down I
suddenly perceived two bright eyes glaring at me from a
large hole in the ground. I dropped my sardine, and put
my hand to my knife, not knowing what strange beast this
might be, and what were his intentions ; but I soon perceived
that it was but an innocent, amiable creature after all, against
whose character I have never heard any accusation brought
—an unlovely scaly monster, somewhat resembling an
alligator, yet inoffensive enough, being only a poor iguana
that was peeping out of his house with no evil design,
merely wondering what we intruders on his solitude might
be. I presented him with a bit of biscuit, which accepting
gratefully, he retired unobtrusively into his house.

At last we reached a ridge overlooking a vast expanse of
country : to our astonishment, for we were unaware that we
had been ascending so much, and never expected to see
Cordoba so far below us. It was a magnificent view : beyond the jungle that sloped downwards from where we stood,
there lay extended a vast level plain, well watered with many
silver streams, bordered with rows of poplars. Arable fields
and pastures stretched far to a distant range of grand mountains, swelling range behind range. Lofty indeed they
seemed to us after the interminable plains, and indeed some

of the summits of these Sierras are 7000 feet in height; and in the centre of this plain, in the bend of a broad river winding out of sight into distant groves, we perceived the fair white city, with many domes and spires of churches, some of a bright white stone, others of marble, others gleaming with gold. To us, coming straight from the wilderness, this sudden first view of Cordoba was as that of the Delectable City to the worn pilgrim of that quaint history which is so delicious to the mind with its old-world fragrance.

Yes, before us was the world-renowned Cordoba, the Cordoba of the Jesuit fathers, the city of the churches, and the ringing of bells, the sanctimonious town of priests and doctors, the oasis of learning in the wilderness, in whose antique university how many generations of youth have acquired the Aristotelian philosophy, and all the humanities, and inhumanities to boot, if report be true. A mysterious place this ancient stronghold of the much-dreaded society of Jesus, in the heart of South America, with a false-learned and narrow-minded population to this day over which the priests have retained a great deal of their old power. When the railway was first brought up to the gates of Cordoba, the *frailes* felt that the old days had gone for ever, and that the dreaded light was coming, the old order changing for the new. In every church they preached fiercely against the accursed thing, and, had they dared, would have urged the pious citizens to tear up the rails, and cursed the fatal iron way.

But let us linger no longer on the hill that overlooks the ancient city, but ride boldly in, more boldly far than we could have done in the olden days, when the Inquisition with its tortures awaited the heretic *gringo* who dared venture here. From the ridge upon which we stood the track gradually widened until it became quite a decent road; for Cordoba, like all other cities in this land, is a mere oasis of civilization in the wilderness; its streets are continued as roads but a few hundreds of yards outside the town, and then dwindle away to scarce distinguishable tracks.

As we descended we became conscious of a great and sudden change in the Nature around us. No longer the level plain, so stoneless that one could not so much as find the smallest pebble wherewith to threaten a snarling cur, but here, at the edge of the Sierras, the granite peeped out occasionally through the soil, a country of rocks and of running water, and where the feet of horses are shod with iron, as is never the case on the Pampas.

Across the road and alongside of it ran with much sound streams of clear sparkling water. We passed, too, huge waggons, slow, groaning horribly, drawn by oxen—waggons of hard red wood, in the construction of which no iron had been used, not even for one nail or tire of wheel, but the parts of which were lashed and laced together with thongs of raw hide.

Our poor unshodden horses of the Pampas were affrighted at the strange surroundings, they stumbled and shied at every step; never had they before been down so steep an incline, felt such stony ground under their feet, or heard such sound of running water. There was a little water-course that was carried across the road in a sunken wooden trough, or canal, some eighteen inches broad at most; though small, it babbled along noisily enough. The horses could not make this out at all; they sniffed at it suspiciously, shook their heads, became very uneasy, and refused to cross it. Ultimately, by dint of much persuasion of whip and spur, they did jump it; each in his turn pulled himself together, took a tremendous leap, and cleared it by yards and yards—a ridiculous spectacle; the prudent creatures evidently were determined to make no mistake about it, and give as wide a berth as possible to the uncanny phenomenon.

There are no suburbs to this city, the wilderness stretches down to the edge of its mediæval streets and squares. Just outside, it is true, there is a wretched *ceinture* of rubbish—offal, bones, broken bricks, and the like, among which, like jackals, dwells a miserable pack of squatters—a low type of half-breeds, hideous and repulsive in aspect. Their squalid mud ranchos are scattered pell-mell over this disreputable locality without any pretension to order.

We rode into the city, which seems a well laid-out and agreeable place at its first aspect. We traversed long straight streets of one-storied white houses with the usual prison-like grated windows looking on the street; clear water flowing down every gutter. The streets here are paved with stone; on hearing the clanging of their hoofs on these our horses became almost unmanageable in their alarm, and when they did quiet down a little, proceeded with steps gingerly and timid, as if red-hot iron was beneath their feet.

We repaired to the "Hotel d'Europa," to which we had been recommended, and sent our horses to a stable to be looked after during our stay at Cordoba, with injunctions that they should be shod, another new experience for the poor beasts. The genial host of the "Europa," who is a German, made us very comfortable in his excellently-managed hostelry.

CHAPTER XII.

ON the morrow after our arrival we sallied forth to inspect the city. We found ourselves once more in a civilized centre, for tramways, American bars, and French *cafés* have followed the railway, and now relieve the sense of oppression and *ennui* which pervades the atmosphere of the slow, grave old university town.

We had been awakened early by the ringing of many bells in many old churches, so had a good day before us to explore the streets and handsome squares of the city of priests and women. For, indeed, priests and women seem to form the bulk of the population of Cordoba. The *frailes* are a sour-looking lot enough, though some of the young clericals are regular *petits-maîtres* in their way, and seem to have quite a feminine taste for lace and millinery. The women are not gifted with much beauty, with the exception, of course, of those of the high caste—pure white Spanish beauties, who are invariably dressed in the latest Paris fashion. But of these there are but very few; all the others are half-breeds, of a peculiarly disagreeable, dark, muddy complexion, and possessing the harsh Indian type of feature. Indeed, the population hereabouts has no right to rank itself with white men at all; these people are but the mongrel descendants of Indians that have been tamed by the Jesuits. This extensive crossing of the Spanish with the Indian blood has, in the opinion of those who know, proved to be a great curse to these countries, for the result has been a useless breed that cumbers the face of the earth. Not as in North America, where the aboriginal races have vanished like smoke before the advance of the white man and his civilization ; here the Indian blood has mingled with that of the Latin colonists, overpowered it indeed, and imbued it with its own barbarism, so that in many regions the conquerors have adopted the manners, dress, and even language, of the conquered tribes.

The negro and mulatto belles of the West Indies know how to set off and match their complexion and peculiar style of beauty with appropriate dress and gaudy tints; but the Indo-Spanish half-breed and chiña of Cordoba envelopes herself from head to foot in a shabby-looking black shawl, or sheet, which, especially when rusty with age, does not tend to show off to advantage her muddy face. Though her toilette be thus simple, and does not entail heavy milliner's and *chapellerie* bills, the chiña belle is very particular in one respect—boots; she must have a pair of nice-fitting French-styled boots. No more acceptable present can you make your Cordoban sweetheart, should you have the bad taste to possess one, than *uno par de botas nuevas.* Cordoba, by the way, like its namesake in old Spain, is a great place for the working of leather, and its damsels evidently consider that there is "nothing like leather," and despise all other additions to their doubtful charms.

When the traveller has explored the cathedral with its massive gilding, the university, and some of the curious old churches—life is too short to visit them all—he cannot do better than light his cigar and stroll round the two great squares—the Plaza 25° de Mayo and the Alameda. There is a great contrast between these two. The latter is strictly old world and Spanish; a solemnity pervades the severe enclosure, deserted as it generally is, save for some silent stalking *fraile* with shovel hat, or black draped chiña, well harmonizing with the spot. This square is laid out with strictest mathematical regularity ; round it are the usual white, grated-windowed, one-storied houses, with no shop-windows gay with display of goods—lifeless, prison-like. A lake of water occupies the centre of the Alameda, in the middle of which is an island cut into some mathematical figure, with a bright white temple of Greek architecture on it. There is a cold, artificial, confined look about the whole place, that seems strikingly emblematic of the old life of the ecclesiastical stronghold, austere, working in a narrow groove, never looking beyond its own limited horizon of the cloister wall. Rows of fine willows once bordered this lake, but during the tremendous hurricane that swept over Cordoba two years back, all these were uprooted. This must have been a fearful tempest, it bent double every heavy iron and brazen cross that tops the manifold steeples of this city of churches, and thus they still remain as we saw then, sloping all one way, a sign to the traveller of what a South American pampero can do at times.

This dreamy Alameda, so lonely and stern of aspect, that one would imagine it had never been awakened to any show of life, save by the excitement of some *auto-da-fé* of heathen Indians, does wake up in a languid sort of way once a day. Towards the late afternoon when the shadows of the Sierras come down to the city, and the southern cross with a myriad stars begins to illumine the delightful night of inland South America—the haughty Spanish beauties come forth in their carriages, and drive round and round the lake for three-quarters of an hour or so, while a considerable crowd of chiñas and others of the lower orders promenade on foot, marvelling at the white beauty of the upper caste.

The other square—the Plaza de 25° de Mayo, is in the centre of the city, and is far more lively than the gloomy Alameda, for it is here that the energetic money-making *gringos* most do congregate. Fine shops and brilliant *cafés* surround it. At one side is the old Gothic cathedral, perhaps the finest specimen of mediæval architecture in the new world. A pleasant and well-tended garden occupies the centre, with two avenues crossing it diagonally from the corners of the square, as is the fashion of most of the old Spanish plazas; shrubs, splashing fountains, and winding walks fill up the interspace. Here every evening the military band plays excellently the enchanting airs of old Spain.

A visit to the North Market in the early morning is worth the while to the European stranger. Ugly old women and girls, half-bred Indians from the country, sit on the bare ground all over the quaint old enclosure; not chattering overmuch, nor importuning the passer-by to purchase, but rather stolidly sucking the perpetual maté through the bombilla, each wrapped in the black funereal shroud I have described, squatting in front of her small stock of wares. Some have but a little mound of algarroba-pods, maize, or alfalfa before them, about six-pennyworth in all, which nevertheless they have perhaps brought hither several leagues, travelling on foot through the night. Others vend melons, wheaten cakes, and strange fruits; while hide horse-gear, old and new, has its separate corner of the market allotted to it; and boots, of course—that chief production of Cordoba,—are temptingly laid out in long rows before the marketing chiña.

We loafed about the ancient city for three days, made a trip to some of the pleasant vales at the foot of the Sierras, and then prepared for our ride to Tucuman. There is an English photographer established in Cordoba — who alone of any we met had undertaken the journey from here to Santiago del Estero. From him accordingly we procured a description of the old tropilla-track, and a list of the good halting-places. This track, which is a portion of that great route across South America along which in the olden days the strings of jingling mules were wont to bring the bars of silver from the mines of Potosi to Buenos Ayres, has been deserted by travellers since the construction of the Tucuman railway. The caravans of waggons from the interior now alone make use of it. From Cordoba to Santiago del Estero, the capital of the province of the same name, is according to some 130 Cordoban leagues (three and a half miles to a league); according to others, more. The latter, I think are right, for the track winds considerably, and we were sixteen days accomplishing the distance, riding at no mean pace for about twelve hours each day.

The railway to Tucuman strikes straight across the *salinas*, or salt-deserts, an almost impracticable route for horses, for apart from the lack of pasture and fresh water, there are times when, after heavy rains in the Sierras, a strong wind blows the waters towards the desert in a mass, so that they roll over it like the Red Sea during Pharaoh's famous march, and convert the salt plain into a broad inland sea, with no land visible on any horizon. The railway is carried along a raised bank which is always above the level of the inundation.

On the other hand the road to Tucuman *viâ* Santiago sweeps one hundred miles to the eastward of the railway; skirts the salt-desert, and winds among the undulating hills of the province of Santiago, one of the poorest and most thinly populated of the republic, a mere jungle for the most part, lying between the salinas on one side, and the Indian hunting-grounds of El Chaco, beyond the great Rio Salado, on the other—a province between two deserts.   This country, according to our friend the photographer, would not fail to interest us, for its scenery is picturesque, and it is inhabited by a primitive people, poor yet hospitable, dignified and courteous, and preserving all the manners and customs of their ancestors, the old *conquistadores*, who came here under Pizarro, ages ago.

The Santiagenas, however, are much hated and feared by the Argentines of the south, having acquired an unenviable reputation as bandits, murderers, and cattle-lifters.   Let me anticipate somewhat by stating that among this ill-famed people we met with greater kindness and hospitality than in any other of the five provinces which we traversed in this expedition.   The Santiagenas, it is true, return the compliment, by accusing the Cordobans of being the greatest assassins and thieves in South America.   The Cordobans, in their turn, heartily abuse both their neighbours of Santa Fé and Santiago, and so it is throughout the republic; but all unite in giving a very bad character indeed to the men of Santiago.   As far as my experience, and that of others who know these countries better, goes, the reports as to the dangers of travelling in this part of South America are grossly exaggerated.   I do not suppose it would be quite prudent to walk all over the republic alone and unarmed, but it would be still less prudent to do so in many countries in Europe I know of.   Organized bands of banditti, as they have in Mexico, are quite unknown here, unless it may be in revolution times, when every South American becomes more or less of a brigand for the nonce.   Considering how impotent the arm of justice is in these remote provinces, that there is practically no police, and that these vast montes could shelter large bands of robbers and enable them to defy the authorities with absolute impunity, it is wonderful that there is so little crime.   It is indeed creditable to these poor half-breeds, that, left to themselves as they are, they should be so law-observing and orderly.   Mule-trains laden with silver dollars often make enormous journeys here without an armed escort being deemed necessary to accompany them.   If the people that inhabited these wild steppes were of Anglo-Saxon blood, it strikes me that this would hardly be the case, and that in the absence of other law, that of Judge Lynch and the Vigilance Committee would soon become necessary.

We were now to leave the land of paper, so we had to supply ourselves at the Cordoba branch of the London and River Plate Bank with *chirolas,* small silver Bolivian coins which are current in the northern provinces, and others of anything but pure silver, bearing on one side an impression of the blessed cinchona-tree. The value of a very few sovereigns in this spurious metal weighs somewhat, so we had to divide these coins among the party, and no small addition did they make to our baggage.

We were strongly recommended to take a native peon with us, and a friend at the bank found us the very man— " A regular ruffian," he said, " doubtlessly an old horse-thief, and therefore the very one to see that your horses are not stolen ; a native endowed with that wonderful instinct every true gaucho possesses, which enables him, when yet afar off, to detect the presence of water or pasture, to tell where a river can be forded with the least difficulty, and the like—a very useful man. You will find, perhaps," he continued, " that he will like to hurry over some portions of the road, as he is wanted in more than one place." This, indeed, we found to be the case ; on one occasion we became aware that he was taking us by a very circuitous route to the place we wished to reach. The following conversation then ensued :—

" Is there not a way shorter than this one, Manuel ? "

" How no, senor, there is a road a little shorter."

" Then why have you not taken it ? "

" Because, senor, I know some one on that short cut." He said this simply, without further comment, as if this was the most natural reason in the world. I suppose he once had a misfortune there—a South American euphemism for having murdered a man—and was being looked out for by revengeful relatives of the deceased.

This worthy called on us at the "Europa," and much disappointed us by his appearance. We expected to see a regular cutthroat-looking bandit in poncho, chirippas, and massive silver spurs, with a long knife at his back. But Manuel was a very different-looking person. With the exception of the alpagatas on his feet, his dress was in no respect that of the orthodox South American bravo. He was clad in a light tweed cutaway coat and trousers—the present of some Englishman—very worn and ragged. His face, dark and bearded though it was, had no ferocity in its expression; his smile was bland and amiable as that of the heathen Chinee. Here we had a pleasant-looking, weather-beaten, middle-aged man, rather down at the heels, disreputable undoubtedly, but no fit model for a melodramatic villain.

There was something in the face of this terrible being that pleased us, so we soon struck a bargain with him. He engaged to ride with us to Tucuman as our peon, and supply his own horse.

"Have you got a horse, Manuel?" asked Jerdein.

"*Como no, senor.*"

"Then we will start to-morrow morning."

This Manuel did not seem to approve of. "My horse is twenty leagues from here," he said. "By the day after to-morrow I can bring it and be ready to start."

Thus was it arranged. Jerdein uncharitably suggested, when Manuel had turned his back, that he was not in the possession of any definite, distinct horse, but looked upon all horses as more or less his property, and only required this space of twenty-four hours, to enable him to pick out from the neighbouring camps a steed to his liking. Poor Manuel! I hardly think this was fair; though suspiciously enough, he did have no *guia* for his horse, when the said beast turned up; anyhow, if he had appropriated another's, he had made a good selection, for that horse proved to be the hardiest of our troop. Manuel himself, too, turned out to be a most excellent fellow, very useful, honest, and obliging; we parted with sorrow on both sides, when the journey was completed.

As Arnaud's horse showed some tendency to sore back he purchased another, a big black ex-racer, and we converted his old Colorado into a baggage animal. This change of duty the animal much appreciated—Arnaud, to begin with, is no feather-weight; now he had but a light burden to bear, and had it much his own way on the journey. He could trot on ahead and feed on some clump of delicate grass till we came up, then trot on again at his own sweet will; so long as he kept up with the rest of the party, and showed no tendency to roll and disarrange his burden, as he generally did after his girths were tightened up.

We formed quite an imposing troop as we fell in early on the morning of the 17th of March in front of the hotel. First came the baggage animal with our saddle-bags on his back, also a sack of necessaries for camp life we had purchased in Cordoba—*matés* and *bombillas,* an *asador,* a yard and a half of Bologna sausage to fall back upon in the wilderness, a supply of sugar, *yerba maté,* pepper, salt, and sulphate of quinine (for it was the season of *chuchu* in Tucuman), goodly ribs of beef, and some of the little flat loaves of the country, and, of course, tobacco. A kettle dangled melodiously at his neck. After this animal, who thus bore on his responsible back all that appertained to the baggage, commissariat, and ambulance departments, came we three *gringos* in top boots and ponchos, each armed with a big revolver and a big bottle, the latter to be filled, when occasion offered, with caña and water. Then followed the sage Manuel armed with his perpetual cigarette, looking, in his seedy cutaway, far less bandit-like than the rest of the party.

He was mounted on a strange, lean, black horse, with bloodshot eyes—a dissipated-looking beast, and seemingly quite incapable of accomplishing so long a journey. But Manuel knew what he was about, and when we criticized his mount, he would smile and say, " *Es muy guapo* "— " You will see."

We did see, and wondered. This was a horse from the Pampas, and, unlike our own, had never been taught to eat hard food ; thus, in the pastureless lands we traversed the poor beast positively starved for days. He stood and looked on with astonishment when our horses greedily ate algarroba or maize, but he himself disdained to satisfy his hunger with these. It was but occasionally he came across edible grass, yet, marvellous to say, this horse that seemed to exist on air was fresher every night, and in better condition when we reached Tucuman than our own better-fed animals. He was *muy guapo* with a vengeance. A gaucho's horse, like the gaucho himself, is as tough as nails, and capable of enduring with stoical resignation hunger, thirst, and fatigue.

We rode down to the Primero, the broad river which runs along the north side of the city, crossed it by a fine stone

bridge, and soon found ourselves in the open uncultivated
country, on the old tropilla-track, marked by the deep ruts
of the lumbering waggons.

When we were still near the town, Manuel rode up to my
side, and, pointing to a cluster of mud ranchos some few
hundred yards off to the right of our road, said rather
shyly,—

"I have a sweetheart up there."

The gaucho, I must tell you, is like the Eastern European,
rather bashful when alluding to his love relations.

"Well," I replied, "I suppose she would like you to say
good-bye to her as you pass by."

"*Quien sabe?*" said Manuel, with a shrug of the shoulders;
"but"—this hesitatingly—"she is very poor, is Anita."

He then explained that this damsel was under his sole
protection, and that he should like to have an advance of a
few dollars of his wages, to enable her to live during his
absence. This Dulcinea was certainly not very extravagant
in her *menage*, for Manuel said he only wanted about fourteen shillings, this would quite suffice her while he was
away (about a month). We gave him his fourteen shillings,
and off he galloped to the rancho of his love. After, no
doubt, an affecting farewell, he returned smiling, and told
us that the senorita sent us her respects, and wished the
caballeros a safe journey. I am grieved to say another lady
turned up in Tucuman, who likewise had claims on Manuel's
purse. Our attendant was evidently a regular *roué*.

It will be very difficult to avoid monotony and repetition
in my narrative of this ride. Each day's journey, it is true,
showed us some new features to admire in the scenery and
vegetation; but it cannot be expected that the reader will
appreciate the meagre description of the ever-changing
beauties of this summer-land as we did the delightful
reality. Monotony we found none, all was fair, strange, and
new to us.

This morning we passed a tropilla, a picturesque and old-
world sight. Slowly it came towards us, a long train of
huge lumbering waggons drawn by mules, solidly built of
the hard red wood, with no springs or iron in their construction, creaking and groaning horribly. Miles off one
could hear the weird lamentation of the tortured timber.
These waggons were laden with hides; strange and wild-

looking men in the gay-coloured ponchos of the north rode alongside them, and behind followed a large number of spare mules. The chief of the caravan was better dressed than the rest, wore boots with silver spurs, and a valuable poncho of vicuña hair, while a brazen trumpet swung by his side, with which he sounded his orders from one end of the caravan to the other. As we passed, the two parties greeted each other in stately Spanish fashion, and Manuel asked a few questions from the chief as to the state of the road, the rivers and fords, as to how many days they were out, whence they had come, whither they were bound, for travellers on these great steppes hail each other and exchange news very much in the same way as two vessels meeting in mid-ocean. The discipline of a tropilla indeed very much resembles that of a ship. This South American caravan has its captain, whose powers over his wild subordinates are as great as that of the sea captain, nay, greater, for there is no inquiry on reaching port, in this lawless land, should he even have inflicted death while chastising a mutinous peon. There is no South American Plimsoll for the crews of the caravan.

These tropillas undertake enormous journeys, extending over many months, journeys whose length may be measured by thousands of miles. The men are generally armed so as to be able to resist any hostile Indians they may encounter on their lonely way. When attacked they form their waggons in a ring and fight behind them, somewhat in the fashion of the South African Boers. The foremost waggon of the line of march is often provided with a small cannon on a swivel. The railways, however, have now to a considerable extent done away with this, as with many other of the picturesque features of Argentine life.

About midday we came across another small tropilla halting by the side of the track among the mimosas. The men in their picturesque garb lay about lazily smoking; while a juicy asado was grilling temptingly over their fire, and a huge demijohn of red wine from the Andes lay among the flowers ready for the meal. The physiognomy of the men and the whole scene recalled vividly to my mind the wayside descriptions one reads in "Don Quixote" and "Gil Blas." So lonely is the land we now traversed, that we only came across one more tropilla for the next 300 miles of our journey; other travellers none.

Just as our appetites told us that it was time for our own midday meal, we came to a public-house. This was a mud hut shaped like a sentry-box, about five feet high and four feet broad. The side towards the road was open, and there stood a little table covered with a very dirty bit of native lace. On this were laid out all the resources of the establishment—the whole capital of the enterprising owner. This consisted of one square-faced bottle of vile gin, a tumbler, three wheaten cakes, some tails of strong black tobacco, and several water-melons. At first this establishment seemed to be deserted, but on looking over the table we perceived the attendant barmaid; for there, squatting on the mud floor, was a very ugly half breed girl, apathetically sucking maté through a black bombilla, evidently troubling herself very little as to whether travellers patronized her restaurant or not.

These Argentines are a very independent lot, and won't go out of their way to ask you to employ them. If you purchase anything at a store, they serve you with an air as if they were conferring a great favour on you; the servility and importunity of a London tradesman would astonish and disgust them. The lady rose from the mud with a gesture of annoyance at being disturbed, and for a *real* sold us a large water-melon, delicious this sultry day. We gathered some wood, lit a fire by the side of the track, and over it cooked a succulent asado of the ribs of beef we had brought with us in the commissariat sack. We invited the bitter barmaid to join us at lunch. She melted, and smilingly acquiesced; so we all sat down and fell to with our fingers, native fashion. The caña we had brought with us washed down the roast; then the maté was prepared and handed round from one to the other, our horses the while rolling in the grass and enjoying the rich herbage. The barmaid now waxed quite loquacious. In reply to our queries, she sighed and said she was " *solitaria*," her husband was serving as a soldier on the Indian frontier; "forced into the army for merely stealing a miserable horse," she indignantly explained.

Having enjoyed our meal and our siesta, we collected our gear, saddled our horses, and bid adieu to the ugly grass-widow, who insisted on standing us a glass of her vile gin all round.

We went at a hand-gallop over the undulating plain of

bush and flowers, whose sole inhabitants seemed to be parrots, vultures, and bizchacas, until we reached Jesus Maria, a small village thirty-three miles from Cordoba. This is an old decayed Jesuit settlement. There is a fine old church in it; and the ruins of a convent, solid and grand, towering over a clump of sordid ranchos and grass-grown streets. Just outside the town are a few small plantations of maize; beyond, the wilderness of thorn. It was curious to see this stately ecclesiastical edifice among such surroundings, as foreign to it as were its builders, the old Jesuit missionaries, to the savage natives of the country.

There is a very fair *tienda* at Jesus Maria, quite a luxurious hotel for this country, where our horses and selves were well fed and lodged for the night. One is very lucky if he gets a bed at all when travelling in these provinces. The Argentine of the camps does not need such a thing; he sleeps anywhere—out of doors by preference—and if he have a warm blanket, he considers that he has all that the most fastidious could require. When the traveller does get a bed, as we did this night, it will be what is called a *catre*, which consists of a wooden frame with strips of hide strapped across it. The catre is generally too short for a decently tall man. His head will hang over one end, his legs over the other, unless he curl himself up like the domestic whiting. As in the East, the traveller is supposed to bring his own bedding with him. As the native saddle consists of a mass of ponchos and blankets lashed on to a wooden frame on the horse's back, what was saddle by day serves admirably as bedding by night.

Our this night's bedroom was an apartment striking for its unostentatious simplicity; the walls and floor were of mud; there was no fireplace, no window, no furniture, nothing indeed but four catres arranged in a row. There was no door either to the doorway, so we enjoyed ample ventilation. Privacy is not valued much here. If one feels dirty in the morning, no uncommon matter with the filthy Britisher, one must sally forth to the horse-pond, or to the well, to perform one's ablutions. But this country is not intended for the over-fastidious traveller.

CHAPTER XIII.

March 18*th.*—At daybreak, Manuel gathered some sticks, lit a fire on the floor of our bedroom, and prepared our matutinal maté. This is indeed a grand drink to pull one together; it beats coffee altogether. It has, I believe, another property, that of acting as a substitute for vegetables, and correcting the evil effect of a meat diet, for the native of the Pampas is exclusively carnivorous, gorges himself with beef like a wild beast, when he can get it, eating no vegetables, nor even bread; but he fills up all his leisure moments between meals in sucking up from the bombilla this marvellously sustaining decoction of the Paraguayan yerba.

This day we rode across a charming country, more undulating than ever, for we were skirting the outer ridges of the Sierras. We crossed many dry beds of rivers—

> " Where oleanders flushed the bed
> Of silent torrents, gravel spread; "

and traversed, to repeat an expression I have before used, a land of birds and flowers, a *bocage* of many shrubs, all in blossom of many colours, of many scents, with fruits, amber and purple. Among others we observed the various mimosas, the honey-tree with its snow-white blossoms smelling of honey, cacti, and prickly pears with large ripe fruit. Below our feet was soft grass in places, everywhere beautiful flowers, gorgeous as if cultivated with greatest care in a British hot-house.

We were very hot and thirsty by midday, for the parching north wind was blowing; but all the river-beds we passed were dry, so we had to ride on. At last, about two p.m., we reached a small shallow pool of foul water left by the last rains. We had to make the best of this, so called a halt, unsaddled, lit our fire, and got the asado under weigh under the shade of a large algarroba blanca. The muddy water of the pool was not very nice, rotten and hot as it was. However, we enjoyed the asado, which we flavoured with the little red peppers which grew plentifully at our feet. Then came the usual siesta, very necessary in this climate, under the drowsy shade of our tree, among the polyanthi blossoms, while insects kept up a perpetual hum around, and the parrots a screaming aloft at our intrusion.

9

We reached this evening a little place called Las Talas, which is important enough to possess a judge, a worthy man who keeps a store and a billiard-room. We put our horses in his corral for the night, and gave them a feed of afalfa. He kindly let us have a mud outhouse, inhabited by frogs, lizards, and fleas, for our own accommodation. He would have let us occupy the billiard-room, had it not been for a great match that was coming off therein this night between the two great billiard-players of the district.

March 19*th.*—This day's journey was across a similar country; at long intervals we passed a house—no rich estançia, such is not to be found in this poor province, but a mere rancho of some small proprietor or squatter. Round each, as a rule, was a small plot of maize or afalfa. We slept this night in the village of Avellaneda.

March 20*th.*—This was a lovely day, hot of course, but tempered with a delightful breeze. We were now in the Sierras, and the track wound down pleasant wooded valleys, and over ridges whence we looked over many leagues of undulating jungle and pasture. We passed through a forest of charcoal, where a monte [1] fire must have been raging fiercely for weeks, the ground being still uncomfortably hot beneath our horses' feet.

Our midday halt and asado was by the banks of a stream of clear water running over a sandy bed; here, too, we found a deep, cool pool, wherein, to Manuel's surprise, we bathed.

In the afternoon we came to a new country. We left behind us the monte, with its various shrubs, and traversed a land where hill and dale was covered with pampa grass, while clusters of dark, stunted palm-trees were scattered here and there. By-and-by these became thicker, till at last we penetrated a dense forest of palms ; from the hill-tops we perceived that as far as our vision could reach, the whole landscape was black with this gloomy-looking species of that graceful family. Here and there rapid streams crossed our path, cleaving steep channels through the dark, loamy soil.

[1] I trust that my readers by this time understand that "monte" does not signify "mountain," as one would not unnaturally suppose, but what the Australians understand by the term "bush,"

At sunset we reached a solitary house on a height, which is known by the name of Santa Cruz. It is a large and straggling building of unbaked brick, and served as the post house in the days before the Tucuman railway withdrew travellers from this route. It stands alone on a bare hill, and commands one of the most solemn and melancholy views imaginable. All round it one looks over a seemingly illimitable expanse of black palm-heads, covering mountains and vast plains, right away to the horizon.

The owner came out as he saw us approach—a dark, handsome, pure-blooded white, with all the sternness and dignified politeness of his Spanish stock. A wild-looking lot of domestic animals, pigs, children, and two or three cut-throat-looking fellows followed to stare at the strangers in the garb of civilization—relatively speaking, for Bond Street would have stared for other reasons. We saluted him in the ceremonious manner of the land, whereupon he invited us to dismount. After a little conversation and maté, he placed a mud outhouse, far inferior to an English pigsty, at our disposal; herein we arranged all our impedimenta, but slept outside in our blankets. Our horses were safely lodged in the corral.

The ladies of the house brought us the maté, and we were much struck by their remarkable beauty. At times in the wildest parts of the republic the traveller comes across the most perfect type of refined white beauty among poor people like these were. One of these was the loveliest woman of the Spanish type of beauty I had ever seen, with splendid complexion, teeth, and eyes, and long raven hair hanging in two tails almost to her heels. There was evidently no Indian blood in this family ; here was the old Spanish stock of the *conquistadores*, unsullied by mixture with lower races.

A regular patriarchal house was this, where all the old-fashioned customs of the grand colonial days when Spain was great were still rigidly observed. Our host was surrounded not only by his stalwart sons and beautiful-eyed daughters, but by his pretty grandchildren and his now aged and helpless father and mother—a happy and upright family of the good old style, over whose heads the peaceful years pass by uneventful and uncounted, as the sons tend their herds and grow their maize in the clearings of the forest of waving palm, unmindful of the revolutions and the ambitions that stir the hearts of the citizens of the great cities by the sea.

When we had rolled ourselves up in our blankets for the night, we heard our host, good Catholic that he is, reading out the evening prayers to his assembled family, while at intervals the hum of their subdued voices, joining in, was heard above the shrill cicala and the crackle of the palm-leaves.

In the morning Jerdein asked our host to what amount we were indebted to him.

"Give me what you think right, senor," said he. "Of course you were my guests last night for supper, what may be the worth of the afalfa we gave your horses in money I know not, you from the city know better than I what things are worth in money."

We knew what this "leaving it to you, sir," means in England; but here our host spoke in all simplicity, for after we had given him what we thought to be right, he held a consultation with his beautiful wife, and then insisted on returning it all with the exception of twelve reals, saying that he was sure the afalfa was not worth more than that, and that sum, at any rate, would pay him very well. Such was the primitive country we had now reached, a land where hospitality is still as much a duty as among the Arabs themselves.

Here, where inns are almost unknown, the traveller as a matter of course rides up to any house, rich or poor, doffs his hat and asks for hospitality for the night. The host responds by bidding him dismount, and informs him that all he has is at his disposition. In the house of a wealthy man, as wealth goes in this poor country, you would insult your host by offering payment. In the house of a poorer man, the traveller if he can afford it pays for the afalfa for his horses, maybe for the beef he himself consumes, but never for his lodging. A man without a cent can travel from one end of this republic to the other and never want, for no one dare refuse food to the stranger if there be any in the house. The Argentine has his vices; and they are great vices; but he has his virtues also, and they are also great.

March 21*st.*—This day's ride was across a desolate country —an undulating waste of dark palms, with here and there, in strong contrast with their gloom, extensive barren stretches of salt sands glaring in the sunshine, for we were now travelling along the narrow strip of land that lies between the Sierras and the salinas, and partakes of the character of both. We passed no house during the day, and having taken no beef with us, had to content ourselves with Bologna sausage and water for our first meal.

At sunset we came across a solitary house, the estançia of Rosario, a more substantial-looking place than we had yet seen in this province. The owner also had shown a tendency to please the eye when planning out his dwelling; a very rare thing in a country where a man builds his ugly mud house for use alone, and considers it very foolish to waste his sweet leisure in any superfluous ornamental work.

As I have before remarked, the native's estançia is rarely surrounded by any attempt at a garden. He is far too lazy as a rule even to cultivate vegetables, far less flowers and ornamental shrubs. But here we found a very delightful residence indeed, with many signs of refinement within and about it.

The house was built on an eminence overlooking an extensive landscape of hill and dale, jungle, pasture, and palm forest. Beautiful creepers wound about the pillars of the wooden portico. A really pretty garden with well laid-out beds spread in front, surrounded with a hedge of cactus and prickly pear. As we rode into the enclosure of this model farm of South America, a regular menagerie of dogs, geese, ducks, and hens saluted us.

We perceived, sitting under the flower-covered portico now glowing in the setting sun, a comely matron of the true Castilian caste of countenance. Busy over the lace she was working, she yet had time to superintend all the little country duties at which her group of pretty daughters and the Indian servants around her were employed. A large fire of wood blazed in the centre of the courtyard, over which hung a huge copper cauldron, from which came forth a pleasant simmering and gurgling and a not unpleasant sweet smell. The girls stirred, fed, and tasted the contents at every instant; great expectancy and excitement seemed to centre in that preparation, and no wonder, for, like the Primroses, mother and daughters prided themselves on being the most industrious housewives and the most clever fruit-preservers of the province. They were making nothing less than *ropa*, that is prickly-pear jam, and what little country family is not excited when comes the important preserving season?

The Indian girls came in constantly from the bush with huge baskets of the wild fruit on their heads, while the daughters of the house deftly peeled them; no easy matter for a novice to do this without filling the hands with millions of irritating, almost invisible, darts. Figs, too, from the patriarchal fig-trees were being laid out to dry on raised platforms of plaited reeds.

As we rode in there was a flutter of alarm among the girls, and they gathered round their mother like chickens round a hen, and gazed at us wonderingly with their big black eyes—for a body of armed strangers is not always a welcome sight in this wild and revolution-ridden country.

The lady of the house rose stately from her chair, and returned our salute with a dignified bow. We explained to her that we were only poor harmless, benighted *gringos*, who craved her hospitality for the night. As a matter of course she offered her all at our disposal; so dismounting, we sent our horses to the corral with Manuel, and sat down with the handsome girls and their comely mamma to drink maté. Our story much interested them; they had read of the yacht in the Cordoban papers, also of our intended ride; "Therefore," our hostess said smilingly, with true Spanish grace, "you are not strangers to us, but at home." She told us that they were citizens of Cordoba, where her husband now was; she and her daughters were passing a few months in this their country farm for the benefit of their healths. For the second time in twenty-four hours the Falcons all irrevocably lost their hearts.

March 22nd.—On the morrow it was with reluctance that we gathered our impedimenta together, in order to leave this oasis of civilization and the pleasant society of fair and gentle ladies. But we were not to start quite so soon as we expected. Manuel came up to us and informed us that our horses had broken through the corral in the night, and had decamped. This was startling news; they might have wandered leagues away by this time, and small chance of recovering them in that case, or—the terrible thought flashed across our minds—stolen!

"No," says Manuel confidently, "they are not stolen. See," pointing to their fresh footprints in the soft soil of the corral, "they have gone through that break, and that too not three hours ago, and none of the men's footprints about here are nearly as fresh as that."

To have distinguished the prints of our horses' feet, iron shod as they were, from the others was easy enough; but it required the instinct of the gaucho to detect that no man had been in the neighbourhood at the time of their departure, for some of the human footprints about seemed quite as fresh to us as the marks of our animals.

Manuel was confident though, and he proved to be right, for after tracking the horses some two miles through the bush, we found them quietly grazing by the side of a stream; so we captured the deserters and brought them back.

Having saddled our runaway horses, we continued our journey. The undulating country was now densely overgrown with cacti, prickly pears, palms, and thorny mimosas; a land of poor and rare pasture, but of plentiful water, for down every valley a little *arroyo* of limpid water runs over the yellow sands.

At midday we came to a mud rancho. The woman who seemed to be its sole inhabitant permitted us to rest awhile under the huge carob-tree, which, as usual hereabouts, spread its broad branches some twenty yards in front of the threshold, and whose shade serves in this primitive land as a sort of spare-room for friends and travellers.

This lady provided us with some algarroba for our horses, for ourselves *charki* and maize ears; which latter, roasted over the fire, are a very fair substitute for bread. Here, away from the perennial pastures of the Pampas, it is usual for each ranchero to cultivate his little plot of maize or afalfa; necessity forces him to become, against his instincts, somewhat of an agriculturist as well as a shepherd. We lit our fire under the carob, cooked our meat, and made merry during the sultry noon of this torrid land.

For those of my readers who have never tasted charki, a few words on this widely-consumed delicacy will not be amiss. Charki is merely beef cut into long, thin strips and dried in the sun; when fresh it is not bad, but it rarely is fresh; and after these lean shreds have been hanging outside a rancho in the hot, dusty air, for I am afraid to say how long, they form anything but a luxurious diet. The charki then becomes so much third-rate leather; all the juices have been completely dried out of it, and the grilling of it on an asador over a wood fire does not tend to soften it. The toughness that beef thus treated can acquire is a thing to be experienced, not told. Conceive first the ideal abstract, " stringy toughness ;" then, as to flavour, imagine a sort of charnel-house, fly-blown taste—for be it remembered that all these months that the charki is hanging in the sun, an average half-inch deep layer of flies is settled on it ; lastly, do not forget that this is one of the dustiest regions in the world, and that you will consume your ortho- dox peck of dirt before you have got through half a dozen meals of these delectable rags, and you will have formed some idea of what charki is—a teeth-testing dish with a vengeance.

Having torn, and worried, and masticated some particu- larly choice, old, high-toned fragments, we lay down under our carob-tree to enjoy our well-earned siesta, and rest our aching jaws. But we were soon awakened by an approach- ing sound, a confused murmur coming from the north. Then we distinguished the lowing of a vast multitude of oxen, the tread of thousands of hoofs, and the shouting of men. At last the great herd appeared out of the bush—a thousand head of cattle at least, lean, and halt, and weary with their long journey over the herbless, waterless country that lay to the north of us. About twenty wild-looking horsemen were in charge, with gay ponchos fluttering in the breeze ; some were barefooted, others had their feet en- cased in the raw skins of foals' legs. This is the orthodox gaucho *chaussure*. It is prepared by simply cutting off the hind leg of a foal, and withdrawing the bone and the flesh. The man's foot and leg are then thrust into this natural boot. To guard the legs of the riders against the fearful thorns of the northern jungle, each horse had two shields or breastplates of stout raw hide, extending like two wings in front of the saddle and falling to below the stirrup-irons. About eighty remount horses followed the herd.

The cattle were rounded in for their midday halt just above us ; then the chief—a great swell with silver spurs, rich poncho, polished top-boots with very high heels, and mounted on a splendid horse—rode up to the rancho, and craved permission to take water from the laguna for his beasts. An introduction was soon effected between this gentleman and ourselves, and he insisted on our joining him at breakfast. Vain was it to declare that we had just completed our meal—breakfast again with him we must. There was one little bull in the herd that was very lame, so our new friend had him lassoed, pithed, cut up, and converted into asados in an incredibly short space of time. We sat down with him, ate the sweet beef with our fingers, and drank the red wine he had brought with him with much pleasure; luxurious, indeed, were these to us after our charki and tepid laguna water.

Bidding farewell to our hospitable friend, we rode on till we reached the first township we had seen since Jesus Maria. This was Chañares, a wretched little place in the midst of an uninhabited, untilled plain of palm and thorns. The *raison-d'être* of a town in such a spot is more than I could discover.

There were only from twenty to thirty houses, and half of these seemed to be deserted and in ruins, for the unbaked mud bricks of this country do not form very substantial buildings; they soon fall to pieces when left to themselves. We dismounted in front of the solitary store, entered it, and called for a tot of caña all round before commencing business. The bottle was put before us and one glass—water they had none on the establishment.

We inquired of the storekeeper if it was possible to find accommodation for ourselves and our horses for the night in this city. He thought that to find this would be a matter of difficulty, as most of the houses were one-roomed. By this time half the population was around us, for the news of our arrival had spread like wild-fire, the visit of travellers, and what is more, foreign travellers, being a very rare occurrence indeed here. Some made suggestions as to where we might possibly get what we required. One little Indian girl, carrying a naked, very open-eyed baby, said she knew of a house that belonged to a recently deceased gentleman; this mansion was now deserted, as the defunct had left no testament or kin behind him, and it might suit us.

We visited this eligible villa, which was in the outskirts of the city. If in the days of the late lamented proprietor it was anything like it is now, I do not wonder that he decided to leave it for a more comfortable mansion in another world. It was a mud rancho; the roof and two of the walls had fallen in, and the ruins had evidently been considered by the neighbours as a most suitable deposit for all sorts of household refuse and filth. Better to pitch our camp outside the town than here, and this we accordingly determined to do, after purchasing a stock of provisions.

But at this juncture an important personage attracted by the crowd, and imagining that this was a revolution that must be nipped in the bud, came on the scene. This was no less than the commandante, who was only distinguished from his humbler fellow-citizens by having a rusty pistol and an ancient cavalry sword stuck into his broad belt. A pompous man as became his dignity, but a very well-disposed little person was this. Robust, well-fed, and oily, both in countenance and manner, he much resembled my idea of the renowned Sancho Panza—that worthy, when governor of his long-promised island, must have been something like this magistrate. He shook hands with us, waved his hand in a patronizing manner round the village, and said, "Welcome to our town;" the *our* sounding much as if it signified *my*, for he evidently never forgot that he was the presiding genius of the place. "Our town is at the entire disposal of the *caballeros*; our herds, our horses, our domestic hearths." There was nothing that was not ours, we were lords of all we surveyed, according to him. We explained that we really could not trespass so much on his generosity as to accept the whole city, but were very much obliged to him nevertheless; we would be content with food for ourselves and horses, and cover for the night if possible.

Brought down from this florid Castilian talk to matter of fact, the poor fellow looked perplexed. It was evidently more difficult to satisfy this simple want than to give us the entire town. He stopped his discourse, looked anxious and doubtful, scratched his head, made and lit a cigarette; then he placed his forefinger to the side of his nose, and with a thoughtful frown contemplated the weather cock on the church steeple. So he stood for some moments, while the little children, silent and with open mouths, gazed with awe at their pondering ruler.

Suddenly he slapped his thigh, rubbed his fat hands merrily, and said, "Come! senors, come! I know now."

He took us to a house where dwelt an old lady and her two daughters. She had one large, bare, mud room on the street, which she kindly placed at our service. It was quite a sumptuous apartment, for it even had a floor of wooden planks, and the mud walls were whitewashed to the height of six feet. Windows of course there were none; but there was a doorway big enough to answer all purposes.

This was a very garrulous old lady; she tried to monopolize us altogether, and would not permit her comely daughters to come near us. A most Argus-eyed duenna, she cruelly took the young ladies altogether out of the establishment as soon as we arrived, and locked the poor things up somewhere at the other extremity of the town.

We tied up our horses in the courtyard for the night; but as it was impossible to procure any algarroba or alfalfa for them, the poor beasts had to content themselves with a large pile of the branches of some tree. However, they seemed to enjoy their frugal repast, even Manuel's horse fell-to heartily; at lunch-time he had patiently fasted, gazing contemptuously at the others as they munched their algarroba.

Our hostess drove the bats, cockroaches, snakes, lizards, and other tenants of our apartment into the street, and swept and garnished this room till it looked so large and beautiful, that it inspired the usually stolid Manuel with a most luminous idea. "What a fine room this would be for a *baile!*" he said. The very thing, we cried, so we determined to give a grand ball to the whole town this night.

In this quaint country it is quite the thing for a passing stranger to do this—and the people will not be shy at accepting his invitation. A musician will easily be found; and two dollars' worth of vile gin is all that is necessary in the way of refreshments. We impressed a blind and villainous-looking gaucho, who could play *baile* music on the guitar, and after dinner proceeded to decorate our room. We stuck about thirty tallow candles round the walls, borrowed some wooden benches, and got a few bottles of square-face from the store, and all was ready. We then issued our invitations. Our hostess was in raptures over the whole thing; she even released her daughters, and permitted them to accept our invitation. Of course all the aristocracy was invited—the judge, the commandante, the store-keeper, and any of the other sex that might to them belong.

The dancing was soon in full swing, and a merry time we had of it. The chiñas had donned their feast-day frocks, had adorned themselves with cherry-coloured ribbons, and looked pretty enough, as their dark eyes flashed with delight and excitement.

Twang, twang-twang, twang all night flowed out the old Spanish airs from the guitar, and as the people danced the

ONE OF OUR GUESTS.

guitarist sang, in a nasal drone, words to the tunes he played, as is the custom here—words generally of his own composition; love-songs; translating the subtle meanings of the figures of the dance.

For many of these quaint and stately dances are whole stories of a love. Such is the zampa, the handkerchief dance, and the gato, in which the fingers are snapped like castanets.

Only two persons take part in these dances—a man and a woman. The man is wooing the woman. She is coy and turns away. He follows, implores. All the gamut of feeling and passion is traversed in this dumb-show, in which each movement of the supple, lithe forms of these marvellous dancers is full of expression. And all the while the guitar-player sings in rough, but often powerful, words the story of the dance, the passionate wooing of the man, the coyness, the subtle by-play of the woman, love sick, yet feigning indifference; again the lover's despair, and ultimately his triumph, when at last the girl can hide her heart no longer, returns his passion and confesses her love. It was an awful and rare sight to see Jerdein in his top-boots dancing the gato with our venerable but jovial hostess as a partner.

There was no sleep for us that night, for our indefatigable guests did justice to our entertainment and kept it up till dawn; as is the nature of their race, winding themselves up to a madness, a Terpsichorean delirium. It was a demoniac whirl of supple limbs, with at times a Bedlam shouting. The atmosphere of the room was hot and stifling with the heavy clouds of dust raised by the twinkling feet, and the fumes of tobacco. Those who did not dance themselves sat down, clapped their hands in time with the measure, and shouted incoherently to encourage the frenzy of those that did. It was a strange spectacle, and showed us that in the dance, if in nothing else, the Indo-Spaniard can be more than energetic.

CHAPTER XIV.

March 23rd.—Having closed the ball, we saddled our horses and resumed our journey. I am afraid that some of our guests could easily have been taken for Anglo-Saxons this morning, for unfairly enough any one at all disguised in drink is at once put down as one of that bibulous race by the South American. Our gin, too, was strong, and to tell the truth vile, but the beverages supplied at balls are not pro-verbially of the best quality even in England. A choice deputation of revellers accompanied us a good way outside the town; then we shook hands all round, or rather two or three times all round, for the deputation was singularly short of memory. The commandante came up to me with his clanging sabre and his beaming face at least six separate times. On each occasion he came back to the attack, saying, " Ah, Don Edouardo, I have not embraced you, nor bidden thee farewell yet. Good-bye, dear friend ; good-bye."

At last we broke away from the kind and friendly people, and proceeded to brace ourselves up with a smart gallop after our night's dissipation. The country was now becoming poorer and more thinly inhabited as we progressed. We were approaching an almost waterless and rainless region, utterly unfit for cultivation of any kind. From dawn till the late afternoon we travelled on this day without seeing any sign of human life. We had now crossed the frontier and were in the ill-famed, poverty-stricken province of Santiago, almost a desert itself, surrounded by veritable deserts.

At last we saw before us a little rancho with a corral by it, but no pasture anywhere, no plot of maize or alfalfa, or indeed any sign to show on what the inhabitants of the hovel subsisted. We rode up to it An Indian woman with a child in her arms came out.

" Have you got any charki to sell ? " we asked.

" No, senor."

" Any maize ? "

" No, senor."

" Have you any food at all in the rancho ? "

" No, senor."

We were parched with thirst, as were our poor horses, so we asked the woman if she could supply us with some water.

"I have got no water, senor," she replied.

There is in the neighbourhood of nearly every rancho in this part of the country a laguna or little artificially dammed-in pond, in the which stink the hot and putrescent dregs of the last rains ; but the laguna here had been dried up for weeks.

" Where is the nearest water, then ? " we asked.

" *Quien sabe ?* " was the reply. " Who knows ? They say that the laguna two leagues further on is also dry."

These people are certainly not unlike the animals they breed in many of their habits, as hardy and enduring as the beasts of the field. Often, as in this instance, a native will find himself in the dry season at many leagues' distance from

the nearest water. This troubles him but very little. Notwithstanding the dry, thirst-giving nature of his diet, he can
exist without drinking for days comfortably enough. Twice
a week or so he will go down to water with his cattle to the
nearest laguna, and then slake his thirst. How unlike the
poor bibulous white man, who has such an unfortunate
tendency to get thirsty at all sorts of odd moments !

So we had to ride on without food or drink all day until
sunset, when we reached a comfortable-looking house. A
plantation of prickly-pears and a plot of alfalfa were on
one side of it, a muddy pond on the other. The master
came out to greet us with the usual stately politeness ; he
was a man of some substance, for his broad hide belt was
adorned with many coins, a gold condor gleaming in the
midst of them, and he wore at his back a long knife in a
heavy silver sheath. He was able to supply us with as much
alfalfa and water as we required, and told us that we were
at liberty to sleep under the large paradise-tree in front of
the house. So we unsaddled our horses and placed a
welcome feed of alfalfa before them, and then bethought
us of our own supper, which was also not unwelcome,
considering that it was our first meal this day.

We had mutton for a change this night, for we purchased
a plump live sheep from our host for twelve reals (= about
four shillings). We took him under our tree and made all
ready for a truly Homeric repast. We lit a glorious fire,
while Manuel, now quite in his element, cut the sheep's
throat, deftly skinned and disembowelled it, and then hung
the carcase on a branch.

As we had now more than sufficient meat for two days,
we did not care about keeping the " innards," so Manuel
took these in his hand, walked up to the señora of the
house, bowed, doffed his hat in stately fashion, and with
a neat little speech presented them to her as a small token of
his gratitude for all her kindness. A don of the old Spanish
court could not have presented a necklace of pearls to a
great court lady with more polished courtesy than Manuel
his strings of raw tripes to the buxom Dulcinea of the
Estançia Algarroba. We really appreciated our splendid
roast mutton this night, unaccompanied though it was by
bread or vegetables. Our host, Don Innocentia Acosta, could
not supply us with these. It was, I suppose, beneath the

dignity of his stock of shepherd gentleman to plant a potato.

We turned in under our blankets to leeward of the fire, so that the smoke might keep the mosquitoes from us, for these pests were numerous this night. As we were making our preparations for the night our host came out to us, and advised us to sleep with our revolvers loaded at our sides, "For," said he, "this is a wild part of the country. Who knows what bad men may pass by to-night? A month or two back two young fellows who had brought some cattle to the south for sale, and were returning with the money, slept one night under that very tree where you are; the next morning we found them lying there robbed, and with their throats cut from ear to ear."

However, we slept snugly by our fire under the paradise-tree, undisturbed save by the dogs, who, smelling the blood of our sheep, prowled about our camp constantly. Manuel had placed the sheep's head under his own head for safety. At midnight three or four big, bold dogs crept up, made a sudden rush at him, rolled his head aside, and decamped in a moment with the delicate morsel—the sheep's, not Manuel's head. A fearful uproar ensued, and sonorous Castilian oaths fell like a cataract from our faithful peon's mouth. We all leapt up and seized our revolvers, thinking that an Indian raid at the least was on us. On Manuel's explaining the adventure, to his disgust, for he would not be consoled for the loss of his sheep's head. Then we rolled ourselves in our blankets, lit our pipes, and smoked ourselves to sleep once more.

March 24th.—At daybreak our fire was still alight, so we made some maté, and cooked some appetizing kybobs of the kidneys and other choice morsels of our sheep. Then we saddled, slung the remains of the carcass over Manuel's horse, and galloped off. At an early hour in the afternoon we reached the township of Ojo del Agua, consisting of one large square, a church at one side of it, and about twenty mean houses scattered round. Through the broad spaces between these one perceived the wilderness, whose luxuriant growth ran through and overflowed all the square itself. Yet this is the *pueblo* that our last night's host spoke of as *muy linda*—very pretty—and possessing *mucho gente.*

We put up at the most respectable store, where some awful-looking ruffians, gauchos of gauchos, would insist on our drinking with them. These were weather-beaten, cut-throat-looking fellows, with knives ostentatiously long: *Monteneros*, who came down to town occasionally to purchase maté or other necessaries, when, as now, they knew that there were no soldiers about. The montes about here seem to have a very bad name. I suppose there must be some fire where there is so much smoke. Our host, rather a timid fellow, told us that these men were banditti when chance offered, prowled about the tropilla-track, attacked small parties of travellers, and cut camp to unknown fastnesses when they were pursued after some more daring outrage than usual. We were warned to be careful, when camping out by night especially.

The coinage in Santiago is curious in itself, and there is but little of it. I drank a glass of caña at the store, and presented the smallest coin current, the silver chirolla of Bolivia, worth two reals. I received in change a little triangular bit of silver, which, on inspection, turned out to be the quarter of a chirolla—for here, in default of smaller change, the people cut up their coins—two cigars, and a *vale*, or I O U, for another quarter real, with the storekeeper's stamp and signature on it. The storekeepers in the remoter provinces often do this petty banking, and issue these *vales* to a large extent in lieu of giving small change. A very good business, too, it must be for them, for not only do they thus derive the banker's ordinary profits, but indirectly others also, for the holder of the *vale* generally, I should imagine, feels himself rather a mean cuss when he enters the store to get it cashed, and ends by becoming ashamed of himself, and taking it out in drinks, or other "kind," instead of in specie.

Our host informed us that the country ahead of us was very rough, that the old tropilla-track was quite impassable, as there was no food to be found on it for man or horse for at least eighty miles—a land of rocks and deserts uninhabited and waterless, traversed only by gaucho bandits when escaping pursuit. He therefore advised us to leave this track for a time and make a détour to the eastward, so passing through the *pueblo* of Salabina.

March 25th.—The vegetation, as I have before remarked,

10

ƒ

had been gradually changing as we advanced, becoming more and more of the tropics. It reached its climax of luxuriance in the country we traversed during the next three days, before becoming stunted and ugly again on the borders of the salt-desert we had subsequently to ride across.

The colouring of the jungle seemed now of an almost unnatural brilliancy. Strange thorny shrubs, flowers, and capsicums, with leaves of all shapes and hues, thickly covered the ground, but nearly all were of a dazzling metallic lustre, some gleaming like blue steel, others like burnished yellow gold, or red copper, or still darker bronze. The snakes and birds and beetles, too, that fed on the acrid juices of these seemed to have acquired from them the same mineral sheen, so brightly flashed their gorgeous wings and scales. Glorious convolvuli, with large blossoms of various colours, wound luxuriantly over every bush. One creeper, with white waxen flowers, sweet scent, and bright emerald leaves, struck us for its remarkable beauty. We procured some seed of this, and sent it home. Perchance the child of Central South America will flourish in an English hothouse. The prickly-pear-trees, covered with delicious ripe fruit, were everywhere. This was the only food-producing plant of the monte. Not only we ourselves, but our horses also, appreciated the cool pulp when we were thirsty. Giant cacti at intervals soared above the lesser growth of the jungle.

After riding some few leagues this day we came to some open spaces in the bush — clear spots of bare, dry earth — where we perceived, growing in patches, a low, insignificant-looking plant with soft, white-petaled flowers and leaves of vivid green. "The *chuchu*," said Manuel. Yes! this was the fatal plant against which we had been so frequently warned. Further on we saw acres of it. It grows only where no other living plant is, on the bare desert spots of the country; in solitude, as if all other herbs avoid its poisonous influence, forming little bright-green isles of verdure on the yellow earth. I do not know whether it be poisonous to man, but if a horse swallow but a few leaves of the deadly plant the symptoms of violent intoxication will first be declared, and the poor beast will die within an hour, raving mad and in great agony. The fact of its growing only in pastureless districts makes it particularly dangerous.

The horses that are native to the sub-tropical plains where it grows know it and avoid it instinctively, but strange horses, like our own, from the Pampas will greedily devour it when they come across it. We had, in consequence, to look carefully after our animals, and never let them wander about to graze when any of this was near. *Chuchu*, by the way, not only signifies this horse-poisoning plant, but also the man-poisoning fever of Tucuman and the northern provinces.

We were in luck this day, for at noon we reached a rancho called Aigulla, and found that we were in time for a grand feast. An ox had been killed—a great event—so the people of the place were making merry. Like vultures, the gauchos and others had smelt the blood from afar, and had gathered here to participate in the luxury of a feed of fresh meat. Of course we also were invited to fall to with our fingers at the sweet asados, and to help them drain the bottle of square-face as it went its rounds. Ultimately we departed, content and happy, for had we not enjoyed a very square meal.

In the evening we reached Quebrachos, a town which, like all these pretentious Santiagan settlements, was laid out in a huge square, not by four-fifths filled up with the mud houses. At one end was a church, a curious edifice, ambitious in design, of unbaked mud, unfinished, but half-fallen in. The architect had tried too much ; crumbling mud is far too unstable a material wherewith to construct a pretentious Gothic cathedral like this promised to be had it held out. The inhabitants of this bleak mud square were exceedingly hospitable. The commandante lodged us for the night, and a courteous and handsome old gentleman invited us to dinner. He was a colonel in the army, but as a follower of General Metri, the ex-president, out of the service *pro tem.*, and in receipt of no pay ; for as I have already explained, in these enlightened and go-ahead republics there is a clean sweep of the broom with each change of Government. When one party goes—out, too, go all the subordinates—down to the ticket-clerks of the Government railways, and even—I should not be surprised to hear—to the licensed shoeblacks of the capital.

The colonel was a very genial old gentleman and cheerful, notwithstanding that Providence had been playing at Job with him with a vengeance of late. Not only was his party out of office, but everything had been going wrong with him, he said. A recent flight of locusts had devoured all his maize ; a few days back a jaguar had robbed him of a valuable horse ; and now he had received very bad news indeed from his estate on the Rio Salado, eighteen leagues to the eastward ; the Indians had made a raid on his cattle there, driven off some hundreds of head, and lanced some of his peones.

We were informed that we were the first foreigners that had visited this town save one, and this latter was so pleased with it, that he had taken up his residence here ; what he found to be so pleased at our informant could not tell us. Anyhow, this eccentric individual, on hearing that there were some European travellers in the *pueblo*, called upon us, and welcomed us with great warmth. He proved to be an Italian, and, according to his own account, a ne'er-do-weel who had tried many professions in his day. He was a garrulous yet solemn little fellow ; he plucked us by the sleeve, and rushed off into a detailed narrative of his former life in the true " ancient mariner " style. He had been for eighteen years a soldier in Italy ; then deserted : after this he was a sailor in the Spanish navy for so long; deserted again : next he became the husband of a shrew; deserted once more : and so on through a variety of professions, finishing off always with a desertion or abrupt running away.

"And what are you now ?" I inquired, imagining that he kept a little grog-shop, was the cobbler, barber, or something of the like nature ; but he gravely replied, " I am the Government schoolmaster of the national school of Quebrachos. He was the village dominie of this little hole in the desert, and was now seriously contemplating yet one more desertion from this not over-lucrative post.

It rains but seldom in the central portions of the Argentine Republic ; but when it does rain, it is to an English shower what the Niagara is to the falls of the Upper Serpentine. This night a fearful storm swept over the land, a hurricane of wind, terrible thunder, and such a deluge of water as quite accounted for the deep fissures and rents that cut the monte we had recently traversed in all directions.

The dogs of Quebrachos were as hospitable as the inhabitants, and not wanting in kind attention to the strangers. They came from the four corners of the square, and mustered in front of the open doorway of the room in which we slept, to guard us through the perils of the night. They told themselves off in two watches, about twenty to each watch, and so relieved each other in the awful chorus which they kept up diligently till morning. When we rose at dawn, they came up to us with forty wagging tails, and looked up to our faces with self-satisfied looks, as if waiting for the thanks which were their due. We did not feel very grateful to them for their noisy guard, but assumed the virtue though we had it not, and expressed to them our undying gratitude for their generous conduct. The officers of the guard dismissed the other dogs, and consented to join us at breakfast over the remains of our sheep; then, with expressions of mutual good-will, we parted.

March 26th.—We did not set off very early this morning, but waited to see whether the weather would clear, for it still rained heavily. This, the autumnal, is the rainy season here. It is only during these two months of February and March that there is any rainfall at all; when this fails, as not unfrequently happens, there is great distress in these provinces, and the cattle must either be driven eastward to the rivers by the Indian Chaco for pasture and water, or southward for sale.

Our Italian acquaintance called on us at about ten o'clock; he was a casual pedagogue, conducting his school on free and easy principles. He said,—

"I must now show you round the town, besides I want to have a chat with you about Europe; come to the school with me and have maté."

"I am afraid we will disturb you at your duties," I remarked.

"My duties? nonsense! I won't ring the bell for school as long as you are in Quebrachos. We'll give the urchins a holiday. Besides, I am tired of working for nothing. Can a man work unless he be fed? *Bueno!* the provincial government have not paid me for nine months; they give me paper instead of salary; paper will not buy bread."

He showed me one of these despised bits of paper; he receives one each month, a large elaborate printed document gay with stamps and seals, an acknowledgment that the provincial government of Santiago del Estero owes him so many dollars (*fuertes*) for a month's salary.

In the original agreement with him the Government contracts to pay him his salary each month, in gold, or its equivalent in bank-notes at the then rate of exchange. But these wretched I O U's, which the Government will never redeem, which no storekeeper will take—utterly unnegotiable, in short—are all the poor wretch is receiving. No wonder that he contemplates another desertion from such a thankless office. It suits the venal heads of departments very well, in more than one way, that Government debts should be paid in these I O U's, for the following trickery is notoriously practised. The Government *employé*, the poor ignorant holder of the paper, finding that he cannot cash it—that it is next to useless to him—will in many cases be only too willing to part with it at any sacrifice, for a sum far below its nominal value. Then steps in a third party, who buys the paper from him for a mere song—a speculator who has a brother, or a brother-in-law, or a cousin, who is a *compadre* of some big man in office, or is possessed of some such backstairs key to that so mysterious an abstraction for the unlearned—the Government. This influence being brought to bear, the treasury winks and cashes the paper at its full nominal value, when the speculator, his relative, and the big man in office share the spoil and hold their tongues. Large fortunes have been acquired in this manner in this enlightened republic.

Quebrachos is but a very small place, at the very outside possessing twenty houses and huts, and yet within these narrow limits we have three public-houses, an imposing store where you can buy English pickles and beer, half a church, a school, a commandante, a judge, a schoolmaster, and an idiot beggar. A Santiagan settlement is like a San Domingan regiment, where all are officers and there are no privates; or the old *Falcon* where we had a self-dubbed admiral, a captain, a first lieutenant, a second lieutenant, and a crew composed of one small boy.

Our friend the schoolmaster did after all summon his pupils before we left; not to study, however, but to take a lesson in practical engineering. The flood of last night had invaded the schoolroom, and a bank of sand had formed outside the door, preventing the escape of the water, so there was the good-natured pedagogue, bare-legged and in shirt-sleeves, spade in hand, directing a lot of half-naked, ragged, half-breed urchins to dig a canal through the sand into the square, so as to drain the flooded academy.

We bid adieu to our kind hosts, and rode off in a lull in the storm. It soon, however, broke on us again with all its fury of thunder, wind, and rain. We were of course drenched in a very short time. Manuel utterly despised the rain, for, as he said, "See my coat; it is an English coat, and water cannot go through it—at least not much." He had evidently great faith in the tweed cutaway of the white man; and, though he did become as wet through as ourselves, he insisted that the water found its way only through the numerous rents of the old garment, the impenetrability of the material he never doubted for a moment.

It rained so heavily that the sandy-floored *monte* was soon covered over with two feet of foaming water. It thus became impossible to distinguish the track, but we followed the current of the waters, which we knew was in our direction, for the brown roaring flood was rushing to the North to swell the Rio Saladillo into wild *crescentes* with these millions and millions of tons of water—water, difficult though it was to imagine, that would never reach the salt sea, but dry up beneath the hot sun in the vast Laguna de los Porongos, an inland sea in the desert that has no outlet to the ocean.

From a balloon some hundred yards or so above, the whole plain we were now traversing would, I imagine, have presented the aspect of a shoreless murky sea, with many bushes rising above its surface. We progressed with difficulty. Our horses became alarmed, and stumbled continually in the rapid water, whose bottom they could not see. At times we suddenly found ourselves in holes, where the whole of our saddles were under water, and the animals were carried off their legs by the rapid tide. Indeed things looked far from pleasant, and, more or less lost as we were, there was a probability of night overtaking us while we were floundering about in the flood—a not agreeable prospect. Of a sudden the sky cleared and was blue again. The sun shone brightly, and all the birds burst into song. Lovely, indeed, this wild *monte* now appeared. All the vegetation was fresh and dripping with diamond-like drops. The tropic evergreens were greener than ever after the welcome moisture. The huge cacti, twenty to thirty feet in height, were the chief feature in the landscape, pointing their gaunt arms, with their rectangular elbows, heavenward, like some huge polypi—quaint and weird growths, very aged some of them, rotten and brown skeletons, with all the outer green pulp long gone, lying on the ground, or standing only till the next strong wind blew them down.

Beautiful convolvuli wound around all of them, while air plants depended like hanging gardens from every branch with their delicate blossoms. Below, the yellow sands were hidden by the rushing waters, but the patches of golden-blossoming camomile rose like little islands here and there. At last, to our delight, we came across a hospitable house on a slight elevation overlooking the flooded land.

On riding up a gentleman came out with an unmistakable Teutonic cast of features. We introduced ourselves to him, and craved hospitality for the night. He told us to off-saddle and enter within. We found ourselves, to our surprise, in a well-furnished room, with good engravings on the walls, and a book-shelf full of standard German works. We seemed to have been transported of a sudden to Europe and civilization once again.

Our host then, before making any further remarks to us, called to a native hand-maiden, and ordered her to bring in some hot water and sugar ; then he opened a mysterious cupboard, full of curious instruments and bottles. From this he drew a decanter. Then turning to us he said in good English, deliberately and with pauses between the sentences, as he poured out with much delicacy, and in exact proportions, the contents of the decanter and hot-water jug into four tumblers,—

" I, too, am a gringo—Dr. Scharn—a medical man in practice at Santiago ; and now, as a doctor, I am going to prescribe for you after your wetting. Hot water and sugar —that is enough. Now, then, the rum. I think that's about the right dose. Come, now, drink this down while it is hot."

Bowing to his superior knowledge as to what was good for us, we swallowed the medicine heroically and that, too, without making wry faces over it.

We found the doctor to be a very well-informed man, who spoke French, English, and Spanish as well as his native tongue. We were lucky in finding him on this his country estate, where he was now passing a few weeks—a pleasant change after the sultry, unhealthy city of Santiago.

We got all our clothes dry, and enjoyed a sleep in beds for a change this night; for this was a very Capua.

CHAPTER XV.

March 27th.—It was not till noon this day that we saddled and rode off, for we had but a short journey before us to the banks of the Rio Saladillo, where we had decided to pass the night. After traversing some six leagues of sandy glades, we reached our destination, just as the sun was setting. The mud rancho, where dwelt the ferryman, was some hundred yards or so from the river, which was invisible from it on account of the lofty cane-brakes that intervened.

As we approached this habitation we heard a sound of voices and music, and, on riding through an opening in the bush, we burst suddenly on a village festival. In addition to the ferryman's, there were two other ranchos here, the white rag flying over the roof of one declaring it to be a *pulperia*, perhaps the only grog-shop for a day's journey around. Each of these miserable huts stood in its own little enclosure, surrounded by a fence of prickly pear and cactus, to protect the cattle within from the tigers and pumas that are so numerous in these *montes*. Along a sandy glade in front of the grog-shop a primitive racecourse had been laid out, and a great race-meeting was now evidently being held; for here was a gathering of mounted men—some 200 at least—and such a gathering!

All the gauchos for three days' journey around must have been collected here—half-breeds most of them, though not a few were half-naked pure-blood Indians. A more cutthroat-looking lot of ruffians I never beheld; ragged, weather-beaten outlaws, each with his long knife at his back, many with *bollas* and *lassos* ready to bring down any stray cattle that might come by to tickle their appetite on their lonely wanderings. In front of the pulperia a *baile* was being energetically carried on.

Right down the middle of it was a row of posts supporting a hide-rope. It is the custom here for but two horses to race at a time, and this barrier is intended to separate them from each other. There was only one match to-day that had been arranged beforehand, the others were scratch-races got up on the course. This, the race of the day, was for twenty dollars, for 420 yards, between two great swells, the only present who wore boots.

It had just been run when we came on the scene. It seems that one had come in three lengths ahead, but the loser disputed the result, and refused to pay up. One of the barrier-posts had been knocked down, as he alleged, by the winning horse. Now to foul this rail invalidates a race. The winner denied this, and accused the other of riding against the post purposely, when he saw he had no chance of winning. There seemed to be no judge—none, at any rate, whose decisions any one paid the slightest attention to—so the dispute waxed hot. All the wild horsemen grouped round the two infuriated jockeys. Each gaucho, of course, stuck up for the horse he had laid his money on, and a good deal of perjury was knocking about in the air. It happened that he who had come in first was a stranger, so nearly all the money, and hence the sympathies, of the spectators were with the other. Therefore, finding himself overpowered, and his protestations against the cheating vain, the winner leapt on his horse, swore a great oath, and galloped furiously away into the jungle, followed by the jeers of the crowd.

This matter settled, preparations were made for another race. The would-be competitors, some mere boys, half-naked on bare-backed steeds, rode about in the throng, shouting out challenges in regular bookmaker style; some wanted to back their horses against special animals, others against the field, or the field bar one, somewhat thus, "Ho! ho! I'll race my *colorado* (chestnut) for two squares, for two dollars, against any horse save Jose's big *saiño* (bay). Ho! ho! *caballeros.*"

In the interval between the races we looked round to see what substitute they had here for Aunt Sally, nigger minstrels, and other Derby-day amusements. It was rather a serious meeting; we saw in one place three men sitting round a fire, and silently, sadly playing at some game with a very greasy pack of cards, as they sucked their maté. About two dozen gauchos stood round them, watching the game with a solemn apathy. By the way, the peculiar seriousness of the half-breed is not indicative of a contemplative mind, but of a torpid indolence; his indeed is the "*réverie qui ne pense à rien.*"

Farther on we came across a ragged minstrel, playing on a cracked guitar. There was a jabbering idiot on the course, too, whose ears had been cut off, by Indians probably, and whose costume consisted solely of a thin, torn poncho, and thick dirt. He groaned and wept and wrung his hands energetically, and evidently was reaping no small harvest.

"Another race; make way! make way!" A long, lean, lantern-jawed fellow, looking like a Don Quixote in bad circumstances, with only one leg, rode to and fro on a hard-looking black horse; he carried a long staff on his legless side, which he stamped on the ground as he rode along, like Peter the Hermit in the old woodcuts. He was very eager indeed to race his horse. "I'll run any one four squares for a patacon!" he shouted continually with a stentorian voice. Many present evidently considered that they had a very fair chance of success if matched against this one-legged sportsman. "*Bueno!* I'll race you on my bay," cried one, and four or five others also accepted his challenge. But that one-legged structure of skin and bone knew what he was about. He affected not to hear these, but continued to yell out his challenge like one possessed, so drawing on more and more to answer it, for all now doubted his earnestness, and looked upon him as some poor, half-daft fellow. But at last, all of a sudden, he turned sharply round and pounced on one jovial-looking fellow mounted on a black horse, who had just then jestingly accepted the challenge. "Good, my friend then we will race," he said, to the discomfiture of the joker. He had waited his time, until one whom he thought he could easily beat had shouted acceptance to his offer—cunning old turfite that he was. The jovial one was rather taken aback, but could not withdraw now, and race he must; so the two dismounted and prepared for the contest.

It seems strange to a gringo to see a jockey take off his trousers in order to ride a race, but the jovial one did this; the one-legged one did not happen to have on even one trouser, so could not. It is the custom in this country to strip nearly naked on such occasions. Our two friends divested themselves of drawers, ponchos, and sombreros, fastened handkerchiefs round their heads, and stood in their shirts. They then withdrew the heavy saddles from their horses, and rode bare-backed to the starting-point.

Now commenced the betting among the crowd, and bet they did with a vengeance; there is no more reckless a gambler than your gaucho; when the fever of play is on him he will gamble away his bridle, his blanket, his horse, his knife, his all, and then walk away, stolid, taking his reverses like a philosopher—a ruined man, yet not cast down, for he will soon steal another horse, and may be luckier next time. We walked to the starting-point, to see the start, which is managed here very differently from the way it is managed in England. The riders start themselves. There are a dozen false starts at least to every race. "Are you ready?" says one; "Good!" then by mutual consent off they go. If one be dissatisfied with a start, he draws up short after a few yards, and they begin again, not without a preliminary wrangle.

At last both drop their *rebenques*, and they are off in earnest. The horses are at their full speed from the very first stride—they are specially trained to this—there is no pulling in, no making a fine race of it, but slash, slash, go the hide *rebenques* from the beginning to the end of the race, and at a tremendous rate they do go over the small distances they generally run here.

The knight of the rueful countenance won this race easily. Many more races followed, some for as low stakes as fourpence or fivepence; but all very exciting to the spectators, and productive of much gambling. Cockfighting filled up the intervals.

But the red sun had now set behind the horizon, and the sudden night of these latitudes was upon us, so the meeting broke up, and the crowd returned to the open space by the three ranchos to carouse and make merry. After a good deal of half-scorched, half-raw beef had been devoured by the fires that were now scattered over the camp, a very witches' ball, so fantastic it appeared, was started in the pulperia, overflowing, so many were the dancers, to the limits of the tiger-haunted monte. The band consisted of a haggard and ferocious-looking gaucho guitarist, and a crazy, almost naked Indian boy, who accompanied him on a drum, which he beat in a monotonous tom-tom fashion.

The young ladies who were present at the ball were plump,

dark, not uncomely, but smacking somewhat of the immortal Dulcinea; fat and garlic being the chief reminiscences I have of them. They were all barefooted, and danced wonderfully, lithesome as snakes, in the rather licentious native dances. The sole ornaments each girl wore was a flower behind her ear, or a glow-worm picked up in the monte gleaming among her raven tresses.

The guitarist turned out to be rather a celebrated *Majo*, or troubadour, one of the wandering minstrels of Andalusian type, that have long died out in old Spain, but are still not uncommon on the Pampas. This bard chanted to us, in a nasal tone, some of his own compositions, plaintive *tristes*, stirring *vidalitas*, with choruses to them, in which drummer and bystanders loudly joined—songs in which the exploits of gaucho heroes are told—all the while he twanged his cracked guitar not unskilfully. Most of these native airs are of a melancholy wildness, monotonous, but of a strangely impressive monotony, like that of many primitive races; airs, too, that curiously affect even a civilized ear, for they seemed to awaken and stir in the soul far vague memories, the buried instincts and sentiments of a remote barbarian ancestry.

The dance waxed mad and furious, the dancers were beside themselves with frenzy, but neither man nor supple damsel seemed to weary, and all the while these ragged beggars, these out-law cattle-thieves, were as smilingly courteous, as polite, as well-behaved, as dignified as the proudest hidalgo of old Castile.

At a late hour we retired to rest, sleeping in our blankets, *à la belle étoile*, with our horses, under the clear dewy sky, with our revolvers under our saddles, which served us as pillows; but all night long the camp fires burned, and the mad orgie continued, the dance, the shouting, the gambling, the gin-drinking, the guitar, and the monotonous tom-tom of that dreadful drum. How weary that wretched little Indian boy must have felt!

March 28th.—When we awoke the next morning at seven, and prepared our maté, the revellers were still hard at it in front of the pulperia; the tom-tom still banged away, while crackers were let off at intervals, as if to revive the flagging energies of the dancers up to the proper pitch.

We went down to the river, and found it to be a wide,

rapid stream, with steep earth banks on either side, and
sand-banks and quicksands rising here and there in the
midst of it—not by any means a nice place to ford.

The natives call this portion of the Rio Dulce the
Saladillo, but the maps designate by the latter name a
tributary stream which here joins the main watercourse.
The Rio Dulce is a considerable river ; it rises in the lofty
sierras of Tucuman, and, after traversing the Salinas, flows
by here towards the Chaco, pouring its waters into that extensive inland sea, the Laguna de los Porongos, which lies in
a depression in the great plain, draining it, but having no
outlet to the sea. By the bank we found the *chata*, a very
rough sort of ferry-boat, awaiting us. Several men and
women, and a harpist, all very dishevelled, half-drunk, and
showing unmistakable signs of having " kept it up " all
night, were to cross with us to their respective homes
beyond the river. The boat was far too small and rickety
to carry our horses across, but three dusky half-breeds
volunteered to swim them over for what would be equivalent to three shillings.

It was a gloomy morning, with a cold south wind blowing ;
the river was a quite quarter of a mile wide, swollen and
rapid with the rain, so they earned their money well. The
fellows were more than half-seas over, and had a powerful
tot of raw gin all round after they were stripped, to keep
the cold out. We hardly liked to trust our animals to them,
and the wife of one of them shared our fears ; she vainly
endeavoured to drag her inebriated lord back into the boat,
but he eluded her. The lady then made us hand over his
share of the pay to her, as she said that he was not to be
trusted with it, and would be murdering her or some one or
other if he imbibed any more square-face. The men, drunk
though they were, took our horses across very cleverly ; they
were strong swimmers, going hand over hand, dog-fashion,
one ahead, with the halters of two horses in his teeth,
leading the way, the other two swimming after, rounding in
the other animals, and urging them the way they should go
with shoutings and splashings. We crossed in the *chata*,
resaddled our shivering steeds, and pushed on at a gallop
across a very desolate and dreary country.

We were now traversing the eastern corner of the Salinas.
and could form a good idea of the character of those salt

GIANT CACTI ON THE SALT PLAINS.

deserts. No grass or herb of any kind grew on the sandy soil, but huge cacti, whose trunks two men could scarcely span with their outstretched arms—giants of their tribe—were frequent. I believe that in no part of the world do these plants attain so great a size, their rectangular arms branched out like those of huge candelabra, and for the most part, so ancient were they, the green covering was entirely stripped off them, revealing the hard wood beneath—decaying monsters that stood like weird skeletons, gaunt and stark, and unhealthy yellow of hue, all over the unfertile plain. The thorns of these cacti were fully seven inches in length, their fine points easily pierced the stoutest boot, and inflicted nasty wounds that healed with difficulty. The only other plants that we came across on this wilderness were a sort of espinas, or thorny shrubs, whose leaves had a saline flavour.

As a result of the recent rains, we came occasionally upon extensive shallow lagunas ; but where the sand was dry it glistened with dazzling brightness with the salt deposit that covered it. The reflection from this would soon have peeled the skin off our faces, had not sun and exposure pretty well hardened and darkened us by this time.

In the damper places we were besieged by millions of mosquitoes, that literally covered overselves and our horses. There were three distinct species of them. There were some that I could scarcely recognize as our old enemies, nearly as big as wasps, and striped like them, yellow and black ; ferocious beasts, that pierced even through our clothes (and through Jerdein's boots, according to him), with their diabolical suckers. They were wonderfully tame, too, never flying from the avenging hand like their wily cousins in Europe ; but what availed it to immolate a dozen or a thousand in this land of *bichos* ?

We reached our night's halting-place before dark—a curious little settlement. First picture its surroundings : a plain of dry mud, in places covered with salt, and everywhere cleft with deep, broad sun-cracks, and cacti scattered here and there, alone in the way of vegetation. In the centre of this not over-cheerful prospect was one of the ordinary unfinished squares of low houses of unbaked mud that I have had so frequently to allude to ; the square, the buildings, the plain, the inhabitants, were all of the same depressing yellow colour. Such is the jaundiced pueblo of Salabina, among whose prosperous fleas we passed an uneventful night.

March 29th.—This day we forced our way through hostile legions of mosquitoes and thorns, to the village of Juanilla. This is indeed a spinous region. The thorns of this day's bushes beat anything I have ever experienced in the way of thorns; I cut some and carried them off as trophies, and am now writing this with one converted into a pen-holder. It would be the envy of any porcupine; it is a foot long, and its base is larger than a sixpenny bit.

At midday we came to a miserable rancho, whose sole occupants were a woman and her child. She gave us permission to light a fire under the mimosa-tree in front of her door, and we soon grilled the beef we had brought with us from Salabina. As we sat by the fire, eating our succulent asado, a bundle of brick-coloured rags sauntered slowly down to us. This was the lady of the house, who led by the hand her little naked, fly-blown child. A lean spaniel bitch followed, also with its offspring, a still leaner, most melancholy-looking puppy; indeed a miserable procession. The woman was pretty, or rather would have been pretty had she been fed, washed, and combed out. Two long raven plaits of hair hung down her back to her heels; her eyes were black and large. She came down towards us slowly and stately, with all the Spanish *hauteur* of mien and carriage. Then she sat beside us, and, with a long nasal drawl and slow delivery of speech, which the Spaniards of South America have acquired from the Indians, she asked—not begged—for a bit of bread for her child. He was ailing, she said. Bread, she thought, might be good for him; she had none in the rancho, *charqui* alone (dry leather! what a diet for a sick baby!). Miserably poor the woman seemed to be, scarcely able to drag along her existence. Famine had dimmed her fine eyes, and weakness had reduced her to a half-daft condition. She did not pay attention to any remark we made till it was repeated three or four times. She was subdued by want to an utter apathy and torpor, a not uncommon state of things in poor Santiago, notwithstanding that its people are so hospitable and ready to share their little all with the stranger.

"Will the senora do us the honour of joining us at our meal?"

" *Como no, senor ?* " she replied; and I think our fresh beef, biscuit, and caña did the poor soul good. The spaniel, too, came up, and with plaintive patience waited for an invitation to have a share in the good things. She, too, had an ailing puppy who would be benefited by bread, and she found means to tell us as much in her own pathetic way.

We made the woman a little present of yerba and sugar before we left, and she insisted on giving us a bottle of prickly-pear jam in return, for with all her poverty, she was far too proud to accept anything in the way of alms.

After crossing eight leagues more of salt plain we reached Juanilla, where were three or four houses and a store. Outside this store were sitting several very stately gentlemen, chattering and smoking. They rose, and politely begged us to dismount. We piled up our impediments under the eaves of the house, and entered into conversation with the gossiping *compadres*, who were evidently the big men and elders of the place.

The people about here are for the most part of pure Spanish blood, many tracing back their descent to the old conquistadores, followers of Fernandez Pizarro; but, curiously enough, the language spoken hereabouts by all is not Spanish, but the Indian dialect, *Quichua*, the ancient tongue of the Incas of Peru. These elders all conversed in this language, but of course understood Spanish as well, as many of the lower orders do not. The Quichua tongue is only spoken in the northern provinces of the Argentine Republic, on the frontier of Bolivia. Our new friends of Juanilla were all fine types of the antique colonist, reminding one of the portraits by the old Spanish masters. Velasquez painted heads like these, long, fierce-eyed, stern, and bearded. In the becoming native dress they looked like men of a long-past age, as they verily are in all their manners ; tall, gaunt, angular men of the true Don Quixote breed.

We chatted and drank gin with these antique Santiagenas, while a small boy was sent in search of maize for our horses. In the midst of the slow dignified conversation, a sudden commotion was heard in the pueblo, and even these stolid sages showed unmistakable signs of excitement. What extraordinary event was it that could so stir these profoundly still natures ? Nothing less than the racehorses—two of them—that were being brought out for their afternoon gallop. The whole population of Juanilla—some thirty, including women and babes—turned out to inspect the beautiful animals. This was the one event, the sole excitement to break the sleepy dead-and-alive day of this dull South American village. These two horses are the pride, the hope of Juanilla, the objects of the greatest solicitude. They are tended with minute care, fed at intervals, day and night, in a scientific way, till they become as hard as nails, or as *charqui*. Before their alfalfa is laid before them, every unwholesome bit or particle of foreign matter is carefully picked out. In fact, they have a fine old time of it, and are treated as gods, even as some sacred Bull of Memphis, kinging it in his manger.

We saw the horses gallop, and agreed with the proud owner that the *tordillo* (grey) was a likely animal to put one's money on. When the maize arrived—very dear it is, by the way, in this province of the desert—we found it was ungrained, so we had to sit down and disintegrate the tough ears ourselves. This is no easy work, and would inflict sore havoc on a delicate-skinned hand, which ours are not, anyhow. After a square meal of puchero we turned in, in the primitive way of the country, under our blankets in the middle of the main (and only) street, for there were no policemen here to disturb our slumbers and bid us "move on."

CHAPTER XVI.

March 30th.—On leaving Juanilla, our route lay across a rather less desert country. We were off early, and before the mosquitoes had slept off the last night's orgie. But they got up soon after us, when the sun warmed their wings, half-paralyzed by the cold of the morning dew. We cooked and devoured our midday asado in the middle of the village of Atamisqui, in front of the butcher's house. This was a typical dwelling of the country: a one-roomed rancho, with no window. Inside was nothing save fleas and dirt, but outside was all the careful housewife's apparatus. First, in front of the door, was a mud structure like a bee-hive—this was the oven wherein the bread is baked ; near this was the hollowed stump of a tree, forming a big mortar, in which a woman was crushing maize, or algarroba pods, with a wooden pestle. The meat (charqui) hung in festoons from the branches of a large mimosa.

This is certainly a most out-of-door people. In this province the cooking of a household is done outside, the family eat outside, at night lock up the house and sleep outside ; in short, exist altogether outside—wisely, seeing what worse than pigstyes their ranchos are. But why do they take the trouble of constructing houses at all, since they apparently make no manner of use of them? I cannot imagine, unless, upon mature consideration, it be for the laudable object of becoming householders, and so having a vote ; but I forget we are in enlightened, universal-franchised South America, not in feudal England. Here we found that the inhabitants understood but little Spanish, and spoke Quichua exclusively.

In the evening we reached Loretto, the largest town between Cordoba and Santiago, but that is not saying much. The photographer of Cordoba had spoken to us of Loretto, and marked it down on the road-plan he prepared for us as a "town of women." Such towns, where men are few, the population being almost exclusively made up of the fair sex, are not rare in some parts of the Argentine Republic. In all parts of this province the traveller is especially struck by the disproportion of the sexes. This I have heard attributed to the revolutions, and to the sweeping conscriptions the tyrant governor of a province often decrees, in order to strengthen his personal power. This Argentine confederation has been, and still to a lesser extent will be, until the Unitarios get the upper hand for good, a collection of almost independent states or provinces. Each has its separate provincial government, its provincial army, its local satrap, who, as often as not, sets at nought the impotent edicts of the central National Government. In this province of Santiago, some few years ago, reigned almost as kings, or, more exactly, as powerful feudal barons, the Taboadas, a noble family, haughty and ambitious. The flower of the land was taken by these to serve in the provincial army, which they maintained on a far higher footing than was necessary to protect the Indian frontier. Thousands of gaucho cavalry were kept ever in readiness to advance against the neighbouring provinces, when disputes arose between the Taboadas and rival satraps.

It was this state of things, I am told, that accounts for the now paucity of men in Loretto and other towns. The Nero-like cruelties and lusts, the unbridled tyranny of these Republican presidents, dictators, and governors, would hardly be credited by folks at home. These men, ignorant as a rule, mere gauchos some of them, raise themselves to the little brief authority by the means of assassination, treachery, and crime; and with these same they protect themselves through their rapacious career, until the assassin's knife makes way for some greater tyrant. The Monteneros, or organized bands of gaucho outlaws, become the ready tool of any would-be despot who offers hope of plunder, and the wild hordes of the Pampas are brought down to overrun the civilization of the city. It is this system that has ruined what would otherwise be flourishing towns and centres of commerce and industry. The stranger is struck with astonishment, and is at a loss for an explanation when he comes across so many towns, considerable and ancient many of them, in this Republic, that are now falling in ruins, and whose grass-grown streets are almost deserted by man.

About half a mile or so outside the "town of women" was a rancho. Here, indeed, was a man, but he was not a whole one, for he was lying very pale and weak on a *catre* in front of his hut, having been severely wounded by a jaguar that he had hunted and driven at bay. He was feebly sucking maté when we approached. Two small, naked, brown children sat by him on the ground, each with two broad rings of flies settled round his eyes, like the black rims of spectacles—for, like the Egyptian infant, the Argentine country child never bethinks him of brushing away these flies, but sits down, seemingly perfectly comfortable, with fifty or sixty thus roosting round his optics. There the two pot-bellied little urchins squatted, stolidly chewing algarroba-pods, which seems to be the sole diet of the poorer children of this province—not a very nourishing one either. To procure enough sustenance in this way necessitates about thirteen hours of persistent chewing a day ; thus the stomachs of the young here, like those of all savages who live on vegetables and roots alone, are bulky and oxlike in proportion.

This man could sell us alfalfa and charqui, and behind his house was a small pond of muddy water, so we determined to camp here for the night, instead of thrusting ourselves on the hospitality of the Lorettanas ; besides, it was far from certain if forage would be procurable within the walls of the town ; and yet, again, would it not have been an over-adventuresome and perilous thing to have passed down those mud streets, and found ourselves alone and un-protected males among so many women ? Caramba ! It was too perilous, and legends of fierce Amazons rose to our memory, and the fearful laws of that city of fair girls where Tennyson's Princess held her sway, so we off-saddled and prepared our camp by the side of the mosquito-haunted laguna—smoke could keep off their sting—but women ! not that we Falcons are misogynists. Heaven forbid !

But from the watch-tower of the city did the sentinel maiden perceive the four horsemen from a far country, and she reported us to the governess. Then was a consultation held, and the elders said, " Let us send some forth that they may slay these gringo intruders—gringos and males to boot ! it is horrible ! " But the younger women were loth that this should be done, for they had perceived that the horsemen were not uncomely, and, being women, they felt much curiosity to know what these men in so strange apparel and stained with long travel might be.

Now, happily, the younger women were the majority in the council, so there were sent forth to invite us as friends within the walls two delegates—one an elder and stately matron, one a graceful, dark-eyed girl. Afar off we saw them approaching, so we tried to look our best, shook the dust off our ponchos, gave our sombreros a gay, cavalier-like askewness, twirled our moustaches, and put on our most superior smiles. They came up, and then we felt small indeed, for they paid no manner of attention to us ; they had walked hither, not for us, but to visit the sick man, who was their relative, and to bear him grateful delicacies. All I have written above was the mere offspring of our wanton imaginations, the conjecture of our vanity, when we perceived the two black-draped figures coming out of the town towards us.

After these ministers of mercy had seen to the wants of the wounded man, they condescended to notice us, and inquired of him what we were. On hearing our tale, the elder woman came up, and, with a very pleasant manner, invited us to her house in the town.

" Señores Caballeros," she said, "I have an apartment in my house, which is not in use, and which I shall be happy to place at your disposition for the night, if you will accept of it. There is a well hard by, and I can supply you with a sufficiency of beef, maize, and alfalfa."

We accepted her gracious offer, resaddled, put our baggage on the pack-animal, and followed her into the town. The poor horses evidently did not relish this, for we had ridden them fifty-five miles this day, and they naturally thought the time for repose had arrived; but they had not far to go ere they were again unsaddled and at ease.

While our asado was cooking in the courtyard, we took a stroll through the town. The small number of men in the place was certainly extraordinary. At last, in one of the stores, we did find quite a considerable group of our own sex drinking—cutthroat-looking gauchos, all with long knives, some with revolvers, but who politely insisted on our drinking with them.

Here, too, was an individual who deserves particular mention—a dark man, beardless, with bright, beady eyes, and much of the Indian in his blood. He was well-dressed, but in a barbaric fashion, that differed considerably from that of the gauchos round in its details : a scarlet kerchief was round his head below his sombrero; his poncho was of gaudy colours and strange pattern; his silver spurs were massive, and gold earrings were in his ears. When he spoke it was with a pompous nasal drawl, very deliberate, and offensive to ears unaccustomed to it.

This man was a Bolivian Colla, a travelling herbalist or quack doctor. These Indian and half-breed Collas have a great reputation all over South America; they travel with their packs of drugs to the southernmost camps of Buenos Ayres, and northwards to the shores of Panama. They are looked upon with much reverence by the gauchos of the Pampas as great medicine-men, conjurors, and miracle-workers. That there is much humbug in these Collas is true, but there is much besides; there is a sort of primitive college in Bolivia where the would-be Collas receive their diplomas. This college has no buildings, no books, the primeval forest serves for both. The elder Collas take the young aspirants out into the midst of that glorious Bolivian vegetation, and expound to them, day after day, the properties and secret virtues, the poisonous effects, of all the herbs and animal distillations, as handed down by tradition from generation to generation, from Colla to Colla, long ere the Spaniard stepped on the American shore. All the instruction is oral; none of this lore has ever been committed to writing. I doubt if one out of twenty of the learned dons and doctors of the college of Collas can read or write. When the young man has imbibed all this antique wisdom, a wand, painted in spiral stripes, is given to him, he is solemnly called by the name of Colla, and he is sent forth to wander over the wide continent on his healing errand. Not to be despised is the medical science of these unlettered men; that traditionary system, that empirical wisdom of many centuries, contains many wonderful and useful secrets unknown to our European schools. I have heard of several extraordinary cures performed by them on sceptical Englishmen, not at all likely to be taken in by a common quack. For all fevers, snake-bites, and diseases peculiar to this country, give me the Bolivian Collas with their striped wand. They know the leaf that is the magical dispeller of fever; they can extract charms from innocent-looking insects that will allay the pains of rheumatism; they can teach you how to mix your mother-in-law's maté with an essence that will bring peace to your household; they will sell you chips of wood, the which, if you throw them in a stream or pond, will poison or intoxicate all the fish, so that they float on the surface and can be easily caught; but as a surgeon the Colla is not to be relied upon; of anatomy, physiology, or any other ology, of course, he knows nothing whatever, though he will talk all sorts of incomprehensible jargon about them for your benefit.

March 31st.—From Loretto a two-days' journey brought us to Santiago del Estero, the capital of the province. Our route lay across a much pleasanter country than that we had left. The vegetation, more tropical in nature, was fresh and green after the recent rains; below the bushes was spread a soft carpet, not of grass, but of lovely flowers—verbenas, polyanthi, tulips, camomile, and others. Towering above the lower bushes were stately trees—the Quebrachos colorados—betokening that we were near the limit of the monte, and at the commencement of the tropical forest. The bushes were not too near each other here, as in the denser montes further south, but scattered, so that through the interspaces the eye was relieved by extensive views over the sea-like spreads of flowers. The convolvuli and creepers, too, that overflowed the bush, the trees, the bushes, were all in manifold flower, and in fruit as well; all bore fruit. There was the prickly pear, with its heavy load of juicy orbs, and the ancoche, with its pearl-like drops, sweet to the taste and wholesome. There was a huge cactus, too, hereabouts, that bore plentiful fruit, somewhat like that of the prickly pear in outward appearance, but larger; some of these were bursting open with ripeness, and disclosed the delicious pulp within, cool as spring-water, and of a blood-red colour. This is called the oukli here, a lovely fruit, and one of the most useful in South America.

In the rainless, arid district of the Andes, in Santiago, and other provinces remote from the sea-coast, where the rainfall is irregular and rare, and where, after long months of cloudless, burning skies, the pastures wither up, the lagunas dry, and the cattle perish of drought; in rocky regions, too, baked by the vertical sun, where no other plant can find sustenance, the blessed oukli flourishes. Those stout, prickly stems and manifold round fruit, covered with thick, green rind, blushing slightly with the red pulp within, are fleshy and juicy to excess, full of an insipid sap sucked in from the heavy dews of the night. These plants are admirably constructed for the absorption of the floating vapours.

In the *seca*—the drought—the ranchero will go out and cut down with his machete a quantity of these soft, pulpy cacti, which the cattle will eagerly devour, both stem and fruit, therein finding an abundance of both food and drink. Were it not for the oukli, many portions of this province now inhabited would have to be left utterly desolate. We found the cool fruit, which can be eaten with impunity, very grateful.

In the pleasant fields we crossed this day, all the winged people of the province seemed to have gathered; never did I behold so many birds together: thousands of cooing doves and chattering parrots, and strange rainbow-coloured little creatures that never rested; coranchos, vultures, and owls were there too in legions, but preserving a more dignified appearance, and seeming to despise the frivolity of their cousins.

A land of fruit and birds and flowers, but of bichos and espinas too!

We heard from people that we met that the Rio Dulce, which we had to cross once more, was swollen by the rains, and not practicable at the passage of Gauchana, so we had to follow a longer route, and ride by the banks of the river to a point about a league distant from the city of Santiago, where there was another chata.

We passed by a little town called Mamodo, where was the usual square, this one more unfinished than any we had yet seen. There were but six houses scattered round it, and the jungle grew so dense and tall in the centre of it that it was impossible from one side to see the houses on the other. I do not know how these pueblos are founded, but the august founders, whoever they may be, evidently, as a rule, expected that enormous cities were to rise on the spots of their choice, on so extensive a scale did they draw out the skeletons of these future Babylons. This they told us was an ancient pueblo, yet jaguars and pumas roamed unmolested in its square. At a rancho here we tasted a new and strange drink, which we all pretended to like—algarroba beer. To make this, the pods are well mashed in a hollow tree-stump, water is poured on them, fermentation takes place, and in twenty-four hours you have your foaming ale. I cannot say much for algarroba beer, but algarroba spirit is by no means to be despised, and the cakes made from the pounded beans are very nice indeed.

After riding about forty miles we entered a forest nearly entirely levelled to the ground by what must have been a most terrific hurricane. On emerging from it we came to an estancia called Roblez, where we passed the night, being received with true Santiagenan hospitality. There was a Frenchman staying in the house, an engineer, who was engaged in constructing canals of irrigation for the sugar plantations near Santiago. He was in possession of a Paris paper three months old, which we devoured eagerly.

April 1st.—This morning we rode down to the ford on the Rio Dulce, which was but a few leagues distant. We found the river in high flood. It here flowed between sandy shores

sloping up to a dense jungle, and was of considerable breadth.
There were some men willing to swim our horses across,
perilous work in this *crescente*, for heavy trees floated down
rapidly on the turbid water. These men drove the horses
into the stream nearly a mile above the spot they proposed
landing at on the other side, so strong was the current. We
in the rough chata accomplished the voyage in the same
manner. When we reached the other bank, we were landed
on a quicksand. Several Indians now commenced to run
rapidly backwards and forwards over this, and so soon
formed a fairly hard road for ourselves and horses. This
method of making a temporary solid path across a quicksand
is very effectual. In Africa they first drive the oxen across
a river, that the sands may so become sufficiently hard to
allow the heavy waggons to cross without danger of their
sinking permanently into the treacherous bottom.

When we were beyond the river we beheld, at about a
league off, the ancient city of Santiago del Estero. The
gleaming dome of the old cathedral dominated all, contrasting
strangely by its size, and the wealth lavished on its construction, with the barbarism and poverty of the broad province
it looked down upon.

We were now entering a new country. As we approached
the city the untilled wilderness vanished, canals of irrigation
flowed sluggishly on either side of the road—for there was a
road—and all round us, with a rustling and a crackling sound,
waved great plantations of sugar-cane; we were in the
tropic north again, with a sudden burst, as it were. No
longer were around us the parched montes and salinas, but a
damp, rainy, steaming land, covered with a rank vegetation,
the unhealthy tepid tropics of Central South America.

We rode into the city, a largish town, but thoroughly
Argentine; there are but few gringos here; a mean place, so
mean that there is not even a tramway in it, and no South
American city can even pretend to be respectable without
that. The miserable houses are of mud, brick being the
exception. Paving there is none to speak of. The streets
are of soft black mud. A disreputable, dishevelled-looking
sort of a capital, whose inhabitants have a large proportion of
Indian blood in their veins, the indolent, useless Indian
blood, that is the curse of this Republic.

As we rode in we saw the children, mahogany-coloured,

with bright dark eyes, and straight black hair, wallowing naked in the rich mud of the streets. There was a wild, barbaric look about the dirty city and its inhabitants that struck us much. We rode to the one hotel, the " Hôtel de Paris," a new institution. Of old the traveller had to throw himself on the hospitality of the inhabitants or camp outside. A native keeps this—the first native hotel that we had experienced in this Republic ; may it be the last ! The land-lord was a haughty aristocrat, who would not condescend to look after the comfort of his guests in the least, but stalked like a monarch through his palace, eyeing his guests as if they were so many intruders on his peace.

The hotel was a strange old place, and not wanting in magnificence ; the house once of some governor or great man, a tyrant Taboada maybe. The patio was large, with a beautiful columned gallery around it, delicately-painted, but now crumbling to pieces from neglect. There was something of the ruined Moorish palace in the look of the whole building. There was a large courtyard behind the patio, in the centre of which was a huge wooden structure like a hencoop. This was the cock-pit, with its tiers of seats.

We were divided into different bedrooms overlooking the patio—large rooms with gaudy draperies on the walls, now hanging in mildewed shreds, but betraying former grandeur and ostentation of wealth. I was quartered with another traveller, a Bolivian, who was driving cattle south, but was here laid up half-way with a very bad attack of chuchu, or intermittent fever ; not a pleasant companion, for he groaned awfully when the shivering fit came on him. He told me he was taking eighty grains of sulphate of quinine a day, which is a largish dose, but not unfrequently ordered here by the doctors.

The *plaza* of Santiago is fine in its way, and surrounded by rather imposing public buildings. A white-plastered column, commemorative of Liberty or somebody else, is in the centre of it, of course tumbling to pieces, for here, as in China, dilapidation is but rarely repaired.

The day of our arrival the municipality had awoke to a spasmodic fit of cleaning up : some gaucho prisoners, guarded by stunted, dirty, half-breed soldiers, were (smoking the while) hoeing up the grass which had been allowed to rankly overgrow all the flags of the desolate Plaza, wherein no human being ever seemed to walk, fine promenade through it would make.

The street sights of Santiago are of the country—chiña girls, wild and half-naked, ride cross-legged on mules laden with alfalfa for sale. Sandaled gauchos loaf about solemnly and noiselessly. At intervals in the gloomy streets are stores where cheap Brummagen and Manchester goods, gaudy, and of bad quality, are exposed to view. With the exception of these last, the houses are like prisons, with grated windows admitting but a feeble light from the street. Outside some of the best of these dungeons, white high-caste ladies, bonnetless, with their two raven tails hanging to their waists, and in dainty high-heeled shoes, sit on chairs in the street, chatting, fanning, drinking maté, and smoking cigarettes, in a very free and easy manner. These are the noblest of the land, wives and daughters of deputies and generals—and in this fashion do the *élite* of Santiago take the air. It is a very out-of-door life that of this people; and, indeed, the habitations are not such as would tempt one to stay indoors much—an out-of-door life, but not a French out-of-door life —there are no brilliant *cafés* here, no splendid shops, no *flâneurs*. The citizens have no cheerful promenades, so stand and sit—a melancholy-looking race—outside their prison-like houses, like so many prisoners out for an airing.

From here to Tucuman is a three days' easy journey on horseback by the usual route, but on account of the flooded condition of the Rio Dulce, which we had yet once more to cross, we were recommended to make a *détour*, and follow its banks to a point some fourteen leagues from here.

CHAPTER XVII.

April 3rd.—Having enjoyed a day and a half's rest in the not very interesting capital of the province of the desert, we rode off at daybreak on the 3rd of April. We went through the town in our usual picturesque procession, with the baggage-animal trotting on ahead, with kettle and asador swinging under his neck rattling merry music; and the sack on his back well full of sugar, maté, biscuit, and beef, a four-days' store, for as we were not following the regular route, who could tell how far we might have to travel ere finding a place where we could re-victual ?

We rode all day; first through the canalized sugar-plantations in the neighbourhood of the town, then across a wilderness of trees and flowers. The deadly chuchu plant was plentiful at our feet, so, too, thick-growing white poppies and variegated tulips. We followed the river, generally about a mile from it, a dense jungle intervening. At mid-day we halted to feed in a small peublo, where a laguna provided us with tepid muddy water, but there was *nada mas* to be got in this place in the way of provisions, as Manuel, after diligent inquiry, informed us, not even cana or gin ! What a barbarous country ! Far, indeed, from civilization must be the spot where fire-water cannot be procured. Then we went on again across the plain, steaming and dank with its rich black loam—how different from the dry south. The atmosphere was that of a vapour bath ; it was late autumn, and the rank vegetation was rotting all around us, unhealthy and leprous-looking. We understood now how it was that this country was famed for its pesti-lential chuchu, being a prolific mother of fevers, while the Pampas and the arid montes further south are quite healthy, where, as in the Sahara of Africa, hunger and thirst and old age are the only diseases known.

It demonstrates how little the natives here know of their own country, to say that we found that the chata, or ferry-boat, fourteen leagues off, the people of Santiago had told us of and recommended, was not in existence, and had not been so for nearly ten years. So after riding all day, we found that we had to follow the bend of the river still further to the south-west out of our direction, in order to find some other *paso*. About an hour after dusk we came upon a house by the river bank, standing alone in the wilderness. The whole family was sitting outside maté-drinking—a patriarchal-looking tribe. The head was a stalwart, hale old man, straight as an arrow, in gaucho dress, shod with colt's feet, and belted with many dollars, with a head that might have belonged to Abraham, Isaac, or Jacob. He had several sons round him, one, a youth of about fifty, was married, had married daughters, and was already a grandfather ; thus our host was a great-grandfather ; but, to our surprise, huddled up within the rancho was another very aged man, with long

12

white hair and beard, and blind, with his palsied head wrapped up in a white cloth. This was our host's father, the venerable ancestor of all the little colony, the great-great-grandfather of the little babe there at his handsome mother's breast. This old gentleman lived in a world of his own, in a time about three-quarters of a century back at least. He would talk to no one, ignored his descendants and all present things altogether, and was wont, so our host told us, to tie himself in a knot there in the corner, and shiver and moan on day by day, with eyes that, though blinded, had yet a far-off look, and mumble to himself all sorts of ancient memories. He would talk often of the king of Spain, whom he evidently considered still ruled half the New World, and of many events of long-past history that his grandsons had not even heard of.

This was a handsome family, from the old Conquistador, as we called the ancient, downwards; there was no taint of the Indian blood in them. And so the happy and peaceful life of this little community of five generations of men flows on its even way in this remote waste, with only the season of the marking of cattle and such-like rural excitements to vary its uneventful calm; for out here even the outermost wave of the revolutions of the cities is unfelt, and those lawless bands of armed men that fatten on pronunciamenta, robbing men and violating women, do not extend their raids thus far.

At night the preparations for rest were made in a way that would surprise an English farmer. Although the night air was cool, almost cold, our host bid his sons bring out the beds. Three *catres* were then arranged in a row outside the house, which, emptied of every one, was locked up for the night. The patriarch turned into one *catre*, the host and his wife into another, the damsels into the third, while the men, the children, and ourselves, camped out alongside in our blankets. This curious habit of locking up the house and turning out for the night is common in these northern provinces; even in chilly weather the native prefers to sleep under the stars to within doors, lulled into slumber, as we were to-night, by the lowing of cattle, the hum of cicala, the cry of wild beasts, and other manifold sounds of the forest and the wilderness, not to forget the snores of patriarchs, for the great-great-grandfather raised a nasal trumpeting this night that drowned that of all his five generations of descendants, his oxen, and the strangers within his gates put together.

April 4th.—When we had ridden but a few miles this day, we perceived that ahead of us the monte, for leagues, as far as the eye could see, was of a red colour, like that of burnt bricks. Earth, tree, and bush had all assumed the same curious hue, the effect being something like that of early winter on some of the vegetation of northern Europe. We could not at first conjecture what the strange appearance signified—it was as if some pestilential blast had withered up all the life of the land ! On approaching, we found this to be a vast multitude of locusts, that were settled so thickly on everything that no twig or leaf, or inch of bare earth was left visible. There was nothing to be seen anywhere under the sky but the mahogany-coloured bodies of these fearful creatures, they covered all. They had nearly finished up this district. As we rode through them they rose from under our feet in thousands, with a multitudinous crackling sound as of a huge bonfire, and then, when we had passed, settled down again, but having revealed in their short flight the devastation they had wrought ; little but bare barkless stalks were left of tree and bush, even the grass had been devoured down to the ground.

After riding over several miles of locusts, we reached a hut by the river, where were two men, who made their livelihood by burning charcoal and ferrying stray passengers across the stream. For this purpose they had constructed what they rather boldly called a boat. Imagine two rough logs, about three or four feet long, lashed together with hide thongs in the shape of a V, then a plank nailed on top of these, so converting the V into an A ; here you have the boat. The apex of the A was of course the bow of the vessel. Only one passenger could be carried at a time on this rickety craft, and he had to balance himself gingerly, as he squatted down on the transverse plank, and held on to the two logs.

One by one we were ferried across. The Charon would launch the boat each time with its nervous occupant looking exceedingly ridiculous, and then swim behind it, pushing it on with his hands, so steering it diagonally across the current, till ultimately he beached it on the opposite bank. The river was much swollen, very rapid, nearly 300 yards wide, and big trees kept floating down, often threatening to collide with the little raft, thus there was no small element of danger in this passage. No accident occurred, however. We were all safely landed, and then the men proceeded to swim our horses across.

We had not ridden half a mile beyond this when a strange sound was heard suddenly, coming from all round us, a sound low and ominous, terrible to the husbandman; it was the noise of the wings of myriads of locusts. The word had been given forth by the captain, and, with one consent, in a moment the vast army rose up with the sun after their night's feed, as is their custom, to renew their journey of devastation. The light was obscured by the number of them, and the sky was reddened. We rode through several leagues of them, all bound in a contrary direction to ourselves, so we had to meet them in the face, a most unpleasant sensation. Our horses evidently had the strongest objection to riding against these dense living showers, that pelted against us without intermission.

We passed a rancho, by which was a small plot of maize. The family were all out, endeavouring to drive off the invaders with branches of trees and shouting, but in vain, for they crowded on over their dead, and would not be repulsed or checked by any slaughter; so the poor people stood in despair, and hung down their hands, as they beheld the speedy ruin of their little farm.

By midday we reached a deserted rancho. In its ruined corral was a well, from which we managed to draw out some rotten water, but we saw that there were so many dead and swollen snakes and other beasts in the well, that we dared not drink, fearfully thirsty though we were, for the day was very hot. Neither could we find pasture for our horses. Between Santiago to Tucuman the stages were long, and we were unable anywhere to procure algarroba or other hard food, so our animals had a very hard time of it.

Rather late this night, very thirsty, we reached a farm that is called Chourki; here there was water and some pasture, so we rested by it for the night. We camped out under a carob-tree in front of the house, together with the farmer, his family, some tame ostriches, and a little flock of goats.

We returned his hospitality by doctoring a horse of his

that had been frightfully clawed in the back by a puma. He told us that his place was in the province of Tucuman, so we must have crossed the frontier some time this day.

April 5th.—This was our last day's ride, and brought us to the city of Tucuman, which is about fifty miles distant from the farm of Chourki. We saw ahead of us a range of giant mountains looming, these were the Andes of Tucuman, the Sierras of Aconquija, whose highest summit is 17,000 feet above the level of the Pacific Ocean. After riding some leagues we reached an extensive swamp, of the perils of which we had heard some exaggerated accounts; we had been told that it might easily befall us to lose a horse or two while traversing it.

We found it to consist of treacherous soft black mud, in some places covered with water, in others with bright green grass, forming a quaking crust over the morass; canes and other swamp-loving shrubs, six feet high and more, grew all over it, rendering progress slow and difficult. A nasty, unhealthy place, a nest of chuchu, where only mosquitoes could resist the poisons of the malarious atmosphere, for under the hot sun the black mud was rotting and fermenting and stinking, breathing forth pernicious fevers. Once beyond it we reached Naranquita, a pueblo consisting of a store, a few ranchos, and a sugar factory with its lofty chimney; a sugar plantation surrounded the village, and a grove of oranges. It was an unhealthy spot that should be left to the mosquitoes that infest it. Nearly every one in the place seemed to be prostrated with the fever more or less, and those who were not suffering then, were sallow, emaciated, and haggard from old attacks of it. We rode on towards the big mountains until late in the afternoon, when we perceived signs that we were nearing an important city. In the first place, the foot-track broadened into a road, and on either side of us were great plantations of sugar-cane, with deep canals and hedges of prickly pear dividing them one from the other. Large orange-groves, too, were frequent. Above all towered huge sugar factories, by which were the mud ranchos of the peons, grouped in little villages; by the roadside were canteens for the use of the men employed on the plantations, presided over by Indian women.

On reaching an eminence, we saw before us a long straight road, and at the end of it a fair city with glittering domes and snowy-white houses, backed by the distant Sierras, rising range behind range into the clouds. Between us and the town was a rapid shallow river, the Rio Tati, a branch of our old friend the Rio Dulce. Here we found a long wooden bridge of considerable height, so as to be above the level of the frequent floods. This bridge is peculiar in its way; its architect certainly has hit upon the most original idea in the way of bridges possible, in so much as this ambitious and solid structure, after starting from the level of the lofty *barranca*, crosses the lower plain for several hundred yards, and then suddenly stops short, just where your common every-day bridge generally begins—at the bank of the river, at the water's edge! We rode along without observing this at first, and were loudly praising the high state of civilization of the country we had now reached, where the rivers were spanned by bridges, and were congratulating ourselves on a passage dryshod, when we were surprised to find the wooden roadway slope suddenly down to the water, leaving us to ford the stream saddle-deep.

Once beyond the foaming Tati, we ascended the steep street to the centre of the town.

Now we enjoyed a spell of luxury for a space, and surrendered ourselves to a gentle life; for in this city, among others, is a hostelry yclept the "Hôtel de Paris," kept by one M. Doucet, a Frenchman; and surely this is saying enough to indicate that it cannot but be an oasis of gastronomic comfort in this monotonous land of puchero and asado. This was a very Capua for us; our host was erst of the "Café de Paris" at Rosario, an establishment frequented by the Anglo-Saxon, so he knew how deftly to mix the insinuating cocktail and the matutinal egg-nog. Contact with the white man had also civilized the native waiters of the hotel.

There was one, a fresh hand, but intelligent, who had found time already to study and commit to memory many of the principal habits of the white man. N.B.—By white man, of course, is signified Englishman, to the exclusion of niggers, Spaniards, and all foreigners whatever; this is the common and proper definition of the term. I rung my bell for something or other the day after our arrival; this particular waiter promptly turned up, and before I had time to say a word, the varlet jerked out,—

"Cognac con soda, senor ? "

" No," I replied with virtuous indignation, for I flatter myself that there is nothing in my personal appearance, no nasal flush or grogginess of eye that betokens habitual morning dryness. " No, why do you ask me that ? "

" Ah, senor," he said with a childlike smile, " there have been several English here, and whenever they rung the bell they asked for a brandy and soda."

Such are the pitfalls that the rash inductive logician is apt to fall into, I meditated; this knave has formed this hasty generalization as to the habits of all my countrymen from the eccentric and vile practice of a few individuals, and thus unjustly. . " But stop," this aloud, " on second thoughts I think I will have a brandy and soda, waiter, if Senor Jerdein will join me." After all, the poor fellow had been doing his best to formulate into laws the mysterious Anglo-Saxon nature. It might confuse his intellect, cause him to despair, and renounce his laudable design, were we thus at these early stages of his study to place before him glaring exceptions to what he considered to be the most elementary and general rules of Anglo-Saxonology.

We had now to dispose of our faithful horses, and entrusted Manuel to sell them for us. He took up his abode under a cart in the stable-yard, and there received the would-be purchasers of our steeds. There were some sharp fellows, who tried hard to do our worthy follower; but he was on his mettle, and, with his bland and simple smile, was quite up to these Tucumans, who fancied their own cuteness, and imagined themselves much more knowing than a Cordoban. We stayed at Tucuman some days, and visited the neighbouring country.

We had evidently arrived at the wrong time of the year to enjoy the beauties of Tucuman, for it was now the rainy season, no make-believe one in this province. A perpetual pall of inky cloud obscured the skies, the rain fell continually, beneath our feet in street or orange-grove was stinking, deep, black mud, suggestive of fever and rheumatism. We found that expeditions into the country and the cordilleras were just now provocative rather of bad temper and grumbling than of enthusiastic admiration of the glorious nature around us. When we were taken out to do anything, we would not admire it at all—nothing was wonderful in our eyes ;

the plain of Tucuman was but "an unweeded garden" to us and the Andes detestable nuisances; such is the effect of weather on the travelling mind.

One day our host took us out for a drive round the neighbouring sugar factories in a tumble-down, vermillion vehicle drawn by no less than six horses, with two outriders on the leaders, dirty, bare-legged, half-breeds, each armed with a tremendous whip. The several portions of the carriage, the driver, the outriders, the horses, were all lashed together firmly with strips of raw hide, so as to obviate all chance of disintegration on the way.

In this bone-jolter we were carried along some terrible roads; for so civilized is this province that roads actually exist between the several plantations, but they are not of a high class, our six horses could scarcely drag us through them. Tall sugar-canes waved on either side of us, a ditch and then a cactus fence in all cases dividing them from the road, which was but a space left between two plantations, unmacadamized, and untended in any way, its natural swampiness being increased by a remarkably intelligent custom. The mud that is dug out in the construction and constant dredging of the ditches is piled up on the sides of the road, forming two banks, sloping down towards its centre. Thus the highway, instead of being slightly convex, as with us, and draining into the canals, was concave, and very much so; indeed, all that can be said in its favour is that, though a very inferior road, it would make a passable ditch. We were ever and anon getting into some more fearful slough than usual, when our coach would refuse to advance, and commence to sink gradually into the bowels of the earth, until the long whips and the tall language of our Jehu and outriders stung the horses into supernatural efforts, and they tore us out. We visited several large factories, all provided with expensive machinery from England, and the processes of sugar and rum-making were explained to us. We tasted several samples of caña. One was a 44 caña, not an A.D. 44, or a 44 shillings a dozen, but a 44 above proof—fire-water, with a vengeance, calculated to make even a Quilp cough.

We brought a new pet for the *Falcon* back with us in the carriage, no less than a young lion, a six-month old puma, that we purchased on the way from an Indian for five shillings ; playful as a kitten, about the size of a New-foundland dog, and with a purr as of a trombone.

We enjoyed ourselves much in Tucuman, and actually learnt a new vice, one that is much indulged in throughout the north-west provinces of the Argentine Republic—coca-leaf chewing. We have heard a good deal about this drug in England lately, and one of our professional walkers is said to have kept up his strength by its use during a recent sensational walk. The following is what I learnt concerning it in this, the land of its use and abuse. The Indians of Bolivia discovered the properties of coca ; they either chew the leaf or drink an infusion of it, and their white conquerors have acquired the vice from them. That it does possess the wonderful sustaining powers attributed to it is certain. When an Indian undertakes a long journey on foot he takes with him a little bag of these leaves, and as he goes, perpetually chews them and swallows their bitter juice. He will traverse many hundreds of miles of country thus, without taking any other sustenance or requiring rest ; but when the gigantic effort is over, he lies down on the ground utterly prostrated, and so remains without moving for days, until he has slept off the wearisome and terrible reaction of the drug. From what I heard from intelligent men here, possessing some medical knowledge, it seems that, taken in moderation, it is a stomachic, and has really useful sus-taining powers—would not be a bad substitute for tea or coffee, and is probably better than these. But those who exceed in the use of coca experience the most disastrous results ; the intemperate enjoyer of the drug becomes apathetic, an utterly useless wretch, impotent in mind and body ; his energy dies, his digestive organs become seriously impaired, the worst symptoms of dyspepsia are induced, and helpless idiotcy not unfrequently occurs. Mr. Ledger, of Tucuman, the discoverer of that most useful species of quinine-tree that bears his name, the Cinchona Ledgeriana, told me that in his opinion the injurious result of excess in coca are more rapidly brought on, and are more terrible in consequence, than those attributed to excess in any other drug—opium and Indian hemp included.

I purchased a pound of coca-leaf at a chemist's (every chemist here sells the drug) for four shillings, and started chewing vigorously, to see what effect it produced. I certainly took a large quantity of it, but experienced no appreciable symptoms whatever ; perhaps it only affects the simple-living Indian, and cannot touch the gringo.

CHAPTER XVIII.

WE stayed about a week in Tucuman and its neighbourhood, and then returned by rail and steamer to Buenos Ayres. As we had to traverse five provinces on this journey, each having a different paper currency, we provided ourselves with a load of Chilian and Peruvian silver dollars, sols, as they are called, which are everywhere taken for eighty-two cents gold.

From Tucuman to Cordoba we were carried by the Government railway, and the evils of its administration were everywhere apparent ; it compared very unfavourably with the other railway companies of the Republic under the management of Englishmen.

A railway accident is the ordinary incident of travel on this line, for it is now so rotten and dilapidated that the train runs off the metals two or three times a week, notwithstanding that there are no curves on the way, the rails being carried in one perfectly straight line across the level plains. However, passengers are but rarely injured by these accidents, for there are no high banks for the train to roll over. They even manage to get up a collision occasionally, an ingenious and extraordinary feat, requiring some calculation to bring about, seeing that one train only starts every other day from either terminus, and the rate of progress is so slow that it is almost possible to see the other train approaching when it is still half a day's journey off across the plain.

Of course we had our little accident ; we ran off the line and took a trip into the Salinas, till we were brought up, and, after some hours' delay, put on the rails again.

We were advised to carry a sufficiency of provisions with us ; so we victualled our carriage with a demijohn of Mendoza wine, some cold fowls, and other luxuries, and made ourselves very comfortable during the two days' tedious journey to Cordoba. The stoppages were frequent ; we passed half a night at a place called Recreo, for what object I know not, save it be for the purpose of putting money into the pockets of the exorbitant proprietor of a buffet that is there. We were continually halting at other little unnecessary stations in the salt-desert, where there were no villages, no goods or passengers to be discharged or taken up, nothing indeed but a station-master, sand, salt, and cacti. The delay at each of these stations was enormous.

The engine-driver and guard of our train would get out at each, light up their cigarettes, and look dreamily across the burning desert for half an hour or so, as if in search of some impossible passengers that were coming up from the far horizon.

Had we anticipated these delays, we would have brought an ox with us, and made Manuel get out and cook us an asado on each platform as we travelled along. As might be expected, we took up no passengers at the stations on the Salinas—at some of the other stations we did. Then there was a double or treble delay, but this was not surprising to me after the following experience at the station of Tucuman.

I had found out that our united fares amounted to seventy-five dollars gold ; so, before presenting myself at the ticket-office, I had calculated what this would be in sols at eighty-two. I counted out the proper number and presented them to the ticket-clerk. But to him this calculation was a very serious matter, and not to be hurried over ; so he called me into his office separately, keeping all the other passengers waiting, and said solemnly,—

"Come, senor, let us calculate this," at the same time producing a large sheet of foolscap, a pen, and a horn of powder.

So we calculated ; he was not what one would call a ready mathematician, over and over again he attacked the difficult problem, irritated, perplexed, impatient, yet ever polite. At each attempt he brought out a different sum ; I worked it out for him, but he utterly despised my result. I had arrived at it too quickly, with too few figures. I could not be right ; it was not such a simple matter as all that. At last some new way of reckoning—an inspiration of genius—flashed across his brain, and after covering another sheet of paper with a row of five-barred gates with a lot of figures running a steeple-chase across them, he came to a conclusion. The number of sols he asked for was less than that I had computed, but he insisted he was right, and would take no more. I paid him and off he rushed to repeat the process with others who were bringing him the moneys of different provinces to puzzle further his addled brain.

When I was settled down in the train, he flew back to me, informed me that he had just discovered a new and infallible way of calculating, which, applied to my case, showed that I still owed him two sols. He was almost right this time, not quite, so I paid him the additional demand ; I believe, as we now stand, he owes me twopence.

It certainly must be a maddening profession, calculating fractions before a wild, jabbering, impatient crowd of half-breeds, who by the way are exceedingly suspicious of the clerk's arithmetic, and squabble with him fearfully on principle, for they are far too mathematically obtuse themselves to have the remotest conception of how much change they should receive.

It was early in the morning of our second day's journey that we entered the province of Catamarca and traversed the Salinas. Waggon-tanks of water are attached to the train while crossing these arid wastes, to feed the engine and supply the rare stations. Just now, however, of water, salt though, there was no lack. It was the rainy season in the distant Sierras, and, as often occurs, the floods had poured down and almost entirely covered these wide flat expanses. As viewed from the train, the Salinas presented in places the appearance of a shoreless sea, for all round, the horizon was of water rippling before a strong north wind ; the stations, which are built on raised spots, stood out like islands in this sea, on to which the little salt waves dashed constantly. With these exceptions nothing rose above the waters, save here and there the tall gaunt cacti, looking like ships at anchor with their yards squared. Scarlet flamingoes seemed to be now the only inhabitants of this waste, for the deer and other beasts of the desert had been driven back by the waters to take refuge in the higher lands.

We stayed a couple of days in old Cordoba, bade farewell to faithful Manuel, and then took train to Rosario, where we arrived on Good Friday. This day is observed with great solemnity in South America; we found that all the shops were closed, and the inhabitants were dressed in universal black. The yards on all the schooners in the river were crossed, and the roughs and gamins were letting off crackers in the streets to the peril of passers-by—burning Judas, as the custom is called.

We sailed to Campana in the steamer *Tridente*, one of a new company, the Argentine Lloyd.

Cold and keen seemed the wintry morning air, when we reached Campana, a great change after tropical Tucuman. Buenos Ayres too was bracing, to say the least of it, not withstanding its bright sun. When we reached the Estaçion Centrale, we left our puma, who had behaved excellently during the voyage, save once when he wished to eat a white baby, in the cloak-room for an hour or so. He was tied up with a cord to a ring, and could only promenade round a circle of about three feet radius, but he somehow managed to get into plenty of mischief even within that space, and run up a nice little bill for his owners during their absence. He devoured a porter's shirt that was hanging within reach; then a fellow-prisoner, a foolish turkey, that came too near his well-clawed paw; then he wound himself up with his rope in an inextricable fashion, so that he could not move an inch. We found him thus, lying down, tied up, blinking patiently, purring, and licking his blood-covered chops.

And now, leading him with a cord, we went off to the Tigre to see how our poor old *Falcon* had got on during our absence. Our home and *Penates* we found to be all right, but we heard that there had been strange doings on board while we were away. It seems that our boy Arthur had got into a row with some drunken sailors on shore, a police-man interfered, whereon the urchin knocked him down, jumped into the river, and swam on board. The assault was too serious to be overlooked, so the captain of the port sent off some of his men in a boat to arrest him. On seeing them approach, our crew dived down below, brought up a rifle, and threatened to exterminate his pursuers and bombard the port if they did not leave him alone. For many hours he kept the whole of the Tigre, with all the naval and military forces of the Argentine Republic, at bay. The people locked themselves up in their houses, terror seized all souls, and Arthur, master of the situation, proudly strutted up and down the deck, pointed his rifle instantly at any one who was rash enough to show his head. But, alas! the enemy by stratagem effected their purpose of taking prisoner that gallant crew. They knew that he would never surrender alive, and that his motto was that of the old French guard, so they waited till night. Under the influence of excitement and the caña he had drunk, Arthur at last fell asleep on the deck. With muffled oars a large body of men rowed off in boats from the *capitania;* they boarded the *Falcon*, and, before he was awake, the unconquered one was firmly fettered and carried off to a deep dungeon, where he was left to sober at his leisure, which he did with head-aching and lamentations. They soon released the drunken little rascal, and the authorities of the port behaved very well in the matter, kindly looked over the offence, and laughed at it as rather a good joke.

We now set to work to fit out the *Falcon* once more for a lengthened cruise up the tributaries of the river Plate. We found that the fresh water had stripped all the barnacles off her bottom ; she was as clean and bright as a new guinea. We took most of the chain and other heavy articles out of her ; by this lightening her draught to six feet, six inches, which is quite enough for the shallow Parana, and more than most of the steamers draw. This made her rather cranky, but not dangerously so.

It is impossible to ascend the ever-shifting channels of the Plata without a pilot, so we made an expedition to the Boca in search of one, for all the up-river pilots are Italians and dwell in this seaport, which is so entirely foreign a settlement, that Spanish is scarcely ever heard on its quays ; gruff Genoese, rapid Neapolitan, and oily Greek being the most used and abused languages. Every *café* has its rough lithographs of Garibaldi, or Italian men-of-war on its walls, and quite a fleet of vessels is necessary to bring from Europe the annual supply of maccaroni and fonghi, that are necessaries of life to these luxurious mariners from the Mediterranean and Ægean seas.

In the Boca we ordered a new boat to be built of cedar and other native woods, to replace the dinghy we had lost in our collision with the steamer ; we also purchased an old flat-bottomed canoe, such as the river schooners carry, for use on our cruise up the Parana.

We heard of a first-rate Genoese pilot who would come with us for 1000 dollars, 6l. a month, and therefore engaged him.

Having lost Andrews, it was necessary to find some sailor to take his place; so I went down with Jerdein to the beach of Buenos Ayres, where the foreign sailors, the shipping-masters, crimps, slop-tailors, and other people whose business in life is connected with the salt water do most congregate. A wonderfully cosmopolitan loafing-ground is this; beachcombers of all nations, mostly sulky and down-at-heel, lolled about lazily outside the grog-shops, and ship-chandleries; Italians, Greeks, Bascos, bronzed, cutthroat-looking rascals most of them, with scarlet sashes and gold earrings; British runaway sailors, too, far the most disreputable and debased-looking of the lot. An English sailor we determined not to get, for all such as are to be picked up in these South American ports are worse than worthless, as any master of a vessel knows. If we had engaged one of these drunken shirkers of work, we should doubtless have had to throw him overboard within a few days.

Through a shipping-agent we found a very decent sailor-boy of seventeen, an English subject, it is true, but hardly an Englishman; he was of Malay parents, and born in Mauritius, so spoke both Creole-English and Creole-French.

On the 7th of May our pilot, Don Juan by name, came on board; he turned out to be a great dandy; he brought an umbrella with him, an article quite unknown with us; also lace-covered pillows for his bed, and a looking-glass. He had a gigantic trunk of clothes, his *maté* and *bombilla*, and his dispensary consisting of a roll of sulphur. I have noticed that Italian sailors invariably carry an enormous amount of bedding and luggage with them on board ship, very unlike our own improvident mariners, who so often report themselves with nothing save what is on their back, even when bound for a voyage round the Horn in winter-time.

We were now all ready for sea; but from May the 7th to May the 12th we were stuck hard on the mud by the Tigre bank, waiting for the waters of the river to rise. This was a time of impatience for us; we stayed on board, and only on one occasion went down to Buenos Ayres, for at any moment the *crescente* might come and float us off.

The rest of these days on the mud I passed in reading Kingsley's "Westward Ho!" It was some years ago, when I was a boy, that I read this charming work last, but I remember well how it made me yearn then for a little ship and a wandering freedom on the salt seas ; and yet, now that I was in mid-fruition of that then so impossibly glorious a dream, it seemed quite an ordinary commonplace sort of a life after all ; but so is it with all our hopes and their realizations. I hope such philosophizings as the above are not symptoms of my becoming *blasé*, but it is impossible to be gushing and enthusiastic and so on, when one is stuck on a mudbank for days, waiting for a high tide, with half a dozen grumbling, sulky, impatient companions round one—there is not so much of the bold-buccaneering-life-on-the-ocean-wave sort of a feeling in one under these circumstances, as there should be in the skipper of a thirty-ton yawl on a roving commission for two years.

CHAPTER XIX.

THE following facts concerning the navigation of the rivers Parana and Paraguay will be of interest to any who purpose ascending these majestic streams. The average rate of the current between Buenos Ayres and Corrientes is two to two and a half knots an hour. The current of the Paraguay is less strong than that of the Parana. The navigation of both rivers is obstructed by constantly-shifting sandbanks. The height of the waters varies much, and irregularly, according to the rains in Matagrosso and the Chilian Andes ; sometimes there will be but six feet of water in the passages between the shoals, and at other times the Indian Chaco will be flooded for a hundred miles from the river-bank.

Cuyaba in Matagrosso, the very heart of South America, is the limit of the navigation. The flat-bottomed schooners occupy the best part of a year in sailing there and back. To accomplish the outward journey in six months is considered good work. These vessels, as a rule, have excellent pilots on board, and travel day and night ; when there is no wind they pole or warp.

It is only within the last few years that the upper rivers have been navigated by these Italian golettas, for the exclusive policy of the tyrants of Paraguay closed that portion of the stream to foreign bottoms, and in Paraguay itself vessels of any description were quite unknown. But now the whole majestic river-system of the Parana-Paraguay is open to commerce from the tropic forests and llanos of Matagrosso to the bleak steppes of the Buenos Ayrean Pampas. The following are the distances by water in English miles from the chief places on the river to Montevideo, which can be considered as at the mouth of the La Plata.

	Miles.
Buenos Ayres	150
Rosario	430
Diamante	507
Parana	552
La Paz	692
Bellavista	911
Corrientes	1053
Rio Paraguay	1081
Humaita	1109
Villa Pillar	1133
Villa Franca	1189
Formosa	1210
Villa Oliva	1228
Villeta	1294
Asuncion	1312
Cuyaba	2365

As the current is perpetually contrary, and it is rarely possible to tack against a head-wind, the upward journey is generally tedious for a sailing-vessel; thus, as will be seen, our voyage from the Tigre to Asuncion, the capital of Paraguay, occupied ninety-one days; but it must be remembered that, unlike many of the traders, we invariably came to an anchor at night, and rarely took to poling or warping when there was a calm.

On getting off our mudbank on the morning of the 12th of May, we found that there was but a very light breeze; but we were anxious to make a start, so, by dint of sailing, poling, and rowing, managed to travel about thirty miles before sunset. On getting out of the Tigre, we ascended the Capitan, one of the numberless channels of the Delta; it wound much and was very narrow, not more than eighty feet or so broad. All this day we were travelling through a lonely and beautiful forest of willows; in the midst of it we passed the *quinta* or country-house of ex-president Sarmiento, where that hardworking littérateur loves to retire in the summer months.

In the afternoon a large Genoese goletta came up with us, overhauling us with ease. We found that these vessels always did so going *up* the river, their shallow draught and enormous spread of canvas, towering above the trees, being in their favour. But coming *down* the river especially when any beating had to be done, our draught told, and we were more than a match for any of them. We also spoke two *ballandras* or smart river-sloops bound for Buenos Ayres from Paraguay ; these were laden with oranges, which not only filled their holds, but were piled seven feet high on their decks.

At sunset we dropped our kedge and made a bow-line fast to a tree on shore -- thus ended the first day of our cruise to that mystic and beautiful land of Paraguay.

May 13*th.*—The wind being fair, we sailed out of the narrow Capitan into the wide Parana de las Palmas, one of the mightiest of the mouths of the Parana ; there was quite a choppy sea on this broad water, so the old *Falcon* became quite lively, and began to imagine she was on her beloved ocean once more, but the freshness of the water must have puzzled her.

We had some capital spinnaker drill this day, as on many other occasions on this voyage, for we had to be continually jibbing the main-sail and shifting over the former sail, according to the windings of the river, which brought the wind now on this, now on that, quarter. The scenery was as that of the whole of this delta, low broad islands covered with rank jungle and forest, and intersected by numerous streams. Many *camelotas*, or floating islands of a species of lily, passed us ; it is these that join together and form the islands of the delta, binding the soft alluvial soil that is brought down by the river. Quantities of eagles and turkey-buzzards hovered over the rank foliage of the swampy country.

On the 14th of May we reached Campana, when the wind fell away and we were obliged to come to an anchor. We were now becalmed for nearly four days, a prey to mosquitoes and ennui. We passed our time in grumbling, and fishing with cotton and bent pins, in the manner of the Serpentine anglers, for a small fish that abounds here, and which, when fried, we pronounced to be as good as whitebait.

This enforced idleness tried all our tempers, especially those of our lion and the two boys, Jim and Arthur. The two latter were always squabbling, and the lion became so irritable and ferocious that no one dared to approach him ; he bit and clawed several of us, and growled perpetually. At last he lost his appetite, and showed symptoms of insanity and distinct homicidal mania, so we had to execute him and cast his corpse into the river as an example to the two lads.

While we were becalmed and at anchor a government steam launch came to us from Campana, and the officer in charge took it upon himself to reprimand us severely for not hoisting our ensign before eight o'clock in the morning. As he was rather abrupt in his manner, we became obstinate, and positively refused to show our colours before the orthodox time. The Argentine naval officers are inclined to be rather arbitrary, and are very punctilious about the respect that is due to their flag. A few weeks before this the passenger-steamer *Inca*, of the Brazilian River Company, was steaming down the Parana, flying the Brazilian flag ; there happened to be a small Argentine gunboat hidden in the jungle under the bank, the captain of which, observing that the steamer did not dip on passing, snatched up a rifle and deliberately commenced to fire shot after shot at the Brazilian captain as he stood on the bridge, and it was not owing to want of will, but of skill, that he did not kill him.

On May the 18th a favourable breeze sprang up, and under all canvas, spinnaker included, we reached the port of Zarate before evening. Above on the hill we saw the little white gleaming town of the same name nestling among the fine willows; so, with Jim following me with a huge basket under his arm, I walked up to it in order to do some marketing, for we had run rather short of stores. I called at the *capitania* on my way to report myself, for every hamlet on the river has its captain of the port. This functionary here had little to do ; there was but one schooner anchored off the town, laden with hard wood, so he kindly offered to accompany me and show me the best stores. We found Zarate to be a considerable place, neat, clean, and full of gringos. We found a French butcher and a French greengrocer, and sent Jim down to the beach, tottering beneath a great load of delicacies, beef, potatoes, pumpkins, apples, and onions.

The 19th was another day of sultry calm, and bad temper—so was the 20th ; but on the 21st it blew a gale from the south-west, and we sailed at a great speed till nightfall when we made fast to a tree on the bank, and caught some fine fish for supper.

This day we passed several southward-bound golettas, chiefly laden with charcoal. These Italians sail up to the riachos of the Chaco, and moor alongside the forest, while the crews are on shore cutting down wood and burning charcoal, until they have sufficient to load their vessels and return. Our pilot seemed to know, and hailed, all these skippers from the Boca as we passed each other.

On May the 22nd the wind was northerly, so, after sailing up one reach close-hauled, we had to come to an anchor again. The shore near us was low and swampy and overgrown with huge reeds. We saw a great many geese flying inland, so I went up the masthead to see what sort of a country lay beyond. Some two miles inland there was a cliff parallel to the river, and I saw that at the foot of this there stretched an extensive laguna, upon which were feeding thousands of ducks, swans, and other birds. The morass extended from the river to the edge of the lake.

Tempted by all this prospective sport, Arnaud and myself took our shot-guns and proceeded to wade through the swamp towards the cliff, and a most distressing wade it was too; we sunk up to our waists in the thick black mud which sent up bubbles of foul-smelling gas as we stepped into it. The mud was quite cold, so protected was it from the sun's rays by the horrid tangle of aquatic growth that covered it. In places there were two or three feet of water over the mud, and often we sank so deeply in the slime that we became alarmed, and thought of turning back, for what danger can so terrify the imagination as that of being inextricably stuck in such a slough as this. The reeds and other plants grew far above our heads, so that we could not see where we were going, and had to judge our direction by the position of the sun in the heavens. The mosquitoes troubled us terribly, as did the camelotas that wound their stems round our legs, and seemed to try to drag us down.

After travelling in this exceedingly unpleasant manner for upwards of an hour, we suddenly came to the end of this obstructive vegetation, and were in the open air once more with nothing but a quarter of a mile of bare festering mud between us and the laguna. And now came our reward : geese, turkeys, golden plovers, black ibis, snipe, teal, and

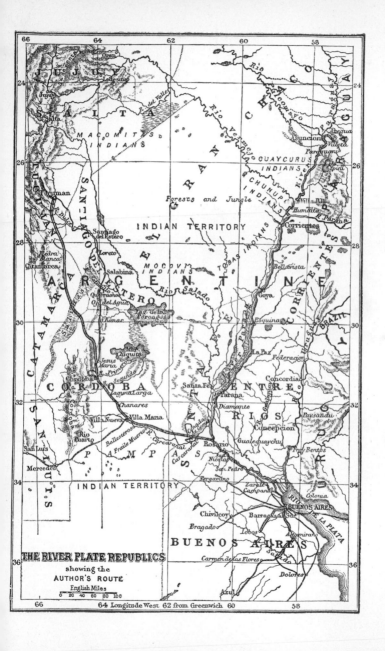

THE RIVER PLATE REPUBLICS
showing the
AUTHOR'S ROUTE
English Miles
0 20 40 60 80 100

Longitude West from Greenwich

some other species of aquatic birds, whose very names I do not know, were feeding here in incredible numbers. They were rather wild, but we managed to kill quite as much as we could manage to carry back through the swamp. We were now both very tired with our exertions, almost faint, but could not possibly sit down in this soft mud, into which our bodies would have sunk never to rise, for to recover one's feet again would have been quite impossible; so we waded across the lake, which was shallow, and to our delight reached dry and solid earth again under the cliff on the other side. Here were some trees that swarmed with noisy and gaudy-plumaged parrots, of which I shot a few to skin as specimens. We were pretty well done up by the time we got on board, but a bumper of Carlon wine soon set us right again.

While becalmed, or delayed by head-winds, as we often were in the course of this voyage, we generally found that sport of some kind for gun or rod was to be obtained in the virgin forests and savannahs, and on the numerous riachos; so time rarely hung heavy on our hands.

Even on this night we had the excitement of some more and rather unusual sport. As we lay moored alongside the bank, we heard a sound as of some large animal breaking its way through the rank vegetation close to us; there was much noise of snorting and splashing and of breaking reeds. It was intensely dark, so we could not perceive what manner of beast this could be. Some one suggested that it was a tiger, but, considering the marshy nature of the ground, we concluded that it was a carpincho. Of these animals we had already seen several, and knew them to abound hereabouts. The carpincho, I must explain for the benefit of most of my readers, is an amphibious animal that can best be described as a river-pig; its flesh is esteemed as a great delicacy by the riverside folk.

When the unknown monster was, judging by the noise, just in front of us, we fired a volley at it, seemingly without effect; so we reloaded, and standing in readiness, ordered Arthur to strike a blue-light, so as to to illuminate the neighbourhood.

Then by the unearthly glare we were surprised to behold staring at us fearlessly with fiery eyes a huge being, whose black head was topped by two great horns. "It is the devil," whispered Jim in horror, and his fingers wandered

nervously about his neck for the blessed relic that some padre
of far Mauritius had given him ere he had started on his
wanderings over the seas. It certainly looked uncommonly
like the traditional devil, and we hesitated, bold buccaneers
though we were, to fire again at his diabolical majesty. With
a last spurt of haggard flame our blue-light died out, and we
were left in darkness. Then was heard Jerdein's gruff voice,
"Jim, bring up the bull's-eye." With shaking hand Jim
brought it, but absolutely refused to throw the light on to
the shore, and reveal once more the outlines of that dread
form ; so Jerdein, the undaunted one, snatched it from him,
and with as much *sang-froid* as if he had been a London
policeman flashing his bull's-eye on some small street-arab
sleeping on a doorstep, he directed the bright disk of light
full on to Satan's coal-black visage, and lo, it was a bull!
How a bull had strayed across this league of treacherous
morass I cannot say, but there he stood, blinking in the light,
and evidently puzzled at our strange conduct.

Jerdein now proposed to send a rifle-bullet into him, cut
him up and salt him. We felt much tempted to accede to
the proposal; stolen fruit is sweet, and sweeter still is stolen
beef, but we hesitated, our insular prejudices, I suppose,
making us rather shy of felony ; so we sat down and argued
the question out in our usual warm and eloquent manner.
On one side it was argued that the owner of the bull was a
wealthy man and could easily spare him, that cattle-stealing
was the custom of the country, " the most respectable men
in the Republic," said Jerdein, " the generals, doctors, states-
men, and the presidents, without exception, have been cattle-
lifters in their day, so why not we, when a bull comes and
puts himself right in our way ?" The bull was spared, however, and in despite of these unanswerable arguments ; but I
am afraid the high tone of our morality had little to do with
our abstention from felony. The fact was the temptation
was not a strong one; we had eaten well, and were not
hungry, and we had already more beef on board, as it was,
than would keep fresh. Had we been hungry or short of
meat, I fear that that bull would have replenished our larder.
Thus was it that we were preserved from committing a great
crime that would have hanged us, even in civilized England.
not so many years back.

I will not go into all the details of our most tedious voyage to Rosario. Sometimes vessels occupy several months between Buenos Ayres and that port. One barque, a short time back, being as much as 120 days on the way; but that is, I believe, the longest time on record. The reason is that vessels are delayed by the constant windings of the river, so that the wind that is favourable for one reach is a head-wind in the next; and, as I have before explained, to beat up the river against the wind is impossible, even for a smart fore-and-after like the *Falcon*, save in one or two places where the current is feeble.

Nowhere does the river wind anything like so much as between the sea and Rosario. There is one most tantalizing series of bends about half-way, known as the Nuevas Vueltas, or nine turns. To pass these, unless you pole or warp, you may have to wait for six or seven successive changes of the wind. You run up one reach beneath a slashing pampero; in the next reach this is in your teeth, and there you have to wait at anchor for days, perhaps weeks, until the wind shifts, though you know all the time that, were you once beyond that reach, the pampero would be a fair wind again for a long distance.

Between calms and flaws of wind it is always down anchor or up anchor in this river, entailing no small amount of labour to the mariner. And so it was with us till the last day of May, when, having been twenty days out, we had not accomplished more than two-thirds of the distance to Rosario, and began at this rate to despair of ever reaching Paraguay.

Since Zarate we had passed no town or village, uninhabited swamps and jungles everywhere lining the banks; thus we had run short for the last three days of sugar, rum, and biscuit, and were anxious to reach some settlement.

On this twentieth day out we did see a town, but only saw it, alas! for we were not to approach it, as it was on another arm of the river—this was San Pedro, built on an eminence, with a lofty church tower that is visible for many leagues around. This town stuck to us all day, though we were sailing at a good rate—it seemed as if we should never pass it; it was worse than Netley Hospital is to a yacht going up Southampton Water.

The Parana here wound about so much that it really appeared as if we were going round and round San Pedro;

sometimes it was in front of us, sometimes behind; now on the port hand, now on the starboard. "And to think," as Arnaud dreamily remarked, that up there there is plenty of rum and sugar and biscuit," and he sighed deeply.

A large Italian river barque passed us this day; she was fifteen days out from Buenos Ayres and had been warping through all the calm weather. Later on in the day we overtook her again, for we were then in a bend of the river, up which we could only just lay close-hauled, with our sheets flattened right in. She, of course, could not manage this, sagging to leeward as she did with her shallow draught, but was obliged to take to warping once more. This part of the channel was nearly two miles wide, flowing between plains of lofty pampa grass. We took the ground in the afternoon, running on to it with a violent shock, for we were under all canvas at the time, and the wind was blowing fresh; we managed to haul the vessel off again easily enough by taking out an anchor astern.

On the 1st of June it blew a strong gale from the S.S.W. —a pampero; now this was a fair wind for us all the way to Rosario, so we made up for lost time, and after sailing for fifteen hours came to an anchor not more than twelve miles below that port. It was not by any means a pleasant day, the rain fell in blinding torrents, and the lightning and thunder were more terrible than I think I have ever experienced. Occasionally squalls of extreme violence struck us, in some of which we were obliged to lower all our sails on deck.

Throughout the day we had three reefs in our main-sail, and that was quite as much as we wanted, though the wind was nearly right aft. We flew by Obligado, a little port, and St. Nicholas, a considerable place, but did not stop to procure provisions; we could not waste so glorious a wind as this.

In the afternoon we came to a point where there was a rapid bend, which we just lay through close-hauled. But at the commencement of it rode at anchor no less than fifteen schooners, some of which we recognized as having passed by us on the way; for none of the river craft could hope to weather that point with this wind blowing.

This day our pilot walked the deck with a prouder gait than usual, for he had now outstripped all the other craft;

it was with a voice of importance, too, that he shouted his orders to tropical Jim, shivering with cold at the tiller, green of complexion and miserable. The very babel of tongues in use on board the *Falcon* during this voyage was curious enough. Spanish, Italian, Genoese, English, and Creole-French were combined into one common language. Jim would occasionally swear in Malay and Hindustani for variety, and a good many Gaurani words crept into our vocabulary later on in Paraguay. This is a specimen of the manner of giving and replying to orders on board; Jim is at the tiller, pilot looking out:—

Pilot. " Arriva ! " (Bear away !)

Jim. " Arriva it is, sir ! "

Pilot. " Horsa un poco !—bueno ! " (Luff a little !— steady !)

Jim. " Horsa un poco, monsieur !—bueno it is ! "

We passed a barque this afternoon laden with marble : she was thirty-eight days from Buenos Ayres, so had more cause to grumble than we had. We could not afford to waste this glorious breeze, so broke through our rule, and sailed on till midnight, by which time Don Juan computed that we had made nearly forty leagues, an excellent day's work. We should have reached Rosario before morning, had we not, just as eight bells sounded, run hard up on a sandbank. We had to work diligently throughout the night before we could haul the vessel off again : we lay out our big anchor, but dragged it home twice, and not till we had got two anchors down did we succeed in hauling her off into deep water. By this time the pampero had blown itself out, and a dead calm followed for twenty-four hours.

On June the 3rd there came light catspaws of wind from the south. We got up anchor and sailed slowly before them against the here strong current. Between the puffs we went astern again and had to drop our kedge. At last, by watching our opportunities as closely as if we had been sailing a race, we reached Rosario, and came to an anchor among the shipping, exactly opposite to the custom-house, being twenty-three days out from the Rio Tigre, not an over smart passage it must be confessed.

CHAPTER XX.

WE went on shore and purchased a goodly supply of provisions, mutton, half an ox at twopence a pound, potatoes, pumpkins, onions, and other luxuries, three demijohns of wine, and a sufficiency of Havannah caña to replenish our rum-cask withal. We also purchased some paint, so as to make the *Falcon* beautiful before reaching the capital of Paraguay.

The tradesman who sold us this addressed his bill to *El Senor Don Milor Inglese, abordo del Jot.* I have seen yacht spelt in many curious ways, such as yatch, yot, and yat, but never before as jot.

We procured some Bolivian and Peruvian silver from the bank before sailing, as we were again to visit paperless regions. We made yet another very useful investment, a large accordion and a noisy hurdy-gurdy, which latter reeled off four tunes: the Blue Danube waltz, a Cloche de Corneville gallop, a reminiscence of the Grande Duchesse, and a boisterous, furious cancan. These purchases were made at the instance of our pilot, Don Juan, who said they would be quite necessary in Paraguay, where we should be obliged to give balls occasionally, as is the custom for all distinguished travellers like ourselves.

It was late when we returned to the beach this night in order to go on board. Arthur and Jim were asleep, so could not hear our loud "*Falcon*, ahoy!" We looked for a shore boat to take us off; boats there were plenty, but no men, and what was more important, no oars. There was a large low building on the shore, which we could see was brilliantly lit up, and in the which, from the noise that issued from it, a merry baile evidently was under way. Here we thought we might come across some of the owners of the boats; we were not wrong in our surmise. We went to the door of the ball-room, at which stood two serenos or policemen; these felt all the people as they entered, to see that they carried no knives on their persons, for these had to be left outside. This precaution is generally taken at these not over aristocratic public bailes in the low parts of a South American seaport; neither are they idle precautions, judging from the physiognomy of the frequenters of these places.

We entered the ball-room, a large whitewashed apartment decorated with bits of coloured paper. At the deal tables that served as bars ugly half-breed Hebes vended vile gin and viler caña. The guests were Italian and Greek sailors, all in their shirt-sleeves, and a few young Chiña girls of anything but dazzling beauty, but making up for this by the extreme affability of their manners—some might call them too affable.

We picked up a boatman, and persuaded him, in consideration of a dollar, to desert for a space the buxom partner he was dancing with, and row us off to the *Falcon.* At first he absolutely refused to go, and explained his reasons. He could not trust the lady of his affections by herself—she would go off with some one else while he was away. But we were not going to be left boatless at this hour of the night without an effort, so we explained the matter to the young lady, who stood by fanning her hot face, and implored her to promise her mariner not to elope faithlessly with another lover in his absence. The nymph indignantly refused to bind herself by any such vows, and was walking proudly off with her little nose in the air, when, as a last chance, we reminded her that through her flightiness and obstinacy the boatman would lose a dollar. The mention of so large a sum startled her; she turned and said thoughtfully,—

"A dollar!"

"Yes," I continued; "a Bolivian dollar."

I saw that she hesitated and was lost. She was wrapt in meditation for a while, when suddenly a happy thought suggested itself to her, and she said,—

"Provided that Don Alfonso will promise not to spend any of the dollar until he comes back here to me, I will wait for him."

The love-sick swain joyfully undertook to do as she wished; so, after half an hour's diplomacy, we were rowed over to our vessel.

On Monday, the 5th of June, a strong E. by S. wind sprang up, enabling us to proceed on our journey. We were told that it would be advisable to take a bill of health from here for Paraguay, so I called early in the morning at the Paraguayan Consulate. A stupid negro girl opened the door to me, and drawled out that the great Don who represented the inland republic was not in the habit of arriving at his office till eleven o'clock. This day he did not arrive till nearly one. He asked me to follow him in, and, throwing himself in an armchair, deliberately rolled himself a cigarette. Having made himself generally comfortable, he sighed deeply in anticipation of the hard day's work before him, and asked me in a languid and aggrieved voice what I wished that he would do for me. I explained that I required a *Patente de Sanidad* for Paraguay. " Show me your papers," he said. I produced my Admiralty warrant and another Spanish document which the captain of the port of the Tigre had kindly furnished me with.

Now he saw a chance of making an honest (?) penny without much trouble, and, before I could imagine what he was about to do, he pounced down on my papers with his official seal, leaving a huge blue impression on each, and glibly said, " It is a patacon for each seal, senor, if you please; I will now draw you out a bill of health, six patacones—that is eight in all " (thirty-two shillings). I grew wrath at this gross imposition and disfigurement of my papers. Vain it was for me to expostulate, to urge that I had never asked him for these stamps; his only reply was to shrug his shoulders and say, " It is done, sir," all the while holding the documents and admiringly contemplating his handiwork. Evidently he considered that this sealing, whether it was useless to me or not, was a piece of hard work for which he, the worker, must at all events be paid.

However, I would not pay up, whereon he waxed nasty, and commenced to throw doubts on the authenticity of my Admiralty warrant. His objections to this were ingeniously absurd and abstruse. He pretended that he could not understand the Admiralty stamp on it—being a colourless impression standing out in relief, unlike his own gaudy blue concern;—he thought it must be humbug; he rubbed it suspiciously with his finger, smelt it, and at last let me go in sheer weariness of me, and then turned fiercely to inspect a row of Italian river skippers who were waiting their turn, looking like a patient rainbow, for they wore no coats, and their flannel shirts, as is their wont, were of gaudy colours— one of orange-yellow, one of scarlet, and so on. Leaving these poor fellows to suffer their share of Paraguayan block-headedness, I hurried on board, and in a few minutes we were under weigh and once more scudding rapidly up the stream.

We anchored for the night off the mouth of our old friend, the Rio Carcaveñal.

We sailed all the next day by the ever-changing swamps and jungles, past mouths of tributary creeks, alive with duck, teal, and geese; by capes and wooded islands and floating camelots until evening, when we anchored in the midst of a wild and beautiful scenery.

Throughout the 8th of June we were becalmed in this spot. After breakfast Jerdein, Arnaud, and myself, taking with us our shot-guns, revolvers, and knives—a ruffianly-looking crew—started in the canoe in search of game. Coasting down a little way, we came to a narrow opening where a small stream clove the densely-covered bank. Let us paddle up that creek, suggested some one. So we shot our canoe within it, and then, to our amazement, found that we were going, not *up*, but down it; the current, and a strong one too, was with us; the little stream did not flow into the broad river, but out of it. As we floated farther on we passed other small riachos branching from this one, they not feeding it, but all drawing away its waters. This seemed an entire reversion of the ordinary course of things, but on a little reflection we solved the problem. In this part of its course the Parana is thirty miles wide, and, as is its characteristic throughout, it flows through an intricate network of channels that divide its islands. The broad river in which the *Falcon* lay at anchor, two miles wide though it be, is but one of many, is not even the principal of these many branches. Innumerable riachos, like the one we were now descending, wind tortuously among the untrodden jungles that lie between it and the mighty parallel branch, the Parancito to the right, and the Rio Colastine to the left, joining them in unexplored water-labyrinths. This will give some idea of the magnitude of this stupendous Parana, with its myriad shifting isles drifting on to fill up channel here, swell promontory there, till they compel the waters to force out new passages through the great alluvial wilderness.

Lovely, indeed, were the shores we beheld as our canoe idly drifted on with the current, deeper and deeper into the secret haunts of carpincho, waterfowl, and tiger. On the banks was a vegetation of incredible luxuriance, not the jungle as of arid Santiago, but a growth full of sap, gigantic, drawn by warm suns from the dark soft mud—the richest soil in the world—never dry, but overflowed at short intervals by the fat and feeding waters of the Parana. Though satiated with tropical scenery, we could not but gaze with enthusiastic amazement at the beautiful nature around us this warm, still day. It was mid-winter, but of the season there were no signs, no decay, no brown leaf, no death ; the leaves and flowers were fresh and bright as of an English spring. Great white lilies, with broad dark leaves, floated on the water ; on the banks rose mighty reeds, aquatic plants, and trees of various foliage ; but that which made the wonder of the place was the mass of flowering creepers, lianes, convolvuli, and others, that overran all, covering the other vegetation like a great blanket thrown upon the country, climbing over the highest tree-tops, and then hanging over in festoons and curtains, forming the loveliest bowers and dark-shaded caverns of leaves and flowers, such as fairy gardener could alone contrive ; little sheltered houses with floors of soft brown earth, dwellings for the lucky carpinchos only, fitter to be summer palace of Titania herself, or Undine fresh from the warm river. We landed and wandered awhile in this glorious garden, wondering and enjoying the loveliness of it, and gathering beautiful orchids and flowers strange to us with as much delight as if we had been children once more, until animals that were good to eat came to look at us, when sentiment vanished, and the murderous instincts of the hunter took its place.

We spared the parrots, kingfishers, monkeys, and other innocent inhabitants of this paradise, who, judging from their fearlessness, knew little of cruel man, but shot several monte hens—pretty birds with russet wings, red legs, and green beaks,—a welcome addition to our larder. We also robbed a wild bee's nest, and caught a few pounds of a sort of small silver fish. We drifted on and on down this fascinating little stream that wished to bear us away who knows whither, and into what unknown wilds ? and were loth to turn ; but we had the current against us on our homeward journey, so reluctantly we took our oars, and rowed back to the broad river where the *Falcon* lay snugly at anchor, with the blue smoke issuing from the galley-chimney, to welcome us and remind us it was tea-time, and a most appetizing smell of grilled turkey's legs scenting the air around. Those were happy days we spent on the Parana, days that, when we recall them years hence, will doubtless bring sighs of regret for their vanished pleasures.

I have now related but one of our very many wanderings on these wild shores when becalmed. Tedious this journey was, but not a waste of time. Nothing in all my voyages delighted me so much as this river cruise, for here the traveller when he lands walks in perpetual excitement, is exploring the unknown, and cannot tell what new strange sight will present itself next, what wild beast he may not at any moment encounter.

There is a mystery and a loneliness that pervades the scenery of the Parana, that agreeably affects the imagination; a mystery—for are not its shores unexplored forests, its sources indefinite, in an unknown region that is still a sort of fairy-land of fable and romance, even as it was when the first Spaniards came and sought the Eldorado? a loneliness too—the towns on its banks are far apart, and there are no roads across the swamps and jungles that divide them.

For days of journey on this river the traveller sees no sign of human life on the shore, only interminable stretches of palm-groves and forests and morasses. So complete and irreclaimable a wilderness extends on the Chaco shore of the river, that it is only in certain spots, far apart, that the wild Indian himself can find a way to the bank from the inner forests to fish; the rank dense growth is altogether impass-able. It is the utter desert as far as man is concerned, intoler-able to him with mosquitoes and ague. If he penetrate it but a little way, awe seizes him to behold that gigantic net-work of plants that shuts him in as in a prison. In these dark depths one is oppressed by a feeling of suffocation, of restrained freedom, as in a nightmare.

The sublime Pampas, with its boundless horizon, impresses man with a sense of its immensity, an immensity of freedom; likewise does the solemn Chaco impress one, but with a different sense of immensity, as of an immense prison, a dark tangle of boughs that goes on for ever, and from which there is no escape.

On the 10th of June the rain fell heavily, but a fresh pampero was blowing, which continued for nearly three days, enabling us to make good progress up the river. All this time we were ascending reaches so broad and long, that always in one, often in many directions the horizon was of water, as on the ocean ; the water, too, was quite rough on these vast lake-like expanses, so that the little floating camelotes, now hove to (the wind being against the tide), rolled and pitched in the choppy waves, like ships at sea, their broad sails of lily-leaves being all taken aback and showing their light-coloured under-surfaces, while the stems, but slender masts, bent to the strong wind.

At last we saw far away on our starboard hand, on the hills of the mainland of the province of Entre Rios, divided from us by leagues of great islands and swamps, the massive cathedral of the ancient city of Parana, and on our port hand, beyond other wastes intersected by a thousand winding channels, the city of Santafé, the two old provincial capitals, nearly thirty miles apart, looking across at each other from the two banks of the mighty river.

It was but little beyond this that we entered the main branch of the Parana, which is the most eastward, skirting the mainland of Entre Rios ; so now we had on our starboard hand no longer swampy deserts, but the Barranca, as it is called, a precipitous range of forest-topped cliff that descends abruptly into the river, so that in many places no landing is possible.

We crossed the Banco de la Patientia—the Bank of Patience—a sandy accumulation that in one place fills up the broad bed of the Parana, and through which the narrow deep-water channel winds in sharp zigzags. A wind that is thus fair for one reach may be a head-wind in the next, and the river-craft are often delayed for weeks on this well-named shoal.

But our Jobian virtues were not to be tested here; our luck had changed since Rosario, for the wind was such as enabled us to lay right through the channel, though in some turns we were as close-hauled as was possible. The pilot kept his lead ever going as we skirted the shallows, and he shouted out his Arriva! Horsa ! and Bueno ! in the most rapid succession. No other sailing craft on the river could have crossed the Patientia with one wind, as we did ; and Don Juan was ever boasting of this great feat to every skipper and pilot he met during the voyage.

At midday of June the 12th the pampero died away, and

a calm, followed by a head-wind, detained us at anchor until the evening of the 16th. We lay close under the Barranca in twelve fathoms of water. This cliff was here of a sort of chrome-coloured earth, full of curious fossils, so we named a steep point below our anchorage Fossil Bluff. The summit of the Barranca was clothed with elephant grass, prickly pears, palmettos, aloes, tree-ferns, and other sub-tropical vegetation. There were no signs of man or his works anywhere on this mainland, but some wild horses approached the edge and gazed at us with evident curiosity.

We went on shore with our guns the morning after our arrival, shortly before daybreak. We beached our canoe at the entrance of a profound and beautiful ravine, or gully, that clove the Barranca. The fossil cliffs, fantastically shaped, overhung it on either side, a rich vegetation covering every irregularity in them that offered a holding-place for roots. Below, a little stream followed the windings of the ravine, losing itself in swamps and pools shaded by willow-groves and dense cane-brakes, the large white lily that is such a feature of the Parana scenery of course covering every sufficiently moist spot.

Arnaud and Jerdein went up to the higher land, where they shot some partridges, ducks, and pigeons. I went down into the swamp, to try my luck with the carpinchos, whose footprints were everywhere on the soft mud, and whose pig-like splashings and gruntings I heard among the canes. These animals are very shy of man, and it is difficult to approach them without giving notice to their keen senses, so I lay in ambush among some myrtles on a dry spot overlooking the cane-brake, and, with a charge of double zero in my gun, patiently waited for some unwary hog to pass.

As I sat here at sunrise, all the life of this solitude awakened around me. The songs of many birds began to break forth, some sweet of notes, some harsh, as if from little throats hoarse and sore from too much feeding on the hot acrid juices of the tropic berries. As I lay motionless the birds showed little fear of me, considering me a harmless sort of animal; they perched and sang on the bushes close to me. There were funny little paroquets—very gossipy,—staid little grey owls, with big round hazel eyes contemplating me solemnly, very musical canaries, and others. It was amusing to watch their pretty antics in this free aviary.

There was one little bright-plumaged fellow, with an impudent orange and pink beak, and cocked-up tail, that was perched on a twig within two yards of me, on one leg, still asleep, not the " early bird " this, but a little sluggard.

Of a sudden rang forth an ominous sound, high up in the sky—ka-waak, ka-wa-a-k—a long-drawn, melancholy, hungry cry that the little birds knew but too well. There was for a moment a fluttering, a frightened chattering, and a trembling among the tiny people, and then there was a dead silence where a few seconds back was so much joyous song. The little sleepy fellow woke with a start, gave a little shrill scream, and nearly fell into my lap with terror. Ka-wa-a-k, ka-wa-a-k. It was a huge cha-ha, or turkey-buzzard, slowly soaring above. The birds of prey had arisen, and were looking out for their breakfasts among the other " early birds." Ugly coranchos—the vultures of South America,— kites, eagles, and hawks now crossed the sky over us at intervals. All the bird world was awake. The kingfishers, storks, ibis, and other so numerous fish-eating birds of this region were hunting in the inky slough in front of me, and when one hooked up some fine prize there would be a regular fight over it between three or four of them, accompanied by angry yells.

The ants and the beetles had also now turned out of bed. I was surrounded everywhere by a teeming animal life that was most interesting to watch, and was being lulled into a sleepy reverie, when suddenly there was a crackling of bush, a loud grunt, and there, some twenty yards off, among the reeds, I beheld the dark form of the object of my patient waiting, a carpincho, and a very big one too.

I fired my charge of double zero into him, and quickly reloaded ; but, alas ! this beast is hard to kill. For a moment he was stupefied, the blood was pouring from his nostrils, he shook himself, and with a grunt of pain and rage plunged into the morass, and was far away before I could fire again. I tracked him some way by his blood, but at last came to a place where he had taken to the water, so was obliged to give up the search and return to the *Falcon* with empty hands.

I employed the afternoon in repairing our Berthon collapsible boat. This was rather an old one, and was pierced by several holes. When a Berthon boat is stove in, it has the advantage over other boats in not requiring a ship-carpenter to repair it. The best person to put it in serviceable condition again is a lady's maid. I took ours on shore, turned it upside down, and mended it very nicely with one of Arnaud's shirts.

While we were anchored in this place we caught many fish. We passed a stout line from our stern to the shore (about fifty yards), and hung it at intervals with lengths of copper wire, terminating in large-sized hooks baited with beef. We caught for the most part armados and patis, both excellent eating, and averaging about three pounds each. The monster dorados, however, that defied our attempts to catch them, bit many of the fish off our lines, leaving nothing of them but the heads.

The fish we caught were all very fierce, biting at everything they came across when landed on our deck, and barking like dogs. The finny inhabitants of the Parana seem to be all of a very ferocious disposition, and much inclined to bark and bite in this way. It is dangerous to bathe in the River Paraguay and Upper Parana, on account of a tiny fish that infests some parts of these rivers. If you jump overboard anywhere where these voracious little creatures are, a thousand or so will attack you, and simultaneously take a bite each out of you, so that you are worse than flayed, and leave the water one quarter inch thinner all over your body than when you went in, a most unpleasant way of Banting.

On the 16th of June the wind was northerly, but there were signs of a change of weather in the threatening sky. There is no country where the health and spirits of man are so dependent on the state of the weather as in the River Plate, and this is not difficult of explanation. This is said to be the most electric region in the world, and certainly nowhere else are the phenomena produced by electric disturbance more beautiful and terrible.

No one can reside here, even for a few months, and fail to observe one very general rule in the meteorological changes over this portion of the continent. For days, or for weeks even, the wind will blow from the north, and all this time the weather will become sultrier and sultrier, and more and more oppressive with the pent-up electricity, until at last, to the relief of all nature, there will be a crash of thunder and torrents of rain, and the cold hurricane of the pampero will sweep over the parched land, more or less violent, according to the previous duration of the north wind, and hence the greater or lesser intensity of that exceptional electric condition of the atmosphere.

For four days the norte had been blowing, and now, on the 16th, the weather became intolerably oppressive. The hot parching wind seemed to dry up the pores of the skin, and so enervated us all with its poisonous breath that we were too languid and uncomfortable even to eat our breakfasts, or row on shore, or undertake the slightest exertion. And thus was it, not only with us, but with all animal life. The shores of the river, ordinarily so noisy with the songs of birds and chirping of shrill cicalas, and a thousand mingling cries, were as silent now as if death had suddenly fallen on the land. All nature was in suspense.

In the afternoon the stifling sensation was more intense, the air was suffocating, and the wind entirely died away. The barometer fell rapidly, and at six in the evening a ruddy light came up in the south-west. The tension was about to be broken; the stillness was full of awe; then, with a hissing sound, the hurricane came rushing up the river with its accompaniment of plentiful rain, vivid lightning, and loud thunder. The sky assumed an extraordinary lurid colour that was reflected by all the landscape. What was the most remarkable was the instantaneous and violent change of temperature, and general sensation of relief. We were now shivering with cold before the bracing gale, and all our langour was dispelled in a moment.

When the first burst of the pampero, a terrific squall that lasted for about ten minutes, had subsided, we weighed our anchor, and scudded up merrily before the favouring wind, till some time after dark, when we came to an anchor under a promonotory of the Barranca, called Cerrito Point.

For several days after this we progressed but slowly, letting go and weighing anchor at short intervals, in consequence of the frequent calms, but occupying the many periods of enforced delay pleasantly enough with various sport on the ever-changing banks, though I am rather surprised that none of us ever caught fever after our long wadings under the hot sun among these poisonous swamps.

The skill of our pilot in guiding our vessel up the intricate channels of the Parana was marvellous. For fourteen hundred miles he knew every feature of the stream, where deep water was always to be found, and where the channel across the more shifting shoals was constantly changing from one side of the broad river to the other, and had to be discovered by his experienced eye from appearances that conveyed no intelligence to us.

Even with a vessel drawing two instead of nearly seven feet, a pilot would be necessary to ascend the Parana. No

ON THE PARANA.

stranger could find his way among this labyrinth of islands and branch streams; he would most probably take one of the false channels, as they are called, and find that he was ascending one of the many rivers of the Chaco instead of the main network of channels, being brought at last to a cognizance of his error by a flight of arrows from the bank, or a threatening band of naked spear-brandishing horsemen coming down upon his wood-parties.

CHAPTER XXI.

On the night of the 18th of June, as we lay at anchor under the bank, we heard the noise of a chain rattling through hawse-pipes, and on looking up found that a downward-bound schooner had come to an anchor close to us.

The captain and pilot happened to be friends of Don Juan, honest Genoese sailors, so they came on board of us for an hour or so, and a merry concert, as is the pleasant custom of the Parana on such occasions, was improvised. Most of these Genoese and Neapolitan mariners have rich voices, and know how to use them; all seem to have an inexhaustible *répertoire* in their heads of sea-songs, Venetian gondola chants, and operatic selections, so it is really very good fun to bring up when possible alongside one of these golettas.

Don Juan and the other pilot talked a good deal of shop in the Genoese dialect, as is the custom of their class; how, on one voyage, he sailed from Rosario to Corrientes in so many days; how, on another, he scraped such a bank, and so on.

The skipper of the schooner had a very nasty scar on his forehead. Don Juan, who knew the history of it, begged him to narrate it to us, which he did as follows:—

"Five years ago, having saved a considerable sum as captain of river vessels, I purchased a fine new schooner of one hundred tons, built of hard Paraguayan wood. My first voyage was to have been to Corrientes for a cargo of oranges. I left the Boca hopefully enough, being now for the first time owner as well as captain of my vessel. All went well till we had been about a month out; then, being becalmed, we brought up along the Chaco bank, not far above Goya. It was a hot and lazy day, all hands were below, or lying about the deck asleep, except the cook, who was preparing the dinner outside the galley. Of a sudden, as I was lying in my cabin, I heard such a terrible yell as I have never heard before or since. I rushed on deck, and there I saw a scene whose every detail seems to have been instantaneously photographed on the back of my eyes, and there to have remained ever since, for I have only to close my eyes to see it all again. The cook lay dead on his face, with an arrow in his back; there were about twenty Indians on deck, who had already killed four of my six men, probably even before they had awaked from their sleep. On seeing me, one struck me with his lance on the head, severely wounding, but luckily not stunning me. I leaped into our canoe, whose painter that moment became, I think miraculously, unfastened, and with a shower of arrows following me, drifted down with the tide. Not having a boat with which to follow me, they let me go. I then fainted away, and was picked up by a schooner later on. Other schooners reported having found my vessel at anchor. On boarding her the sailors beheld a horrid spectacle: my murdered crew lay naked on the deck, hacked in a thousand places, fearfully mutilated. The Indians had taken away all that could be of any use to them—the sails, fittings, and other property useless to them they had cut up or burnt, venting their rage on all they came across, as is their custom. So here I am once more, a poor river captain on another's vessel, with all my savings of years lost."

Such disasters have frequently happened to river craft that moor to the trees on the Chaco shore, and carelessly keep no proper watch; but the Indians are not alone responsible for these outrages. Outlaw gauchos, runaway criminals, and other renegade whites, find too easy an escape from justice by crossing the river to the Indian Chaco, where pursuit is quite impossible. These men are a hundred times more dangerous than the maligned Indian. By the superiority of race, they become caciques and leaders of the aboriginal tribes, and urge them on to the raids and piratical atrocities that are the terror of the frontiers and the river.

On the night of the 19th of June we came to an anchor off the little town of La Paz, which is built upon the Entre Rios barranca. Here, though 700 miles from its mouth, the river seems to preserve its volume undiminished. To a vessel anchored in the Parana near La Paz, the horizon both before and behind is a shoreless stretch of water.

On the morrow we went on shore, to lay in necessary stores—wine, meat at three-halfpence a pound, pumpkins, beans, &c. The river being flooded, the butcher's shop on the beach was under water, so we were able to row right inside it to buy our beef, which was highly convenient. We also purchased a quantity of coarse salt for purposes of barter, for this is a valuable commodity higher up the river, and the inhabitants are very glad to exchange eggs, cassava, and other produce, for a few handfuls of it.

As is usual after the prevalence of this wind for some days, the Pampero now gradually died away, the cloudy skies and bracing weather that accompany it disappeared, and we lay at anchor some fifteen miles above La Paz for several sultry, cloudless days, during which time light northerly winds alternated with calms.

We were anchored close to the Chaco shore, here covered with a fine forest; but the trees were joined together with such strong and close networks of lianas and other parasites, that to walk into the country, even with the aid of a machete wherewith to cut a way, was quite impossible.

We did manage, after considerable labour, to clear a small space alongside the *Falcon* with our hatchets and cutlasses, and on this we kept a tremendous fire burning during our stay, doing all our cooking on shore. As there was no game to be found hereabouts, we employed our time in cutting an abundance of fuel, sufficient for a month, and stowing it in our vessel. We also boiled down the feet of the ox we had bought at La Paz, and manufactured some excellent neat's-foot oil. Charcoal-burning was another of our experiments, and in this we were also highly successful. How much I would have enjoyed this Robinson Crusoe life on the edge of the virgin forest when I was a boy! The water was deep right up to the bank, and the *Falcon* was so close that we were able to jump off and on to the shore. Day after day passed without any change in the weather, and grumblings at our bad luck commenced once more to be heard. The impracticability of penetrating the forest prevented us from obtaining any sport, save a stray shot or two at a carpincho or lobo (fresh-water seal) as they swam by us, and we were anxious to progress to some more open country.

It was not until the 27th of June that the wild Pampero came up once more from the south-west. This strong gale drove us in a few hours into quite another and more tropical country. We hugged the Chaco shore, which soon assumed quite a different character. The land, no longer swampy, became slightly undulating, and the rich vegetation that covered it was not dense, but leaving open spaces and glades that afforded easy passage to man. Tall and graceful palms, the palmistes, and vicunas, were here in thousands bending to the strong breeze; numberless little streams traversed the country, running down beds of golden sands to the Parana. It was a lovely land, inhabited by tigers and other wild beasts alone, and untraversed save by the roving Indians, who often come down here to fish.

I went aloft, so as to command a more extended view over this charming country. It offered many varieties of landscape; forests of palm were succeeded by leagues of Pampa grass; then there were broad gleaming stretches of sand, and lakes swarming with duck—a land after an Indian's own heart, I should imagine. This Pampero had evidently blown us into a new climate, and a new vegetation; we noticed, too, that its breath was more mild and genial than it had been further down the river. Should the brave south-wester but last another twenty-four hours, we said, we would by that time reach the land of crocodiles and monkeys. It did not last twenty-four hours, but left us becalmed this evening off the mouth of the riacho that leads to the town of Esquina.

In the evening of the 28th, a light Pampero sprang up, which carried us some fourteen miles to the mouth of the riacho called Tala, on the Chaco side of the river.

The next day a regular gale was blowing from the south-west, so we joyfully prepared to get under weigh, anticipating a run of nearly 100 miles before nightfall. We had weighed our anchor, and were dropping out of the narrow mouth of the riacho before tide and wind under bare poles, when a sudden squall from another direction struck us, and in a moment drove our vessel beam-on to the shore. It was now seven o'clock, and for eight hours, until three in the afternoon, all hands were hard at work endeavouring to drag the vessel off again. It was of no use, she would not move, so firmly was her keel imbedded. We had our big anchor out on splendid holding-ground, but with every purchase at our command applied to the windlass, we could yet do nothing There was a downward-bound schooner at anchor close to us waiting for a fair wind. Now it is the good custom of the river craft always to assist each other under such circumstances as these, even though the one assisting loses considerable time by so doing. So the captain of this vessel, having first moved her further out in the river, put two anchors down, and then taking a very stout warp to our bows, set all his men to work on his capstan. These schooners are specially provided with capstans of immense power, in view of their taking the ground, as they invariably do more or less frequently on each voyage. But the good fellows laboured in vain: the warp stretched, and our timbers creaked with the strain; yet the *Falcon* would not budge. The only thing we could now do was to take our anchor out into the river again, and keep a constant strain upon the chain, whereby in time the vessel would eat a channel out for herself. It was horribly annoying, however, to lose all this valuable wind in this way. Our pilot nearly cried with rage, and stamped about the deck, frequently exclaiming, "If we had run on a bank under full canvas, I should not have minded so much, but under bare poles to stick so fast!"

By putting a watch-tackle on to our capstan-bar, we kept up a very considerable strain on our anchor, and by the afternoon the gale raised a sea that did more for us than all the labour of ourselves and the goletta's crew, with all the capstans and tackles put together. For now the vessel rolled about till she had so loosened her hold in the mud that we were enabled to drag her off a few inches at a time towards the deep water. At last it was only her stern that held her, so, hoisting our heavy canoe on to our bowsprit end, we made her rise aft, and then with a haul altogether on the watch-tackle, we floated her off. After these eight hours of constant hard work, we took three reefs in our main-sail, for the gale had increased rather than diminished in violence, and sailed a good eight knots an hour up the stream till nightfall; the Pampero following us with its usual accompaniments of heavy rain, thunder, and lightning.

The following day the same south-wester was blowing, but with moderate force, so that we were enabled to shake our reefs out and set the spinnaker. After sailing some twenty miles, we came to a portion of the river where navigation is attended with considerable difficulties. The bed of the Parana, here very broad, is filled with an accumulation of ever-shifting sands, just covered with water. The channel across this, which rarely has more than seven feet of water in it, winds considerably, and often changes its position. Our pilot had been informed by a brother *pratico* who had recently sailed down, that since the last crescente it was necessary to steer from a certain clump of trees, which is a well-known mark to another clump right opposite on the other bank. However, there was some mistake about the direction, for we ran hard upon the sands right in the middle of the river. We let all sail fall on deck, lowered the canoe from the davits, and lost no time in getting out an anchor, but it was not till after three hours of work as hard as that of the previous day, that we got off and continued our voyage. We anchored this night off the riacho of Caraguyta, which is not far from the town of Goya.

We were becalmed here throughout the whole of the 1st of July, so we're enabled to go on shore and explore the country awhile, which we now had not done for many days.

On our right hand was now the province of Corrientes, a land of palm forests, swamps, and many lakes and rivers.

On landing, we traversed a broad morass that lay between the river and a fine forest. We saw many alligators basking on the drier spots, but being only provided with shot-guns, could not kill any of them. On reaching the wood, we broke through the lianes and creepers, clambered over the fallen trees, and soon found ourselves surrounded by the veritable South American forest. No words can possibly convey any idea of the solemnity of these virgin wilds. The lower growth was of bamboo, wild coffee, dense lianes, and other plants, while above all, towered the ancient and gigantic trees that produce the most valuable hard cabinet-woods of export. We were in the haunt of beasts of prey and carrion. Storks, eagles, and foul vultures, flew over us with hoarse cries; parrots screamed, and hundreds of monkeys looked down on us with their human faces from the branches above. We saw many fresh footprints of tigers, and the lacerations on the trunks of trees showing where they had recently sharpened their claws.

While lying at anchor here we amused ourselves with some more exciting sport than usual. In the daytime we succeeded in catching some dorados, a fish we had long been trying to hook in vain, and in the night we organized a general tiger-hunting expedition.

I have already told how these dorados would bite other fish we caught off our hooks: now it was our turn. We happened to have some oranges on board, and these, the pilot declared, were the best possible bait for these voracious monsters. Acting in accordance with his instructions, we baited some large-sized hooks with half an orange each, bending them on stout copper wire trebled; even through this their sharp teeth would sometimes bite, and we would lose our hooks. In half an hour we caught one great big fellow, five feet long; we got him into the canoe. In his rage he bit the bulwark till his teeth nearly met in the stout wood. We passed a rope's end through his gills, and hauling him on deck, examined him at our leisure. The dorado may be described as a gigantic goldfish; his shape is that of the little creature familiar to us in bowls at home, and his colour is that of the outside of an orange, with a more reddish tint in places; his mouth is large and cruel, like that of a shark, and I do not doubt that a full-grown dorado could bite a man's arm off. We managed to catch three of these great fish this day, the smallest of which was three feet long. We cut them into strips, salted and sun-dried them, and found that their flesh was really most excellent eating. We lit a fire on shore, and extracted the oil out of one of these fish, which proved to be the very best material for preserving guns from rust I have ever tried.

We found a spot on the shore so thickly covered with the spoor and footprints of tigers, that it was evidently a favourite watering-place for these animals, and not only that, but a fishing-place also, for we saw the remains of dorados lying about. The jaguar is a great fisherman; he crouches in the dense undergrowth by the river bank, and deftly hooks up passing fish with his claw, somewhat in the manner of an English boy tickling trout.

To secure some of the beautiful skins of the South American tiger was a great ambition of ours, so we consulted how best to tempt the wild beasts to visit our neighbourhood this night. We had nothing but salt beef on board now, and as this might not be to the taste of the monarch of the forest, I set forth in the canoe up a riacho to kill some of the shag that abound on the Parana, or any other animals that might be suitable for tiger-bait.

I shot as many black shag as was needful, wounded a carpincho—a beast we never could secure, though we wasted much powder and ball on him, and was drifting back noiselessly with the oars on board, when I heard a sound on the bank close to me that made my heart suddenly beat some-what quicker.

It was a loud breathing or snoring of some evidently large animal. I guided my canoe to the opposite side of the riacho, here only about twelve feet broad, and quietly made it fast to the rushes. Then I loaded my rifle, which I had with me, and tried to make out who this gentleman enjoying his siesta might be. The jungle was so dense that this was impossible, and I thought it hardly prudent to force my way through and disturb his slumber. He might be of a choleric temper, and object. So not knowing what else to do, I fired straight at the point from whence the noise came, which could not have been much more than twenty feet from me, in the hopes of hitting him in some fatal spot. This may have been rather foolish, but I could not bring myself to go away without letting that conical bullet have its chance. The noise of the discharge, if nothing else, did disturb him, for it was followed by a howl of anger and surprise, and a sound of something crashing through the jungle. I forced my way through the canes to the spot where he had been lying. There was his bed, a large one, too, and still hot with his body, but I could see no blood or other signs about to show me that my shot had taken effect.

We cut open some shag, and hung them, together with some dorado-flesh, on the branch of a tree some three feet from the ground, and close to the watering-place I have mentioned. At sunset the forest resounded with a con-tinuous and awe-inspiring din, the chorus of wild beasts, terrible and exciting to one who hears it for the first time; the shriek of tiger and puma, the drum-like chatter of baboons, and strange and weird cries that we had never heard before.

Jerdein, Arnaud, and myself, settled ourselves comfortably among the branches of three separate trees, each armed with rifle, revolver, and knife. We were so disposed as to be able to converge our fire on any animal that should come near our bait.

We remained perfectly noiseless in our respective trees for three hours. Then, I imagine, we began to consider our position ridiculous, and our attempt at jaguar-catching a vain amusement, but no one liked to speak first and suggest this. The wild beasts seemed now to have turned in, except one,

who occasionally still disturbed the still night with a wild
sardonic laugh, full of insanity and cruelty, the most blood-
curdling cry of the forest, that no one would imagine to be
uttered by a bird ; yet so it was, for this was the screech of
the foul buzzard of South America.

Four hours passed away, and we still remained on our
perches, immobile and silent, when suddenly Arnaud sneezed.
The charm was broken : we burst into a simultaneous
Homeric peal of laughter, and, with no dissenting voice,
moved an adjournment on board the *Falcon*.

The tigers never came that night, for the bait hung un-
touched in the morning.   Had we possessed a *live* sheep or
other animal to tie up as bait, we might have had better
luck.

On the morrow the north wind was still blowing, so I was
enabled to visit a large island covered with trees that was
near our anchorage.

I found it to be densely overgrown with bamboos, mangoes, coffee, and venerable *Quebrachos Colorados*, of whose
hard red wood—so heavy that it sinks in the water like lead
—the river schooners are constructed.   Beautiful orchids or
air-plants in blossom hung from the trees like aerial gardens.
Of these we tore down some, and stuck them on our own
rigging, where they flowered and throve for some months, so
that the *Falcon* presented quite an æsthetic appearance.   On
the soft soil of this island were the fresh marks of tigers and
deer, but we did not come across the animals themselves.   If
we had only brought some dogs with us, I believe we should
have found some good sport among the larger game ; not to
have procured some at Buenos Ayres was a great oversight
on our part.

This morning's bag was composed of two turkeys, two
monkeys, some parrots, and an alligator or caiman.   The
turkeys and parrots were shot for the larder, the alligator
and monkeys for their skins, though alligators' tails are
esteemed as a delicacy in Paraguay, and a dish of young
monkeys is not to be despised by any one.

CHAPTER XXII.

On the 6th of July we came to a portion of the river where, for the first time, we saw both banks at the same time, the wilderness of El Chaco being on one side, the not less wild province of Corrientes on the other, no islands as usual intervening between us and one or other of the two mainlands. We beheld at last, after all these labyrinths of isles and channels, the whole volume of the Parana concentrated in one stream ; and a noble river it seemed here, of considerable depth, and I should say about two miles in breadth.

At nightfall we came to an anchor off a rancho of mud and bamboo on the Corrientes beach. It was the first sign of man we had seen since we were off the riacho of Esqina, ten days before. The owner of this house came forth when he heard our chain rattle out, and endeavoured to strike up a conversation with us. But we were sulky, and stood on our dignity at first, not responding heartily to his friendly overtures—for, if the truth be told, we felt very annoyed and aggrieved when we beheld this hut and its holder.

We had lately taken to looking on all these deserts and forests as our own happy hunting-grounds, and this fellow seemed to us an intruder on our solitude. He at any rate owed us a humble apology for having dared to build himself a house in the centre of our preserves, and just in front of our night's anchorage too.

But when he came off to us in a little canoe with a peace-offering of cassava, sweet potatoes, and eggs, and only wanted a little bag of coarse salt in exchange, we melted, and magnanimously forgave him.

We went on shore, and found that there were several ranchos behind his. Round one was a plantation of orange-trees covered with fine ripe fruit. Wishing to purchase some of these, we went up to the hut, and found there two women swinging lazily in grass hammocks, smoking huge cigars. We addressed them politely, but found they could not understand a word of Spanish, being only cognizant of the Indian dialect Guarani. However, our first acquaintance could speak a tongue that bore some distant relationship to Castilian, and acted as interpreter. The women drawled out in the soft vowels of the Indian language that we could have oranges at a dollar a thousand, but must gather them ourselves. As it was nearly our dinner-time, this we could not do, but informed them that we would willingly pay more if they would pluck them for us. This they declined to do; they were far too comfortable there in their soft hammocks, dreamily watching the wreaths of smoke as they rose from their mouths, to think of descending, were it for forty dollars. But a happy thought occurred to the inspired Jerdein, and he said, "Fair ladies, if you will but pluck for us 500 oranges, we will give a grand ball in this village to-night, at which we will hope to have the pleasure of seeing you."

When this was interpreted into Guarani, we could perceive by the expression of their faces that they were at last moved by our entreaties—the prospect of a ball excited them greatly; but they were not to be humbugged, so these indolent beauties (beauties by courtesy) would not get out of their hammocks till they had inquired into all the details of our entertainment. "But there is no music here," urged one. "O yes there is," explained the persuasive Jerdein. "There is a concertina, and a box full of dances; you turn a handle, and out they come," and he demonstrated in pantomime the action of a hurdy-gurdy. "There will also be gin," said our interpreter, "and tobacco," continued Jerdein. Before all these temptations the fair ones could not but yield, and they consented to pluck us our oranges on the understanding that —no oranges, no ball.

This little settlement is called Rincon de Sota, and the inhabitants of it are about as numerous as the letters of its name. The poverty of the place can be imagined when I state that it does not support either a commandante or a judge!

As we had progressed northward, we perceived that the population became more agricultural in its pursuits; thus these poor half-breeds of Rincon de Sota cultivated the ground around their bamboo huts with considerable care, producing cassava, potatoes, oranges, and maize—very unlike the shepherd aristocrats of the Pampas, who scorn to till the soil.

Of the dozen inhabitants of this little place, about nine were of the other sex; these, on hearing of the coming ball, became excited to a degree, and forthwith set out to wash themselves in the river, and otherwise adorn themselves in a rather public manner for the great event.

The ball was to be held in the rancho of our first friend, which was large and had a fine mud floor, admirably adapted for the purpose. At about nine in the evening we went on shore with the concertina, the barrel-organ, and three bottles of gin. We, too, were in ball-dress, that is, we wore top-boots, had sailors' guernseys on, handkerchiefs round our necks, and revolvers and knives at our backs. None other but ourselves wore boots. We left Jim to keep watch on deck with a musket during our absence, and Arthur, with a cutlass as big as himself, stood by our canoe on shore, for of course we could not know that our new friends were not of a piratical and brigand disposition; anyhow, this is a rough and dangerous part of the river, and it was as well to be prudent. But all went on well, and there was no grand finale of stabs and shots to mar the harmony of the evening.

Women as well as men smoked long Paraguayan cigars all the time they were dancing, as is the custom of this province, where the smallest child indulges freely in the strong green weeds, and where a baby crying in its mother's arms is soothed by having a plug of tobacco thrust into its mouth. Our host was an *Indio manso,* or tame Indian—a very ugly but sprightly old gentleman, who, becoming *medio obscuro,* as Don Juan euphemistically termed his condition, sat in a corner, with an expression of intense satisfaction on his leather features, clapped his hands, and exclaimed at intervals, " *Es muy superior! muy superior!* " He, at any rate, appreciated our efforts to amuse the population. His ugly squaw was highly pleased with a keepsake I presented to her, being an old wooden pipe. The barrel-organ, of course, was an object of great interest ; every one insisted on having his turn in revolving the handle, and the smiles of astonishment, pride, and delight that illumined those simple ugly faces when a real *bonâ fide* tune resulted from their efforts, were worth seeing.

It was not until the evening of the 12th of July, having been sixty-one days out from the Tigre, that we came to an anchor off the town of Bellavista. The aspect of the scenery around us at that moment was extraordinarily beautiful. We were between the sun and the moon ; on our left hand was the former setting gloriously behind the Chaco,

15

throwing over all that wild country a peculiar crimson glare; while to the left of us, over the Corrientes shore, hung the full moon, casting a silver light upon the white houses of the ancient city. Very remarkable was the contrast of colour between the two coasts under these circumstances, and apt to recall to one's mind the still sharper contrast in another respect between the two lands thus separated by the mighty river. On the one hand the Spanish settlements, the countries of the men that live in houses; civilization of a poor kind, but civilization all the same, and progressive. On the other hand barbarism, for there lay the vast Indian hunting-ground of El Gran Chaco, where the aborigines defy the white man, and wage perpetual war against him. For three centuries the two races have looked at each other across the broad Parana for upwards of a thousand miles of its course with the same irreconcilable hatred; and nothing so strikes a stranger when standing in the streets of such a town as Corrientes, with its tramways, its men in black coats and top-hats, and other outward signs of civilization, as to look across the gleaming Parana and remember that that fair country so near to him is yet the uncontested terri-tory of the savage, as much as it was before the Spanish keels first clove the waters of the River Plate.

We had to remain at Bellavista throughout the next day in consequence of a calm. This town, though the second of the province, is a wretched place, but beautifully situated on the summit of the Baranca, commanding an ex-tensive view over the Parana and its islands, and the Chaco beyond.

The river as seen from the Plaza is very majestic; even here, and far above this, it stretches in such broad, seemingly-shoreless expanses, that an explorer coming from overland upon its banks would easily imagine that he had reached some bay of the sea, were it not for the freshness of the water. Bellavista is embowered in a grove of oranges; each house is surrounded by a plantation of these dark-foliaged trees, now covered with golden fruit. No region in the world so abounds with oranges as do the province of Cor-rientes and the Republic of Paraguay. It is not worth the while of the people to gather them, save where the trees are in the vicinity of the river-bank for there it is easy to dispose of them to the Italian schooners that sail up the Parana at this season to take in cargoes of the fruit.

At Bellavista we were enabled to lay in a fresh supply of beef, salt, maté, wine, and vegetables. We also covered our decks with mountains of oranges, which we devoured from morning till night, to the horror of Don Juan, who told us we should all die of a horrible death if we committed these excesses. Said he, " It is the fever (chuchu) season now on the river ; nothing gives a man fever so soon as eating oranges."

But we would not be persuaded, being unable to see any connection between malaria and oranges, and we did not catch fever, whereas abstemious Don Juan did, though but mildly.

After leaving Bellavista, we sailed for two days, when the wind rather suddenly veered to the north, and we were obliged to anchor off the mouth of a large *riacho* that penetrated the Chaco. This change caused the thermometer to rise from 65° to 85° in the shade, within a few hours. In the canoe I ascended this riacho for some miles with Jerdein. A forest of fine trees, but impassable on account of the dense undergrowth, lined either bank. At last we came to an encampment of some twenty wild-looking half-breeds and tame Indians, who had two long canoes moored to the bank. They were occupied in cutting down bamboos for sale in Bellavista, where they are much used for building and other purposes. They were fairly armed with old-fashioned muskets, knives, and bollas, to defend themselves in case of attack by marauding Indians. Their wives and children were with them, and performed all the domestic duties of the little camp. When the dogs had been quieted with sundry kicks from their owners, and objurgations which I suppose were Indians' curses, we saluted each other, and entered into conversation. They told us there was an open savannah some three leagues up the riacho, where there was great plenty of game and wild beasts, but that by the bank between us and that, on a " campo muy rico," there was a tolderia or village of Tobas Indians, who were far from being friendly-disposed to the white man. One old fellow that was spokesman of the party was a professional tiger-hunter ; he had an ugly and many-scarred dog with him that was the hero of a hundred fights with the jaguar, and which he said he would not sell for five ounces of gold.

In the night of the 18th of July, a gale of wind sprang up from the south-west, and raised such high waves that we rolled about at anchor as if we had been lying in the Solent instead of on a river 1000 miles from the sea.

On the 19th the pampero was still blowing with such fury that we sailed under mizzen and fore-sail alone, going very fast even under that short canvas. There was quite a heavy sea running in places, so that we felt anxious, for to have run on a bank under these circumstances might have involved the total loss of the *Falcon.* Hereabouts, too, the bottom is not altogether composed of sand and soft mud, but blocks of tosca rise up at intervals ; this is a sort of natural concrete, nearly as hard as rock.

But the pilot was very careful, sounding every moment as we crossed the perilous shoals with often not more than half a foot of water under our keel ; we were continually turning and jibbing our sails, till at last we were greatly relieved by Don Juan saying, as he coiled his lead-line on the hatch, " All right now, we have three fathoms of water all the way from here to Corrientes." Before dark we came to an anchor off the city of Corrientes, the capital of the province of the same name.

This is a curious old place, rising from a shore of rough, lumpy tosca. Both beach and town have a slovenly, unkempt appearance ; the streets are of loose sand, with big stones and deep holes here and there, straight, lifeless streets fragrant with the many orange-trees, unlit by night, and then not over safe to promenade in, for the population of Corrientes has a lawless, murderous reputation.

Several campaniles of old Jesuit churches dominate the dilapidated-looking city, and there is a college, a really fine building, that would be worthy of a European university town. I was the pupils turning out from lecture, when I was here. They were of the age of English schoolboys, small boys, too, for the most part, but in their manners very different indeed from those at home. There was none of that boisterous, tumbling out of school—those irrepressible animal spirits that distinguish the British urchin—these sallow youngsters walked out staid and solemn, old men in all but years, each, even the smallest, puffing away at a gigantic native cigar.

On landing in our canoe on the tosca beach, we found ourselves in the midst of a crowd of half-naked women washing clothes and chattering, as is the manner of washer-women all over the world, very fast in the soft Guarani. A little higher up on the beach was an encampment of men, women, and children, whose barbaric costume and hideous faces betokened them to be Indians of the Chaco. They were Guacurus, a ferocious tribe, and spoke a harsh, guttural language, sounding very unpleasant after the tongue of the civilized Guaranis. These Guacurus had come over the river in a huge canoe which they had drawn up on the beach; they had brought firewood and skins of wild beasts to exchange for salt and other necessaries. They were of a very dark colour, with long coarse black hair hanging down their backs; some had tiger-skins, but most had merely filthy blankets wrapped round them. The women were, if possible, uglier than the men. The married women were distinguished from the maidens by large round patches of black or dark-blue paint under their eyes, giving each one the appearance of having received two very thorough black eyes at her husband's hands.

Corrientes is really more an Indian than a Spanish city, for not only do the savages from the Chaco often throng its streets, gazing with wonder at the gaudy blankets and cheap trinkets that are exhibited in the stores to attract them, but, as far as I could judge, quite three-quarters of the in-habitants are Guaranis, and speak that tongue.

Arnaud and myself were going off to the *Falcon* this same evening at about eleven o'clock. We stood on the beach and hailed her until we were hoarse. For upwards of half an hour we shouted, so that we woke most of the Indians camping round their fires. All the cocks in Corrientes commenced to crow, all the dogs to bark, and the police to yell challenges and answers to each other in different parts of the city, as is their custom, to show that they were awake and heard the disturbance, and, as is also their custom in a row, they took very good care not to come any-where near us. Though we had stirred up a din as of many revolutions, our sleepy crew would not wake; so, as there was no one else about, we applied to the Guacuru Indians for assistance. I gently poked one with a stick, whereon he rolled out of his blanket with a grunt. I tried to explain to him that we wished to go on board the *Falcon* in the canoe of his people, a huge craft that required at least four men to row it. He would not understand. Then I showed him a silver dollar, and he evinced signs of intelligence, and proceeded to wake up some of his fellows. But now a difficulty arose. The squaws and children were already awake and sitting up in their blankets, staring at us with their black, beady eyes, but it seemed that our friend was too gallant to ask the ladies to row us over, or perhaps too jealous to trust these questionable beauties with us. Anyhow, he insisted on trying to wake the men. But these sons of the tropic forest had, after completing their barter, invested most of their gain, as is their wont, in the fire-water of the white man, the insinuating square-face gin. Dead drunkenness is the only term that can express the condition of most of these noble savages. Our friend, who was comparatively sober, failing to awake the others, went up to the cacique, a huge ruffian, rolled up in a white blanket, and reclining his head on a half-empty bottle of gin as a pillow. He proceeded to stir up this great man with a ceremoniously and respectfully administered kick in the ear, as befitted his high station.

The savage, with his wild-beast instincts, fearful of danger in every sound, leapt to his feet in a moment, as if he had received an electric shock, with a sudden start and a horrible yell, as his right hand clutched his long knife. Having appeased him, our Indian tried to explain our wants, and put before his chief all the arguments in our favour : how many drams of gin could be purchased for a dollar, and so on. But the cacique was too far gone to understand anything, even gin ; so, after glaring savagely around with his blood-shot eyes, and muttering sundry guttural blood-curdling remarks in Guacuru, he fell down and relapsed into insensibility. Finding that we could not get a boat, we presented our friendly barbarian with a few cigars, and repaired to an almacen to beg a bed, having succeeded in awaking the savages, dogs, cocks, police, and citizens of Corrientes—all indeed save our sleepy boys.

I have already alluded to the many curious substitutes for coins that a South American store-keeper will give you in change, such as the vales or IOU's, tramway tickets, chopped up Bolivians, and so on. In Corrientes and all the Paraguayan towns you will receive in lieu of small change, as I found on paying my hotel bill the morning after our adventure with the Guacurus, boxes of matches, bundles of cigars, and drinks; very cumbersome, save perhaps the latter, which are a sufficiently portable currency; and yet have we not seen men totter even beneath the weight of these?

On going down to the beach, we walked over the prostrate forms of the still " drunk and incapable " Indians, whose lank, black locks were alone visible above their dirty blankets. The squaws, however, were awake, smoking cigars, and sadly contemplating their lords, who, in a night's spree, had thus wasted all that the women had earned by months of hard work, reserving nothing wherewith to buy the little household necessaries, such as salt to flavour the Sunday joint of alligator-tail, a blanket for the new baby, or tobacco for the old wife.

Our boy Arthur was an independent and mutinous young ruffian, who, like most of us, would not hearken to and profit by the experience of his elders. So it happened that, in consequence of neglecting the sage advice of Jerdein and myself, he received a rather practical lesson on the night after our arrival at Corrientes. Having obtained permission to stroll about the town for a few hours in the afternoon, he proceeded to dress himself out in the costume in which he most fancied himself, being the Sunday apparel of a North Sea fishing-boy : thick pilot coat, woollen stocking round the neck, and so on, more adapted to the Arctic regions than to latitude 26°. Thus accoutred, and with the biggest cigar he could procure in his mouth, he commenced to roll about Corrientes in the regular Jack-ashore style. To cut the story short, he broke his leave, and never returned all night. We went off in the canoe to look for him in the early morning, and there on the beach we beheld a miserable, half-naked object that we could not at first recognize as our gallant crew. He had nothing on but a pair of trousers. His face was swollen and bloated, and his teeth chattered with cold. We took him on board, where he explained, as well as he could, but vaguely, what had occurred. He said he had been drugged by some Spanish sailors in a public-house, then robbed of his coat, money, boots, hat, belt-knife, pipe, &c., and cast out in an insensible condition to pass the cold, dewy night upon the beach. He had been afraid to approach the Indian fires when he awoke, and so must have had a very uncomfortable time of it.

CHAPTER XXIII.

NORTHERLY winds detained us in Corrientes for several days, so we were enabled to see a good deal of the neighbourhood. One excursion we made is worthy of mention. This was to the Colonia Resistantia, a small settlement of Italian agriculturists in the Chaco opposite Corrientes, one of the few spots where the white man has established a footing in the Indian hunting-grounds beyond the river. Don Felice, a jovial store-keeper of Corrientes, who owns property in the Resistantia colony, invited us to go there with him; so one fine morning we embarked in a small, lateen-sailed boat that carries passengers across the Parana to the new settlement. We were very much over-crowded, there being twenty-six of us altogether. With the exception of ourselves, all were Italian colonists. There were several pretty girls among them, and two musicians to enliven our journey with guitar and flute.

The voyage was a stormy and even a perilous one, for the north wind blew hard. In the middle of the broad river a choppy sea was running, and the waves toppled over the sides into our deep-laden vessel in most alarming fashion. We were all soon drenched; the women shrieked and prayed, whereon Don Felice at the helm shouted to the musicians, "Toca la musica! toca la musica!" thinking with lively strains to soothe the terrified damsels; but, alas! the harpist and flutist, haggard and pale with sea-sickness, could not even talk, far less harmonize.

Then our admiral drew forth a bottle of rum, and ordered tots to be served round to all hands. This inspired the crew with greater confidence, and a pretty little Italian girl sitting next to me so far recovered as to wipe the tears from her eyes, draw forth her fan, and commence a little flirtation with the writer, which Don Felice noticing, he cried out, "Bravo!" and called public attention to the pluck of the

Donna Julia, holding her forth as an example to the rest, at which she blushed and simpered, not unbecomingly, behind her fan.

As a matter of fact we were not very far from foundering on several occasions during this voyage, but, baling out all the while, we managed to reach the other side of the broad, rough Parana, and entered the calm waters of a riacho that pierced the jungle of the Chaco. All these amiable Italians now recovered their spirits, and fanning, flirting, laughing, and music became once more the order of the day. After ascending the riacho, along whose banks basked many alligators (yacarés) for some miles, we came to the colony. We found quite a decent road traversing it, and seeing the tidiness, cleanliness, and signs of industry everywhere around us, we did not require to be told that this was not a native but a foreign colony.

The settlement consists of small farm-allotments, whereon a hard-working, handsome, cheerful race of Piedmontese, Tyrolese, and Lombards raise from a fertile soil nearly every produce of the temperate and sub-tropical zones. Round each pretty house is a flower-garden and a little plantation of potatoes, turnips, peas, a common sight at home, but a very rare, and therefore pleasing one in this republic. Beyond these are the fields of maize, plantations of cotton and sugar, groves of oranges and bananas, and the cleared pastures for the cattle. None of these pleasant people are rich, but all are in a comfortable position. They are sufficiently numerous to defy the Indians, and live contentedly and undisturbed, save for the impositions of a vile government.

On sailing back to Corrientes on the 25th of July, we found that the north wimd had freshened to a strong gale, so a shift to the southward within a few hours was more than probable. " *Norte duro pampero seguro* " is the proverb of the Parana pilots. This was one of those hot, electric days that accompany the termination of a northerly,—90° in the shade, 125° in the sun, a good temperature for midwinter ; but this had been an exceptional season for these latitudes, "*un anno de norte* " as Don Juan called it in disgust, and very unfavourable for the ascent of the Parana. " *Un anno de crescente*," too, it had proved, for the river was exceptionally high, and the larger game had retreated inland from the flooded shores of the Chaco. Hence the comparatively poor sport we had encountered. As a rule the river-banks swarm with deer, tigers, and other animals.

On the morning of the 26th of July there was a dead calm. It was terribly close and hot, a silence as of death hung over all nature, and man and beast lay listless and depressed in suspense beneath the incubus of the coming storm. Suddenly a dark mass of cloud rose rapidly from the southern horizon, and then the fierce pampero burst down upon us with great fury; its first blast was hot as of a furnace, being the dry air of the recoiling norte; but in an incredibly short time this had passed, and instead of an atmosphere of the Sahara when the simoon blows, we had above us the cloudy rainy sky of the autumnal equinox at home, and the cold, moist breath of the wind in our faces was exactly that of our bracing, blustering south-westers of old England. On no occasion have I experienced so very rapid and great a change in the climate as on this day.

Early this afternoon, having run at a great rate before the strong pampero, we reached the junction of the rivers Parana and Paraguay, and here leaving the former we proceeded to sail up the latter mighty stream, with the forests of the Republic of Paraguay on our right hand, and the Indian territory of El Chaco on our left.

At last, after a river voyage of seventy-four days, we found ourselves at the gate of that fair land of Paraguay, of which we had heard so strange things, and which we had so desired to see; the country of women, a very fairyland of romance, of which so little is known in Europe; a region the most favoured by nature under the sun; a beautiful, tropical garden, well watered by many lakes and rivers, and yet now the poorest and most unfortunate of states.

The history of Paraguay does not go far back, and yet it is one of the most remarkable in the world, and full of instruction to communists and other theorizers on the perfect social state.

Here remote from the sea, in an earthly paradise, dwelt a mild, kindly, but brave race, that of the Guarani Indians. To them in the commencement of the seventeenth century came the Jesuit fathers, who, notwithstanding the jealousy of the Spaniards, succeeded in founding here the most important of all their missionary establishments. Paraguay became an ecclesiastical commonwealth. The fathers taught the Indians the arts of peace—and war too, for no little fighting had to be done at times with savage Indians and San Paulist slave-hunters. The people held all their property in common, and were taught a blind obedience to their clerical rulers; they were kept in a state of perpetual pupillage, as mere children, not being allowed to acquire the art of writing or reading, and being compelled to speak the Guarani language alone. By these means the Jesuits thought to insure the perpetual submission of these docile savages, and to prevent the ingress of any new ideas from abroad.

Such was the education and such the dependent condition of this simple people for a century and a half. Then the Jesuits were expelled from South America, and anarchy and pestilence sadly thinned the Guarani population. Next that new spirit of revolution that had so shaken all the thrones of Europe crossed the seas, and the watchwords of political freedom were echoed from the Pampas to the Andes and even up to remote Paraguay. Not one of the Spanish-American races was in any way prepared for self-government, nor are they so to this day, but far less than all, poor Indian Paraguay. But little could these docile children of the good fathers understand these new theories about liberty— what did they want with liberty? Thus when all the states around them declared their independence from Spain, the Paraguayans did nothing, but wondered in their usual stupid way, and waited for something to turn up. Something did turn up in the shape of one Francia. Seizing the reins of government, this man constituted himself the first of the dictators or tyrants of Paraguay. His policy was similar to that of the Jesuits in many respects. Under his administration all foreigners were excluded from the country; if any wretched stranger did venture across the frontier, he was not permitted to return, and was most probably imprisoned for life. This exclusiveness was indeed if anything stricter than was that of Japan until recently.

To Francia succeeded Lopez I., who followed in the footsteps of his predecessor; and then came the infamous Lopez II., his son, who in his short reign succeeded in converting the once cultivated garden of Paraguay into what it now is, a jungle roamed over by tigers that have become man-eaters since their glut of human flesh in the late terrible war; a land of women and children, for nearly all the men were slain; whose population numbers but one-sixth of what it did but twenty years ago.

Lopez II. commenced by converting the so-called Republic of Paraguay into what may more appropriately be termed one huge slave estate of his own. He enforced the old laws prohibiting any native to leave the country, but encouraged foreign engineers and artificers to come to it, that they might be subservient to his ambitious schemes; though towards the latter end of his administratorship he was wont to imprison and otherwise ill-treat these on the slightest pretext.

The river Paraguay was closed to foreign bottoms; when an Italian schooner came up the Parana from Buenos Ayres, it was obliged to come to an anchor at the mouth of the Paraguay. The tyrant would then send an agent on board to inspect the cargo and offer a price for it. If this was accepted the goods were stored in the government magazines, and retailed to the people at a high profit. If Lopez and the skipper could not come to terms, the latter had to return to Buenos Ayres with his cargo, for he was not permitted to sell it to any private party. All the commerce of the country passed through the dictator's hands, who thus amassed an enormous fortune. If Lopez had contented himself with tyrannizing over the docile Guaranis, no one would have meddled with him; but in an evil hour for himself and Paraguay he visited Europe. At Paris he learnt all the vices of civilization and nothing more. There he took to himself a mistress, an English woman, another man's wife; clever, ambitious, and unscrupulous, she flattered the vain, ignorant savage, and led him to believe that he was destined to become the Napoleon of South America. He greedily drank the poison, returned to Paraguay, spent the whole revenue of the little country in preparing her for a gigantic struggle, and then set to work to conquer the southern continent.

Hence that five years' war, which only terminated twelve years back with the death of Lopez at the hands of a Brazilian lancer, one of the most terrible wars of history, between one plucky little Indian state and three such formidable allies as Brazil, the Argentine Republic, and Uruguay. Few know what those five years were; what suffering, what atrocities, what oceans of blood attended that literally war to the knife, and all to gratify the ambition of one madman, the half-breed Lopez. The Jesuit-taught, docile Guaranis followed him devotedly to the death, blindly, not loving him and yet not fearing, but with unreasoning, dog-like fidelity.

For five years the unequal contest was prolonged, until the Guaranis were nearly exterminated, and to this day there are nine women to one man. Towards the latter years of the war Lopez became little better than a dangerous madman, as was his prototype, Nero, before him. An insane suspicion of all, even his relations and dearest friends, possessed him. He was liable to sudden accessions of violent rage. He put to death all officers that were unsuccessful in battle, or who were unable to carry out his impracticable orders. It is said that he had a cage of wild beasts in his palace, to whom he threw his cousins or other people that annoyed him. He ordered his own mother and sisters to be publicly whipped for expostulating with him for executing some innocent relative. He put to death his bishop-brother, and the noblest of the land, in his jealous hatred of any that might be considered as equal to himself.

If any man was praised before him as being good or able, it was sufficient to arouse the tyrant's suspicion, and a death-warrant was issued. It seems almost impossible to imagine that this reign of terror was in the nineteenth century ; nay, but twelve short years back.

After the final defeat and death of Lopez, the allied armies occupied the country for a time, and it is but recently that the last Brazilian regiments have evacuated Concepçion and other towns. Such a tremendous war indemnity was demanded by the conquerors from the vanquished republic as will cripple her energies and render her perpetually bankrupt; for it is quite impossible that she will ever pay it, or her public loan, for the matter of that, which was fraudulently contracted for her in Europe, and of which poor Paraguay received so little.

At the present day matters are drifting along tranquilly enough in the desolate country. The form of government is as nearly as possible that of the neighbouring republics, and the rivers are as open to foreign vessels as the Thames itself.

Such is the history of Paraguay, the only South American

Republic that has no sea-board, and the only country in the world in which the conquerors have universally adopted the language of the conquered, for Guarani is still the spoken tongue, Spanish being only used by the upper classes, who are not very numerous; even the country priests can only speak the Indian dialect. But Spanish words are used for European luxuries and for numerals above five, for which there are no equivalents in Guarani, this not being a mathematically-minded race.

Paraguay is indeed a beautiful and voluptuous land; a tropical forest cloven by broad, fair rivers, with gardens fair as those of the Hesperides intervening between the places of denser-growth—a realm of lotus-eaters, where the worn mariner might well be tempted, like the followers of Ulysses, to wax weary of the "fields of barren foam," and cry,—

> " We will return no more; our island home
> Is far beyond the wave; we will no longer roam."

There are, indeed, certain men who have come here from Europe, and the lazy influence of the soft, beautiful climate has eaten into their souls, and they have stayed in the " land of streams," unwilling to return, settling on these gentle hills that slope to the broad Paraguay, amid groves of orange-trees, bananas, and papaws, with white-robed, silent Indian women serving them as slaves.

There is no useful product of the tropics that is not to be found in Paraguay : sugar, coffee, yerba, cassava, tobacco, cotton, and rice, all flourish on the fertile red soil. It is a land where there is an unbelievable profusion and variety of game of all sorts for the sportsman. For the explorer, too, there is on the Brazilian frontier, in latitude 24°, the half-fabulous cascade of La Guayra, where the whole volume of the Parana falls from a great height. The old Jesuits had visited it, and describe it as the most stupendous cataract in the world, even greater than Niagara. No white man has ever seen it in modern times. The Indians say that no man can dwell within thirty miles of the falls, for even at that distance the roar is so great as to produce complete deafness in time. Expeditions of whites have attempted to reach La Guayra, but have all failed, so dense is the under-growth of the forests through which they had to cut their way, so pestilential the swamps that have to be traversed.

Strange, indeed, are the tales that the Indians tell of some of these inner solitudes : of the gold, the jewels.   One is reminded, on hearing them, of the fairy tales of the Eldorado that first urged the old Spanish adventurers to their bold explorations.

The women of Paraguay, for so few are the men that of the fair sex alone is it worth while to say much, are not uncomely ; they have well-moulded limbs, voluptuous lustrous eyes, and are of every colour, from mahogany to the white and pink complexion of the fairest Anglo-Saxon.   The dress of a Paraguayan woman consists merely of a snow-white tunic, coming down to the knees, and a white shawl ; a much prettier costume than the dingy black robe of the Argentine.   These women are bare-footed, only the upper classes wearing boots.   " The shoed people " is the Guarani expression for the aristocracy.

This mild race lives principally on oranges, pumpkins, cassava, and other fruits and vegetables, being almost vegetarian, unlike the almost exclusively beef-eating and more ferocious Argentine of the Pampas.   There can be no doubt that the Guarani is one of the higher branches of the Indian family.   The Paraguayans are incontestably a hand- somer race than any of the half-breeds of the neighbouring republics.   I have seen in this land as perfectly beautiful women as in any part of the world, but, it must be confessed, they are the exception.

Many are the virtues of these poor, brave Paraguayans ; they are hospitable, kindly, honest, and though marriage is looked upon as an unnecessary prelude to two young people starting housekeeping together, they are remarkably constant in their attachments.   The Paraguayan girls are, like Byron's savage heroines, faithful unto death, soft as doves, but ready to give up their lives for their mates.   Fiery, passionate little creatures these, and woe to him who gives one cause for jealousy, for in love and hate they have the tiger in them —the fierce Indian blood that produced a Lopez throbs in the veins of these tropical Haidées.

In this land none see any shame in unlawful love.   Every country priest keeps his mistress, generally more than one, and this openly, without any attempt at concealment, every parsonage containing its harem and its nursery.   In a recent work on South America the Paraguayans are reported to excuse the errors of their clergy by saying that the Pope has, in compassion for the now unpopulated condition of poor Paraguay, been pleased to grant to the priests there, dispensation from their vows of chastity. This excuse is a very good one, but from all accounts this people were not famed for their morality even in the days before the war.

Not a few European travellers have visited Asunçion since the war, but none, I believe, have explored the interior of the country. Paraguay is indeed now, for the most part, an unknown country, even to its inhabitants; and yet there are few so charming regions for the traveller, be he sportsman or naturalist, or merely an admirer of what is grand and beautiful in nature. What more delightful than an expedition of a few friends in a properly-furnished and light canoe upon these glorious rivers and lakes, many of which have been hitherto undisturbed by the frailest bark-boat of the Indian ? At times the explorer will, to his amazement, suddenly come upon a stately stone ruin in the dense forest, overgrown and half-hidden with the rank creepers. It is the remains of a Christian church, marking the site of some old Jesuit mission, long since deserted to the tigers, all signs of the ancient clearings and maté plantations wiped away, for the rapid growth of tropical vegetation soon fills up the scars of man's handiwork.

CHAPTER XXIV.

As we entered the mouth of the river Paraguay, we saw before us an island that is called Cerito, on which, though we could perceive no houses, there were several white-clad damsels standing, who waved their hands to us and laughed musically as we sailed by, as if to welcome us to the land of women.

We noticed that the Paraguay was considerably narrower than the Parana, and that the vegetation had suddenly changed in character, being more tropical. Possibly this is due to the waters of the Paraguay being of a higher temperature than those of the Parana, for it flows from due north, straight from the burning regions of Central Brazil, whereas the latter river pursues a westerly course.

The navigation of the Paraguay is much easier than that

VIEW IN PARAGUAY.

16

of the Parana, notwithstanding that it winds like a cork-screw, but it is generally deep and unobstructed by sandbanks, while its current is much less rapid than that of the other stream. At nightfall, having sailed a great distance before the strong pampero, we came to an anchor along the Paraguayan shore, with a line from our bows to a palm-tree in the forest.

During the next day, July 27th, the south wind blew hard, so we accomplished another good day's work. We sailed between magnificent tropical forests, that even roused our enthusiasm, accustomed as we were to such scenes ; we passed occasional brakes of the most gigantic canes I have ever seen, stout as our own main-mast. Both banks were alive with parrots and monkeys, and the alligators lay basking in rows by the water edge, looking like so many stranded logs.

This night we anchored again under the Paraguayan shore. One of those terrible thunder-storms peculiar to these countries broke upon us, and lasted for several hours. We, too, became rather electric and stormy after tea, for we discussed the Irish question so warmly that we kept the poor pilot awake for more than half the night with our decla-mations, and effectually frightened all the monkeys away from that part of the forest.

The next morning the weather was damp and close, with a yellow fog hanging over the jungle, very suggestive of fever.

As there was no wind, we had to remain where we were, so I determined to set foot on the Paraguayan shore and see what manner of country it might be. Taking my Martini-Henry rifle with me, I landed, and found that beyond a morass and jungle of cane and bamboo that lined the river there extended a splendid wood of huge trees, from whose depths I could distinguish the cries of wild beasts, and over whose dark foliage flew multitudes of large green-and-gold-plumaged parrots. After penetrating this jungle, I found myself surrounded by that wonderful production of tropical nature—the virgin forest, with its tangled mass of intricate creepers and its monstrous growth of secular trees. The most thoughtless man is strangely awed and impressed by this gigantic and mysterious nature that appeals at once to his every sense. Like a cataract of sound ring out around him the manifold new and terrible noises of the solitude.

strident cries of rainbow-birds, the angry, hoarse shriek of
others, the fearful wails of various beasts, the shrill, ear-
piercing song of cicala, and at times a fearful crash in the
unseen depths of the woods as of thunder, that hushes all
that noisy life for a moment—it is the fall of some ancient
giant of the woods, a huge tree dead long ages ago, but only
now breaking its way through the dense growth around it to
the ground.   Most impressive is this teeming life, vegetable
and animal, but not human, for nature here is too great and
rank for man.   Here life springs up fierce and monstrous,
drawn up from the warm alluvial swamp by the all-com-
pelling sun of the tropics.   One can almost imagine that his
senses perceive — that he hears the tremendous flow of sap,
the intense generation, a growth so great and rapid that it
goes beyond death itself.   The great tree outstrips itself, and
while one half is green and full of life, the other is rotten
and dead ; strange creepers with metallic-lustred leaves
wreath round skeleton branches with their graceful festoons.
A life, reckless, profligate, despising death, familiar with and
embracing it on its way.   Out of leprous-looking tangles of
rotten trunks and leaves spring in horrible contrast the
ghoul-like plants feeding on decay, rich, rank, gaudy of
colour.   The tree endeavours to force its way for life to the
upper light and air above the dark smothering undergrowth
—so for sixty feet it puts out no leaves, but employs all its
strength to rise upwards to the open heavens, where at last
it sends forth branches to breathe the fresh winds, and feel
the bright sun.   Then the parasitic creeper from below
ascends the tree, fighting also for the light and air, and winds
round the trunk and branch till it chokes its helpmate and
they both die.   Among this vigorous life, death meets one
at every step.   Plant and animal prey on each other and live
by death.   The vulture awaits it on the tree-tops, the wild
beasts below crouching in the jungle, all are on their guard,
each preying on another, each fearing a greater.   The
habitant of temperate lands where life is less strong and
profligate, but more careful and provident, is awed by this
perpetual presence of death.   It is everywhere— pestilence
is in the air—the hectic berries are poisons—the rare savage
of these wilds knows not what security is, he creeps with
stealthy, fearsome steps through the confused growth, uncertain what next danger he will suddenly come upon, what

hideous reptile, what new death lurking among the brilliant flowers.

In these forests of Paraguay is to be found a wonderful variety of strange plants of every kind, and the *feræ*, unhunted by man, abound in incredible numbers. Besides the jaguars, pumas, and deer, are tapirs, bears, hogs, while among serpents the deadly rattlesnakes are unpleasantly common. Huge vampire-bats, too, flit about these wilds, and often prove worse than disagreeable to the traveller that camps out in the open.

Later in the day a light wind sprang up which enabled us to sail as far as Humaita, off which little town wo anchored, alongside a schooner whose main-mast had been struck by lightning in the last night's storm, and had broken off short a few feet above the deck. A drizzling rain was falling as we neared Humaita, and miserable the place looked.

We saw a congregation of a few low huts, not more than sixteen. But high above all soared a monument of misery— the ruins of a great church that must have been a grand building in its day, but is now a weird-looking wreck, having evidently been pounded to pieces by heavy cannon. It is wonderful that so much of it does remain, and that it was not entirely levelled, for this now dismantled fortress of Humaita was the chief stronghold of Lopez. For three years was fierce battle waged here, and the Brazilian gunboats in vain poured their heavy balls upon the devoted earthworks. For three days even after the evacuation of the place, when not one inhabitant was left in it, did the iron hail fall on the church and town, so fearful were the conquerors of landing among those wonderful men and women who fought so fiercely. The Brazilians made themselves pretty sure that not a Paraguayan was left among the ruins before they dared occupy the troublesome fortress.

Notwithstanding so prolonged a bombardment, the grand church still towers bravely over the huts of Humaita, for those old Jesuits built for all time, unlike our modern architects, and the stout walls could not fall utterly ; the tower, though riddled and torn, still stands a ghastly monument of the five years' war. It was here at Humaita that Lopez put his celebrated chain across the Paraguay to stop the Brazilian gun-boats. Here, too, he sank blocks of tosca in the river for the same object, which still impede the navigation.

When the water is low a plentiful harvest of cannon-balls, guns, and other weapons is to be gathered in the bed of the Paraguay, in front of the town. The population of Humaita consists, as far as I could see, of a crowd of women and girls, who live in ranchos scattered about the remains of the old pueblo. As soon as a vessel brings up off here, these flock down, twenty or thirty of them together, each with something to sell, eggs, cassava, sweet potatoes, and other produce. This afternoon it rained so hard that only two or three ventured forth. Ladies who possess but one garment in the world, and that a light one, and dwell in highly-ventilated bamboo-and-mud huts, naturally do not care to expose themselves under a tropical rain.

Here we heard that a revolution had broken out in the province of Corrientes, and that there had been a "little killing" at Esquina. This in no way surprised us, though but three days back when we were in Corrientes all was quiet, but revolutions break out very suddenly in these countries, especially when the north wind blows.

The captain of the port came off to us—a very pleasant fellow, who was delighted to see the first yacht that had ever sailed to Paraguay. He gave us strict injunctions not to anchor on the Chaco side of the river at night, between Humaita and Asunçion, as the Indians that come down the riachos to fish are of a very dangerous class, and wage perpetual war against the whites.

During the 29th of July we sailed by the solemn forests and cane-brakes that characterize this river, seeing as usual no sign of human beings on the banks, save one encampment of wild Indians on the Chaco shore at the sandy estuary of a little stream. These yelled discordantly at us as we passed. We observed that some of these Indians were employed in skinning what appeared to be a large serpent.

"It is an anaconda—a water-snake," said Don Juan; "there are many hereabouts."

He told us these monsters of the river often attained an immense size. He had seen the skin of one on a goletta that was twenty-four feet long and eight broad. I remember reading a translation of some old Jesuit's journal in Purchase's Pilgrims, in which the gigantic size of the anacondas of the Paraguay is alluded to.

At midday we came to a bend where a considerable river

joined the Paraguay.   This was the Vermejo, a stream that, rising in the highlands of Bolivia, flows by the city of Tarija, and thence winds for upwards of a thousand miles across the Indian Chaco to this point.   This great river has never been fully explored, for the dense forests on its banks are inhabited by ferocious Indians who nurse an undying hatred against the Spaniard, and, themselves unseen and safe in the trees, let fly their poisonous arrows against any rash whites that venture into their fastnesses.   The Vermejo is not more than fifty yards in breadth at its junction with the Paraguay, but higher up they say it is shallow and very wide.

Above the estuary of the Vermejo the river Paraguay flows with so little velocity that we found it possible in most places to beat up against wind and tide ; the shallow river-schooners, however, cannot do this

The next day being calm, we were forced to remain at anchor under the Paraguayan shore.   Across the river we beheld a very typical scene of the Chaco wilderness.   We saw four Indians come stealthily down to the bank, armed with long lances.   Then, lying down among the reeds, they gazed silently into the water till they saw some big fish pass by, when, with wonderful skill, they speared them one after the other and threw them on the bank.   Next they lit a fire, roasted the fish they had caught, and devoured them. This done, they picked up their weapons and crept back into the woods as noiselessly and stealthily as they had come.   The whole time—some three hours—that they were on the river-bank not one of these men spoke a word ; they gave the necessary directions to each other by slight inclinations of the head only.   As soon as they had gone, the kites and vultures that had been waiting patiently around came down and finished the remains of the fish.

In the canoe I ascended a beautiful stream in the Chaco this day, but the vegetation was too dense to allow a landing in any spot ; however, I succeeded in killing some duck and turkeys.

The business of the next day, the 31st of July, commenced with what the pilot called a "diversion."   Arthur and Jim, while preparing the morning coffee for their masters, fell out over some discussion on the Irish Question or Woman's Rights maybe, as the skipper and mate were wont to do. But from windy words the two lads came to blows, and created a din that awoke us all, whereupon Jerdein, who is not fond of having his slumbers disturbed, informed them that if they wanted to fight, they must do so on deck. As they seemed very anxious to have it out, they were marched up, and allowed to exhibit their pugilistic skill through a few rounds; then, their officers deciding that each had received a sufficient punishment, they were sent down again to their duties. The monotonous life, good food, and light work of the river cruise had made the boys wax over-plethoric and hence irritable. They were always wrangling, and this contest was necessary to clear the atmosphere. Arthur was the smallest but the pluckiest of the two. Jim the half-breed was the heaviest. Arthur got Jim's head in chancery, and then set-to to pummel it lustily, being quite unware of the toughness of the nigger's skull. Jim on this commenced to butt his adversary's stomach with the top of his head, as is the fashion of his race, much to Arthur's surprise and discomfiture. Jim was very anxious to discontinue the fight, though he was really getting the best of it, and amused us much by constantly calling out in his Creole-English, as he fought, "Artur! now you beat me or I beat you quick, for I in much hurry; I must go make captin's coffee."

The morning being calm, the pilot, myself, and Arthur, with his black eye, paddled some miles up a riacho, but shot nothing but a carpincho and a cayman, who both escaped.

In the afternoon the wind freshened, blowing right in our teeth, but we made good progress tacking against it. The water was deep right up to the banks, so we never went about until our rigging brushed against the palms and other tropic trees. The river was here literally covered with lilies, through which our vessel clove its way, tearing up and casting them away from either side of her stem like the unæsthetic yawl that she is. Towards evening we came to a rich and beautiful country, pretty farm houses were seen occasionally peeping through the oranges, palms, and guava bushes that lined the river bank. We were evidently approaching some large settlement, and soon on turning a palm-covered promontory we saw it before us, the picturesque Paraguayan town of Villa Pillar, one of the most considerable places in the Republic.

These townships of Paraguay present a much more pleasing

appearance than the dismal Argentine pueblos of the Pampas with their ugly, flat-roofed houses. The houses of Villa Pillar, for instance, have wooden verandahs in front of them, and sloping roofs of palms, looking something like Swiss cottages. As seen from the river this pretty settlement presents rather the appearance of a garden than a town, for the habitations are scattered, and nestle in groves of papaws, bananas, palms, and orange-trees.

On the morrow of our arrival I went on shore to do some necessary marketing, taking Jim with me, who carried a large sack on his shoulders, into which the provisions were thrown as soon as purchased. We traversed several silent, sandy streets that were strewn with the oranges that fell from the frequent trees; on looking round, my first impressions of a Paraguayan town were certainly of an agreeable nature.

Numerous women passed us, each clad in the snowy white robe of the country, bare-footed, and bearing something on her head, a jar of water, a pumpkin, a bundle of cigars. I have never seen a Paraguayan woman without some burden, be it only a box of matches thus placed; I do not think she considers herself dressed or decent without one. Every one of these fair damsels was smoking a long native cigar, also quite indispensable to the women of this race, the smallest female children of three years old that toddle at their mother's heels are inveterate devotees of " ye holy herbe," as old Purchase calls it. Few Paraguayans are really remarkable for the beauty of their features; but their figures, the modelling of their small hands and feet, are such as no other land can I believe show. They stalk through the streets with a soft, supple, panther-like tread, that is most beautiful, for they do not indulge in high-heeled boots and stays, but step out as Eve herself might have done, quite unimpeded by their simple dress, which is merely a short tunic tied round at the waist, and adorned with the pretty native lace. These tunics have short sleeves and very low necks, and reveal the statuesque shoulders and breasts rather more than would be considered delicate in Europe. Nearly all the Paraguayan women have large dark and fine eyes, and I think they know this.

What I particularly remarked was the jovial, gay nature of this amiable and innocent race, so unlike the sombre dignity of the Argentine character. These Paraguayan women seem to be always happy and laughing, and their kindness and good-nature towards each other is very discernible. The few men we met possessed the same jovial, kindly nature, but they are more indolent and selfish than the ever-sprightly women, who, being now so much in the majority, do all the work in the country, and pamper and support the nobler sex. Thus the men become considerably spoilt, and degenerate into lazy drones dependent on the generous fair, which cannot but prove sadly detrimental to the nobility of this once fine race.

We came to an open place backed by groves of oranges, and sloping to the broad river; in the middle of this was a fine market-place, a large covered building, such as I did not expect to find in Villa Pillar.

Here the white-robed houris vended meat, mandioka, sugar-canes, sweet potatoes, cigars, and the various coloured liqueurs for which this land of Paraguay is famous, and which the old Jesuits, I suppose, taught their children to distil from the oranges and canes; some of these liqueurs are flavoured with rose leaves and other flowers.

These market-women were all laughing and most good-naturedly importunate; how different again from the silent *china* market-girls of Cordoba that I have described further back! One would catch me by the coat, and try to stammer out in Spanish, persuasions to buy her goods, then the whole market would resound with shrill laughter at her failure in the foreign language: " Come and try my fine cigars, patron," or " See this fine mandioka," " How nice is this fat meat ! " about exhausted their knowledge of the Castilian, whereupon they would commence to jabber away in the soft Guarani. The way I was pestered by these fair damsels was very trying to a modest man like myself.

After I had completed my purchases and filled Jim's sack, my fair butcheress, a plump little woman whom I had selected from all the other butcheresses on account of her superior beauty, insisted on giving me the customary *japa* or parting gift of a glass of liqueur. On this all the other women in the market tried to make me take *japas* with them; I tasted a few green, blue, pink, and yellow compounds to their great delight, and departed to the sound of clapping hands and feminine laughter.

The market-place of Villa Pillar is certainly a most amusing sight for a stranger. I found that nearly all Paraguayan markets were conducted on the same merry principles. There is always an immense amount of joviality and good feeling between vendor and purchaser.

CHAPTER XXV.

On August 2nd we made good progress before a cold and moisture-charged southerly wind. Throughout the day we saw no signs of human life. In the evening we passed Villa Franca, once a flourishing town. We could only see one rancho on the beach. The pilot said he landed there two years back and found the population of this city consisted of two women. Thus have the banishment of the Jesuits and the wars of Lopez depopulated and ruined these once flourishing regions.

From the mouth of the Paraguay to Asuncion, nearly 300 miles, there are but two settlements now that are worthy even of the name of villages, Villa Pillar and Villeta. We passed by many deserted ranchos on the forest-clad banks. Our pilot once found a fine tiger-skin hanging up in one of these. It was difficult to say what had become of the inhabitants. The common explanation about here is that they were eaten by jaguars, for these beasts are very numerous in Paraguay, and have become man-eaters since the war; they are much bolder here than in most parts of America, even walking coolly into the streets of a town like Villeta occasionally, and taking off some child or woman.

This night we did not cast anchor, but made fast with a hawser to a palm on the Chaco shore, for there were many sunken trees about here which our anchor might have got foul of and so have been lost.

We were close to the sandy estuary of a little riacho, which the pilot said was much frequented by Indians. Further in, he told us, this stream opened out into a great deep-water lake, which he once explored in a Spanish schooner, that had sailed to the Chaco to take in a cargo of hard wood. He was no less than six days sailing round this inland sea, but found no timber, jungle alone on the banks. From the centre of it no land was visible on either side even from the top-mast of the vessel, so extensive was this sheet of water. It is not marked on any of the maps, but indeed the Chaco even close to the river banks is but little known. The pilots call this lake the Loguna Ojo.

No marauding Indians molested us this night, but we were kept awake some time by the roaring of many jaguars in the bush.

During our next day's voyage we were much astonished at seeing another very strange phenomenon in the Chaco, which also was unmarked in our maps. This was no less than an important fortified town. There on the edge of the Paraguay was a congregation of log-houses and stores, with the backwoods just behind them—no clearing having yet been made even of the immediate forest. There was a battery, too, facing the river, with half a dozen small brass guns on it, and the white tents indicating the encampment of a full battalion of troops. Off this settlement rode at anchor two gun-boats, and to our amazement we perceived that both fort and men-of-war flew the Argentine and not the Paraguayan flag.

All this was an exceeding puzzle to us, and also to our pilot, who had never seen this military establishment before.

" Why," he said, " when I was here last that was a settlement of Indians ; the tolderia of one of the greatest Caciques of the Chaco was on that spot."

It was not until we reached Asunçion that this mystery was solved. We were told that since the war the Argentine Republic as well as Paraguay laid a claim to this portion of the Chaco, and the former had thought proper about twenty months back to establish this fortified post as a menace, I suppose, to the Indian Republic. It is called Formosa, and will, I suppose, form the nucleus of a prosperous colony in time. At present it is merely a military post, and rations are served out to the civilians daily as to the troops. Thus vessels cannot easily victual here, as we found on our return voyage.

On the 4th of August we sailed a great distance before a fresh south wind. We passed Villa Mercedes, an important town with only one rancho that is not in ruins, and that

one is uninhabited.   Here also we saw the wreck of the old
military telegraph of Lopez that connected Asunçion with
Corrientes.

As it was possible to tack up the Paraguay, we were only
detained by calms during this part of the voyage, not by
head-winds.   We were detained by dead calm, or an in-
sufficiency of wind, during the 5th, 6th, and 7th of August.
Luckily, we were at anchor in an interesting portion of
the river, and were enabled to amuse ourselves with sport
and exploration, both on the Chaco and Paraguayan shores.

Arnaud, Don Juan, and myself in the canoe ascended a
broad stream that penetrated the Chaco.   On the way we
shot a lobo (river seal), and picked up a derelict Indian
canoe.   After paddling several miles up this river we found
that it opened out into a broad lake surrounded by fine
forest, and studded with many islands of lilies and other
aquatic plants, floating gardens, whose sole inhabitants were
gorgeous butterflies.

We circumnavigated the lake, but could nowhere discover
a landing-place, for the country seemed to be flooded for
leagues inland.   We paddled up between the great trees,
and the intricate lianes far up into the recesses of the forest.
The aspect of this wilderness was grand in the extreme.
In places the still water reflected beautifully the glorious
vegetation, the evergreens with their lilac and red flowers
and the towering palms.   In places the dense growth above
hid the sky, and we progressed slowly, winding among the
trunks of huge trees through the inky water, along caverns
of dark branches, above us the noise of the unseen parrots
and monkeys, and below the ugly roar of the crocodiles.
Then we burst out once more into an open glade of the
forest, glowing under the sunshine, where the spread of
water would be entirely covered with the Victoria Regia,
the queen of lilies, forming a fairer carpet than can be
imagined by any one that has not seen the wonders of these
lands.

We came to a certain large tree, with dark green leaves,
which Don Juan told us was always a favourite of the pavos.
He told us that he had never seen one of these trees on
which half a dozen or so of these birds were not perched.
The pavo, both in shape and in the cackling sound it makes,
is very similar to a large domestic fowl, but its plumage is

something like that of a partridge. It is excellent eating. Don Juan told us that the pavo was rather a wild bird, but if you succeeded in shooting one on a tree, none of the others would fly away, but remain to be quietly killed in detail. Likewise if one took flight and flew away, all the others would immediately follow, these birds possessing much family affection, and never separating in life or death. There were six pavos on this particular tree, so here was a good opportunity of discovering whether this bird is quite so idiotic as our *pratiquo* made out. We paddled up cautiously, and succeeded in bringing down the necessary first one, and true enough not one of the others moved, but they simply flapped their wings and looked around them in an uneasy and foolish manner, as if they thought something was not quite right, until we had secured the whole six, not a very much more sportsmanlike feat than firing into a poultry-yard might be; but great was the rejoicing on board when we produced this welcome addition to the larder, for salt meat had been our diet for some days.

I have often read of vessels being ice-bound, but never lily-bound; and yet this was our plight while we lay at anchor during these three days of calm. Camelotas, big and small, were floating down in thousands at this time. These got across our chains, and gradually accumulated, till we became the centre of one great island of beautiful lilies, in leaf, in flower, and fruit. Finding that these were causing us to drag our anchor, we left off hanging over the bows, "living up to the precious things;" and waxing unæsthetic, commenced to ruthlessly cut them away with cutlasses and hatchets, a long and tedious process; but we had no desire to be carried away to sea by our floating island, which would soon have taken charge and dragged us off, so big was it becoming.

We visited the Paraguayan shore of the river, which was hereabouts some forty feet high, far out of reach of the highest crescente, so on it we found once more the spinous underwood, the dull-hued thorns and cacti of a waterless land, like that we see in the province of Santiago del Estero, a great contrast to the rank and glorious vegetation of the opposite Chaco, with its often flooded alluvial soil.

The 8th of August was ushered in by a little excitement

in the shape of the ship on fire. A paraffin stove came to grief forward, and caused the mischief. There was a tremendous blaze, but we soon got it under, and little damage was done. This day we killed several patos reales, royal ducks, and I succeeded not only in killing but securing a crocodile. I sent a Martini-Henry bullet into one of his eyes as he lay on the bank. Even this did not immediately render the beast insensible, for he commenced to crawl into the river, but shoving the canoe up towards him, I managed to take a turn round him with the painter, and we hauled him on board. He then flapped about his huge tail in a way that threatened to break some of our logs and smash the canoe, but a few blows on the skull with a hatchet soon quieted him.

It occupied me a good afternoon to skin the monster, no over-pleasant work on a sandbank in the blazing sun, for nothing can be more nauseous than the rank smell of alligator flesh. This day our thermometer registered 87° in the shade, and this in midwinter. The mosquitoes were becoming insufferable, and were it not for the mosquito-nets we had brought with us, and under which we used to sleep on deck at night, travelling would have been quite impossible.

On the 10th of August, the south wind blew strong and enabled us to reach Asunçion, and complete our upward voyage. After sailing some hours we saw far off on the Paraguayan shore blue undulating mountains once more, pleasant after the level swamp and forests we had been among for the last three months.

We passed by the little town of Villeta. Here was the schooner *Aconcagua* lying along the bank, taking on board a cargo of oranges. Two gangways connected the vessel with the shore, along which coming and going were two streams of jabbering, laughing, white-robed girls, who brought down the golden fruit in large baskets on their heads, from the orange groves on the neighbouring hills, and poured them into the schooner's hold.

As we sailed on, the Paraguayan shore became more hilly, swelling up into great forest-clad domes, one behind the other to the purple mountains on the horizon far inland. From the very bank of the river rose one very remarkable sugar-loaf-shaped peak, covered with fine timber; this was the Cerro Lambaré, famous for the gallant defence of the Indian

Caique Lambaré against the Spaniards. The river hereabouts is still of great width, and to one looking from the deck of a vessel the horizon up and down the stream is generally of water, as if it were an estuary. In the afternoon we beheld before us what seemed to be a considerable city, with two Brazilian ironclads and many schooners at anchor off it. We were at last at our journey's end; after having ascended the great rivers for ninety-one days, we had reached the capital of Paraguay, which is distant by water upwards of 1300 miles from the Atlantic Ocean.

Wretched as is this city of Asunçion on nearer inspection, it presents an imposing appearance from the river; for on a little promontory that juts out slightly from the ruined quays, there towers a grand palace, a haughty structure that dominates all the mean streets; lower down, too, is a great building that is, or was, evidently the naval arsenal of an ambitious state.

But all else is squalid and in ruins, and on looking once more it is perceived that the palace is a mere wreck, with broken windows, gutted as by a fire, a mere empty shell within, and without, torn and pierced by many a shot, and that the ambitious-looking arsenal is deserted and falling also into ruins. For that glorious and massive palace, reminding one somewhat of the Tuileries, and now in the same pitiful condition as those imperial Tuileries actually are, is the palace of one who also assumed imperial honours—the would-be Emperor of South America, Lopez. This and that other ambitious ruin, the Arsenal, where the shot and shell and cannon were turned out, stand as relics of one of the most fearful tyrannies since Nero, one of the most annihilating wars since Carthage fell. It was from this palace that the tyrant swayed the mild Paraguayans with a rod of iron; and now it stands a monument of his despotism over the unfortunate city that he made desolate, and which, though twice as great in extent as Rosario, numbers but about 16,000 inhabitants, for half the houses are in ruins, and many others deserted and tenantless.

Such is the condition of the ancient capital of the great Viceroyalty of La Plata. It is a melancholy place, full of the wrecks of the ambitious schemes of Lopez, who certainly would have made a fine city of it in time. On the north side is a shallow bay that he intended to deepen and convert

into a port, a most useful design, but now this bay is entirely
covered with the beautiful Victoria Regia lilies, with leaves
so large that a child can walk upon them and be supported.
Out in the river opposite this bay the top-masts and yards of
a sunken ship are visible—another relic of the war, for the
stains of battle are not quickly washed out in this land.

On landing and exploring Asunçion, we were much struck
by the desolation that reigned everywhere. Few men were
visible in the streets, and these for the most part were
foreigners—the crews of the Brazilian gun-boats—Italian
storekeepers and others; but of barefooted, graceful-walking
women there were many. The streets are unpaved, and so
one sinks deep into the soft red sands, in which holes full of
water and running springs are frequent. In some places
banks of stones are built right across the road, so as to act as
dams, and prevent the sand washing away with the rain, and
leaving deep ravines behind; indeed, most of the more hilly
streets present the appearance of the profoundly-fissured beds
of mountain torrents.

In addition to the palace on the beach and the arsenal,
there are several other public monuments, constructed by the
late tyrant, rising in strange contrast to their mean surroundings. All of these are more or less in ruins. Everything
that Lopez planned was on the most ambitious scale, but was
never completed, for the war burst out in the midst of these
great works. There is a noble theatre, and a Pantheon
destined to be the last resting-place of a long line of empe-
rors. But no actors ever find their way to this impoverished
capital, and the house of Lopez fell even before its founder
was enabled to wear that imperial crown which he had com-
missioned a Parisian jeweller to construct for him.

There is an hotel too which we frequented occasionally,
the Hotel de Roma, a most pretentious building, though
somewhat dilapidated, a palace with its doors opening on an
unpaved street of sand and shards. Seeing its magnificence,
I knew that this, too, must be some other monument of
Lopez; on inquiry, I found that this was the case. This
palace had been built by him to serve as the residence of his
mother. Papaws, bananas, and palm-trees grow in quantities
about the town and somewhat relieve the monotony of its
red, silent streets. The native men of Asunçion seem an
indolent lot, and pass their whole life in smoking. They

wear white linen trousers, frequently scarlet ponchos, and are barefooted like the women. These latter, as they stalk by with their white robes and mantles, harmonize well with the ruined city around them. As they pass some unfinished, yet ruined temple of Lopez, with its Grecian architecture, the resemblance of these women in costume and walk and figure to the women of ancient Greece irresistibly strikes the traveller. Their white robes are worn in the same fashion, theirs is the same grace of movement; but they are always smoking cigars, and Grecian dames, I believe, did not resemble them in this.

A well-known writer has pointed out how much an interior at Asunçion resembles one at Pompeii in nearly every respect; there is the same central court-yard, with its fountains, galleries, and painted walls; and the girl who walks silently into the patio to present you with the maté and bombilla is the impersonation of the Pompeian slave-girl; while she waits for the empty bombilla, she stands before you motionless, with her bare white feet gleaming on the tesselated floor; her white robe is fastened up on one shoulder, revealing the opposite breast; her faultlessly-moulded arms are bare; they are dropped meekly in front of her, with the hands clasped. You could take her for some fair statue just stepped down from its niche. You return the bombilla, and with supple, silent tread she goes out without a word.

Asunçion is as much a city of the dead, and of memories only, as are the ruined cities of Greece and Rome; for all her palaces, though not two decades old, are deserted, grass-grown, and wrecked; all the civilization and commercial wealth that the Jesuits and the tyrants after them did, notwithstanding their faulty policy, create, are things of the past; and her brave manhood is no more—slaughtered in an unworthy cause, while women and a new and effeminate bastard youth alone represent the gallant race.

The only dissipation or excitement that this capital offers is its tramway. This is a very unique thing in the way of tramways. It runs but for a short distance, from a certain drinking-place on the beach to another drinking-place near the railway-station. Its only object seems to be to take people from one of these bars to the other. The trains run at such very long intervals, every two days, I believe, that

the carriage of railway passengers to and fro is the least of
its functions.   In the evening a band of three unmusical but
noisy musicians is stationed in the front part of the tram :
this attracts all the members of the *jeunesse dorée* of Asunçion,
who fill the car, and, silently smoking the while, travel backwards and forwards from the one public-house to the other, a
stoppage of ten minutes being allowed at each terminus for
refreshments—the Paraguayans, be it told, being the reverse
of teetotalers.   In an hour you can make about six passages
to and fro in this manner.   The first time I travelled on this
tramway I was much amused by an incident which is highly
characteristic of the way things are done in Asunçion.   The
manager of the tramway happened to be one of the passengers ;
on the car drawing up opposite the café near the station, this
gentleman dismounted, entered, and called for some potable
or other.   The waiter happened to be engaged in an interesting game of cards with the proprietor of the place, and did
not respond with proper waiter-like alacrity to the cry for
drinks, but continued dealing the cards, whereon the irate
tramway manager called out in a stentorian voice to the
patron, " Let that drink be brought me at once, and by, &c.,
&c, blank, blank ! if this ever happens again, I'll take up the
tram rails and lay them down up the other street to Don
Pedro's café, and ruin you."

When tramway travelling from bar to bar loses its excitement, no other form of amusement is left one to fall back
upon, save the public balls, which bear a strong resemblance
to the dignity balls of the West Indies.   Most of the streets
of Asunçion are altogether unlighted at night, and wherever
a lantern with its solitary light hangs outside a door, it
indicates that there is a public baile within.

CHAPTER XXVI.

THE *Falcon* lay at anchor a whole month off Asunçion before
we commenced our downward voyage.   During this time we
made many pleasant excursions into the interior of this
beautiful country, and saw a good deal of the manners and
customs of this simple people, but it will be sufficient to
describe but one or two of these expeditions in order to
convey some idea to my readers of what life in Paraguay is.

Like all others who visit Asunçion, we took train to Paraguari, which is the terminus of the line. Lopez intended this railway to connect the capital with Villa Rica, but only forty-two miles were laid down before the war broke out, so it remains half-finished and most dilapidated, like all other of the tyrant's works. The railway station at Asunçion is of course a most ambitious structure, with a splendid colonnade and frieze, like a Grecian temple, and might be as old as the Parthenon, judging from its wrecked appearance. It over-looks a great square, one of those wildernesses of red sands and weeds that characterize this city, and much add to its appearance of utter desolation.

The train leaves the capital at six a.m. every other morning; we found two first-class carriages, one of which we occupied; it was dirty and ragged, with no glass in one window, and no cushions—this had been the state carriage of Lopez, which he used when he travelled. There were open trucks attached to the train, in which, with bare legs dangling over the sides, were huddled up a chattering, laughing mass of women.

The railway traversès a lovely country, undulating and many-fountained—this Paraguay is indeed a land of running water.

There seemed to be a fairly large population, but chiefly of squatters, among these verdant hills. Pretty little *quintas* and huts, with long, sloping, thatched roofs, peeped out of the glorious groves of oranges and citrons in fruit and flower at the same time; the air was heavy with the perfume of these mingling with that of many flowers, and the ground was strewn everywhere with the golden fruit.

The little one-roomed houses nestled among the oranges, bananas, and papaws, each surrounded with its little planta-tion of cassava, and the women and plump naked children played or swung in their hammocks outside, in the indolent manner of their race, smoking of course. A land of unsur-passed fertility, whose happy inhabitants have, at any rate, always a sufficiency of food, and whose mild climate renders clothing not a necessary of life. Many tall palms rose above the orange-trees, and in places the hill-side was one mass of bright pink, with the blossom of that noble tree, the lapacho, a species of greenheart, whose hard wood is in request for ship-building. Above the more or less cultivated plains and lower slopes rose in the background great domed hills, clothed to the summits with virgin forests. On our left hand lay the extensive lake of Ypacaray, which the railway skirts for many leagues; beyond it is a dark range of mountains, the Cordillera, much infested by tigers, but at whose base a German colony has recently been established.

At each station that we stopped at, was a curious crowd of women who vended fruit, cakes, bits of pork, lace, and what not, to the passengers. The remarkable tidiness and cleanliness of these Guarani women, not only in their persons, but also in the manner they prepare these refreshments for sale, is also very worthy of remark. I believe the Paraguayans are the cleanest people in the world, as well as the most good-tempered. It was very cheerful to see the happy, innocent ways of the childlike little women at the railway stations; we bought some oranges of one, whereon she insisted on decorating us all with flowers in her gratitude.

At last we reached the station of Paraguari. In front of us were two isolated mountains, between which a strong wind nearly always sweeps. The little town is on an eminence, and, like all these old mission villages, consists of one grass grown square, a dead-and-alive place, silent and strange, that commands a wonderful view over a great plain of pasture and waving palms, traversed by silver streams, that stretches to a far range of blue mountains.

On this railway there is a little settlement called Aregua, to which we paid rather an interesting visit that is worth recording. We were accompanied by an Englishman who knew the géfe or chief man of the place, so we determined to give a *baile* to the population, a very good way indeed of acquiring knowledge of the manners and customs of this people. Accordingly, we left Asunçion one morning by the usual six a.m. train, taking with us a couple of demijohns of wine and some beer for the proposed entertainment.

At the station of Leuki we stopped for some minutes, so we purchased from the crowd of women that always awaits the train here some provisions for ourselves, bits of pork and roast parrots laid out on plates with snowy napkins on them, oranges, bananas, and a sufficiency of chipa, or Paraguayan bread, which is very excellent and is made of mandioka flour and eggs.

The station of Aregua is some little distance from the town, which is on a height above it; so we placed our provisions on the heads of some dozen laughing women, who serve as porteresses in this land of Amazons, and proceeded in procession up a steep grassy hill.

We found Aregua to be a very typical old mission settlement, and beautifully situated, as are all towns founded by the clever Jesuits. It is built on a sort of terrace in the mountain; behind rise steep domes clothed with forests and groves of citron and orange; in front of it the land falls down in a grassy slope to the cultivated plain that the railway crosses, beyond which stretches the broad lake of Ypacaray, backed by the dark Cordilleras—an extensive and magnificent view. And the town is so laid out that from every house this fair prospect can be commanded; for it is built in a square, of which the houses fill three sides, the fourth, that opening on the lake, being left open. The houses are all similar, white-washed and containing two rooms each, one looking on the square, the other on to a little garden behind. The doors of all the houses open out on to a common verandah or colonnade that is carried right round the three sides of the square, and which is paved with the strange, pentagonal, basaltic stones that are found in the Cerro of Aregua, a steep peak that towers above the settlement. The centre of the square, like the slope in front of it, is grass-grown, common pasture for the animals of the townsfolk.

In the lovely evenings of this country the gossips are wont to sit out on this verandah to talk, smoke, and enjoy the fresh breeze that comes over the lake.

There is a church that looks like a barn in the middle of the square, and some way off an erection like a guillotine or some instrument of torture, and indeed it is the latter, for this skeleton scaffolding is no less than the belfry, and at short intervals during the day it is customary for two naked boys to scramble therein and ring the bells in most energetic style. After walking round this square, we found that the population of Aregua may roughly be described as two storekeepers, the géfe, the parson, the carpenter, and many women, who occupy their time for the most part in making cigars and lace.

On calling on the géfe, we found him to be a lively, friendly little man, who at once gave orders that a spare house in the square should be hung with hammocks for our reception.

When he heard that we proposed to give a ball, he rejoiced much, and took it upon himself to prepare all the preliminaries. He ordered the largest room in the village to be emptied and to be laid down with the most luxurious carpet that could be found in Aregua; for in this land carpets are laid down, not taken up, in view of a ball, and indeed a carpet is preferable to a mud floor, especially for bare feet. I don't suppose there was another carpet in the town, and that this was kept for such occasions as the present.

Tallow-dips and petroleum-lamps were hung about in the ball-room, and the portion of the verandah opposite it was rendered gay with half a dozen Chinese lanterns. At eight p.m. several crackers were let off outside, for this is the Paraguayan mode of issuing invitations to a ball, and letting the guests know that all is ready. Then the aristocracy of the place poured into the room, with all their little finery about them, merry, determined to be pleased. A few of the women wore in their hair the national golden comb, but there are not many of these now in the poor country, for nearly all the native jewellery was melted down in the cruel war, the patriotic women giving up their ornaments to Lopez that he might mould them into cannon, as was literally done, many of the captured guns at the Parque of Buenos Ayres containing much gold in their composition.

Outside the ball-room squatted many of the poorer women, with bottles of gin and bits of chipa before them, vending refreshments, for these poor creatures never omit a chance of earning a little money, generally to find its way into the pocket of some idle and worthless lover.

Our band of four musicians was really good, for this people is endowed with much musical taste, which was fostered by the Jesuits. The dancing was of course perfect of its kind. The Paraguayans dance even better than the Argentines— and the Palomita, one of their favourite measures, is very beautiful, and, I should say, would cause a furore if produced on the stage of our opera-house. All smoked. It was curious to see a girl and her partner puffing away at their long cigars across each other's shoulders while waltzing vigorously.

The géfe would not hear of our leaving Aregua this day, but insisted on our staying till the morrow—the great feast of the Santa Rosa during which, he said, "there will be great doings; you will not regret having waited with us, you will see."

We were introduced to the clergyman of this little flock, who was certainly one of the most remarkable members of his profession we had ever come across. The padre was a very stout and jovial man, of pure Guarani blood; no article of his attire, save, perhaps, the collar of his coat, betokened his sacred calling. He wore a very broad-brimmed straw hat, no boots, and was an exceedingly slovenly and unshaven old gentleman. He was certainly the very typical Paraguayan parson; he could only speak his own native Indian dialect, and knew nothing of Spanish, save the names for beer and a few other luxuries. He had been a brave soldier under Lopez, they say; for priests as well as women and children fought in that terrible war; but had degenerated into one of the most profligate, lazy, drunken old rascals it was possible to imagine. His head was very much too big for his body, as is not uncommon among this people, and was illumined by a perpetual smile. He had a parrot in the verandah outside his house, whom he had taught to imitate the sound of the weeping women at funerals, the mumbling of the Latin Church service—which the bird, I am sure, understood just as well as his owner,—and several indecencies and blasphemies. The way in which this reverend gentleman passes his life is somewhat as follows. He gets drunk regularly twice a day, and is on each occasion put into his hammock by the young women who dwell in his house, and who bear relations towards him which are of far from a doubtful character, to sleep off the effects of the caña; his children—for of these he has a nursery full—the meanwhile fanning him into a refreshing slumber.

Between these orgies, unless they have been too severe, he delivers mass at his church, but generally with a full stomach, and not fasting, as the canons order.

As he waddles off to church, he is always followed by fifty women or so, clad in white, and droning hymns in Guarani.

The mistress of the priest is one of the great ladies of Aregua, for this post is considered an honour in this queer, demoralized country.

The padre is great at raising collections, and combines with his pastorship the profession of usurer, for he advances

VIEW NEAR OLINDA: BEACHING A CATAMARAN.

sums to his parishioners that have good security to show at the moderate interest of sixty per cent.

Notwithstanding all his faults, and his gross ignorance about everything, he is loved, revered, and thought much of by these poor deluded people. I may state that in honour of our arrival he got very drunk, and publicly notified that he would be incapacitated from opening the church for mass during our stay.

August 30th was the feast of the Santa Rosa. This is in the River Plate an ill-omened day, fraught with storms and disaster; but in Paraguay it is always the occasion of much merry-making.

The géfe undertook to take us to a great festival and baile that was to take place some four leagues off. My readers will doubtless complain that all I have to describe of my Paraguayan experiences are the perpetual balls, and that I really saw nothing else of the customs and habits of the people. This may be true, but, be it remembered that dancing *is* the life of this race, the one object of existence to which all else is subservient: a woman will save penuriously for months that she may contribute to one of the great public balls, such as this one that I am about to describe.

It was arranged that we should travel with the aristocracy of Aregua in a trolly to the festival, and that each of us should take charge of a lady. My partner of the last ball, who gloried in the possession of boots and a golden comb, kindly honoured me by selecting me as her escort.

Early in the morning we Englishmen waited at the railway station for our companions. Soon we heard a tremendous din of bells on the hill, and beheld the whole population of Aregua flocking into the church. The service was of about three minutes' duration only—I don't suppose our padre was given to long sermons;—then all the people poured out again, and forthwith forming into procession descended the grassy hill towards us. It was a curious sight. First came the fat padre on his palfrey; then women, bearing aloft a little, gaily-dressed doll, the Santa Rosa; then all the white-robed women of Aregua, chanting a melancholy dirge, and lastly, the géfe, the carpenter, and others, who seemed to think themselves too important to mingle in a religious procession.

On reaching the railway all the people, save the few who were to travel by trolly, hurried off to the scene of the festival on foot; some bearing the image of the saint, the others carrying on their heads provisions of different kinds. They stalked out grandly along the line, a good-natured, laughing mob, bent upon pleasure.

The trolly was drawn up. First two cases of beer, our votive-offering, was placed on it; then we ascended, the four Englishmen, the géfe, the carpenter, the padre, who preferred travelling with us to leading the procession—being, as he himself confessed, more partial to beer than to Santa Rosa,—and seven ladies, one for each gallant to look after; and very pretty they appeared to be, as they sat there excited, happy, and laughing, with all their finery on and roses in their raven locks.

Our motive power consisted of two men, who pushed the crazy trolly along the ill-laid metals. The padre much pitied their labours, and was continually calling for a halt, that they might rest, and that he himself might indulge in another bottle of his favourite beer.

At last we reached a point on the railway that was the nearest to our destination, and the trolly was brought to. Here we found seven horses awaiting us, which the seven men mounted, each taking a fair one behind him. The ladies thought this great fun, though they were rather timid at first, and made many excuses in the soft Guarani that we could not in any way understand, but their pastor soon conquered their scruples, and himself leaping on a horse, took a buxom girl up behind him, and galloped on to show the way. After riding a few miles through the odorous groves of orange and citron, we came to an open place where there was a great white crowd, and a sound of music and merriment. There were here collected about 500 women and 100 men, all clad in white, save for the occasional scarlet ponchos that some of the men wore. Very few had boots. It was a happy, childish assembly; there were no quarrels, and none of the men seemed to carry knives behind them— very different, indeed, from the wild, murderous race-meetings of the gauchos of the Pampas. The revellers, indeed, bore far more resemblance to clean children at a school-treat in an English village than to anything else I can think of.

Here was a people well in harmony with its constant associations of perfect climate, birds and flowers and fruits —innocent and natural; and these are heroes, too, though they evidently know it not, too perfectly brave to be aware of the fact. The women are proud in a simple manner of their beauty and skill in the dance; the men seem to be proud of nothing; yet these are the enduring stolid men and women that in the war, as Surgeon Skinner tells us, bore amputations without cry or wince of pain, though no chloroform had been administered to them.

This was what may be termed a subscription picnic, for all here had contributed something towards it; each woman had brought on her head provisions of some kind, were it only a bowl of milk or a little mandioka, and all shared alike when the dinner was laid out at the long deal tables under the palm-trees.

Many a one of these clean and tidy women had nought in the world save the dress she wore—no house, no bed,—and yet supported some lazy lord on the profits of her lace-making. Perhaps she had toiled for months, in order to save enough for this festival of the Santa Rosa; for not only had she her own contributions to think of, but she must needs turn out her rascally lover on that day in a clean shirt, a new pair of pantaloons, and a pocket-full of silver Bolivians, to lay on his prize fighting-cock in the pit, for the Paraguayan is far from free from the usual South American passion for gambling. I believe that nine out of ten men at that festival were thus dependent on the industrious women who wash their clothes for them, cook their chipa, and give them all their little earnings.

The first thing we did on our arrival on the scene was to pay our respects to our host, an old gentleman who occupied a small house, and had the honour of sheltering within it the doll Santa Rosa during the feast.

We seven men and seven ladies, whose aristocratic and booted forms seemed to inspire the revellers with great respect, dismounted and crawled into the house, which was something like a big beehive, with a door not more than three feet high. We then found ourselves in a small, windowless room, at one corner of which was a little table on which stood the image of the saint with three lit candles before her, and around, many not untasteful decorations composed of flowers, native lace, and the feathers of gorgeous parrots and humming-birds.

Not much respect seemed to be paid to her saintship, for padre and all drank, smoked, and sang Bacchanal and other very secular songs in her presence—the latter not badly accompanied by the padre on his guitar.

We were glad to escape from the stifling atmosphere of this room to see the fun outside. The baile was being vigorously carried on under a large palmetto-thatched open shed, notwitstanding the intense heat. It had commenced as nine this morning, and would doubtless continue all through the sultry day, all night, all the morrow, and indeed till food and drink for this multitude fell short, when each merry girl would trudge back to her home to work like a slave, while the men slept until the next fiesta.

Besides the dancing, there were other amusements to attract the pleasure-seeker, such as scratch horse-racing, cock-fighting, and tilting at the ring at full gallop—a pretty pastime, at which some of the men were very skilful. The ring used is not much bigger than a wedding-ring, and the lance, a small wooden skewer, not much more than a foot long.

When it was time for the midday dinner, the people sat down at long deal tables to a very substantial repast. We aristocrats were forced to dine in the stifling room where the Santa Rosa was. Our meal was a luxurious one; chipa, roast parrots, and stewed iguana or lizard being but a few of the many delicacies that were spread before us.

The padre did not dine with us, as he had drunk himself into a state of imbecility, as is his wont on every such occasion. The women of the place had tucked his fat carcase into a hammock, and were engaged in fanning his apoplectic-looking visage. Women in all lands show much affection for the ministers of the Church, but the devotion of the Paraguayan women towards their pastors altogether outdoes anything in the way of curate-worship at home. It was very sad for us to observe what a lot these kindly girls made of that horrid old man.

While he thus lay drunk, a boy crawled through the door to ask for his blessing; whereon the priest swore softly, but horribly, and waved him off—" Not to-day, not to-day those farces," he said, " to-morrow ; to-day is the Santa Rosa, and

I am drunk—very drunk," and this in the very presence of the illuminated saint!

As is the custom of the country, our seven fair companions did not sit down with us to dinner, but stood by, serving us silently with all we wanted. When we had concluded our repast, the damsels sat down in their turn, while we stood behind them.

From time to time one of them would take up a delicate morsel on her fork, and hand it up to her cavalier to eat, a pretty little attention that is another custom of the country.

At six in the evening we rode away to the station, so as to catch our trains into Asunçion. The young ladies saw us off and presented us with flowers and sweetmeats to take with us ; then came the farewells, which brought tears into the eyes of these sympathetic daughters of the tropics, and the train started.

CHAPTER XXVII.

THERE was a race-meeting at Asunçion while we were there, an important one too—a sort of Paraguayan Derby ; but all seemed very unfamiliar to our eyes. Imagine a tropical moor with palm-trees and bananas scattered about it, and wastes of red sand here and there. The course was worn bare of vegetation by the feet of many horses, and was of soft earth, something like that of Rotten Row.

As is usual in South America, but two horses ran at a time, divided from each other by the partition that I have before described. As is also usual under the South American system of racing, there were about fifty false starts to a race, but no impatience was manifested by the quiet spectators. There was no grand-stand, no book-makers, no merriment, or debauch. Twenty white-draped women were squatting in a row with bottles of gin, dulces, or sweetmeats made of guava, prickly pear, and other fruits to vend. Very few of the people, and none of the jockeys, wore boots. There were many of the soldiers about, these too, non-commissioned officers as well as privates, bare-footed, as is the economical custom of this army. The uniform of the Paraguayan Tommy Atkins is not costly ; a cheap kepi, a coarse blue blouse, and white pantaloons complete his outfit.

As I watched the racing I noticed that there was a white man, far taller than any Paraguayan, and clad in the dress of an Argentine gaucho, who was watching me intently. At last he addressed me,—

"Do you feel inclined, sir, to back any of this here crowd as is going to run now?"

Surprised at hearing my native tongue spoken by a gaucho on a race-course in the centre of South America, I stared at him speechless for a moment, and soon recognized through the deep tan unmistakable Anglo-Saxon features.

"Well," I said, "I should not have taken you for a fellow-countryman!"

"No, I suppose not. I've been in this country some years now, and don't think I shall ever get out of it; it's too much trouble. One gets lazy-like up here; besides, my little woman there"—pointing to one of the vendors of gin and dulce—"is not a bad sort. I don't much care about leaving her."

As I evinced some curiosity to learn how he first came to the country, he continued,—

"It's not a long story. During the war I was a sailor on a British gun-boat lying off Montevideo, deserted, shipped on an Argentine man-o'-war, came up here to fight these poor devils, and somehow, between this and that, I never got back again. Here I am still."

The lazy lotus-eating spirit of the land had evidently, after all these years, completely possessed the man, and, like Ulysses' mariners, he had foresworn the stormy seas, and put out of his mind his far island-home and all that he held dear therein, succumbing to the soft dreamy influences that were ever around him in these regions of perpetual summer, where,

"Sooth to say,
"No living wight could work, ne cared even for play."

General Caballero, the president of this republic, on whom, as in duty-bound, we had paid our respects on our arrival, expressed a desire to visit the *Falcon*, the first yacht that had ever navigated Paraguayan waters. So one afternoon, after giving us due notice, he came off to us in the presidential barge with Don Jose Segundo Decoud, the Minister of Foreign Affairs, the Chilian minister, and others. The first magistrate of Paraguay is a fine-looking man with no Indian blood in his veins, indeed more like a good specimen of an

English squire than a Paraguayan. The expression of his
face is kindly, and no man in the country is more respected
and loved. This is the same Caballero who, as general under
Lopez, showed such high military qualities, and routed the
Brazilians in many a bloody battle. He is not a great diplo-
matist, but is the very man for Paraguay in the present day
—a plain, straightforward trooper without any of the wild
ambitions, or impossible political schemes of his predecessors.

Even the Brazilians like Caballero, though he thrashed
them so frequently and thoroughly, for he bears a character
for humanity, and has never been accused of committing the
fearful atrocities that disgraced nearly all the other generals
of the tyrant.

After enjoying ourselves very much for about a month in
the capital and the country round it, it was proposed that we
should up anchor and descend with the current to the distant ocean once again. But now a strange thing came to
pass. The crew of the *Falcon* had become enamoured of
soft, barbarous Paraguay. Jerdein, Arnaud, and even the
boys, were loth to leave the land, and declared their intention of deserting the *Falcon* when she reached Buenos
Ayres, and returning up the river. The boys had a rather
vague idea as to what profession they would take up, but
Jerdein and Arnaud talked a good deal about coffee and
tobacco-planting, and were exceedingly sanguine about their
prospects.

Such was the enervating effect of a month's dwelling
among the lotus-eaters. I felt the charm of the land myself;
but at the same time an impatience after old associations,
the civilization—dingy and ugly though it be—of old London
came upon me.

The European cannot long be a lotus-eater. There is an
unsatisfied, melancholy expression on the faces of most of
the English gentlemen that are settled in Paraguay and cannot get away. That dyspeptic recluse, immortalized by our
great poet, who, sad under dark English skies, hungered for
the soft savage

"Summer isles of Eden lying in dark-purple spheres of sea,"

was foolish only for a moment, and knew that—

"Better fifty years of Europe than a cycle of Cathay."

I do not believe that Paraguay is altogether the country to recommend a young Englishman with some capital to emigrate to. Land is cheap, it is true ; but labour is not easily procurable, and the distances to the nearest marts for any produce are immense.

On Sunday, the 11th of September, we bid adieu to our friends at Asunçion, weighed anchor, and proceeded under all canvas down the river before a dry and hot northerly wind that raised the temperature to 90° in the shade. Our upward journey had occupied ninety-one days, but we accomplished the downward voyage in twenty-two. The river-schooners, with their light draught, had nearly invariably out-sailed us against the stream, as I have explained farther back ; but now that the current was with us, our deep draught was in our favour, and not a single homeward-bounder could keep up with us, even when we were running free. When we had to tack we of course defeated the golettas still more easily. Had we chosen to sail by night as well as by day, I am confident that we would have made the fastest voyage on record down the Parana.

Just before we started we were visited by a strange scarecrow, a man, lean, and of starved appearance, clad in a ragged blouse and trousers ; his naked feet were sore, swollen, and full of chigos. He took off his old greasy cap, and commenced to address us, with a voice hoarse and indistinct from long exposure to the heavy night-dews, in very excellent French. He said he was a starving Frenchman. He wanted to get down to Buenos Ayres, where he might find employment. Would we give him a passage in our vessel ? He would work his way willingly. We consented to take the poor fellow with us as a deck-passenger. He certainly did work his passage with good-will, always trying to make work of some kind to do, when there was none very obvious at hand.

Washing was his great forte ; he would wash everything without waiting for orders, from the plates to the tiller. His nautical education had been neglected, but he tried his best to become a sailor during the voyage.

To look after the fore-sheet, when we went about, was his especial delight. The fierce, earnest way in which he would tackle it each time was very laudable. He evidently thought that the safety of the vessel entirely depended on his proper handling of this rope. He came to look upon it as an enemy to be bravely attacked, yet cautiously circumvented; but at first he used to charge it with the blind *élan* peculiar to his race, till he was brought to his senses by sundry hard knocks on the head from the heavy fore-sheet block, as it banged about backwards and forwards, while the vessel was coming into stays.

He explained that he was a lithographic workman, and had imprudently left Paris for Buenos Ayres, where he was told wages were high. At Buenos Ayres he discovered there was no room for him, and was advised to go to Asunçion, in which capital he found that there was still less demand for men of his trade, seeing that there is not a single lithographic establishment. His career had been rather a chequered one. He had fought for the commune in Paris, impressed, he said, against his will, and had received a severe bayonet-wound in the leg. He arrived at Buenos Ayres twenty months back, just in time for the last revolution there. Having no papers of nationality with him to prove that he was a Frenchman, he was again impressed, and forced to fight against his will, this time receiving a rifle-ball in the head as a trophy. In Paraguay, being unable to find work, he had lived on oranges in the woods, a not very fattening diet, though the Paraguayan troops often fought for weeks on no other food than this.

We had three other passengers as far as Villeta, friends of ours, who had been invited as well as ourselves to a baile at that town, given in our honour by the captain of the port. These were a money-lender, an ex-minister of finance, and a merchant; for this is a democratic country, wherein presidents, usurers, publicans, and sinners seem to be all on much of a same footing, and associate together in a most natural way.

Current and strong wind both being with us, we reached Villeta in three hours, and came to an anchor off the little town. Like Aregua and many other of the old Jesuit settlements, it is built on the summit of a lofty, grassy down that slopes down to the water's edge; it consists of one square, three sides of which are of low houses connected by a deep verandah, the fourth, that looking towards the river, being open, with four ancient black wooden crosses of huge size planted at equal distances along it.

There was a steamer and several schooners lying along the shore, which were being loaded with oranges by a long stream of laughing white-draped girls. Mountains of the golden fruit lay on the bank, while lumbering bullock-waggons constantly brought down fresh supplies from the groves, a quaint scene very characteristic of Paraguay.

We landed, ascended the down, and found our host, Colonel Godoy, and a sumptuous repast awaiting us. This gentleman, now commandante of the port, and géfe of Viletta, is a very good type indeed of the Paraguayan man, such as there were many of before that war of annihilation. Not tall, but very broad and muscular, with a profusion of curly black hair, bright black eyes, and a broad mouth that is ever opening to smile and laugh, revealing two rows of large white teeth, he presents a remarkable and pleasing exterior. But beneath the joviality that he shares with all his race, it is easy to perceive that there lurks something of the savage, tigerish spirit, that is also in the Paraguayan blood, though it be but seldom awakened. Even Lopez was an amiable man enough, till he had tasted blood.

Señor Godoy is a well-known character; he was one of Lopez's most dashing and valiant colonels, and distinguished himself on many occasions during the sanguinary five years' war. He received in different actions no less than fifteen wounds, of which some were very severe. I may mention that the foreign surgeons that were attached to the Paraguayan forces state that not only did these men bear the most painful wounds and amputations with extraordinary stoicism, but that they recovered rapidly in cases that would have almost certainly proved fatal to Europeans. Of the negro troops of Brazil they report exactly the reverse.

One of the chief traits of the Paraguayan character, brought about by the long training of the Jesuits, is complete submission to any constituted authority, else how can we explain the unquestioning manner in which the decrees of the tyrant Lopez were obeyed? When he ordered every officer that proved unsuccessful in action to be shot, when he put to death so many of the best and noblest of the land, simply because they were such, there was no attempt at disobedience, no symptoms of rebellion displayed themselves. Thus Colonel Godoy, who was narrating some of his experiences to us, said, "When we were marching to X——, there were many women and children with us, weak, half-starving, who greatly impeded our progress; Lopez, hearing of this, enjoined me to cause every man, woman, or child, who could not keep up with the rest, to be shot. Thus in many cases my men had to shoot their own sick relatives: it was butcher's work; I did not like it; but we had received the order, and had of course to obey the chief."

But this evening the gallant colonel was employed in a manner more congenial to his kindly nature. After dinner he brought out his guitar, and, accompanying himself the while, sang to us in a fine deep voice the wild songs of the Guarani; Narancaros, or songs of the orange-gatherers, and war-songs breathing bitter contempt for the "Monkeys of Brazil."

When all was ready for the baile, the colonel ordered his bare-footed soldiers without to fire their muskets and let off crackers, as an invitation to the townsfolk. They were all prepared for this, and immediately responded to the summons; the women flocked in—the booted ladies and the unbooted maidens that had been hard at work loading the vessels with oranges all day mixing familiarly in very republican sisterhood. In this land equality is not merely a political watchword, but here alone it is possible, for all men and women are equally well-bred, all "gentle" in their manners—the ostentation and false pride of the patrician being as unknown as the coarse brutality and vulgarity of the plebeian.

When one wearied of dancing, it was pleasant to leave the stifling ball-room and walk awhile in the grass-grown square. The view from the four old crosses on the edge of the down was impressive. The broad river gleamed under a brilliant moon; beyond it stretched a long streak of flame, where savage Indians had fired the Chaco in a great ring, so as to hem in and destroy the tigers and wild beasts, whose skins formed their clothing. After a pyrotechnic display with some of the rockets and blue lights, from the *Falcon's* stores, the ball broke up. The colonel and his men stretched some hides out in the middle of the square, the usual bed-place of the tough veteran, and lay down to sleep on them, while we returned on board.

The spring was now advancing, and we found it uncomfortably hot in the cabin at night, so throughout the downward voyage all hands were wont to sleep on deck, of course under the mosquito-nets, for these pests were much more numerous than they had been during the upward journey.

Different insects now pestered us at different hours of the day, so we were able to divide our time very accurately according to their visitations. In the morning, when the sun had acquired an altitude of about twenty degrees, the mosquitoes retired; and then turned out in dense clouds annoying little winged insects that possessed long suckers, and left black spots behind, where their probes had entered the skin. In the afternoon these would be relieved by the equally troublesome sand-flies, who would bite vigorously until it was mosquito time again at sunset.

Before leaving Villeta on the morrow after the ball, I was button-holed in the regular ancient mariner style, by a venerable Genoese, with a glistening, fascinating eye, and a tangled mass of snowy hair.

Said he, " I have a disclosure to make unto you ; there is, I believe, gold ! gold ! gold ! unlimited gold ! " and he stretched out his arms as if to encircle a huge sack of the precious metal ; "gold ! and I know where it is ; come with me and get it. The Indians have told me—up the Pilcomayo —the sands are made of gold ; they have cooking-vessels now of gold that their civilized ancestors made. I have no money ; I cannot get a boat to go up the river and get all this gold. O misery ! misery ! all this gold, and I cannot get at it—and now," seizing me fiercely by the arm, and speaking slowly and distinctly ; " you are a milordo Ingleze, you have some gold ; buy a steam-launch ; take me, we will go together up the Rio Pilcomayo, and we will get it all. Gold ! do you hear ? gold. O ! holy Mary, gold ! "

I could not deliver myself from the clutches of this enthusiastic old man until I had promised to think the matter over ; but he shook his head sadly at my half-hearted manner as he let me go. " Gold, gold ! all that gold glittering in the sands for us—and you hesitate ! "

There was unmistakable madness in the glare of the man's eye ; and Don Juan explained that his fellow-countryman, commencing life as a sailor, had become a sea-captain, then an owner of many ships, and lastly had invested all his capital in lands and vast herds of cattle in this neighbourhood.

Now it happened about three years back that the Asun-çion newspaper accused an Italian of having murdered a certain woman in that town. An Italian forthwith proceeded to the newspaper office, and blew out the editor's brains with a revolver. The Italians, of whom there are many in Asunçion, took their countryman's part, and for eight days fought the government troops. At the head of this Italian revolution, as it was called, was my acquaintance of the snowy locks and the glistening eye. When the émeute was put down the government punished him by confiscating all his lands and cattle—utterly beggaring him. This calamity affected his brain, and now he roams about, an innocent but wild and weird old man, with a crazy head chock-full of visionary schemes; not, however, that the Pilcomayo gold scheme is necessarily such, for many of these tributaries of the Rio de la Plata wash down gold, though it is doubtful whether the exploration of this particular stream would prove profitable in that way.

On the 13th of September we again experienced one of those remarkable and sudden falls of the temperature that are such a feature of this climate. We had been sailing all day before a light north wind under a cloudless sky, the thermometer registering 93° in the shade, when suddenly the familiar haze of the dust-storm was seen rising on the southern horizon, and the quick gathering masses of cloud indicated the approach of the Pampero hurricane. We hastily lowered our main-sail, and shifted jibs. We were at this moment sailing close by the Paraguayan shore, and passing a lovely grove of lapachos and oranges glowing like fire under the lurid glare which the sun, shining through flying clouds of dust, cast upon all nature.

In this grove were some ranchos, the occupants of which, three women, with flowing white robes, draping but not concealing the beauty of their statuesque forms, on seeing us, came down to the river bank, and like the maiden of Longfellow's "Excelsior," called out to us in silvery voices, "Go no farther, come and anchor here, safe is this port; see the tempest comes." But, like Longfellow's youth, we were obdurate to the voices of these sirens, and, with reluctance, brushing the tears from our eyes, we shook our heads and shouted back "Excelsior!" or something to that effect, and sailed on towards the storm.

Of a sudden our sails were taken aback, and with terrific thunder, lightning, and rain, the pampero broke on us. From 93° the thermometer fell rapidly to 73°, which seemed quite cold to us. We tacked down the river against the gale until sunset, under mizzen and head canvas alone.

On the 14th of September we anchored for an hour off Formosa, the Argentine military settlement on the Chaco shore. We found here a village of log-huts, occupied by a battalion of troops, of whom many were employed in clearing the forest, digging drains, carpentering, tinkering, and so on. We were told that these were military prisoners, and received no pay for their work. In this case about a third of the battalion must have been prisoners at the time of our visit, a fact not much to be wondered at, for the Argentine soldiery is raised from the dregs of the populace. These men looked like the thorough scoundrels they were, but at the same time had a very hardy appearance, and indeed even hostile critics allow them to be splendid troops, brave, and enduring fatigue and hunger with the fortitude of the Indians themselves.

We had run short of salt meat, but found it impossible to purchase any at Formosa, for regular rations are served out daily to soldiers and civilians by the commissary, and he is forbidden to supply stores to passing schooners or other strangers.

CHAPTER XXVIII.

WE reached Villa Pillar on the 15th of September. We found at anchor off here two schooners, the *Rosa* and the *Fradalanza*—one laden with oranges, the other with hardwood. Don Juan was acquainted with the pilots of these craft, and after holding a consultation with them, advised us, though we might lose a few days by it, to await their departure on the morrow, and keep them company as far as Rosario, " for," he explained, " the Parana, they say, is now very low, and if we do run ashore going down the river, we shall be unable to get off again without the assistance of some other vessel."

Seeing the justice of his remarks, we acceded to his proposition. When the river is low, it is customary for vessels thus to sail in company; that one with the greatest draught and the best pilot leads the way; if she strikes, those behind immediately cast their anchors, and, passing hawsers to the leader, as a rule manage to haul her off. Again, when there is doubt about a channel, a boat is sent ahead to sound, and as one boat can do this for the whole fleet, much labour is thus saved.

On the 16th of September, at a signal from the admiral, the Anglo-Spano-Italian squadron got under weigh and proceeded down the river, in single file, with a space of about 150 yards between the vessels. I must explain that one of the schooners was Italian, the other Spanish. The former, which drew as much water as ourselves, was the flagship, and led the way.

We found that we had to keep the *Falcon* under easy canvas, so as not to outsail our consorts; we were invariably more than a match for either of them, whether in running, tacking, or drifting down stream in a calm.

On the 17th of September, a hot, cloudless, windless day, the fleet drifted out of the Paraguay into the Parana, and we bid adieu to the pleasant land of women.

And now we observed that the appearance of the Rio Parana had undergone a great change since we had ascended it some two months back. The waters had so much receded, that great banks of yellow sand stretched far out into the stream from the jungly shores, or formed long islands in its centre, between which in places were narrow, rapid channels, wherein was scarcely sufficient water to float our craft. And now all the animal life that had been driven by the flood into the inner fastnesses of the Chaco, had come down once more to the river banks, as we perceived from the cries of many tigers, pumas, and other beasts that made each night hideous as we lay at anchor under the shore.

On several occasions we managed to obtain some very good sport during this downward voyage, succeeded in killing some stags, but were unsuccessful in all our attempts to slay the crafty jaguar. The ducks, turkeys, and geese were as numerous as ever, and the alligators at the approach of spring had come out in much larger numbers, and lay basking on the hot sands in rows of twenties.

Our flagship ran ashore early in the day, but we soon hauled her off; later on both the *Rosa* and *Falcon* ran very one vessel or the other), and heard our friends Luigi, Juan, Pedro, Pancho, Andrea, Francisco, and the rest of them, not to forget our Admiral Bartolo, sing the sea-songs of Genoa, the gondola chants of Venice, Spanish and Guarani love songs, and the like. The company smoked largely, and a huge vessel of wine was handed round, which we held high above our heads, pouring the thin purple stream from the small orifice into our mouths as is the custom of the Italians.

Throughout the 22nd and 23rd of September we sailed without the occurrence of any mishap, on the latter day making no less than forty-five leagues, and passing La Paz.

On the 24th of September we passed Urquiza, and taking the Santa Fé channel, not the Parana channel, which we had pursued on our upward voyage, came to an anchor some two degrees below Diamante, in consequence of the flag-ship having run hard on a shoal. After prolonged labour, all the other vessels of the squadron lending assistance, it was found impossible to move her, and as the pilots discovered that the river was still falling, it was determined that we should desert our unfortunate admiral, for our stopping would not be of any use. Accordingly the word was given to up anchor and proceed. The admiral, as we heard afterwards, had to take two-thirds of his cargo out of his vessel before she would float, and was delayed nearly two weeks at this spot, which unfortunate occurrence more than ate up all the profits of his four months' voyage.

On Monday, the 26th of September, we reached Rosario. We found the thermometer was only 66° in the shade ; we had left the regions of perpetual summer, and the Buenos Ayres spring struck us as uncomfortably cold after the climate we had recently been enjoying.

After remaining two days at Rosario, we once more weighed anchor, first bidding farewell to our consorts, for the captains were trying to dispose of their cargoes in this port, and so save the tedious voyage to the Boca and back.

Overtaking and outsailing every vessel of whatsoever tonnage and rig that we encountered, we sailed by Zarate and Campana, entered once more the narrow channels of the Delta, whose willow and peach-clad banks were fresh and green in this glorious spring weather of the River Plate, passed by the pretty quintas of the market-gardeners, whence the Basque and Italian girls waved their kerchiefs to us as we went by ; and on the 2nd of October came to an anchor at our old berth in the Tigre, 143 days since we had sailed from it for our cruise up the great rivers.

And now it was that the old crew of the little *Falcon* was broken up, scattered in different directions, while I was left alone on board of her to ponder how I should proceed on the voyage. Jerdein and Arnaud, enamoured, as I have before said, of Paraguay, prepared to return to that soft climate.

Arthur, the boy, also refused to proceed on the voyage, and asked to be paid off. I accordingly gave him his discharge, arrears of pay, and certain words of good advice, in reference to the dangers of this rough seaport of Buenos Ayres, which I was fully aware he would utterly disregard.

Jim also refused to go to sea in the *Falcon*. He said she was too small for the ocean ; he preferred a bigger vessel.

But when it was known that I wanted men, no lack of volunteers presented themselves : three Spaniards from the Capitania of the Tigre offered to desert and join me, but I did not like the look of them, still less the appearance of the drunken, dirty, runaway English sailors, or rather sham sailors, that loafed on the beach of Buenos Ayres ; so I repaired to the Boca del Riachuelo, the cut-throat Italian and Greek colony that I have before described, but in which I knew I could find as many honest seamen as I required.

To pick up a decent British sailor in these foreign ports is very difficult, as British skippers know too well.

I wandered about the crowded quays and streets of the Boca, a seaport that reminded me of many an old Mediterranean harbour ; for, indeed, all its inhabitants and sailors are natives of the fair shores of that inland sea, and have brought their habits of life and style of architecture to the banks of this little South American river.

Don Juan, our late pilot, accompanied me in my search ; we entered the *cafés* that he knew to be the haunt of Genoese mariners, and after passing over several whose physiognomies were a trifle too cut-throat, we selected three likely-looking fellows.

As the *Falcon* required caulking and a general overhauling before she was fit for sea, I determined to sail her from the Tigre to the Boca, the latter being a very convenient place for fitting out a small vessel.

On the 10th of October my new crew came on board, and

as is the custom of Italian mariners, brought such mountains of luggage and bedding with them that it would have filled up all the cabins of the *Falcon,* so I was compelled to make them put three-quarters of it on shore again, much to their chagrin.   A British sailor generally ships with nothing but the clothes he stands in, in the way of *impedimenta;* but his Italian brother has a very old-clothesman mania for accumulating rags of all sorts.   He never throws away a coat or other garment, though it be so rent and worn that he cannot possibly wear it, but hoards up all, till after some years' service at sea he is the proud possessor of five or six huge canvas sacks of dirty shreds, which he carries with him wherever he goes, though they are not of the slightest use to him.

On sailing out of the River Tigre we found from the tide-metre on the San Fernando mole, that there were but six feet of water on the bar outside.   (The reader will remember that on entering the river we were aground on this bar a whole night during a gale.)   For five days of rain and wind we lay at anchor off the San Fernando, waiting for the rise of the water, the monotony being only broken by a clumsy Argentine man-of-war, or rather old-woman-of-war, that deliberately ran into us, doubled up our davits, carried away a main shroud, and would perhaps have sunk us, had we not promptly given our vessel more chain.   The lubberly officer who was in charge of this steamer, not contented with having inflicted this damage, proceeded to carry away the bowsprit of a schooner that was at anchor below us, and then while endeavouring to turn so as to enter the San Fernando Canal, ran the nose of his vessel with considerable force against the stone mole.

On the 16th of October a change of the wind caused the water to rise about a foot ; so weighing anchor, we safely crossed the shallows and scudded before heavy squalls of rain and wind down the coast, past the long quays of Buenos Ayres to the entrance of the river Riachuelo.

We found that the Boca was full of small craft that had run in from the inner roads for refuge from the bad weather, but we managed to squeeze our way through the crowd and pick up a convenient berth alongside the rickety wooden quay, between a German barque and an Italian orange-schooner.

And now from sunrise to sunset for many days there was

a constant bustle on board the *Falcon ;* caulking, painting, stowing provisions, rigging; in short, thoroughly preparing the vessel for her lengthy homeward cruise.

The Italians in the Boca took great interest in our proceedings, and there was always a little crowd watching us from the quay. Seeing that I had taken a crew of their own countrymen in preference to any others, these earringed and gay-sashed mariners took a pride in the little vessel, and showed us much sympathy.

Jerdein and all other Buenos Ayres friends expostulated with me on the madness of sailing with an Italian crew; my throat, they said, would certainly be cut by these notorious ruffians of the Boca. But I knew more about Italians than any of my friends, and had gained no slight experience of the ways of the population of all the Mediterranean coasts in several previous travels, so felt confident ; besides, the men that I had engaged were all well known in the Boca, and of highly respectable character.

It is true that a little contretemps occurred before the men had been three days on board that led to the discharge of one of them. While I was on shore for an hour or so, this fellow, who it seems was of a quarrelsome nature, refused to obey the orders of the man I had appointed mate, and, on being remonstrated with, or more probably sworn at, drew his knife and attempted to murder his officer, but his object was frustrated by a knock on the head with a capstan bar. On returning and hearing this story, I considered that the " bag and baggage " policy was the best adapted for the circumstances, and packed him off on the spot with his *impedimenta.*

Only once again did anything like this occur while these men served under me, and that also during my absence, for nothing could exceed the alacrity of their obedience and civility to myself.

When the *Falcon* was ready to sail, looking smart enough with her fresh paint and new main-sail, mizzen, and foresail, a ragged and miserable-looking object presented himself on board. The return of the prodigal boy, Arthur, had come to pass as I had anticipated. He had spent all his pay, sold all his clothes, and looked very dirty and thoroughly ashamed of himself. He now of course wished to re-ship on the *Falcon.* After putting before him the heinousness of his offence in deserting me at a pinch as he had done, and warning him as to the results of ever behaving in like manner again, I took him back, but killed no fatted calf for the reprobate; on the contrary, gave him no leave on shore, and plenty of hard work, to counteract the bad effects of his ten days' debauch, during which time he had been living on his accumulated arrears of pay at the rate of about 1000*l*. a year. We did not require him now on the *Falcon*, for I had engaged another man to take the murderously-inclined one's place, and I knew he would be ever quarrelling with the foreigners; but to leave the scapegrace at Buenos Ayres would have been to insure his speedy perdition, so I felt bound to take him away.

The crew of the *Falcon* now consisted of myself, captain; Pellegro Lavagna, mate; Paulo Ciarlo, cook and seaman; Giobatta Panissa, seaman, and Arthur Cotton, boy. The mate was a good-looking young Genoese of twenty-six, a good fellow, a dandy when on shore, but rather a timid sailor, and one who could not inspire the others with due respect, hence frequent quarrels, and in two cases, as before related, the drawing of sheath knives.

Paulo Ciarlo, a piratical-looking, bronzed fellow of thirty, was not only an excellent cook, but an admirable fore-and-aft sailor, a plucky man, and one with whom I never had occasion to find fault during his stay on board the *Falcon*.

Giobatta Panissa, who I afterwards found dared not return to his native land in consequence of having been a ringleader in a serious mutiny on board an Italian barque, did not turn out well. He was a young fellow with thick black eyebrows and a cruel mouth, with a surly and forbidding expression. He was not a good sailor, and could not be trusted at the tiller in bad weather; indeed, I discovered his real profession was that of fireman on board steamers. He was cowardly but quarrelsome, and required constant suppression, which he got. This Panissa was the hero of the second knife adventure. The mate and Panissa took the port watch, Ciarlo, Arthur and myself the starboard.

And now the outward voyage of the *Falcon* was completed, and she lay moored to the Boca quay ready for her homeward departure. The route that I had chosen for myself was rather a circuitous one. I purposed coasting up the eastern shores of the South-American continent as far as the West

India Islands, and thence across the North Atlantic and make for old England. In describing this voyage, I shall have to tell how we sailed to the desert islands of Martin Vas and Trinidad, and there explored strange volcanic peaks and ravines, where, I believe, no man before us had trod, and where the savage birds, not knowing how formidable a foe is man, attacked us with fury as we traversed the rocky defiles which they peopled in their tens of thousands; thence how we once again sailed into the emerald waters of the Reconcavo of Bahia and saw old friends; how we cruised for a week round the beautiful bay and up its tributary rivers, that pierce a tropical paradise; how we visited Maceio, and Pernambuco, the Brazilian Venice; and how doubling Cape La Roque, we were carried rapidly up the coast by a fresh wind that ever blew right aft, and a strong, never-changing current of hot water, the same that thousands of miles further on, after it has traversed the Gulf of Mexico, is known as the Gulf Stream; how we passed by the turbid mouth of the Amazon, greatest of rivers, crossed the equator once more, sailed by unhealthy Cayenne, and the mangrove swamps of Dutch Guiana to Demerara, where we spent a pleasant time, and so on to Barbados, where, for reasons that will be told in their right places, the *Falcon* was hauled up on to the sandy beach, and laid up for a season under the cocoa-palms and poisonous manchineals.

CHAPTER XXIX.

AT half-past four on the morning of the 4th of November, we were outside the Boca harbour, homeward bound at last. We shaped our course for Montevideo, at which port I had to call, having left my chronometers there during my travels in the River Plate Republics. It was blowing very hard from the south-west, so we scudded under three-reefed mainsail, passing the *Chico* light-ship at nine a.m., having run forty-five miles in four and a half hours, a speed which astonished somewhat my Italian mariners.

It was somewhere near here that we hove to and filled our breakers and tanks with the muddy, yet sweet and wholesome, water of the estuary, as is the practice of outward-bound vessels. The water was in no way brackish, though we were out of sight of land, and to all appearance in the midst of a tempestuous ocean.

The pampero had by this time raised the usual steep breaking seas that render the navigation of these shallow waters so perilous, and my Italians expressed great delight and astonishment when they observed how splendidly the little *Falcon* rose to each sea, steering perfectly easily all the while.

Near the *Chico* we passed the new Argentine man-of-war, the *Admirante Brown*. This vessel was constructed in England, and recently steamed over the Atlantic with the intention of reaching some port of the Argentine Republic This she has not done, and never will do, for it is found that this white elephant draws too much water to enter Argentine waters at all, so here she remains at anchor in the high seas, disconsolately rolling about, a constant butt for the caricaturists and comic papers of Montevideo.

At about two p.m. we passed the *Cuirassier* light-ship. The sea near here was tumbling about very uncomfortably, for the tide and wind were opposed to each other. Some ten miles further on we passed close to a barque of about 500 tons that had evidently foundered within a few hours. As the depth of the estuary hereabouts is not much more than five fathoms, her masts were above water, her canvas was still on her, flapping about and tearing in the violent wind, with a noise like that of irregular musketry fire. There were no men to be seen in her rigging, so we presumed some passing vessel had rendered assistance to the crew. This, we learnt later on at Montevideo, had been the case. This vessel was an old Italian wooden corvette of war that had recently been sold to some Italians of Montevideo, who had converted her into a river merchant barque.

At nine p.m., after a fast voyage of sixteen hours, we came to an anchor off the custom-house of Montevideo, where we lay all night, rolling and pitching into the nasty seas that make this so-called harbour so uncomfortable.

I had purposed remaining at Montevideo but four days, which I calculated was a sufficient time wherein to complete all our preparations for sea, but circumstances, in the shape of a violent storm, considerably delayed our departure.

During our outward voyage we had enjoyed singular immunity from bad weather, but during the first month or so of our homeward journey we certainly encountered more than our share of it. It is true that this was the tempestuous season of this portion of the South Atlantic, when fierce pamperos are of frequent occurrence.

The weather had been unsettled for some time. On the 6th of November, two days after our arrival at Montevideo, the barometer commenced to fall steadily. It was intensely close and hot throughout the day, and in the afternoon we observed that our rigging was entirely covered with those fine filaments, like spiders' webs, which sailors that have visited these seas call Virgin's threads. This phenomenon is common on the River Plate, and is said to precede a strong pampero. Throughout the following day there were many clear signs of an impending storm visible, and ancient mariners on shore shook their heads.

On the morning of the 8th of November it was blowing hard, but it was not until five in the evening that the pampero burst upon us, with its usual suddenness, but with a fury that I have never experienced in any wind before or since. The pampero of these seas is a true hurricane, and though not of so long duration as the hurricanes of the West Indies and other seas, it is often quite as violent as long as it lasts.

On this occasion a perfectly clear sky became of a sudden quite obscured to us by great whirling clouds of dust, that enveloped the whole city and the roads. Then the hurricane came down with a great roar, swung all the vessels round with a violent jerk, causing many to drag their anchors, thereby fouling each other, and inflicting much damage. We had two anchors down, with sixty fathoms of chain on each, and dragged but an inconsiderable distance. But the strain on our chains was tremendous ; we seemed to be drawn under water at times during the more violent gusts. We pitched and tumbled about in a manner that threatened to be even dangerous, and as the wind blew off all the tops of the waves, driving solid sheets of water through the air, these flew over our decks, almost drowning any one who ventured above. We pitched our bows, too, so deep into the seas, that I entertained serious fears at times lest we should founder at anchor. This first squall was far too furious to last long; it was circular, as all such very violent storms are, going round all the points of the compass. The dust was soon blown

away, and then, as far as one could see it through the blinding
spray, the aspect of the sea, sky, and city under this fearful
visitation was really awful and magnificent.   The atmosphere
passed through several extraordinary changes of colour, now
brick-red, now pale-green ; the ships, houses, and vegetation
all assuming the same hue.   The lightning, forked and purple
in colour, was vivid, as it perhaps only can be in this highly
electric region.   Other electric phenomena were not wanting.
Each wave in the roads was capped with a flame of fire, and
the large hailstones that fell seemed to be mixed with
showers of sparks.

The numerous casualties on shore and afloat testified to the
power of the wind.   Many people were killed, and the city
was filled with consternation, hundreds of trees were uprooted,
fifteen strong stone houses were blown down in a row on the
sea front, the whole of the new exhibition building at Buenos
Ayres was destroyed, and, among the many other accidents
to the shipping, a large barque, at anchor off Montevideo with
all canvas stowed, was capsized by the first gust.

The *Falcon* was in great peril of being utterly lost, either
by foundering or collision with the numerous craft that had
parted their chains, and were driving helplessly on shore.
Lucky it was for us that this first cyclonic squall only lasted
about half an hour, when the wind settled down to a comparatively gentle, strong south-westerly gale.

We now found ourselves in a most dangerous position.
We had anchored near several of the heavy, iron-ribbed
lighters which are used to discharge the cargoes from vessels
in the outer roads.   These were all much larger craft than the
Falcon.   Now it happened during the cyclone that, in consequence of some, or, as is more probable, all, of us having
dragged our anchors, we had collected together into a dense
group, and collisions were frequent between different craft as
they rose and fell on the heavy seas.   To collide with one of
these tough monsters probably meant destruction to the
lighter and more delicate yacht.   One did come foul of us,
and carried away the greater part of our starboard rail and
the stanchions of the hand-rope, but luckily inflicted no
serious damage.   Then she tried to come on the top of us, and
bringing her bowsprit down on our decks, snapped it off
short.   Before any serious damage had come about, I had
sent Panissa on board of her to pay out her chain.   This he

managed to do, and so she fell away clear of us. The wretched Panissa, however, found it impossible to climb back to the *Falcon* again, so he had to remain wet and blanketless on the deserted lighter until the weather moderated on the following day, and we were enabled to lower a boat to take him off.

But we now observed a far more serious cause of danger just astern of us. We had dragged right under the iron bows of another larger and also deserted lighter. Her bowsprit was not a yard from our bows. As a great wave passed under us and raised her, she seemed to be right over us and about to fall and inevitably cut us down and sink us. I sent a man on board of her, but he could give her no further scope of chain. We could not move from our own position without certainly fouling some lighter, so all we could do was to hope for the best, and wait. We were certainly in a position of great danger. We all knew that if the *Falcon* dragged her anchors but six feet more, she would without fail be cut down and sunk. All through that stormy night and the next day we watched with straining eyes that cruel-looking, iron-bound bow rising and falling behind us, expecting in each fiercer gust of the storm, or after some higher wave than usual, to hear the dull thud and the sound of crushing timbers.

I think that the most speculative of underwriters would have refused to have anything to do with the *Falcon's* insurance, had he seen her then. The poor old vessel's life was not worth much, so little that the men collected their watches and such valuables about them, in expectation of our vessel sinking beneath our feet at any moment. But the old *Falcon* was not yet to die; she had dragged so far, but having got as near danger as she conveniently could, she stopped, and did not go astern another inch all through the pampero. Our escape certainly seemed miraculous, and had the good effect of inspiring my Italians with a profound faith in the luck of the vessel.

Nearly a week went by before our repairs were effected, for during that time a nasty sea was nearly constantly running in the harbour, which rendered carpenter's work difficult on board; besides, the Italian ship-carpenter we had engaged invariably got sea-sick when our vessel rolled about to any extent. But at last the little craft was once more ready for sea. All her stores were on board—tinned meats, rum, and water for four months; a large cask of eggs, preserved in lime-water, on deck; and an abundance of vegetables. All the standing and running rigging had been carefully over-hauled, and replaced where necessary.

On the 15th of November I got a clean bill of health for Pernambuco, brought the chronometers on board, and gave orders for sailing that evening.

All hands were then employed in securing everything on deck and below, lashing the boat bottom upwards on the deck, and so on. The weather was glorious, with every prospect of it remaining so, and we sailed out of the harbour at seven in the evening in grand style, with spinnaker and top-sail set. We saluted the English gun-boats as we passed them; then, having got outside the bay, found that we had a light wind right aft to help us up the coast. All seemed in our favour, and we entertained hopes of being rapidly carried into the calm tropic seas out of this stormy region, for a pampero was not a phenomenon we at all desired to encounter out at sea; we had seen quite enough of the fury of this wind in port.

No sooner were we well outside the harbour than the mate came up to me, and asked me if I had any objection to the voyage being inaugurated according to the usual custom on Genoese vessels. On hearing what this ceremony con-sisted of, I at once assented. He called the hands aft, made a little speech in Genoese, in which he exhorted them to do their duty, be obedient and respectful to the captain, and so forth. Then a glass of rum was served to each, the prosperity of the voyage drunk, and the watches formally set.

The voyage that was now before us was to be a far longer one than any we had yet undertaken during our cruise. Not that the direct distance to our next port, Bahia, at which I purposed calling on my way to Pernambuco, was great. From Montevideo to the Bay of All Saints is, roughly, 1800 nautical miles. But we anticipated a head-wind all the way; and a dead beat of 1800 miles against a confused and choppy sea, not to mention a contrary current, is somewhat of an undertaking.

The south-east trade-wind does not blow home to the Brazilian coast, but, at the distance of several hundred miles from it, is deflected in its course, and pursues a direction nearly parallel to the land. For one half the year this wind blows *down* the coast, for the other half *up* it. These seasons are known as those of the northerly and southerly Brazilian monsoons, a misnomer, as any one who reads the definition of monsoon in any physical geography can see for himself.

Now we left Montevideo in the middle of the northerly monsoon, when that wind blows boisterously from the north-east, accompanied by heavy rains and frequent squalls, so we anticipated a long period of uncomfortable tossing about, with a good deal of water tumbling over our bows at times ; nor were we disappointed.

It is the rule for vessels bound north from the River Plate and South Brazilian ports, during the prevalence of this unfavourable monsoon, to sail some 700 miles to the eastward, or even considerably to the south of east, close-hauled on the port tack, before they go about and make their northering, and, with all this offing, it is not unusual for a clumsy craft to fail to weather Cape San Roque, that bugbear of South Atlantic mariners.

But with a fore-and-after like ours, that could sail a little over four points off the wind, such precautions were unnecessary ; we would make eastering when the wind was favourable for so doing, and go about whenever a shift of wind rendered the other tack the most advantageous.

By making use of every turn of the unsteady, ever-varying monsoon, we made a fairly smart passage. A large barque left Montevideo the same day as ourselves. We both arrived at Bahia on the same day after a voyage of thirty-eight days; but, whereas we sailed considerably out of our course in order to visit the desert island of Trinidad, and there remained at anchor for nine days, I think we can fairly boast of having given that barque a very undeniable beating. The distance to Bahia is, as I have said, about 1800 miles, but with our rather zigzag course and trip to Trinidad, we made over 3000 miles of it.

We passed Flores light at about eleven on the night of our departure. Then the wind fell away, and but light puffs occasionally filled our spinnaker as we drifted on slowly before the easterly set of the River Plate.

On the following morning a five-knot breeze sprang up from the west, before which we scudded east under all canvas. We passed by Lobos Island and Maldonado Bay, and at sunset perceived Cape Santa Maria to the W.N.W., from which we took our departure.

On relieving the watch at eight o'clock of our third morning out, I found we were out of sight of land and in blue water once more. The wind had now veered to the quarter from which it was to be expected, north-east, so sailing full and by on the port tack we were enabled to steer about east.

This wind gradually freshened, a confused sea rose, and the sky became obscured by heavy banks of clouds. This weather lasted for the next three days, and very uncomfortable it was. The *Falcon* continually pitched her nose into the short choppy seas, taking more water on board each time than during the whole outward voyage. She laboured a good deal at times, and we found it necessary to relieve her by taking two reefs in the main-sail and shifting the first for the storm-jib. All our clothing was wet through during this time, as indeed it generally was for a month afterwards, while we battled with the north-east monsoon, our paraffine-stove being, of course, not capable of doing much in the way of drying ; we had to wait for the rare sun to do that.

By this time I had been able to come to a fairly just estimate of my Genoese crew. On the whole I was satisfied with them. With the exception of Panissa they were up to their work, and very willing to do it ; but they were not of over-cleanly habits. I often used to give the mate lectures on this subject, describe to him the fastidious order and cleanliness which distinguish an English yacht, and picture to him the horror with which our slovenly vessel would be regarded in an English yachting harbour, such as Cowes. But it was of no use ; I could not overcome the nature of these mariners. An Italian considers dirt as a comfortable sort of thing ; as long as everything is fairly shipshape for practical purposes of seamanship, he is content ; he looks upon tidiness and the removal of filth as foolish waste of time. After vain attempts to bring my Genoese over to my views, I had to give in for the sake of peace, and contented myself with merely insisting on an approximate cleanliness while in port.

Our cook, Paulo Ciarlo, a very worthy fellow, was much puzzled at first with the paraffine-stove and the tinned meats, but he soon fell into *Falcon* ways, and ingeniously managed to evolve a very fair *cuisine à l'Italienne* out of the preserved meats of Australia. This Paulo Ciarlo was a great fisherman; he would contrive all sorts of quaint machines wherewith to tempt the finny dwellers of the deep. He made one most diabolical-looking apparatus, a sort of wooden egg bristling with spikes an inch and more long. With this he caught polypi, a great luxury to Italians, though I cannot say I appreciate them myself. But we caught better fish than these—palomitas, dolphins, and king-fish, which latter may be defined as giant deep-sea mackerel.

From a small vessel like ours many more fish can be caught than from a faster-sailing vessel. Indeed, during our homeward voyage we were never without fresh fish on board, for the tropical seas of Brazil abound in life. The dolphins were our favourites, and we often caught fine fellows, weighing fifty or sixty pounds. We always towed a stout twenty-fathom line behind us with a large hook, baited, as a rule, with a scrap of white rag merely, unless we had a flying-fish to put on; for this is the greatest temptation one can offer to a dolphin. We found a speed of about four knots the most favourable for our deep-sea fishing.

As soon as some big dolphin or king-fish took the bait, there would be great excitement on board. The steersman would shove his tiller hard down, and the vessel would fly up in the wind with all sails flapping, even the spinnaker would be taken aback at times. The way of the vessel thus checked, that arch-fisherman, the cook, who always rushed on deck as soon as he heard the cry of " a fish," would haul in the line with a face distorted with excitement, till the monster would be right under our stern, darting about hither and thither in frantic terror. Then another hand, who was standing ready with grain or harpoon in hand on the taffrail, would deftly throw it, and, in another moment, a beautiful sixty-pound dolphin, all purple and gold, would be flying about our decks, beating it with its powerful tail with blows that sounded like a heavy hammer. Then the cook would exult and chuckle, and draw his long knife, to prepare the beautiful creature for culinary purposes. When a fish escaped from our hooks, the anguish with which he would stamp about the decks, and the fluency of his swearing, were fearful to see and hear.

CHAPTER XXX.

On our sixth day out, Sunday, the 20th of November, the north-east wind fell away, and we were left rolling about in a calm, under an overcast sky from which a constant drizzle descended. We were about 340 miles from the nearest land, but did not know our exact position, as the weather had prevented our taking an observation of the sun for three days. The barometer had fallen rather suddenly a tenth and a half, but there were no indications of bad weather in the heavens. However, the River Plate pampero is not wont to give much forewarning of this kind, and often comes on with such suddenness, that the sails can scarce be taken off a vessel before she is in the midst of the furious hurricane.

The glass did not fall for nothing this day. At midday the sky cleared, a light north-east wind sprang up. It was the finest imaginable weather, and a tempest seemed a very remote contingency; but at 12.30 there rose suddenly from the southern horizon into the clear blue sky, an inky mass of cloud that spread over the heavens, and advanced towards us with tremendous rapidity. It was a most ominous appearance. There arose a great bustle at once on board the yacht. We lowered all our canvas on deck, stowed the main-sail as closely as possible, and lashed the boom firmly amidships.

On board a full-rigged ship, that was about a mile to windward of us, the crew were taking in canvas as rapidly as possible.

We made all snug, then waited to see what was coming; and not long had we to wait. The mass of cloud was over our heads, and in another moment had covered all the heavens. For the first few minutes there was no wind, but a fearful downpour of rain — bucketfuls of it—almost literally. The conflict between the opposing southerly and north-easterly winds caused a dead calm by us. Then the storm-wind gained the day, drove back the feebler monsoon, and we were scudding rapidly before a heavy south-easterly gale. We put the storm-trysail—a jib-headed one—on the little ship, and the storm-jib, under which canvas she behaved very well. But here let me remark, that every small fore-and-after that is bound for a lengthy ocean cruise should carry a small square-sail of stout canvas for running before strong gales. I much regretted not having provided myself with this sail. Under such a square-sail the little craft can run dead before the wind and waves without any fear of jibing.

During the afternoon the wind came round from the south-east to the south-west, as is the custom of the pampero, and increased much in violence. The sea, too, rose very suddenly, and some of the waves that followed us looked so formidable that I regretted not having hove the vessel to with the floating-anchor out. This would have been the more prudent measure, but now it would have been dangerous to have attempted to bring her up to the wind with such a sea running.

It was not a true sea, either, that was following us, for the waves not only came up behind us before the south-west wind, but occasionally a nasty cross sea from the south-east would worry us, which we had to meet with the helm, so as to avoid taking these dangerous waves broadside on.

The *Falcon* behaved wonderfully well in this the heaviest weather I have ever seen her in. Giant billows, with overhanging, breaking crests, came rolling on us, looking as if they must inevitably overwhelm the vessel; but she would toss up her heels as they approached, and they would thunder by without sending much water on her decks. This was a severe test for her seaworthiness, and she certainly did not belie her old reputation of the English Channel.

During the night, which was very dark, steering was anxious, for it was difficult for the helmsman to perceive in time, and bear away from, the cross seas that came up steeper and higher than ever, at intervals of about ten minutes. During my watches this night I had to do more than my proper share of steering, for the boy, Arthur Cotton, had managed to steal some rum from the barrel below, and had brought himself into a condition of the most helpless drunkenness, to console himself for the bad weather. So he passed the night snoring loudly under the boat on deck. He had to make up these arrears of steering with interest afterwards, and was deprived of sundry luxuries for some time to come.

Throughout the next day, the 21st of November, the gale

blew with increased violence. The sea, too, was higher; we
shipped a good deal of water over our quarter at times, as we
rolled about in the confused seas which came up from the
south-west and south-east alternately, so that the vessel required very careful steering. Panissa proved himself so bad
a helmsman, that we found we could not trust him at the
tiller at all, so he enjoyed a holiday throughout the remainder of the pampero.

It is generally observed that during a prolonged gale two
or four rollers, far higher than any others, occur at long
intervals, say of twelve hours, and it is no doubt, as a
rule, one of such exceptionally lofty and breaking seas
that overwhelms a vessel and causes her to founder.

At four o'clock this afternoon two such gigantic billows
came right astern. I was steering at the time; the cook,
who was on deck, suddenly cried out, "Caramba, qué mare-
cada!" and looking over my shoulder I perceived a huge
wave of green water, with an ugly, over-curling, breaking
crest, rapidly overtaking us. It seemed that it must of a
certainty fall on us, and that it was quite impossible for the
Falcon to rise to such a steep wall of water; that she would
be rolled over and over by it certainly seemed probable to
me at that moment.

I observed, however, that the wave was not breaking
just at the portion where it would strike us, though it broke
heavily at either side. I only took a second's glance, jammed
myself firmly inside the tiller-rope, and steered so that the
wave would strike us dead aft. Suddenly up went our stern
with a jerk that jumped me off my feet, a few bucketfuls of
water tumbled on board, then up flew our bow, till our deck
was at an angle of 45°. The roller had passed us; it had
struck us so true that we remained on an even keel without
the slightest list to port or starboard.

But the peril was far from over yet; another equally lofty
roller followed close, and between the two was a valley so
narrow and steep that it was impossible that the *Falcon* after
her descent could raise her stern in time to meet the second
wall of water.

After a glance over my shoulder, which sufficed me to take
in the danger of the situation, I turned my back on the roller
again, and kept the vessel dead before it. We slid down the
slope of the liquid valley, then our stern commenced to rise

a little as the foot of the second wave reached us, and then there was a crash and a sudden darkness, and I felt a mass of water rush right over my head.

"It is all up with us," I thought, that is if I thought at all, for all this had occupied but a few seconds ; I think, however, all on board imagined that we had foundered ; doubtlessly, to any one looking from above, the masts of the vessel would at that moment alone have been visible, the whole hull must have been submerged But the *Falcon* was strong, the mass of water had not broken through her decks ; just as she had met the first wave she met this, not the least on one quarter or the other, so we escaped broaching to—a probable occurrence in the presence of such monster waves, and one that would of course have ensured our loss.

In another second, as I opened my eyes after the stunning effect of the deluge of water, I saw the bulwarks rise above the sea, then the little vessel gave herself a sort of a shake of relief and the water soon poured out through her scuppers, this being facilitated by the comparatively calm sea that always succeeds to exceptionally high waves.

The cook, I observed, had held on tightly, and had not been washed overboard. Then the companion hatch slid back, and the mate and Panissa came up, with faces very pallid ; when they heard the shock of the mass of water on deck, they said they distinctly felt the vessel go down, and were sure she was foundering.

This was the only occasion during the cruise in which we were in serious peril. Had we taken the first roller on board, the second falling on us as we lay deadened and stunned, with our decks full of water, would certainly have sent us down.

During the second night of the gale steering was more anxious work than ever, for it was too dark to distinguish the perilous cross seas. It is no easy work on a black night to luff or bear away continually to two seas coming up at right angles to each other.

But about midnight there came a change in the weather that was in a way favourable to us. The south-west gale continued, but at frequent intervals south-east squalls of great violence, accompanied by heavy rain, would drive across the sea ; these blew off the tops of the waves into blinding sheets of spray, so that we could distinguish nothing, but so furious were they that they soon also blew down the high and breaking seas, and converted the ocean into a confused mass of short, choppy, foaming waves of little height, and in no way dangerous We had to bear away and run before these squalls when they struck us.

The south-wester now gradually moderated, and veered round to the south, then by the morning of the 22nd of November to the south-east. It was squally and rough still, but the gale had evidently broken, and the glass was rising steadily.

I managed to get an observation of the sun, and found our position to be lat. 31° 58′ S., long. 43° 57′ W., we had therefore run about 300 miles in a north-east direction, before the pampero, that is, nearly parallel to the coast.

At midday we got into a calmer sea, and the wind being now about east we steered north-east, sailing full and by on the starboard tack. The sky was now cloudless, so contentment and joy filled our souls at the contrast between this delicious weather and the recent storm. Our decks presented a very agreeable appearance, and a somewhat picturesque one —a scene of idyllic repose, if the term is applicable to a seascape.

The vessel was sailing her five knots through the dark-blue water, throwing up two wings of silver spray on either bow. Italian garments, more or less ragged, and of rich colours, festooned the rigging, to dry in the warm sunshine. All hands were basking on deck in their several fashions. The cook lying on the upturned boat eagerly scanning his fishing-line that was dragging aft, his whole soul in his favourite sport; the mate mending a pair of pantaloons under the bulwark; Panissa, looking sentimental the while, was sitting on the hatch playing Spanish airs and selections from Italian operas on his accordion.

The captain lay on his back on deck in the sun, drying, smoking, and contemplating the sky, a volume of Balzac by his side. The boy, stubborn and stern and silent, was steering, making up arrears, a suspicious lump in his cheek betokening a quid, a luxury the young rascal was over addicted to.

But we were not long to enjoy this pleasant *dolce far niente* in the sunshine, for by night the wind had got round to the north-east again, and an uncomfortable fortnight was before us of wearisome beating up against the squally, rainy monsoon across a leaden-coloured sea under a sunless sky.

We had now got an offing of about 350 miles, but I wished to increase this distance considerably if possible, for further to the eastward we should probably encounter south-easterly winds.

In latitude 20° 30′ south, and some 700 miles from the Brazilian coast, is situated the group of desert islands known as the Trinidad and Martin Vas. Of these Trinidad is a fair-sized island, about fifteen English miles in circumference, with lofty, rugged mountains ; as our course was likely to bring us somewhere in its vicinity, I thought it would be quite worth our while to effect a landing and explore it if possible.

The description of this islet in the "South Atlantic Directory" was certainly tempting, though hinting at dangers, and there were held out to us in this work promises of good fishing around its coasts, and sport among the hogs and goats in its ravines, not to mention turtles, green food, wreckage, and other attractions. The following is taken from the description in the above-mentioned work.

"Trinidad is surrounded by sharp, rugged coral rocks, with an almost continual surge breaking on every part, which renders landing often precarious, and watering frequently impracticable, nor is there a possibility of rendering either certain, for the surf is often incredibly great, and has been seen during a gale at S.W., to break over a bluff which is 200 feet high.

"Captain Edmund Halley, afterwards Dr. Halley, Astronomer Royal, landed on this island, the 17th of April, 1700, and put on it some goats and hogs, and also a pair of guinea fowl, which he carried from St. Helena. ' I took,' says his journal, ' possession of the island in his majesty's name, as knowing it to be granted by the king's letters patent, leaving the Union Jack flying.'

"When the English went to Trinidad in 1781, in order to ascertain whether a settlement was practicable there, they did not find it answer their expectations.

"The American commander, Amaso Delano, visited Trinidad in 1803, and he, again, describes it as mostly barren, rough pile of rocky mountains. What soil there is on the island he found on the eastern side, where are several sand beaches, above one of which the Portuguese *had* a settlement.

"This settlement was directly above the most northerly sand-beach on the east side of the island, and has the best stream of water on the island running through it.

"Delano got his water off the south side of the island. Here a stream falls in a cascade over rocks some way up the mountains, so that it can be seen from a boat when passing it. After you have discovered the stream, you can land on a point of rocks just to the westward of the watering-place, and from thence may walk past it, and when a little to the eastward, there is a small cove among the rocks where you may float your casks off. Wood may be cut on the mountain just above the first landing-place, and you may take it off if you have a small oak boat.

"All the south side of the island is indented with small bays ; but the whole is so iron-bound a coast and such a swell surging against it, that it is almost impossible to land a boat without great danger of staving it. The south part is a very remarkable, high, square bluff-head, and is very large. There is a sand-beach to the westward of this head, but I should caution against landing on this beach ; for just at the lower edge of it, and amongst the breakers, it is full of rocks, which are not seen till you are amongst them.

"If a ship is very much in need of wood or water, it may be got at Trinidad ; or if the crew should have the scurvy, it is an excellent place to recruit them in, as you can get plenty of greens on the south-east part, such as fine purslain.

"We [Delano] found plenty of goats and hogs—the latter were very shy, but we killed some of them and a number of goats ; we also saw some cats."

When my men heard of my intention of sailing to this lone island of the South Atlantic, they expressed great delight, especially when they learnt that pigs and goats were reported to be its sole inhabitants. On this, the 23rd of November, being our ninth day out, Trinidad was about 1000 miles to the north-east of us.

And now we had a troublesome time of it, the wind was

ever varying. Now we lay up to the north-east on the starboard tack, now could only fetch up to the east or even south-east. We were often going about, and sometimes were considerably puzzled on which tack to put the vessel, both being bad; the one taking us to the south of east—a retrograde direction—the other towards the land which we wished to avoid.

The weather, too, was abominable, the rain was almost constant, and heavy squalls very frequent, so that we had often to lower our main-sail on deck till they had passed by. A very nasty choppy sea, too, was perpetually running, which deadened our way considerably, and kept us constantly wet. We did not average 100 miles a day. For two nights we had to heave the vessel to, so heavily was she labouring.

The poor cook was in great trouble all this while, for cooking was attended with decided difficulties. Now and then, especially when the lubberly Panissa was steering, a sea would come over the bows, find its way down the chimney, extinguish the stove, and spoil the polenta or savoury dolphin-stew. Then would the forecastle man-hole cover be shoved aside, and above the deck would appear the cook's ferocious face and gaunt tattooed arm, which latter he would shake menacingly at the guilty helmsman, while he thundered out sonorous Italian oaths on his head, until another green sea came on board and quenched his ire; whereupon he would disappear suddenly, and the hatch would close over him as on a Jack-in-box. Poor cook! he had many troubles, not least among which were the cockroaches which swarmed in millions on the *Falcon* since her visit to Paraguay; these would devour all the vegetables and the dried fish; indeed, nothing came amiss to them; they supped one night on Panissa's kid boots—for that mariner, like many Italian sailors, possessed a shore-going pair of high-heeled French kid boots! They honeycombed all our biscuits, our soup always came on the table thickened with these filthy insects, so that we had to skim it carefully before eating. They were everywhere, and not to be avoided; to exterminate them we should have had to take everything out of the vessel. But the cook consoled himself for present ills with the anticipation of future bliss, for he was wont to picture to himself all manner of wonderful fun

20

he was going to have at Trinidad, how he would salt down
tons of fish and turtles, cure bacon, collect birds' eggs.   It
was arranged that he should go on shore at daylight each
day to milk the goats for our morning coffee.   He was
pleased and excited at the prospect, and volunteered to
accompany me on a thorough voyage of exploration among
these untrodden volcanic crags, for he had in his blood
some of the adventurous spirit of his fellow-citizen
Columbus.

On looking over my log for this voyage, I find the same
constantly-recurring entries of the following dreary nature :
—" Constant rain "—" Four violent squalls in succession "
—" Still battened down "—" Ship taking much water over
her bows."

We had, indeed, a most uncomfortable time of it.   I
believe, during this fortnight, the *Falcon* jumped about more
and shipped more water than during all her previous
existence.   To be constantly battened down was highly
unpleasant, especially as we advanced northward into
warmer weather.   Although the sky was ever clouded, and
pouring down almost unremitting rain on us, the temperature
was high, 75° to 80°.   The sea, too, was of about the same
temperature, and felt like hot water as it washed over us,
for we were sailing against the warm equatorial current that
flows down the coast of Brazil at the rate of twenty miles
a day.   The atmosphere in the cabin was horribly close,
and after a few hours' sleep below, one invariably awoke
with a headache.   This was not to be wondered at, for
ventilation of course there was none, and the stove poisoned
us with carbonic acid gas.

The compound odour, too, was quite indescribable.   The
strings of garlic and onions that festooned the forecastle, the
reeking garments of the crew, the foul smell of cockroaches,
could be too easily distinguished ; but there were other subtle
and pungent smells besides, that defied analysis.

How we damp wretches looked forward to the time
when we should be running with easy motion again before
the soft trades under sunny skies, instead of this perpetual
jumping into the steep seas, with shock and sound, as if
the vessel was striking a rock, till one's head swam round
with the dizziness of the irregular leapings and fallings.
The health of the crew was affected by this unwholesome

tepid weather; the constant exposure to the humidity, not of the sea only, but of rains and soaking dews, brought on rheumatism, and a great languor and debility. Our sleep was heavy and unrefreshing. We woke with big, aching heads, and pains in the eyes and neck. Some of the symptoms, such as the sense of debility, I was inclined to attribute in the case of the crew to the fact of their constantly wearing their oilskins. In warm weather like this no practice could be more unwholesome. I myself was suffering from a recurrence of old malarial symptoms, and the cook from ophthalmia.

And so we thrashed up against the monsoon, as a rule close hauled on the starboard tack, but occasionally on the other when the wind favoured it, until the 27th of November, our thirteenth day out, when our position at midday was latitude 24° 53′ S., our longitude 39° 57′ W. We were thus distant but 160 miles from Cape Frio.

On the following day Cape St. Thome bore 118 miles to the north-west by west. We had crossed Capricorn, and were once more in the tropics.

We were now so much to leeward of Trinidad, which was 568 miles to the E.N.E., that I determined to abandon the projected visit to the desert island, and sail direct for Bahia, which bore 600 miles to the north of us. But I consoled the cook with a promise that we should anchor a few days among the Abrolhos rocks, which lay on our course. The waters round these are reported to abound with fish.

The wind now became more variable and gusty than ever, sometimes it blew from the north, sometimes from the south of east, and for several days we beat up against a very confused and troublesome sea.

On the 2nd of December Trinidad lay 370 miles to the east by north of us, the Abrolhos rocks 220 miles to the north-west.

On the 3rd of December the weather cleared, to our great delight, and the sun made its appearance, so we were enabled to hang out our drenched garments to dry. Everything, even to our bedding, had been wet through for three weeks. Our rigging now presented a goodly show of gaudy-coloured rags, blankets, and oils, fluttering in the wind, suggesting reminiscences of Ratcliffe Highway slopshops.

On the 4th of December the wind chopped round to the N.N.W., and blew hard right in our teeth, if we continued our course to Bahia; but it was fair for Trinidad, now only 200 miles distant to the E.S.E. It looked, too, as if it would last, so after inspecting the chart, and thinking the matter over, I determined to alter our course once more, and run for Trinidad. I came on deck, and gave instructions to this effect to the mate. The men were delighted at the welcome news, and eased off sheets, and got the spinnaker on with great alacrity.

Delightful to us was the easy motion of our vessel, now running before wind and sea after all our tacking. But this pleasant state of things was not to last long. The *Falcon* seemed to be a very *Flying Dutchman*, for whichever way we altered our course, the wind would turn round and head us. At ten p.m. the wind quite suddenly came round to the E.N.E. again, taking our sails aback, so we had to take in spinnaker, trim sheets, and put her close-hauled on the port tack. Later on the wind got round to E.S.E., that is dead in our teeth.

The mate suggested wearing round, and running for Bahia; but I would not alter my plans again, and determined now to sail to Trinidad, however long it took us to get there. Besides, if we were to alter our destination with each change of the fickle monsoon, we should be ever going backwards and forwards across this dreary bit of the ocean, and never fetch anywhere.

On the morning of the 6th of December the wind got round again to the N.N.E., so we were able to lay up for our island with flowing sheets. At midday Trinidad was 112 miles to the E.S.E. of us, so the cook, wild with eager anticipation, overhauled his apparatus of destruction, and got everything in readiness, fishing-lines, harpoons, casks for preserving pork and goat-flesh in, and so on.

The 7th of December was a calm, cloudless day, and hot. At eight a.m. we were about forty-six miles from Trinidad, at which distance its lofty mountains should be visible in clear weather.

As the sun rose higher we perceived to the south-east, in which direction we expected to discover the island, a bank of cloud on the horizon. We knew that the lonely rock of ocean lay in the midst of this, for all such lofty and isolated islands attract to them masses of clouds. The multitudes of fish, too, that swam around our vessel were a sure indication of the vicinity of land. At eleven a.m. this vapour lifted somewhat, and we distinguished the whole rugged form of the iron-bound island, its pyramidal summits being capped by clouds.

But the ill-fate of Vanderdecken seemed still to attend us, for the wind, that though light had been fair, fell away. We had been allowed to catch a glimpse only of our much-desired port, when heavy banks of clouds rose from the south-east horizon with ominous rapidity, and scarce had we time to take in our spinnaker, and reef our main-sail, before the squall was on us, blowing right in our teeth from the direction of the island, and accompanied by a regular tropical downpour of rain. The whole heavens were now covered with rolling vapour, and of course the island became invisible to us.

The south-east wind blew throughout the rest of the day, and a steady drizzle set in that promised to last some time, but taking short boards we sailed on against wind and rain undiscouraged, for we were so near to our destination that we now could afford to laugh at the foul weather. Already we smelt the smell of the roast pigs, and our mouths were watering at the thought of the delectable crisp crackling thereof.

At night the sky cleared, and in the bright moonlight we once more perceived Trinidad standing out black and distinct with rugged ontline before the blue starlit sky, one solitary white cloud crowning its highest peak. The wind blew steadily from the south-east. This is the prevailing wind off Trinidad, for the island lies outside the region of the Brazilian monsoon, and within the zone of the south-east trades.

CHAPTER XXXI.

At daybreak of the 8th of December we were becalmed under the lee of the island, about three miles from the beach, upon which we could hear the sea break furiously. Trinidad certainly appeared a wild and uninviting spot, a precipitous mass of barren volcanic rock, with lofty inaccessible summits, the whole surface being studded with sharp needle-like peaks.

We got out sweeps, and with their aid slowly approached the south-west corner of the island. I recognized many of the landmarks that previous navigators had described ; the huge Monument—the Sugar-loaf and others—and on opening the south-west bay I perceived a considerable issue of water leaping down a rugged, barren ravine in a series of cascades into the sea. This I soon concluded must be the one described in the Directory, and I determined to come to an anchor off it.

After having got our chain and anchor up from the hold, I sent the mate out in the boat to take soundings, and choose a suitable anchorage. He returned at midday, and reported that he had found bottom—coral, and broken shells—in eighteen fathoms, at about half a mile from the shore. Further in he said there were many dangerous rocks.

It was now a dead calm, so we towed the vessel towards the bay with our boat. As there was a slight current against us, this was pretty hard work, under the rays of a vertical sun. At 2.30 p.m. we came to an anchor off the cascade, the south-west point of the island bearing south-east, and Bird Island, N.N.W. Bird Island, so named by us, is a rock of considerable size, peopled by thousands of sea-birds, that lies off the north point of South-west Bay.

Glad we were to hear our chain rattle out once more, even though in an open roadstead in mid-ocean, off a small desert island, after our weary twenty-four days of battling with the rainy monsoon.

Having made all snug, I decided to dine first, and then search for a landing-place in the boat. It did not look much like landing at all from our deck or masthead, for the great smooth ocean swell in which the *Falcon* now rose and fell so gently, broke heavily on the coral-fringed shore. There seemed to be one unbroken line of great breakers even on this the lee side of the island, and the roar of them reverberated among the rocky ravines like loud thunder, that did not sound encouraging to the explorers.

We enjoyed a very varied fish dinner, for the cook had not been idle with his lines. I was aware that the sea round any desert isle rarely visited by man and far distant from any main, always teemed with fish, but I had no idea that any portion of ocean ever swarmed with life to such a marvellous extent as is the case round this islet.

There was a species of black pig-fish, as the Italians call them, that surrounded us in vast shoals, so dense that the clear water presented an unbroken inky appearance in every direction for a time. There was another species of pig-fish, too, that was beautifully striped with broad bands of violet; there were fish of every colour of the rainbow, of every size and shape.

"Too much fish, Mistare Niti!" exclaimed the cook, who gazed with an amazement almost mixed with fear at this more than realization of his very wildest piscatorial dreams He rubbed his eyes and cried, "Is it not a vision? but I will try." And he forthwith cast his lines, and no sooner did the hook touch the water than hundreds of fish were at it, and the chief, indeed only, skill required by the fisherman, was to haul the line quickly back before the secured prey was devoured by his cannibal brethren.

There were eight distinct varieties of fish, and all edible, crowding the waters around our hull, and none were timid and shy, for what knew they of the insidious hooks that lay buried in the tempting morsels that these strange monsters that had visited their island for the first time were so kindly throwing to them?

But now sharks, perceiving the unwonted commotion and large crowd of smaller fry that was collected round us, came up to discover what was going on. At one time there were quite thirty of these ugly monsters swimming round us. The other fish dispersed as they approached, and only the very greedy ones remained. The sharks spoilt our fishing somewhat during our stay off Trinidad; but not much, there was enough for all. What we chiefly objected to was their habit of biting some fine fish off our hooks before we could get him on board; but Mr. Shark got caught himself several times in consequence of this unneighbourly practice, and even before our dinner this day we had hooked and slain four fair-sized sea-lawyers.

After dinner I pulled off in the boat with the mate and Panissa to discover a landing-place, taking a musket and some fishing-lines with me. On approaching the shore we found it run steep down, so that the sea only broke when it reached it, there not being two or three lines of breakers as is the case on gently shelving coasts. But though we rowed along the line of surf for some distance, we could nowhere perceive any spot on which a boat could be beached without running a great risk—indeed, certainty would be the proper word—of getting her stove in. There was but a narrow verge of beach between the cliffs and the breakers, and this was composed of sharp coral rocks and huge boulders fallen from the mountains ; there were no sandy or pebbly beaches.

We could examine the shore very close, for the sea broke always so exactly in the same spot that we were enabled to keep the boat on the summit of a wave just before it was about to break, and look down on the beach below us.

We rowed under the Monument, which is a four-sided column of basaltic formation,—quite 800 feet high, I should say,—separated from the cliff by a wide opening. We passed between Bird Island and the mainland, and pulled on for an hour to the northward, but everywhere the sea broke furiously on an iron-bound coast. We observed that little rivulets fell in cascades down every defile in the mountains, so of fresh water there was evidently an abundance on the island.

We could perceive no vegetation on the beach or on the lower slopes of the mountains, which were either precipitous or steep inclines of loose rocks and stones of every shape and size. But we noticed that there were plateaus and great domes at the summit of these hills, which were covered with a bright green grass or other herb, and, in places, forests of some sort of tree.

Amazed as we had been at the quantity of fish that swarmed in these waters, we were still more so when we perceived the myriads of sea-fowl of various species that covered this island. Seen at a distance many of the cliffs appeared white, as if of chalk, with the multitude of the snowy-plumaged birds that were perched on their honey-combed surface. Bold as had been the fish, these birds were more so. Hundreds of kittiwakes and certain great fluffy, hoarse-voiced fowl, whose true name I am unacquainted with, came off their cliffs to inspect us ; they flocked about our boat, and followed us as we coasted along, their number ever increasing. They kept up a continual chatter, no doubt discussing what we strange creatures could be, whether we were fish or birds, a new species of shark or albatross. They approached so near to us that we could knock them down with stretchers, and even catch them with our hands as they flew round our heads.   But we saw no signs of any other life on the island, and commenced to entertain some doubts as to the existence of the pigs and goats.   I think that after our experience with the fish and birds, we had half expected to see these quadrupeds flock down to the beach in battalions to welcome us to Trinidad.

We returned on board considerably disheartened at sunset, but were hungry and did justice to the cook's dinner of rock-cod and pig-fish.   Failing land-pigs, that ardent disciple of Walton had caught " *too mucho fishi-porki*," to use his own words.

The next day was fine, but a fresh south-east wind had raised a considerable sea outside ; this caused a higher swell than usual to run into South-West Bay, so that the surf on the beach was more dangerous than it had been on the previous day.

After breakfast I rowed off with the mate and Panissa in the boat, with the intention of again attempting to effect a landing.   I made for a spot that I had observed on the previous day, and which seemed to me then to be the best, if not the only, locality adapted for a boat landing-place ; this was a promontory of coral formation, that ran out into the sea some fifteen yards or more beyond the breakers.   It was situated in South-West Bay, a short distance to the northward of the cascade.   It was, indeed, a natural pier, for its sides ran perpendicularly down into deep water, and its summit was but six feet or so above the level of the sea. We got alongside of this, and the swell that passed by was so regular, though high, that it would have been easy to have approached close to, and when the boat was on the top of a wave, and so almost on a level with the summit of this coral jetty, for me to have leapt on shore without any danger, for the rough coral was not slippery.

But the mate was a timid boatman, and Panissa a more timid one ; so after several attempts, I had to abandon this method of landing ; for as soon as a wave approached, these fellows would get frightened, and push off so far from the rock that leaping on it was quite out of the question.

I made them row along the coast far to the northward, and I observed that this portion of the island was far the most precipitous and inhospitable.   At last we came to a cove, on to whose beach the sea broke dangerously at long intervals only ; for two precipitous capes that bounded it sheltered it considerably. We observed also that in one portion of the cove there were no sharp rocks to oppose our landing, the shore just there, which seemed to be of coral formation, was flat, and terminated seawards in a steep step. Here landing seemed to be feasible. Our method was as follows : We dropped our anchor some fifteen yards from the beach ; and then, choosing our opportunity, slacked out cable and backed stern on towards the shore. I stood up in the stern, ready to leap on to the beach as soon as the boat was near enough, leaving it to the mate to watch the sea, and choose a proper time between the breakers. As soon as I leapt on to the land he was to haul out again ; my provisions and rifle were to be passed to me by a line. So was it arranged ; but this is what occurred. I was standing up in the stern in readiness, with my face turned to the beach, when I heard a cry, and the next moment felt a mass of water strike me on the back, nearly pushing me overboard.

The clumsy mate had allowed a sea to break over our bows. It nearly filled our boat up ; she quivered, uncertain whether to turn turtle or not. The mate seemed to be paralyzed by the accident, and not till I poked an oar into his stomach, to wake him up, had he sense to obey my orders and haul away at the line, so as to get beyond the limit of the breakers before the next was on us. By balancing the boat carefully we managed to keep her upright, and set to work to bale out as rapidly as possible. It was a near shave, and a nice mess we should have been in had we lost our boat, for she certainly would have been stove in had she been rolled over on these hard rocks by the powerful waves. It would not have been very prudent to have swum back to the *Falcon* through a sea swarming with sharks, and I had left no one on board who would have been capable of navigating her to the Brazilian coast, to purchase a boat with which to take us off. I saw I had committed a very imprudent act, so determined when I next attempted a landing to leave the mate on board the yacht, with definite instructions as to what to do in case of an accident occurring to the party on shore.

We returned on board in time for dinner ; the mate and Panissa were more than discouraged by their morning's adventure. They suggested that we had better sail at once for Bahia, that landing on Trinidad was impossible, the attempting it a serious risk to life ; besides, they urged, " we have been close to it : it is all a heap of stones ; if we did land we should discover nothing worth the discovering." These arguments were just, but I did not like being beaten by Trinidad, and after sailing all this way I thought that we had hardly tried enough yet, and should not give in.

The cook was strongly of my opinion, and volunteered to accompany me on a voyage of discovery after dinner.

So we got under way once more at three p.m., taking with us a rifle, a bottle of rum, some biscuit, a tin of sardines, some tobacco, and of course fishing-lines. I arranged a series of signals by means of which I could communicate from the shore to the mate in case we lost the boat, one signal being an order to bring the yacht nearer to the shore, so that we could swim out to her; another, an order to sail to Bahia, purchase a boat, and return for us, this latter being in view of our finding abundant food on the island and funking the sharks.

This afternoon I examined the coast much more closely than I had done before, and knew that if landing was feasible, land we now should ; for my companion was a thoroughly good boatman, and quite fearless, to boot. Paulo Ciarlo was ever ready for any wild adventure, and was a great contrast to the timid mate and cowardly Panissa.

Just to the northward of the Monument there is a promontory of precipitous rock, honeycombed and full of birds, on to which the sea breaks with fury. On the other side of this cape, and sheltered by it, is a bay hemmed in by barren mountains, steep, and seemingly inaccessible from the sea. There was little surf here, so we determined to land. To beach the boat we saw would be impossible, for the shore was encumbered with huge boulders of rock fallen from above. So we dropped our anchor far outside the breakers in about twenty feet of water, jumped overboard—there were no sharks so near the breakers—and swam to the shore.

We soon found ourselves standing on dry land once again, and rejoiced exceedingly. The next question was to get our stores on shore also. Now as the breakers were higher than they seemed to be from the boat, and the back under-tow difficult to contend against, even for a strong swimmer, we simplified matters by carrying a line from the stern of the boat to the shore; we hauled it taut and made it fast to an elevated rock. We found it quite easy to travel along this, hand over hand, through the water, with our baggage tied on to our heads. In two journeys we had brought all on shore. We put our property under a hollow rock, took a tot of rum each to counteract the dampness of our garments, lit our pipes, and proceeded to look around us. We wished to discover if it were possible to reach the rest of the island from this barren bay; if it were so, I decided to return on board, and get some of the crew to land us here again on the morrow; then they could take the boat away until our exploration was complete and we signalled for them to return to bring us off. We of course dared not leave the boat at anchor in this exposed spot for any time, for a westerly wind might spring up and bring a furious sea into the bay at very short notice.

The coast upon which we had landed was certainly an uninviting one. We could find no issue of water anywhere. The two precipitous capes that shut in the bay to the north and south put insurmountable obstacles to our progress in those directions, so we proceeded to scale the mountains to the back, to see if we could find an exit to a more fertile region.

In four different places in succession we attacked the mountains, and four times were defeated, but not till we had attained a considerable elevation on each occasion.

The lower slopes were formed of *débris*, loose stones of every size, that the slightest touch dislodged, so even this portion of the ascent was not unattended with danger. Above these steep inclines of rolling stones was an almost precipitous wall, hundreds of feet in height, of basaltic formation, rising in shattered regular-shaped columns similar to those of the Giant's Causeway. So many were the inequalities of surface offered to the climber's foot, that to ascend this would not have seemed an alarming feat to any one with a good head, were he sure of his foothold.

But we soon found the mountain to be literally rotten. The columns were broken through at short intervals, and crumbled away when one grasped them. There was not one stone that was not loose and ready to topple down.

Thus, after struggling up to a much greater height than

prudence should have sanctioned, for we had some narrow shaves, we were compelled to give in, weary and disappointed, and confess that we had landed in vain, having fallen on a cove from which there was no escape in any direction, surrounded by impassable cliffs.

As we discovered afterwards, this savage spot afforded a good specimen of the nature of the island. Utterly barren mountains rose from a coral beach, mountains that were rotten—and the whole island is so—burnt and shaken to pieces by the fires and earthquakes of volcanic action.

What struck us as remarkable was, that though in this cove there was no live vegetation of any kind, there were traces of an abundant extinct vegetation. The mountain slopes were thickly covered with dead wood, wood, too, that had evidently long since been dead ; some of these leafless trunks were prostrate, some still stood up as they had grown ; many had evidently been trees of considerable size, bigger round than a man's body. They were rotten, brittle, and dry, and made glorious fuel. This wood was close grained, of a red colour, and much twisted. When we afterwards discovered that over the whole of this extensive island, from the beach up to the summit of the highest mountain—at the bottom and on the slopes of every now barren ravine, on whose loose rolling stones no vegetation could possibly take root—these dead trees were strewed as closely as is possible for trees to grow ; and when we further perceived that they all seemed to have died at one and the same time, as if plague-struck, and that no one single live specimen young or old was to be found anywhere,—our amazement was increased.

At one time Trinidad must have been one magnificent forest, presenting to passing vessels a far different appearance to that it now does with its inhospitable and barren crags.

The descriptions given in the Directory allude to these forests ; therefore, whatever catastrophe it may have been that killed off all the vegetation of the island, it must have occurred within the memory of man.

Looking at the rotten, broken-up condition of the rock, and the nature of the soil, where there is a soil—a loose powder, not consolidated like earth, but having the appearance of fallen volcanic ash—I could not help imagining that

some great eruption had brought about all this desolation;
Trinidad is the acknowledged centre of a small volcanic
patch that lies in this portion of the South Atlantic, therefore I think this theory a more probable one than that of a
long drought, a not very likely contingency in this rather
rainy region.

As we could find no fresh water in our cove we saw that
there was nothing left for us but to pack up our stores once
more, swim off to our boat, and row back to the yacht. We
felt very disinclined to undergo the exertion of all this. It
was now dusk, and we had been toiling hard, rowing or
climbing, all day under a fiery tropical sun, so we were
pretty well fagged out; our several duckings in our clothes,
too, had assisted not a little to the exhaustion of our
energies.

We should have preferred camping out where we were
for the night, but without water this was impossible, for we
were even now parched with thirst.

I had already packed up my bundle and was preparing
to wade out into the breakers with no pleasant sensation,
when a joyful cry burst from the cook, who was prowling
about the shore in an inquisitive fashion.

"Agua! senor; aqui hay agua!"

I dropped my bundle and hurried up to him; he pointed
to where, drop by drop, a crystal fluid was oozing from an
overhanging rock, to be absorbed by the dry volcanic *débris*
beneath. It was but little, but it was enough, and a quart
bottle which we had brought with us filled, on being held
under the tiny issue, in about five minutes, with as cool pure
water as any one could desire.

I tasted it, and then said, "Paulo, we will sleep here
to-night."

"It is good, senor," he replied eagerly, for he was as tired
as I was, and hence funked the plunge into the strong
breakers as much as I did myself.

We now proceeded to make ourselves comfortable for the
night. The overhanging rock under which we had placed
our guns and stores on landing afforded us excellent shelter
from a drizzling rain which had set in. We collected a large
quantity of the dead wood, and soon had a glorious fire
blazing at the mouth of our cavern, which quickly dried our
sea-drenched garments.

Our dinner was a luxurious one, for we had an abundance of biscuit, a box of sardines, and a bottle of rum; besides these we had a few bright speckled sea-snakes we had found among the rocks, and some fine crabs, which when roasted we pronounced to be excellent. We both felt thoroughly comfortable and contented as we smoked our pipes by the loud-crackling fire after the completion of our meal.

We were far from being in sole possession of this little cove; bare of vegetation though it was, it swarmed with life. The hideous yellow land-crabs were very numerous, and attracted by the unwonted light, marched into our fire all night long, to be roasted in hecatombs. But more numerous than even these were the birds: there are several species of sea-fowl on Trinidad, but this cove was peopled only by a pretty sort of small gull like our kittiwakes.

It was now the breeding-season. On every stone and stump of wood the female birds were sitting on their eggs; our presence in no way alarmed them, they permitted us to stroke them, and seemed rather to like our kind attentions. The overhanging rock under which we slept, though not of larger size than is, say, a brewer's dray, must alone have been occupied by one hundred of these gulls, so prodigiously crowded with bird-life is this lonely island.

Every crevice in the rock had an egg or freshly-hatched chicken in it. One mother had a fluffy baby on a ledge within arm's reach of where I sat by the fire. Once when the mother was away I presented this baby with some roasted crab, which the dissipated little creature supped off eagerly. The mamma returned before it had finished the delicacy, and snatched the unwholesome morsel from its off-spring, following up with a shrill and voluble sermon as to the peril of allowing strange beasts to stand one crab suppers.

We slept soundly on our beds of stones and coral, though we were frequently disturbed by the claws of the inquisitive land-crabs that crawled over us in a most irritating manner throughout the night.

At midnight I was awakened by the much increased roaring of the waves on the beach; a high sea was evidently running, and the spray of it occasionally dashed into our cavern. So I turned out to have a look at the weather; I was far from reassured by what I saw. The rain was still falling, the clouds above were of a very stormy appearance, and were travelling in a southerly direction at a rate that betokened a stiff breeze. Even on this, the lee-side of the island, the sea had felt the influence of the wind, as its loud roar clearly proved. I knew that as the sea rose it would break further out, in which case our boat anchored where it was would almost certainly be swamped by the rollers or dashed to pieces on the rocks. The night being dark, I was unable to distinguish it and relieve my anxiety.

To lose our boat and be left on this desert gulf, unable to cross the imprisoning mountains to a point opposite to the *Falcon*, whence we might make signals of distress to her, was no pleasant prospect; it would be quite a question whether, even if the mate sailed round the island in search of us, he would be able to distinguish ourselves or our signals from the distance at which he would be bound to keep the vessel; besides, there was no spare boat on board wherewith to fetch us off if discovered; the "collapsible" had long since been worn out and thrown away. To stay here for a month or so, living on gulls and crabs, was, for me and the cook, I saw, a now not improbable adventure.

However, anything was better than trying to get off to the boat in the dark, tired as we were; so as nothing could be done till dawn, I piled up some more trees on the fire, lit a pipe, and smoked till I fell asleep again, which was not long.

We were awake at daybreak the next morning. "*Es muy feo*"—"It's very ugly"—was the cook's remark, after silently inspecting the ocean that lay before us for a few minutes. Ugly it was, but not so ugly as it might have been, for our boat was still riding safely beyond the breakers, though hidden from us at intervals as it fell into the hollows of the high swell. To reach her, however, burdened as we should be, would be a formidable undertaking. On the sharp slippery coral rocks, offering insecure foothold at the best of times, the surf was dashing furiously. The rock, too, to which we had fixed the stern-line from the boat was now no longer out of reach of the waves, for the tide had risen considerably, so we had not the support of the rope to rely on just where we most needed it, that is in the shallow water among the breakers.

The weather looked very dirty, so we saw that we ought

to hurry back to the *Falcon* without delay. But first we roasted some crabs, and off these, with rum and pipes, breakfasted—a very necessary preliminary, for we had hard and dangerous work before us ; besides which we were fagged, chilly, and aching in our limbs, the result of our yesterday's adventures. Having lashed some of the stores on my back, including a bottle of rum, a hatchet, and my rifle, I proceeded to make for the end of the rope. As I was clad in a thick pilot suit and heavy sea-boots, I found myself to be a very unwieldy mass to guide when I got into the troubled water. I had to watch my time, and hold for life on the sharp coral as a wave approached, allowing it to go over me, a process attended with no few cuts and bruises. Half-drowned, and considerably knocked about, I at last managed to reach the rope, and proceeded to haul myself along it, hand over hand, towards the boat. Breathing between the passing waves I got on very well for a few yards, then the water deepened suddenly. I was out of my depth, and I found that my impedimenta were so heavy that it was quite impossible for me to keep my head above water, and the rope was so slack that my weight at once dragged it under.

I shall never forget that journey, and do not wish ever to repeat it. I was travelling under water. It was a race for life. I hauled myself along the line as fast as my hands would move, with the energy of a drowning man. I felt as if I must have gone over a mile, and yet no boat; and, indeed, the distance was a very long one for a journey of this description. So long was I under water, that the cook, looking on from the shore, thought I had been drowned.

But at last I felt the line tighten, my head rose above the water, and there was the boat just in front of me. Purple of visage, and gasping, I held on to the stern for a minute, then crawled on board, and without more ado lay down until the results of the semi-suffocation had passed, when a tot of rum from the bottle set me right again.

It was now the cook's turn. Not profiting by my example, he, too, overloaded himself. He passed through the same period of torture, and, after dragging his weary limbs into the boat, vomited a gallon or so of Atlantic Ocean that he had swallowed on his way.

After half an hour's rest we recommenced work. There

were still a few things on the shore, so, stripping all my clothes off, I jumped into the water, and returned to the beach. Collecting what there was, I hauled myself back again along the line, this time with my head above water, for I carried but a slight burden. Then the cook in his turn had his second ducking, for the line had to be cast off from the rock.

On his return we proceeded to weigh the anchor. Alas! our troubles were not over yet, for strive our utmost it would not come up, having evidently got foul of some rock at the bottom. After dragging our boat's stern down to the water's edge in our endeavours, we had to give it up, cut our cable as low down as we could, and leave our kedge behind us. We soon reached the yacht, running under our lateen sail before the strong wind. Those on board were much pleased at seeing us again, for they had been rather anxious for our safety.

CHAPTER XXXII.

On the following day, the 11th of December, a rather high sea was running, so I saw it would be impossible to effect a landing; but I coasted along the shore, this time in a southerly direction, to prospect. I satisfied myself that South-West Bay was the best, if not the only portion of the island that afforded facilities for landing.

One's foot once on shore there, it would be easy to ascend the ravine above the cascade to the forest-clad domes above, and thence to descend to the fertile vales that are rumoured to exist on the windward side of the island.

So much I could perceive from the *Falcon's* deck, I have described further back the little promontory, or natural jetty, of coral formation, near the cascade, that juts out beyond the breakers. It was on that I determined to land as soon as the sea should go down.

Coasting this day to the southward I was astonished to discover what really magnificent scenery this little island contains. Passing South-West Point, a low, narrow isthmus, terminating seawards in a small fantastic hill of basaltic columns, we opened out an extensive gulf, narrow at its entrance, shut in by two stupendous precipices, but broadening within. The sea, even in this sheltered fiord, was tumultuous, and dashed furiously on the rocky islets that thickly covered its surface. The volcanic shores appalled the fancy with their strange forms and forbidding appearance. To the back of this gulf were lofty mountains, among others the Sugar-loaf.

Passing this nameless gulf, that probably no keel of boat had ever disturbed, we came to another and still stranger fiord, that caused an exclamation to burst from both of us, when it suddenly and unexpectedly opened before us, framed as it was picturesquely by a great arch in the cliffs. This was a deeper inlet than the other. Surrounded like it by fantastic rocks, its further extremity yet presented a most inviting appearance, for there a beautiful beach of golden sand fringed the white foam of the perpetually-breaking sea. Above this rose gentle slopes of verdure, of what nature we could not distinguish. Behind all rose steep, bare mountains, the great square bluff of South Cape, or Noah's Ark, as I named it from its shape (resembling that of the toy of our childhood), towering to the right.

To land here would be delightful, so we penetrated the gulf for some way; but, alas! had soon to abandon the attempt. For the bottom was everywhere sown with rocks, some rising above the sea as islands, others just awash, and these latter were a source of great danger to us. For at times, as our boat sank down into the hollow between two waves, we were horrified to perceive through the clear blue water some sharp rock just beneath us, on to which we were rapidly falling, appearing, though, as if itself were rising upwards to pierce our fragile craft. The danger from this cause was so great that we found ourselves obliged to reluctantly return, having feasted our eyes on the strangest and grandest scenery, but having convinced ourselves of the impracticability of landing in any of these rough and rock-sown fiords to the southward of Trinidad.

On the next day, the 12th of December, success crowned our efforts, our perseverance was at last rewarded, and we landed in South-West Bay, without any difficulty whatever.

It was a glorious day, hot indeed, for it was midsummer in this latitude, and the fierce tropical sun was vertical at midday. The wind had almost altogether fallen away, and it was very apparent from the *Falcon's* deck that there was far less surf on the shore than on any day hitherto. I determined now to make a final attempt at an exploration of this island, and of course chose the cook to be my companion. The boy also volunteered to join us, and was so eager that I foolishly consented to his doing so, for, though now seventeen years of age, he was not strong enough to endure the fatigues we were about to encounter among these burning crags and stifling ravines, and as the sequel showed was considerably knocked up by his journey, though behaving pluckily enough throughout.

We did not wish to encumber ourselves with much baggage, so, in addition to the clothes we wore, we carried between us three days' rations of biscuit, a cake of tobacco, a bottle of rum, a rifle, and a hatchet. The mate and Panissa rowed us off to the coral jetty by the cascade, which I have described, and we were all astonished at the ease with which we effected a landing. The water was almost smooth, the rock being of coral formation offered so many irregularities of surface that we had no difficulty in climbing on it, and scrambling along its summit to the beach.

Having seen us safely on shore, the mate and Panissa wished us a prosperous journey, and rowed back to the vessel.

I have before described the aspect of the ravine at whose foot we now found ourselves. A small stream finds its way down to the sea, terminating its course in a cascade of some height. On reaching the stream we found its waters to be deliciously clear and cool, as indeed is all the water of Trinidad. We slowly toiled up the ravine, and wearisome work it was ; sometimes on one side, sometimes on the other, of the watercourse, at times floundering through it, according as one or the other offered the safest and easiest route. The ascent was steeper than we had anticipated, and great rocks fallen from above offered constant obstructions. The dead trunks of trees everywhere crossed the stream. Of vegetation there was at first none but a wiry long grass which covered the soil, wherever there was any. But after we had ascended a considerable distance we came across those beautiful products of the tropics, the tree-ferns.

At first, of small growth, they filled up the hollow of the stream only, having exactly the appearance of our common English fern, but higher up we found them extending their fan-like masses of vivid-green leaves from the summits of lofty trunks.

At last we reached the summit of the ravine and were on the Col, for such it was, a gentle depression between two mountains, and here found ourselves in the midst of a very different nature, and enjoyed the loveliness of a scene such as we little guessed stern Trinidad concealed within its encircling wall of wild crags. For now we saw no rocks, we were walking on a soil powdery and soft and dry, into which our feet sank. The mountain that rose above us on our left was a gentle dome of similar soil; and all was covered with a rich and beautiful vegetation. We were walking through a dense grove of tree-ferns, whose branches meeting overhead, like cathedral aisles, allowed but a subdued light to fall on the soft floor below, where millions of land-crabs crawled about; for these hideous beasts swarm on this island even to the mountain-tops. Other life there was none, not even insect.

A gentle breeze blew over the Col from the windward side of the island, very grateful to us after our ascent of the hot, windless ravine. The scene, with its fresh green, seemed very beautiful to us at the time, as beautiful as anything we had ever seen. But after a month on the barren sea, and after the contrast of the dreary coast-scenery beneath us, any vegetation could not but seem very beautiful.

On the summit of the mountain there appeared to be some other tree growing with a darker foliage, but we left the inspection of this for our return journey, for we wished without delay to descend to the windward side of the island, which seemed to hold out a magic attraction for us. We expected, on very slight, if any, grounds, to make all sorts of valuable discoveries in that direction.

We reached the summit of the Col and looked down upon the eastern side of the island. A magnificent view stretched before us. From our great height we overlooked the mountains, ravines, and fiords, a wonderful panorama of strikingly contrasting or rather discordant colours. Dark, barren peaks towered up all around, huge pyramidal cylinders of burnt rock. These were based on gigantic couloirs or slopes of volcanic *débris*, of a bright, ruddy colour. These again were continued towards the sea by downs of vivid green, that in their turn sloped down to bays whose beaches were of the most brilliant white sand. Rugged promontories of coal-black rock divided these bays, and the sea for far out was studded with similarly black islets, on to which the sea broke furiously ; beyond the white foam lay the blue Atlantic, on whose far horizon rose three small islets which we recognized as the Martin Vas, and which are distant from Trinidad about twenty-six miles.

From the summit of Trinidad we obtained several extensive views along the windward coast, and everywhere it seemed that landing in any description of boat was quite out of the question ; this is not a clean coast as is that to leeward, but foul with many outlying reefs and rocks, while the surf is always much more dangerous, for the swell raised by the perpetually-blowing south-east trade-wind breaks on this shore, the first obstacle it has met after crossing thousands of miles of ocean.

I was much impressed by the strange nature of the scenery, which was such as I had never seen before, though common enough, perhaps, in some volcanic districts. There was indeed something awful in the appearance of this island, with its chaotic masses of rock and unearthly lurid *débris*.

After a halt and frugal meal under the shade of the tree-ferns, we proceeded to follow the ridge of the mountain in search of some easy way by which to descend to the sea-shore. Half a dozen times we pursued some likely-looking route until stopped by the edge of some precipice, that compelled us to wearily retrace our steps.

On one occasion we clambered down a long slope of black *débris*, recalling to one's memory the magic mountain of black rolling stones described in the " Arabian Nights." This brought us to the bottom of a steep ravine ; advancing some way down this, we reached a spot where it fell precipitously into depths of utter darkness, and we had to clamber all the way back again.

At last we came to where a red mountain of loose stones and *débris* sloped gradually towards the sea and seemed to join on to the green downs below, no precipice intervening.

The day was now far advanced, and we were anxious to reach a stream by which to bivouac for the night ; for we

THE MARTIN VAS ISLANDS FROM TRINIDAD.

were now weary and very thirsty, having come across no water since leaving the ravine of South-West Bay. Therefore we walked as fast as we could over the rolling stones of this mountain, hoping in an hour at the outside to reach the beach. Since leaving the fern-groves, we had seen no vegetation, but after progressing now some way down, we found the volcanic soil covered with a plant whose name I know not, spreading far and wide with rope-like creepers, bearing large leaves, pink flowers, and a bean about the size of a haricot. This was the vivid-green vegetation that we had distinguished from the summit of the island.

We were now fated to meet a great disappointment. This hill terminated in a precipitous wall of rock, which it was quite impossible to descend. So we had to turn back once more.

We were now in a real mess. South-West Bay, with its water, was many hours of weary climbing from us; weak and thirsty as we were, we could not reach it, at any rate the boy could not, for he now altogether collapsed, and said he could not walk another step, and would stay where he was. But move on we must, to stay where we were for the night meant death ; after a few hours' more deprivation of water not one of us could have made an effort to save his life. So, encouraging and pulling the boy along, we commenced to very painfully drag ourselves back — fearful work up those loose stones, that rolled down on us as if to press us back, and with the soil slipping away from under our feet at each step.

I soon saw that we could never reach South-West Bay, and must make an effort to find water nearer.

This mountain was a projecting spur from the central mass, and divided two ravines from each other. I thought it highly probable that a stream flowed down the ravine which was to our left, and suggested to the cook that we might try to descend to it. The *débris* on which we stood sloped down at a steep angle to the depths of this gorge, but the bottom of it we could not see. On its other side rose steep precipices of black rock.

The cook thought a moment or so, looked at the boy who was lying on his back, pale and breathing hard, and said, " I think we had better try it." He saw the difficulties and dangers of the plan as clearly as myself, but also saw it was our only chance. So we stirred up the boy and commenced the descent. At first it was easy enough, like an ordinary *moraine* in the Alps, but at every step the decline became steeper, until at last we had to lie on our backs and progress inch by inch with the greatest caution. To have slid a yard would have meant a rush ever increasing in rapidity into the depths below—a certain death.

This mountain was not composed merely of loose *débris*, or it could not have sloped at so steep an angle. It seemed rather to be a mass of rotten, or, rather, burnt rock, exceedingly brittle and breaking away when grasped in lumps, whose regular mathematical forms denoted the fiery ordeal the whole had been subjected to. It was but in places that the *débris* covered the slopes in layers of any thickness. So it was that this treacherous mass in consequence of its semi-consolidated state preserved an angle steeper than would be possible in inclines of loose stones or earth, at the same time offering no firmer support to hand or foot than would so much sand. We named this Mount Rotten, not while we were on it though, for then we respected it too much to call it any names.

It soon became apparent to me that to reascend this mountain would be quite impossible. To descend safely consisted of allowing oneself to slide down a few inches at a time with the least possible disturbance of the *débris;* but one ascending could not avoid disturbing these rolling masses, and nowhere would the rock where it jutted out have supported his foot, it was no better than so much dried mud.

Thus if we found, as we might easily do, our further progress barred by precipices, a most awful fate was before us, for there we should have to remain lying on the bare stones until we died of thirst or fell over the edge.

Our position was certainly a dangerous one, and we progressed slowly in silence, startled occasionally by the sound of a shower of rolling stones, caused by the movement of one or the other of us, when we would stop, dig our elbows into the earth, and wait a moment or so, fearful to hear the sound followed by another and more terrible one. Small, but not on that account the less dangerous, precipices occurred occasionally on this slope, to avoid and go round which we had to work our way sideways—a difficult proceeding. But by degrees we approached the bottom without any accident, and

now found that for the last two hundred feet or so we had
to descend a rugged cliff of firm, black rock. The foundations, at any rate, of the Rotten Mountain were solid.

These rocks opposing no great difficulties to us, we reached
the bottom of the ravine, and there indeed over the black
stones flowed a tiny stream of water; in our joy at this we
in a moment forgot all our fatigues and dangers, and lay
down with our faces in the shallow current, taking deep
draughts until our fearful thirst was quite assuaged. After
this we lit a great fire of the dead trees that lay thickly
around us, dined off biscuit and roast crabs, and slept soundly
enough in spite of the drizzling rain that fell throughout the
night.

We were so happy and comfortable, having found water,
the only thing we cared for just then, that how we were to
get out of this ravine never troubled our heads in the least.
And yet we certainly seemed to have descended into a very
prison, from which escape was impossible. There can be but
four ways of getting out of a gorge—to descend it, ascend it,
or climb one of its two sides. Now to climb up the side we
had come down the Rotten Mountain, I have already explained was quite impossible. The opposite side was formed
of precipice above precipice of bare, black rock, rising to a
great height; that, too, was evidently not accessible. To
descend the ravine was likewise quite out of the question,
for just below our encampment the stream fell over a sheer
wall of rock quite a hundred feet high. There was but one
chance of escape left us, that of ascending the ravine ; and
that, too, appeared from our encampment to offer insurmountable difficulties. Great rocks fallen from above filled
up the narrow bottom of the defile, in places opposing steep
walls to our progress ; and we could perceive that, higher
up, the stream fell in a cascade over a precipice, seemingly
similar to that below us, and about thirty feet in height.

We felt fatigued, stiff, and ill, when we woke the next
morning, but commenced our difficult march, or rather climb,
at daybreak. We had to exercise some ingenuity in getting
over the steep, fallen rocks that blocked our path. We found
the dead trees of great use to us here, and when we came to
the foot of the precipice I have mentioned, we found means
of scaling it by piling the timber up against it—a proceeding
that occupied us a considerable time. I believe that we

should never have escaped from this ravine, had it not been for the adventitious profusion of these trees.

After a time our progress became easier; and emerging from the ravine, we were once more on the gently-sloping ridges of the central mountain-mass, where all the ravines have their heads. Proceeding along this ridge to the northward, and so still further away from the south-west bay, we continued to search for some practicable way of reaching the coast, for notwithstanding our yesterday's failures, we were not inclined to abandon our project.

However, I determined not to allow our party to travel more than a certain distance away from water, for I dreaded a repetition of the previous evening's adventures; besides, the day was cloudless and windless, and the heat was intense. It was a genuine tropical midsummer day.

We soon came to the head of a ravine that seemed to promise a way to the beach. It was a gloomy gorge, with sides formed of black rocks piled on each other in chaotic masses; a small stream trickled down it.

We clambered down from one big stone to another without much difficulty. After proceeding some way the scenery became wilder, and the rocks higher and steeper. Far below us we saw the white beach, with the blue sea beyond it, but we scarcely hoped to reach it, expecting sooner or later to find ourselves on the edge of one of the usual precipices that had already so often thwarted us.

Lower down we found that the ravine widened, and a wiry grass grew in patches by the water-side; other vegetation there was none, save, of course, the never-failing dead trees. Here the land-crabs swarmed like ants on an ant-hill; huge beasts some of them, of a bright saffron colour. The birds, too, were in the ravine in greater numbers than on any other part of the island. It was evidently the breeding-place of one particular species, not the pretty kittywakes that inhabited South-West Bay, but large, snow-white, fluffy, awkward creatures. Sitting on their eggs, tending their young, or sleeping, they covered all the stones. The whole valley stank of the fish on which they fed; and foul as the fabled harpies in their manners, they dropped morsels of rotten fish from their mouths when we approached, and attacked us with fury. We had to beat them off with the weapons which we carried; and let me say that it is no joke to have to defend oneself from a half-dozen or so of these angry mothers, flapping, pecking, and screeching about one's head all together. We had even to go round and avoid spots where they were thickest

Certainly the whole nature, live or dead, of this lonely island has something uncanny about it that dismays and appals the imagination. This ravine, with its black rocks, varied occasionally by red volcanic *débris*, its strange vegetation of dead trees throwing out their skeleton arms, and its inhabitants savage, foul birds, and the still more offensive-looking land-crabs, struck us as having a particularly ghastly and spirit-depressing appearance. Among such scenery one felt as if anything horrible might happen at any moment, and a vague feeling of insecurity seized the mind.

We descended the ravine until we reached its termination, which was on an extensive down of soft red earth, covered with the creeping bean I have described before, and with purslain, which we of course ate eagerly.

The stream that had accompanied us down the ravine here left us, sucked up by the thirsty earth, so we had to abandon it, but not unreluctantly, for it was now oppressively hot, and we were tormented with a perpetual thirst. We discovered that there was nothing to prevent our descent from this down to the beach, and soon found ourselves walking over the fine, white sands. We had at last succeeded in reaching the windward side of Trinidad. We were on a bay to the north-east of the island, so proceeded to follow the shore towards the south, as the more fertile and inviting country lay in that direction. Thus we passed by the mouths of the different defiles that we had vainly attempted to descend on the previous day.

A broad margin of flat land, red earth, and then sands, extends between the mountains of this side of the island and the sea ; not as is the case on the leeward side, where the mountains generally fall sheer into the sea. Again, on this side the mountains terminate in great slopes of *débris* and downs, so that the streams are absorbed far up, and never reach the shore. We travelled along the beach from sandy bay to sandy bay, the mountains towering on our right, and the sea breaking on the coral reefs on our left. Spurs thrown out by the mountains divided bay from bay ; some of bare rock, some covered with sand, but all easy to cross. And now we noticed that this coast, though more beautiful-seeming from the sea, with its green downs, was in reality a far less hospitable one for the shipwrecked mariner than would the bleaker leeward coast be ; for, with the exception of the ravine we had descended, it was clear to us that no route lay from here up the mountains ; precipices occurred everywhere above the domes of *débris*, and no issue of water was attainable from the beach.

We met plenty to attract our attention as we walked along the glaring sands and hot coral rocks. Every pool was full of quaint creatures, rainbow-coloured fish, bright, spotted crabs, and azure polypi ; and snakes striped like wasps or gold-speckled crawled among the stones. We picked up some beautiful specimens of coral and shells. We came across the tracks of turtle, they were evidently in the habit of visiting these sands at night, and we promised ourselves some sport later on. But first we must find water by which to encamp, and of this we saw no signs, not even that left by rains in the hollows of rocks.

We wandered on, opening out bay after bay for some hours, till on traversing a rocky promontory we came to an extensive gulf, backed on its further side by the huge mass of Sugar-loaf mountain ; great walls of rock surrounded it, and altogether it was as inhospitable-looking a place as ship-wrecked sailor was ever cast on. Now all the shore of this gulf was strewed with wreckage. Along the whole of this windward coast we had perceived many spars, barrels, timbers, and other remains of vessels, but here they were in much larger quantity than elsewhere, so we named this dreary spot Wreck Bay. From its position in the region of the south-east trade-winds a vast amount of drift and many derelict vessels must of a necessity be driven on to the windward coast of Trinidad, and indeed there was a marvellous accumulation. Judging from its appearance some of this timber must have lain here for hundreds of years, and doubtlessly this beach preserves naval remains of every age since first vessels doubled the Cape of Good Hope. Apart from masts, barrels, and other driftage, we observed that more than one vessel, derelict doubtlessly, had been driven bodily on to the island, for we frequently saw two circular rows of ribs rising from the sand, with the corroded bolts sticking in them here and there, showing where the frame of some fine old ship lay buried.

What struck me as remarkable was that some of this wreckage had been cast up a great distance above what I judged to be high-water mark. Far up, jammed between two rocks, I perceived a huge iron beam that must have weighed many tons.

The explanation probably is that Trinidad, like several other lone-lying South Atlantic islands, notably St. Helena and Fernando Noronha, is subject to that terrible phenomenon known as the rollers. Those who have witnessed this describe how, on a fine, clear day, when the winds are still and the ocean smooth, of a sudden the waters in the offing are observed to become disturbed; billow after billow advances to the shore, gradually increasing in magnitude, until at last the waters are piled up in mountains far higher than the hugest storm-waves, that rush on to shore with fearful impetuosity, driving from their anchors any vessels they may encounter, and hurling them far up on the land, beyond the reach of the highest spring tides. Distant hurricanes and submarine volcanic action are both suggested as the causes of this phenomenon.

Casting a line into the pools left by the ebbing tide we soon caught a much larger quantity of fish than we could carry with us, so we called a halt, lit a fire of drift-wood under the skeleton bows of a small vessel, and prepared a lunch of roast fish that was indeed excellent, but which we should have enjoyed all the more had we possessed water to wash it down with. We kept our thirst down to a certain extent this day by constantly damping our clothes with sea-water.

The boy and the cook became quite excited on seeing all these wrecks, and proceeded to hunt about for any valuables that might have been cast up by the sea. They found nothing but an empty Ackshaw brandy-bottle and a tin of Australian meat, which on being opened proved to be bad. Valuables there doubtlessly are buried among the sands; the heavier portion of the cargoes of these wrecks must still be here; that ancient vessel under whose bows we were lunching may have been some old Dutch East Indiaman, or Spanish galleon from Peru, and untold doubloons and bars of precious metal may have lain hidden within a few yards of us.

Had there been water anywhere near this bay, we should certainly have dug into some of these wrecks; but water there was none within half a day's journey. Had we even come across a sound barrel, we could have filled it from the stream we had left in the morning, and carried it to the scene of our operations.

We crossed over the promontory that divided Wreck Bay from the one next it to the southward, and found ourselves at the foot of Noah's Ark Mountain. There was no water flowing down its perpendicular slopes. Our further progress was barred by a precipitous mountain running out into the sea; but we were now to the extreme south of the island, and all beyond this we had already explored. The next gulf was the one I had visited in the boat four days back, but on whose shore I had been unable to land in consequence of the dangerous outlying rocks.

All we could do now was to return to our stream in the harpy-inhabited ravine, and camp by it for the night. So, loading ourselves with as many fish and fine sea-crabs as we could carry, we trudged wearily back across the sands, and did not reach the foot of the gorge until dusk.

Ascending it until we came to a suitable spot we pitched our camp and lit a great fire. The stream formed a little pool just below, in which I had a most delicious and refreshing bath, while dinner was cooking. An excellent dinner it was—three kinds of fish, biscuit, rum, and unlimited water, not to forget the pipes of tobacco to finish up with.

More weird than even in the morning was the appearance of this ravine, now that the shades of night were falling. It was just such a scene as Doré's pencil would have done justice to: a desert of black stones over which hung a magic spell that killed all vegetation, so that the trees rose as gaunt leafless skeletons, and haunted by evil spirits in the shape of the foul birds brooding on every stock and stone, and the abominable reptiles, the land-crabs.

The huge mass of black crags that towered at the head of the gloomy defile was exactly what one would picture as the enchanted castle of the evil magician, within sight of which all vegetation withered, looking from over the desolate valley of ruins to the barren shore strewed with its sad

OUR CAMP IN THE RAVINE.   22

wreckage, and the wild ocean beyond. We at our encampment, picturesque enough in the firelight, yet hardly realized my idea of the virtuous knights about to release the damozel imprisoned in the castle overhead.

But the land-crabs certainly looked their part of goblin guardians of the approaches to the wicked magician's fastness. They were fearful as the firelight fell on their yellow cynical faces, fixed as that of the sphinx, but fixed in a horrid grin. Those who have observed this foulest species of crab will know my meaning. Smelling the fish we were cooking, they came down the mountains in thousands upon us. We threw them lumps of fish, which they devoured with crab-like slowness, yet perseverance.

It is a ghastly sight, a land-crab at his dinner. A huge beast was standing a yard from me; I gave him a portion of fish, and watched him. He looked at me straight in the face with his outstarting eyes, and proceeded with his two front claws to tear up his food, bringing bits of it to his mouth with one claw, as with a fork. But all this while he never looked at what he was doing; his face was fixed in one position, staring at me. And when I looked around, lo! there were half a dozen others all steadily feeding, but with immovable heads turned to me with that fixed basilisk stare. It was indeed horrible, and the effect was nightmarish in the extreme. While we slept that night they attacked us, and would certainly have devoured us, had we not awoke, and did eat holes in our clothes. One of us had to keep watch, so as to drive them from the other two, otherwise we should have had no sleep.

Imagine a sailor cast alone on this coast, weary, yet unable to sleep a moment on account of these ferocious creatures. After a few days of an existence full of horror, he would die raving mad, and then be consumed in an hour by his foes. In all Dante's Inferno there is no more horrible a suggestion of punishment than this

On the morrow, after an early breakfast of cold fish and water—we had finished our rum,—we proceeded to reascend the ravine. When we emerged from it on to the plateau where the tree-ferns grew, the green dome that forms the culminating point of the island lay in front of us. I wished to explore the mountain, so as to determine the nature of the vegetation that covered its slopes, also to discover the pigs and goats that, if they existed at all on Trinidad, would most possibly be found in this fertile district.

A scramble of a little more than half an hour brought us to the summit of the dome. We found it to be everywhere covered with a dense grove of beautiful tree-ferns and a shrub like myrtle, which I satisfied myself was not the young growth of the species of tree whose dead specimens were strewn over the whole island.

These were still a mystery; having once robed all Trinidad with one glorious forest, they had of a sudden perished as of a plague, leaving no young or seeds behind them. The once vigorous race was now utterly extinct. Of pigs and goats we also found no traces whatever ; they too, possibly like the old trees of hard red wood, had died out, leaving the island to the birds and foul crabs that now alone inhabit it.

We now stood on the culminating point of Trinidad, and held a counsel as we looked down on the calm ocean, and the little *Falcon* appearing like a child's toy-boat, as she lay at anchor so far below. We decided that we should at once proceed to the south-west bay and embark on our comfortable craft ; we had had enough of this lone rock of ocean, and wished to shake the dust of it from off our feet. Besides, we were worn, weak, and had consumed all our stores.

At any rate we had succeeded in very thoroughly exploring the island, and had made ourselves acquainted with all its resources, or rather lack of resources. We had certainly undergone much fatigue and no little peril, without any adequate result. In the course of our explorations we had been nearly drowned, had incurred much risk of perishing from thirst, and had run a very near shave of losing our lives among the mountains. The game had indeed not been worth the candle ; but of course we anticipated nothing of all this when we started. We must now satisfy ourselves with the empty glory of having beaten the island, notwithstanding its vigorous defence and our frequent repulses. As I have before hinted, treasures might be dug from the wrecks on the windward sands. Let some other enterprising yachtsman sail in search of them ; I certainly will not, having had quite enough of Trinidad. These, or something like these, were our deliberations on the mountain top ; then, resuming our march, we proceeded to the head of the south-west ravine, descended it, reached the coral jetty, and lit a fire to attract the attention of the *Falcon*.   Perceiving us, Panissa rowed off for us in the boat; the water being very smooth, we got into it without difficulty, and were soon, weary yet joyful, reposing ourselves in the snug little vessel—this night to dine luxuriously indeed, and sleep undisturbed by land-crabs.

I forgot to say that we wrote a record of our adventures on a piece of paper, and, enclosing it in our empty rum-bottle, left it in the hollow of a stone, just above the cascade.

NOTE.

In the winter of 1884–85, *since the publication of this book, an expedition started from the Tyne in search of supposed hidden treasure on Trinidad.   A ship's captain, who has traded to the Tyne for some years, obtained plans and papers relating to the hidden treasure from an old sailor who had been a pirate in his youth, and had seen the wealth buried.   The vessel reached Trinidad, a landing was effected with some difficulty, but the treasure was not discovered.*

CHAPTER XXXIII.

On the morrow we got all ready to sail.   We stowed away the fish we had salted and dried; a sufficient quantity to last us for many months to come.

For some reason or other all hands were more or less ill on leaving Trinidad; I was myself suffering from symptoms of malaria, which had been troubling me for some time, and which the recent fatigues I had gone through had much aggravated, so that I was debilitated and worn with fever, and almost unfit to work at all.   The crew were no better. What was the matter with them, I could not pretend to say, for they had visited no malarious regions.   I suspect that some of the fish we had caught and eaten were unwholesome, and we certainly had been indulging for some days on an exclusively fish diet.

Illness seemed to be the rule on board the *Falcon* during the whole of this homeward voyage.   On our outward voyage all hands enjoyed constant health.

There was a good deal of imaginary illness on board, too, later on, especially on the part of the mate, who had a most wholesome dread of the fevers of tropical ports, and who frightened himself four or five times into what, he thought, was yellow fever, but which I, as ship-doctor, pronounced to be indigestion, the results of over-eating.

We were now to sail to the Brazilian coast, to the Bay of All Saints ; my crew had looked forward with joyful anticipation to landing on Trinidad, but not so to their arrival at their next port. The countenances of the mate and Panissa wore throughout the voyage an anxious gloom, which deepened as we reached the dreaded coast.

Bahia lay 700 miles to the north-west of us, so this voyage was not to be a lengthy one. At about one p.m. of this day, December 15th, we weighed our anchor and hoisted our sails. As the wind was south-east the island kept it off us, so that we had to take to the sweeps. Having got an offing with their aid, we at last felt the wind, which was but light, so that we did not make more than four knots an hour.

On the morrow, the 16th of December, the wind veered round to the north-east. At dawn we perceived a vessel steering almost as ourselves; at mid-day we came up with her and sailed close by. She was the *Pendragon*, an iron ship of 2500 tons, from San Francisco for Queenstown. She asked us to report her at Bahia, which we duly did on our arrival. This day we only made sixty-nine miles.

On the 17th of December we made 128 miles ; all hands were now more or less prostrated with sickness and fever.

On the 18th December we made 135 miles—the same glorious weather and north-east wind continuing. Being now midsummer, the temperature was high, even at sea— about 85° Fahrenheit in our cabin.

On the 19th of December we made 150 miles.

On the 20th of December we made 130 miles. We were now approaching the land; we passed one of the quaint-rigged Brazilian negro coasting-vessels this afternoon. The temperature in our cabin rose to 90°. This night the heavy dew indicated the proximity of land ; at about midnight we sighted the light on Point Itapuan, and lay becalmed in front of it during the night, the breakers on the beach being distinctly audible to us.

At sunrise on the 21st of December we still lay becalmed.

We were not more than one mile from the coast, near the Rio Vermillio. The rows of stately cocoas that fringed the sands and the hills behind with their dense vegetation looked certainly most beautiful in the morning light, and the rich coast presented the very appearance of an earthly paradise. No wonder that the old navigators grew wildly enthusiastic when such lovely and fresh scenes burst upon them suddenly, after dreary months of sailing on an unknown sea. I called up the mate to see how he would be affected by this to him first glimpse of a tropical shore. He shook his head sadly; his face wore a look of miserable foreboding. "Ah," he said, "the very look of it is enough; you can see the fever there. Look at that curious green of the trees; look at the yellow earth: any one can see it is unhealthy. I can see it, can smell the fever even from here."

Hundreds of curious fishing-catamarans now sailed out from the shore, manned by naked negroes. On beholding these primitive craft, and on hearing the barbaric jargon of their hideous crews, my men now concluded that I had brought them to a land of savages, as well as of fevers. A breeze springing up, we slowly sailed by the coast, doubled Fort San Antonio, and opened out that magnificent bay that is one of the wonders of the world, with its stately city rising steeply from the beach, mingling with the rank and lovely vegetation that only these favoured climates can show.

Exclamations of surprise and admiration burst from all. But these sentiments soon gave way to fear in the minds of two of the crew, as we sailed into the bay, smooth and sultry after the fresh and heavy Atlantic outside. A headache at once attacked the mate, and tears were in his eyes as he informed me that he knew that yellow fever had already struck him. "Take half a tumbler of castor-oil," I said to him, "and don't eat so much." I steered the vessel to our old berth under Fort La Mar, and there dropped our anchor, after a voyage of six days from Trinidad, and thirty-eight days since we sailed from Montevideo.

It was now a year since I had last visited the quaint old Portuguese city of the ever-tinkling bells, and I was glad to meet my friends and enjoy once more the delights of civilization. I determined to stay over Christmas at Bahia, as the vessel was in need of some repairs, and particularly of a good cleansing out, so as to exterminate if possible the

myriads of cockroaches that infested her. I expected re-
mittances at Pernambuco, so thought I should save time if I
left the *Falcon* at Bahia while I steamed to the former port
and back, thus avoiding the necessity of calling there in my
own vessel. My crew of course were much pleased with my
plan, for Pernambuco has a very evil reputation in the
River Plate as being by far the most pestilential of Brazilian
seaports.

Pernambuco is only some 450 miles—looked upon as
nothing in this land of enormous distances—from Bahia, so
the voyage by steamer is not of long duration or costly.

On the eve of Christmas Day I embarked on the steamer
Bahia, one of a very well-conducted native company, whose
vessels run up and down the entire coast of the empire,
calling at every important port. The voyage was a very
pleasant one. I have had some experience of ocean pas-
senger-vessels, but none have I ever found more thoroughly
comfortable in every respect than this Brazilian mail-steamer.
There were no foreigners on board save myself and two others
of the passengers, one a German diamond-merchant, the
other a Capucin friar from Florence. We three therefore
naturally were attracted to each other at the commencement
of the voyage, being, as the priest put it, if not fellow-
countrymen, at any rate fellow-Europeans, and so neighbours.
The German was a thorough cosmopolitan, and so a pleasant
companion; but the poor priest, whose face wore an expression of extreme discontent and sorrow, could talk but
on one subject, that of which his heart was full, his intense
dislike of the manners and customs of the people, of the
climate, and of everything indeed pertaining to Brazil. His
home-sickness was apparent, and the poor fellow said himself,
"Nostalgia will kill me." So far he was plump enough,
though sour-looking—a rather villainous-featured, black-
bearded priest, of the true inquisition-stake-and-fire type.
His conversation was not cheerful, being somewhat like that
of my mate. He spoke with loathing of the blacks, the
savage Indians, the fevers, the wild beasts, the reptiles,
snakes, insects, the terrible dense forests, and the heat ; to
hear his eloquent complaint one would take this glorious
empire to be a very inferno of horrors, instead of the earthly
paradise it really is.

The German and myself soon struck up an acquaintance

with our Brazilian fellow-passengers, chiefly students going home for their vacation from the University of Rio de Janeiro, very nice young fellows, and evidently gentlemen. There were some families also on board, with charming young ladies, and all trying to render themselves as agreeable as possible to their travelling-companions. The Brazilians are indeed, at any rate superficially, a delightful people, from the nobility down to the mulatto peasant-proprietors.

Now that I had visited the River Plate States, I was much struck, as all travellers to South America have been, by the tremendous contrast presented by the Portuguese and Spanish settlements, the Portuguese empire of Brazil and the numerous republics of the Spanish-speaking peoples. Notwithstanding the existence of slavery, and the great degradation of the European race by mixture with the negro, Brazil strikes the stranger as being a really civilized nation. Most of the Spanish republics, on the other hand, appear to him to be but badly-organized hordes of utter savages. To the most superficial observer is this great difference apparent. In Brazil a sense of security is experienced ; a feeling that one is in a well-ordered state. The government, alone in all America, is monarchical, and the old-fashioned system does indeed shine out bright here when compared with the wild democracies that surround it—republics with perfect constitutions framed on the highest principles of Bentham and Montesquieu ; where universal freedom is preached, and the vilest tyranny of unlettered savage chieftains practised.

The Brazilian has one fault, however. He may have more—probably has,—but this is a very great one, or at least seemed so to me while living on this steamer, as it seriously interfered with my comfort ; whereas, whatever other faults he may have did not get in my way ; to them therefore I am tolerant. The fault I speak of is this, the Brazilian does not know how to dine comfortably. This to the Englishman, proverbial for his dining propensities, is simply horrible and unpardonable, for is not dinner one of the greatest duties of life ? But the Brazilian slurs this sacred duty over. All the courses are put on the table at once ; then comes a scramble, every one gobbling away as if for very life—helping himself from any or all dishes, pell-mell and anyhow.

Now, a most excellent dinner of many dishes was served

on board this steamer—a dinner to linger over, and it was
all done in thirteen minutes exactly by my watch. Even
when hurried by business this is inexcusable; but on a
steamer, where one has nothing to do but eat and drink,
and look forward with anticipation to the next meal as soon
as one is finished, such a custom is positively criminal.

Why thus hurry over the chief pleasure of the day? Life
is not so full of joys. Should we not advance delicately
from course to course, dally over the dessert, and then,
softly meditating, linger long over the soothing cigar, coffee,
and its *chasse?* But, alas! the good dinner is all over in
thirteen minutes, though it be Christmas Day. Very little
wine is drunk, the coffee is taken standing, no one follows it
with a *chasse,* every one rushes off, and the German and
myself do not feel that we have dined. However, we
console ourselves by sitting under the awning on deck,
smoking excellent cigars, and watching the glorious coast
scenery as we pass it—leagues after leagues of sandy shores
lined with waving cocoanuts, and green hills studded here
and there with great mango-trees.

So passed my Christmas Day, like my last one at sea. On
the 26th of December the steamer anchored for some hours
in the Bay of Maceio, off the town of the same name, to take
in cargo. This is not a considerable seaport; there were but
six vessels at anchor when we arrived, nearly all Englishmen
loading with sugar, and, like ourselves, rolling about heavily
in the high Atlantic swell, for the bay is exposed to
the prevailing on-shore wind. The glaring white town is
built on the slopes of a hill; in front of it is a fine, sandy
beach, on which there is a perpetual surf. As everywhere
else on the Brazilian coast, groves of cocoanuts line the
shore, and beautify what would otherwise be a rather arid
scene.

The diamond-merchant and myself went on shore for a
while, being landed by a native boat on the end of a rather
rickety pier. We found Maceio to be an exceedingly uninteresting town—a mere congregation, for the most part, of
small huts inhabited by negroes and mulattoes. There was
a tramway, of course, as everywhere else in South America,
and the strings of nearly naked slaves and carts that were
bringing down the sacks of sugar to the beach, not without
much bustle and noise, lent some life to the miserable streets.

The export of sugar from Maceio is very considerable, and this was the season of greatest activity in that trade. We soon had enough of this glaring town, for the heat was very intense. It was indeed seasonable weather—that is for Christmas in the southern tropics.

Early on the morning of the 27th of December we were off Pernambuco, which from the sea appears insignificant enough, huge city though it be, on account of its low and perfectly flat site. Forests of cocoas seemed to surround it. I had heard a good deal of the celebrated recife or natural breakwater which forms the harbour of Pernambuco, but I was not prepared to see so wonderful a freak of nature as it really is.

The recife is a coral bank or reef extending along many hundreds of leagues of the Brazilian coast. In places there are openings or gates in this reef, through which vessels can sail into the smooth lagoons within, and here ports are established.

Here, at Pernambuco, the recife is parallel to the shore, and distant but eighty yards or so from it. It rises in a broad, squared wall of coral, perfectly regular, being some feet above the level of high-water springs. To the north of the town this wall terminates abruptly, and the reef from that point is below the sea-level. At the end of this wall is an old fort erected by the Dutch, just under which is a very narrow channel deep enough for the passage of vessels; but the broadest and safest opening through the reef is still further to the north. Steaming through this latter passage we proceeded up this admirable harbour, which cannot but strike every visitor with astonishment. It is, as it were, a broad canal, thronged with vessels flying the flags of every civilized nation. On our right hand extended a fine stone quay bordered by an avenue of shady trees, behind which were the long rows of houses, the stores of merchants, hotels, banks, and cafés. On our left, perfectly parallel to the quay, extended the recife, a straight wall of dark coral, squared and so regular that one could scarce believe that this was the work of nature and not of man. Cannons captured in the Paraguayan war were firmly let into this wall at short intervals, to which the vessels were moored. Under shelter of this breakwater the water was smooth as glass; while on its other side the great Atlantic waves, driven up before the trade-wind, broke furiously, at times dashing showers of spray right over among the shipping in the still canal. The waves not unfrequently wash over the Recife; but, as storms are almost unknown on this coast, it is rare that much damage is inflicted.

Pernambuco has been called by some imaginative people the Venice of Brazil. The resemblance consists merely in the fact of water being a rather common feature of both cities. The River Capibaribe doubles upon itself several times while traversing Pernambuco, and hence one crossing the city in a straight line comes frequently upon broad, canal-like stretches of slow-flowing water bordered by quays and houses. But the architecture and general colouring is anything but Venetian. These canals present an animated appearance, being covered with the small craft of the country that bring down the produce from the interior. Not here are the gondolas, but long, narrow, native dug-outs or canoes, formed of hollowed trees, paddled by negroes and other swarthy savages whose form of head denotes their Indian blood. The catamarans, too, mere rafts, skim along the water with an astonishing speed under their white, triangular sails. Some of these canals are exceedingly foul— well calculated to breed yellow fever, one would imagine.

Pernambuco, translated, signifies the mouth of hell, and its reputation is well described by its name. Low-lying, as it is, and surrounded by mangrove-swamps and lagoons of foul, stagnant water, it ought to be a most unhealthy place. Indeed, so it once was; being justly reputed, as I have said, the most pestilential seaport of Brazil. But Pernambuco is gradually acquiring a better reputation. Yellow fever does not visit it as often as of old, nor are the epidemics of this plague so severe as they were. An English company has undertaken the drainage of the town, and the increased salubrity is by many put down to this cause. Again, there is but little malaria even in the suburbs and in the vicinity of the swamps, for the fresh trade-wind that never fails by day effectually disperses the deadly exhalations.

For seven days I had to wait at Pernambuco, as no steamer sailed for the south during that period—thus I was able to study the city and its ways. My chief impression left was that of sugar. Sugar indeed pervaded Pernambuco when I was there. The very air was sugar; the city was

paved with it; the heavy smell of it was positively oppressive at times. The gates of great barn-like stores gaped on
the streets, and within each I saw half-naked Indians,
negroes and Meztizzos piling up very mountains of the yellow
crystals with their spades. Clumsy cart after cart, truck
after truck, lumbered creaking from every quarter to the
quays, obstructing the ways, with molasses dripping out
between their boards. Pernambuco indeed reeks of sugar;
from the stores it overflows into the road; under one's feet
is a brown sticky mud, like tar in consistency, and far more
soiling than even our greasy London mud, for the mud of
this city is of unrefined cane-sugar.

The country round Pernambuco, though flat, is exceedingly
beautiful, overflowed as it is with a vegetation of whose
magnificence no one who has never visited the tropics can
have any conception. I went one evening to Caxanga, which
is to Pernambuco somewhat what Richmond is to London,
and about an hour's journey by rail. It was one of those
magical evenings that are common enough in this land of
perpetual summer, starlit and still. Our whole way lay
through a wonderful, fairy-like grove, where trees and plants
that are valuable treasures of the hot-house to us grew in
wild luxuriance. We passed villa after villa nestling in
gardens; and what gardens! what magical colours! what
dark green masses, or light, feathery palms and bright-
flowered creepers! and, more wonderful than all, the frequent
great trees, leafless, but covered for leaves with bouquets of
vivid purple or crimson. The villas were gaudy to an English
eye—horrible would they be under an English sky, but here
quite harmonious to their surroundings, and in good taste;
luxurious palaces of the tropics, where dwelt the wealthy
Pernambucan merchants—open and airy mansions, all of
light colour, many covered with porcelain tiles, most of them
light-blue, picked out with white, as if houses of Wedgwood
china.

Caxanga itself is not much of a place, but there are
splendid baths of cool spring water that are the chief attractions, for a cool bath is not to be found everywhere in this
climate. To the north of Pernambuco is a hill overlooking
the sea, on which is built the ancient and now almost
deserted city of Olinda. Between the two cities extends a
dreary, marshy plain, with lagoons and festering mangrove-

swamps, tufts of palms rising occasionally above the lower vegetation. An excellent road has been carried across this wilderness from one city to the other. Feeling very energetic one day, I walked along this to Olinda. I rather repented of my project before I had got half-way, for it was broiling hot, and shade there was none. The only people I passed were naked negroes, wading in the black mud among the mangroves in search of crabs, and they looked at me with surprise as I passed, for a white man tramping along this road on a midsummer midday was a strange sight indeed to them.

Olinda itself, one of the most ancient of American towns, is now a city of the dead. All the houses are old, of the antique Portuguese style. Churches and convents seem to be the most common buildings; their number is extraordinary. The streets are steep, winding and ill-paved, grass-grown and silent; even the magnificent cathedral appears to be neglected. Great indeed is the contrast between Olinda and modern, bustling Pernambuco. The situation is very fine, and a magnificent view of the distant seaport and of all the country around is obtained from the open places. Great palm-trees rise in every portion of the city, and set off to advantage the austere and massive ecclesiastical edifices.

On reaching the summit of the town, where from a plot of grass in front of what I took to be a monastery the best view is commanded, I sat down to make a hurried pencil-sketch. Hitherto I had walked through silent streets, hearing but the echoes of my own footfall, when now I was suddenly startled by the most fearful and blood-curdling yells just behind me. Leaping up, I perceived they proceeded from a tumbledown-looking building that I had not before observed. It was somewhat like one of the cages in which the lions are imprisoned in the Zoological Gardens, for a stout iron grating was carried along the front of it; within were several men, mulattoes for the most part, with faces like wild beasts, who shook the bars and raised the fearful cries that had startled me. This, as my readers may have guessed, was the pauper lunatic asylum.

CHAPTER XXXIV.

ON returning to Bahia I carried out a project that had long been on my mind.   When I first sailed into this harbour, a year back, I was very desirous of undertaking a cruise among the islands and bays of that beautiful inland sea, the Reconcavo.

My poor mate was of course very sad on hearing of this plan.   "What?" he said; "you are going to take us up those pestilential rivers? we will all die."   It was in vain to tell him that malaria was unknown in the breezy neighbourhood of the ocean.

We procured a pilot, or rather a Portuguese harbour-boatman, who said he was a pilot for the rivers, and sailed away before a glorious sea-breeze on the 7th of January.   As I had already steamed up the rivers Cachoeira and S. Amaro a year before, we made for the mouth of the river Jaguaripe, which, after these, is the most considerable river flowing into the gulf of Bahia.

First we steered right across the Reconcavo to the northern extremity of the large island of Itaparica, which supplies the market of Bahia with fruit.   This island is famed for its beauty, and indeed, when we approached it, we could not but allow that it well merited its reputation.   Gentle hills rise from the shore, covered with a dense, rich vegetation—a tangled forest of cocoas, bread-fruit-trees, mangoes, bananas, jackas, palms, and other trees ; these groves are of a delightful fresh green, and resound with the songs of birds.   Below are beaches of sand, lined with mangroves.   As the water was deep, we kept close to the island as we coasted round it. We passed several little villages, whose negro inhabitants devote their time to fishing and whaling ; small whales are common in the Reconcavo, notwithstanding the constant war that is waged upon them.

On doubling a point we opened the capital of the island, the sleepy town of Itaparica, dominated by an old fort. Sailing from here to the mainland, we entered the mouth of the river, and after ascending it until dusk came to an anchor a mile below the little town of Maragoujipina, and there passed a night among the mosquitoes, surrounded by dense groves, all glittering with myriads of fire-flies and noisy with cicadas

On the next morning there was no wind; therefore, as our pilot told us that we were not far from the city of Nazaret, we determined to leave the vessel at her anchor and row there in the dinghy. On being closely cross-examined as to the exact distance, he informed us that it was about "one quarter of the half of a quarter of a league." I suppose he thought this would sound nice and precise to us, but it hardly tallied with his next statement, that it would require from an hour to an hour and a half's rowing to reach it.

Three rivers met just above our anchorage. Our pilot pointed out one as being the river of Nazaret, so we proceeded to pull up it, taking him with us, so that he might set us right in case of our being at a loss at any other point.

This river flowed across a muddy plain, but ahead of us, at about the distance of three miles, were wooded hills under which, we were led to understand, lay Nazaret. But these hills, though but three miles off as the crow flies, were an unconscionable way off by water; for this stream wound about in a most irritating fashion, so that we were rowing away from our destination as often as not.

We were crossing an utterly deserted country, whose scenery was anything but cheerful. On either side of us stretched great mangrove-swamps; the black mud bubbled, and festered, and stunk under the hot sun; and the mangroves themselves, those most repulsive of all plants that grow, drooped down from half their height in muddy festoons, showing the point to which the sea-tide rose. Over them crawled innumerable crabs, red, and blue, and yellow, and green—the only reptiles that can find a congenial habitat in such a slough. But a mangrove-swamp has often been described before, and all who have seen it bear witness to its loathsome ugliness.

On and on we rowed, and never seemed to get nearer to the hills; then dark clouds crossed the heavens, and the rain fell, as it can fall in Brazil, drenching us in a moment of course. This did not improve the aspect of our dismal surroundings. At last we did reach the hills, and found that the river skirted them; on one side of us now was the swamp, on the other were the fertile, but uninhabited, heights.

The river now wound more than ever, following each irregularity of the hills. We rowed on for a considerable time, but no sign of Nazaret—none of the bells and fireworks that announce to one yet afar off the presence of a Brazilian city. We, so cheerful hitherto, began now to wax wrathful; and the pilot, so very confident hitherto, looked puzzled.

"Are you sure we are right?"

"Certain; in a quarter of an hour we are there," was his constant reply to our often-repeated inquiry.

But we doubted him, and when at last we saw a little bamboo rancho nestling in a banana-grove on the hillside, we shouted loudly, to the evident dislike of our guide, who did not approve of being mistrusted. The negro householder heard us, and came out.

"Ho! Patrice!" called to him one of my friends—it is the custom to address every peasant as Patrice hereabouts, until you know his real name. "Ho! Patrice! how far to Nazaret?"

"To Nazaret!" replied the sable one, chuckling. "This is not the Nazaret river."

"What river is it then?"

"The river Sao Geronimo."

The unfortunate pilot, who had already come to the conclusion that the crew of the *Falcon* were a set of ferocious pirates, turned white on hearing this, and was fain to jump overboard, in order to escape our just anger. But finding that we were not going beyond classical imprecations, he consented to remain with us; and wet, sad, hungry, and thirsty, we rowed all the weary miles back to the *Falcon*, which we reached at about two p.m.

After a meal we set out again in search of Nazaret; this time we did hit on the right river, which did not traverse a mangrove-swamp, but flowed over a bed of silver sand, across an agreeable and diversified country.

Nazaret we found to be a pretty little town, very picturesquely situated on the slopes of a hill. The river is not navigable beyond this; here it rushes noisily over a rocky bottom, and is spanned by a fine bridge.

Of course it was a saint's day, or rather half a dozen saints' days, and the town was *en fête*. Rockets and crackers fizzed and banged all around us, the bells were ringing, the church was illuminated within and without at sunset, and we witnessed a curious ecclesiastical procession of priests and negro acolytes, certain of whom bore censers and danced in

23

front, revolving with slow and stately step, singing the while quite in the old Biblical style. When we had seen enough of all this, and had danced at a mulatto ball, we rowed back, and at three a.m. partook of a digestible supper of cold tinned plum pudding and rum.

The next day we sailed down the river till we were off the town of Jaguaripe, when, the wind failing us, we came to an anchor. This little town is built on the slopes of a hill covered with tropical fruit-trees, and is dominated by a fine old church. I went on shore with my two friends; it was blazing hot, being but an hour after midday, and all the inhabitants were within, enjoying their siesta; we Englishmen were alone abroad. After wandering about for some time, we were passing a large stone house, when an upper window of it opened, and a man, putting his head out of it, most courteously invited us to come up out of the sun and refresh ourselves. Such hospitality to an utter stranger is thoroughly Brazilian. We entered, and were received by this kind person in a large room whose windows overlooked a splendid and extensive view—leagues upon leagues of undulating tropic forest-land intersected by many winding rivers.

Our host produced English bottled beer and cigars, and entered into a lively conversation with us with that unaffected cordiality and charm of manner that so distinguishes the gentlemen of this empire. He introduced us to his wife and children, and also to his two very pretty and agreeable sisters-in-law. He told us that he was the chief of Jaguaripe, which he described as a very quiet, peaceful sort of a place. Just below his mansion was a gloomy mass of masonry, a building large enough to lodge all the inhabitants of the town; that, he told us, was the prison; but do not, he continued, "form an estimate of the number of our criminals from the size of our prison; there are no prisoners in it, and there have not been any for a very long time. Indeed, we have no police here now."

There is indeed very little crime in Brazil; the mulattoes that form the bulk of the free population are of an amiable, gentle nature; in this respect forming a striking contrast to the natives of the Spanish republics. Neither, again, is there to be found in the free mulatto or negro of Brazil that insolence and those other most objectionable qualities that so distinguish the mulattoes and negroes of the United

ON THE RIVER JAGUARIPE.

States, the West Indies, and other Anglo-Saxon countries, wherein slavery has been an institution. The reason is not far to seek. Black blood is a reproach in the latter. The Anglo-Saxon will not marry with the negro, as does the Latin, and more especially the Portuguese colonist. He hates and despises the son of Ham, and all who have the slightest taint of African blood.

The mulatto knows this; feels it deeply; despises himself that he is of a despised race. Though feigning to imagine himself a man and a brother, he is aware that he is a social outcast, that the whites will not eat with him or associate with him; so he revenges himself by insolence and brutality, feeling that it is vain for him to be ambitious, that he can never rise, he gnaws his heart out with his thwarted aspirations and crushed vanity. But in Brazil this caste-feeling does not exist at all, or at any rate to a very slight extent. The best families have negro blood in their veins. The pure whites are an insignificant minority, and the mulatto, taking a pride in himself, feeling himself to be really on an equality with the other citizens in every respect, falls into his natural position, and has no need, like the Barbadian nigger, that worst of his species, to try and pass off his inferiority by unbounded insolence to those of the superior race.

However, may the day be very far off when the Anglo-Saxon, like the Portuguese, feels no degradation in allying himself with the African; for the nigger, though he may be a man, is certainly not a brother, whatever his white friends may say.

We sailed from Jaguaripe at daybreak on the following morning, and tacked down on the top of the ebb tide until we reached the centre of a broad stretch of water within the Barra Falsa or false entrance to the Reconcavo, which, obstructed with reefs as it is, has caused the destruction of many a vessel that has mistaken it for the true passage.

Suddenly we ran hard upon a sandbank and stuck fast. The unfortunate pilot, who had been confident as usual, now burst into tears, and rushed up and down the deck, stamping and raving. On being sternly asked for an explanation of his conduct, he jerked out between his sobs,—

"Ah! senor, it is not my fault indeed; it is the mermaid's."

"The mermaid's! thou idiot."

"Yes, senor; there was never a bank here before. I have sailed ten thousand times across here, but the last time —yes, close here—indeed, just here, I saw a mermaid; I did not throw her a gift, and thus has she revenged herself. Ah, dear! ah, dear! what a miserable wretch am I!"

We could of course abuse him no more after so satisfactory an exculpation of himself. A pilot cannot in justice be held responsible for the acts of a malicious mermaid, who piles sandbanks in his course. Had we known the Reconcavo was infested by these dangerous maidens, I should not have ventured to navigate its waters in my precious *Falcon.*

All the fishermen of this coast have an unshakable faith in mermaids; few among them are there that have not at least once seen one of these beautiful water-people. It is customary to place mirrors and combs on rocks by the sea, as propitiatory gifts to them.

As the tide was still ebbing, we had to reconcile ourselves to a few hours' stay on the mermaid bank; so I rowed off with my friends to the coast, about a mile and a half distant, where we perceived some houses. After landing on the sandy beach at the mouth of a small river, we walked up to the village, the polite, kind yellow people of which informed us that it was called by the curious name of Caixa de Pregos, or Box of Nails. The houses or rather bamboo huts are not built in streets, but scattered through a dense and pleasant grove of bananas, cocoas, mangoes, bread-fruit-trees, &c., winding footpaths connecting one with the other in such a way that the settlement is a very Hampton Court maze. The whalebones that occasionally form the doorposts of these huts indicate the occupation of the people.

We at last, after much wandering in the maze, came to a little bamboo public-house where passable cashaça or white rum was vended: over the bar were pasted two plates cut out of a Portuguese illustrated paper. One was the portrait of Mr. Gladstone, the pendant was Henri Rochefort!

We came across an old mulatto boatman here, who undertook to paddle off to the *Falcon* at high tide and pilot us across the banks. After being introduced to, and then cordially welcomed by, every man, woman, or child, we left the village of Box of Nails, and rowed back to the *Falcon.*

At four p.m. the tide had risen two feet, and we were

again afloat ; then our new pilot came off to us in his dug-out. A long discussion ensued between him and the old pilot ; for the former insisted that the bank on which we had grounded had existed where it now was for twenty years, to his knowledge. This rather shook our faith in the mermaid story, and we led our unfortunate Portuguese, who was now getting rather sick of the *Falcon*, to understand that we should throw him overboard if he played the fool with us any more, mermaids or no mermaids.

Our mulatto piloted us over the shoals, and then left us, when we proceeded without further accident to the whaling village of S. Amarro de Catu, off which we anchored for the night. Of course there was a fiesta, church bells, fireworks, and dancing, at which, being welcome, we assisted.

The next day we sailed to Bahia. First we had to beat down a rather narrow channel ; however, the pilot, though sad, was confident. Said he,—

"There are no more sandbanks now ; there are only a few rocks ahead ; sandbanks may change their position, rocks cannot."

"But a mermaid can move even rocks."

On hearing this all the poor fellow's confidence vanished, and a terrible anxiety, to be easily read on his face, took its place. We, too, felt anxious ; for, after so many specimens of his ignorance, we doubted his accurate knowledge of the position of the rocks ; for our part, he being pilot, we preferred sandbanks. However, all went well ; we sailed down the river with its beautiful banks, passed Itaparica again, crossed the broad Reconcavo studded with quaint native craft, and before night were at anchor once more under Fort la Mar. The pleasant trip was over. The temperature, by the way, during this voyage ranged from 88° to 94° in our cabin.

I stayed in Bahia for another thirty-six hours, and then sailed for the north. It puzzled me somewhat to decide what should be my next port of call on my way to the West Indies. Having seen the principal and most beautiful of Brazilian cities, I did not care to call at any other ports of this empire ; besides which, I wanted to make a lengthy sea-voyage of it now, in order to blow some of the malaria out of myself. Thus I determined to sail direct for distant Guiana, but the question was, whether to make for a harbour of Dutch, French, or English Guiana.

Cayenne, as being one of the most remarkable penal settlements in the world, rather excited my curiosity. Having no charts or pilot-directories for the coast to the north of Brazil, I hunted all over Bahia in search of these. It was in vain; there was nothing of the kind to be found here. This was awkward, for I knew that all the coast north of the Amazon is so obstructed with mudbanks, far out to sea, that charts, and good ones, too, are quite indispensable for a skipper wishing to make any of the harbours, especially if the skipper be an amateur one, like myself. However, I found among the captains, who loafed about the ship-chandlers, an old German, master of a barque loading here with sugar for Hamburg. He knew Demerara well, and gave me such plain directions for making the mouth of that river that I made up my mind to sail for Georgetown, the capital of British Guiana.

The directions of my friendly skipper were as follows : Get hold of the coast near Berbice, and sail on in four-fathom soundings till you sight the light-house and fort at the mouth of the Demerary river ; when they bear S.S.W., sail straight in without fear. For a vessel of the *Falcon's* draught these directions are all that is wanted, but they would hardly do for a much larger craft.

From Bahia to Georgetown is about 2600 English miles, so this was to be one of our long voyages.

On the 13th of January, having taken our water on board and a supply of stores, we got under weigh, the afternoon breeze enabling us soon to get outside the bay among the heaving Atlantic waves. Our old enemy, the northerly monsoon, was still blowing, but not so boisterously as is his fashion further south.

For the first 600 miles of the voyage, that is to near Cape San Roque, I decided to keep hold of the land, taking short tacks, not only that we might enjoy the scenery, but with the object of fishing. For outside the inner reef of the Recife, there extends for a thousand miles or more along this coast, and parallel to it, a submerged reef of coral, known as the Pracel, one of the finest fishing-grounds for rock-fish in the world. We found it so, as we now tacked backwards and forwards across it for a week, securing bonitos, rock-cod, king-fish, dolphins, sword-fish, and a dozen other species with whose English names I am unacquainted, in large quantities.

The weather was fine, though the sea was choppy and sometimes high ; so we enjoyed these seven days—for the mononotony of an ocean voyage is much relieved by being, as we were, ever in sight of a varying and beautiful coast.

We passed the great Cocals, village after village of negro fishermen, with whom, as they came out to us in their strange boats, we often conversed, saw Sergipe, gave Cape Coruripe and the neighbouring reefs of San Rodrigo a wide berth, and took a board up to the mouth of the mighty Rio San Francisco, a river 1800 miles in length, the most valuable watercourse in Brazil, and along whose banks dwell one-sixth of the population of the empire.

On the 17th of January we came to where forest-clad heights fell abruptly in cliffs of red rock into the ocean, and behind them the far purple peaks of the inland Serra Bariga rose into the pale blue sky.

On the 18th of January the coast changed once more, being gently undulating and covered with groves of fruit-trees, unplanted by man. This day we passed the bay of Alagoas and Maccio, and at night sailed along a coast lit up for leagues by a great forest fire.

On the 20th of January we doubled Cape San Agostinho, and soon after discerned the hill of Olinda with its many churches and convents, and the great flat city of Pernambuco. A very bright idea now struck me. I had been rather troubled about my foul bill of health, and feared quarantine in Demerara. Now, if I put into Pernambuco, where yellow fever had not yet broken out, I might get a clean bill for Demerara. It was worth trying ; the Pernambucan authorities, I knew, would not quarantine me, though yellow fever had got under weigh at Bahia. The Brazilians don't mind Yellow Jack ; they are too familiar with him ; besides, he does not attack a native often, but only sweeps off the foreign sailors and such like strangers. Had it been small-pox now, that had been written across my hill of health, I should certainly have been quarantined, for the Brazilian dreads that disease indeed, and rightly, for it commits fearful ravages among the South American populations.

So it was that, to the dismay of my mate, I put into Pernambuco after all (he took precious good care, by the way, not to go on shore during our stay). Refusing the services of a pilot, I took the vessel through the Picao or little passage—the narrow entrance I have described as under the old Dutch fort on the Recife, and brought up within the great breakwater, nearly opposite to my old hotel. Several mail-steamers were anchored without, while within the Recife I recognized, to my surprise and joy, the *Norseman* telegraph-ship, which, as my readers will remember, towed us into Maldonado just a year back.

I succeeded in getting a clean bill of health for Demerara on the morrow after my arrival, and passed the remainder of the day with my old friends of the *Norseman*.

While I was on shore a mutiny broke out on the *Falcon*. Giobatta Panissa refused to obey the mate, drew his knife on him, and compelled him to beat a precipitate retreat into the cabin, where the mate, finding a loaded revolver, in his turn forced the other to retire up the companion to the maindeck. At this stage of the proceedings I arrived on board, and, after settling matters very quickly, pitched into the mate roundly for his impotence in preserving discipline when I was away, explaining to him that it was his duty to at once hit on the head with the weightiest bit of iron handy any one who ventured to question his commands. As for Panissa, I got hold of him by the collar, and informed him that it was my unalterable intention to throw him overboard, whether we were in port or mid-ocean, on the very next occasion he even talked of using a knife.

Having thus restored peace to the vessel, I looked around and found them a lot of hard work to do, so as to keep them quiet for the rest of the day.

On the following day, the 22nd of January, having taken on board an abundant stock of bananas, pine-apples, yams, sweet potatoes, and manioka, we sailed out of the harbour— this time by the larger Olinda passage.

It is 2000 miles from Pernambuco to the mouth of the Demerary. The voyage occupied us exactly ten days, so this is the best log the *Falcon* can show; and, indeed, I do not think it would be easy to find another yacht of her tonnage that had ever kept up a rate of 200 miles a day for ten consecutive days. Our best day's work was 220 nautical, or 253 English, miles.

There were two causes that conduced to this rapid run. In the first place we had done with the northerly monsoon, for about here are its limits; and we sailed away from Pernambuco before a fresh south-east wind, which enabled us to

run for days under all canvas, spinnaker included. We
encountered no calms on crossing the line, but passed straight
from the south-east to the north-east trade winds, which in
their turn were favourable to us, being on our beam.

In the second place we had a strong, favourable current
with us from Cape San Roque to Demerara. It is on Cape
Roque, the easternmost extremity of the New World, from
which the coasts fall away at right angles the one to the
other, that the great ocean current from the Cape of Good
Hope striking, bifurcates — one stream flowing down the coast
of South America to the south-west, known as the Brazilian
current, which, allied to the northerly monsoon, had troubled
us ever since we left the Plate ; and the other stream flowing
up the coast of South America to the north-west—this known
as the main equatorial current, further on, after it has
crossed the Caribbean Sea and Gulf of Mexico, receiving the,
to us, more familiar appellation of the Gulf Stream. This
equatorial current is of great assistance to vessels proceeding up the coast from the Cape San Roque. The rate of
it varies according to the season of the year, sometimes, it is
said, flowing as rapidly as four knots an hour. The greatest
difference we observed between our distance run in twenty-
four hours, as recorded by log and observation, was fifty
miles, which would give a two-knot current.

For the first six days of the voyage the wind blew fresh
from the south-east, enabling us to make about seven to eight
knots an hour through the water. This brought us to the
Equator, when the wind veered rather rapidly round to the
north-east, and so continued till we reached Demerara. We did
not encounter any calm whatever ; indeed, the lowest rate
logged for any hour of the voyage was five and a half knots.

For the first few days we hugged the coast, saw the port
of Parahiba, and passed close to the Rocas, those perilous
reefs that lie off Cape San Roque, and which are so dreaded
by mariners ; but now a light-house is being constructed on
one of the higher rocks ; we could perceive the men working
on it as we sailed by.

During this portion of the voyage we passed many jan-
gadas, the clumsy native coasters ; they sail well, but do not
appear to be built for really bad weather ; but bad weather
is of rare occurrence on this tropical ocean. I suppose when
a jangada is caught by a gale outside it goes down.

After doubling Cape San Roque, we left the land and took a course more to seawards, so as to avoid the variable inshore currents, and to fall in with the main body of the equatorial current. When we were off San Luiz do Maranhao we had an offing of about 200 miles, which we kept till we approached Guiana.

We caught a great many fish during this run, especially dolphins of large size. It was indeed pleasant, though rather monotonous, sailing. As the wind and current were in the same direction, the sea was remarkably smooth, rolling on in long, oily-looking waves of tepid water under a blazing sun.

The temperature in our cabin was high, 85° to 90°. We crossed the Equator on the 26th of January in longitude 42° 28'. On the 28th of January we were off the mouths of the Amazon, but too far out to sea to find ourselves in the discoloured water that this huge river pours out into the ocean.

Now that we had a north-east wind and a beam sea, high and choppy at times, our motion was not so comfortable as it had been for the first six days of the voyage ; we rolled heavily, took much water on board, and on several occasions were under two-reefed main-sail.

On the 29th of January, being off the north frontier of Brazil, and Cayenne bearing west of us, 170 miles, we steered so as to approach the coast once more. This day we came into a very heavy sea, with nasty waves breaking and curling up against the rapid current ; with us the wind was not strong, but a gale must have been blowing somewhere. We had now sailed into a very different climate from that which prevails on the healthy coasts of Brazil. The sky, instead of being clear, was ever overcast ; an unhealthy yellow haze hung upon the sea by night, and the atmosphere was oppressively close. I have since read a work by a naval officer, who observes how debilitating an effect is produced by this great heat accompanied by moisture. He states he often had half his men below on the sick list while sailing off the coast of the Guianas. The crew of the *Falcon*, who seem to have got into a generally bad state of health, felt these influences, and were suffering from fever and those bilious and intestinal disorders that are common in these latitudes.

On the 31st of January, having obtained no observation of

the sun for two days, in consequence of the heavy vapours, but knowing that the land could not be far off, we hove-to at daybreak to take soundings, but found no bottom in forty fathoms. This day we contrived to get the meridian altitude, and an observation of the sun for longitude at four p.m. We discovered that we were but twenty miles to the north of the river Surinam in Dutch Guiana. On taking a cast of the lead, we found that we were in twelve fathoms. The water here was of a dirty soup-colour, as it is far out to sea, all along this coast.

CHAPTER XXXV.

THE coast of Guiana, indeed of all the countries between the Amazons and the Gulf of Paria, a stretch of upwards of a thousand miles, is one of the strangest and most dreary in the world, rich though the inner country may be. For here the silt brought down by many mighty rivers, notably the Amazon and Orinoco, has formed a broad strip of low alluvial land that extends far out seawards from the forest-clad hills. It is difficult to distinguish where these vast plains terminate, and the sea begins, for the slope is so gradual that the mariner can find soundings when yet a day's sail from the coast; and a vessel can drive ashore and be broken up by the heavy rollers on the shoals, though from the mast-head no land be visible. And to mariners thus wrecked poor is the prospect of escape in the boats. For if they are not swamped by the breakers and reach smoother water, they can go on for long leagues, the sea but very gradually shallowing, till there be but a few feet of water under them, and going further they will find vegetation indeed, but not land, for dense groves of mangroves grow out into the sea, and in places forests of huge trees. And now the boat can go no further, nor can the men proceed on foot, for the mud underneath is soft as butter and deep, so that one venturing on it will sink wholly in it. Indeed, it appears a hopeless land of slime and fever, quite unfitted for man, unless it be for the Tree-Indians, a low race of fish-eating savages that, like birds, build their homes among the branches of the flooded forests on the Gulf of Paria. But within this outlying waste of mud there lies one of the most fertile countries of the world. If one ascends any of the creeks and rivers that pierce the outer swamps, and afford the sole means of communication to the interior, he will find himself among the richest plains of earth, where are cultivated sugar, cocoa, and all tropical produce; while further inland are mountains and valleys covered with one dense primeval forest of the rarest cabinet woods; but this latter, yet unexplored, is inhabited only by Indian tribes, cannibals some of them, for the settlements of the few white men are solely on the very unhealthy, but fertile, low-lying coast-region, chiefly at the mouths of the rivers.

At midday, January the 31st, we were, as I have said, about twenty miles from the nearest land, near the river Surinam. The lightship that lies off the mouth of the Berbice river, and which is moored about twelve miles out to sea, was now but 130 miles distant, and for this I now shaped a direct course.

As I had no chart and knew not how far out to sea the tongues of the shoals might extend, I took casts of the lead at frequent intervals. So soft is the bottom hereabouts that it is difficult to feel when the lead reaches it, and about a foot must be deducted from the depth indicated to allow for the sinking into the mud.

A fresh E.N.E. wind, driving us on at the rate of seven knots an hour, blew during the night, yet a heavy haze lay on the ocean. The soundings decreased as we advanced till at three a.m. we found but three fathoms of water, so we hauled two points to windward and got into the line of five-fathom soundings. We were then off the mouth of the great Corentyn river, that divides British from Dutch Guiana.

At six a.m. the soundings quite suddenly fell to three fathoms, and we found ourselves in the midst of very heavy and dangerous rollers. These were so high and steep that we had at once to haul our wind and make for deeper water. For upwards of ten minutes we were in real peril of foundering; a heavy-laden merchant-vessel would certainly have gone down. As we crossed these waves, our motion was so extremely violent that I fully expected to see the mast chucked right over the bows at any moment. Each sea washed over us, filling our decks with water. I was in charge of the deck at the time. The tremendous jerks, the noise, and the alarming angles the vessel assumed, sometimes seeming to stand almost on end, brought up the watch below, who fully expected to find that we had driven on shore among the breakers and were fast tumbling to pieces. But the *Falcon* behaved admirably as usual; and after steering seaward for a quarter of an hour, we reached the six-fathom soundings, and were in comparatively smooth water again.

I learnt afterwards at Georgetown that the rollers, which, breaking more or less heavily, are always to be met with on this shoal, are a well-known danger to the mariners of this coast; and that many a vessel had not come out of them to tell the tale as we did, but has gone down with all hands.

At nine a.m. we passed close to the Berbice lightship, and perceived on our port hand land once more, and, what is more, English land, the first I had seen since I had sailed out of Falmouth Harbour.

We coasted along the shore in four-fathom soundings, the sea being quite smooth, and of a reddish tint. The shore here does not present so desolate an appearance from the sea as it does to the east or west of the British colony. We saw a long low line of forest, above which at intervals rose the lofty chimneys of the sugar factories. We passed many of the colony craft, shallow, but fast, sloops and schooners, very different in build to the coasters of Brazil that we had hitherto seen.

In the afternoon we sighted the lighthouse and the shipping at the mouth of the Demerara river. Following the instructions of my friend, the German skipper, I sailed on till these bore S.S.W., and then made straight for the entrance to the river, finding nowhere less water than three fathoms. At four p.m. we were within the Demerara, and dropped our anchor off the fort. The captain of the port soon came off to us, gave us pratique, and kindly piloted us to a convenient berth, just in front of Georgetown market-place, near the landing-stage of the steam-ferry that affords communication between one side of the river and the other.

Having stowed our canvas, we now looked around us. The town that stretched in front of us on the right bank of the river was certainly quite unlike any city I had yet seen in tropical America, in every respect. At a glance one could perceive that this was a British, not a Spanish or Portuguese, settlement. None of the massive quaint old houses of stone here, none of the irregular streets as of Bahia, the dirt and careless untidiness; but bran-new, unhandsome, but very practical and comfortable, buildings of wood and corrugated iron sheets, cleanliness and order. What chiefly puzzled my crew was, that all the negroes that passed us in canoes and rafts spoke English to each other. It was evidently quite a new idea to my Italians, who imagined that all blacks spoke Portuguese alone. I must confess I felt somewhat as they did. It hardly seemed natural to me, when I went on shore, to hear my native tongue spoken by every one around me, black, yellow, or white, and I was constantly addressing people at first in Portuguese and Spanish.

On the morrow after my arrival in port, I landed on the Stelling by the market, and proceeded to inspect the town. The clean, tidy dress of the black and Creole policeman, the zouave uniform of the soldiers, forcibly brought to my mind that I was no longer in a foreign colony.

The streets of Georgetown are wide and regular, the houses are of wood with corrugated iron roofs, and all are erected on piles, standing, as it were, on stilts; thus the ground-floor, to explain myself by a bull, is some fourteen feet above the ground. The object of this style of architecture is to avoid the malaria that floats along the surface of the soil. It has been found in all these countries, that if the dwelling-rooms be thus raised some feet from the ground the miasma is wholly avoided, or nearly so. In many parts of the north coast of South America, especially on the Spanish Main, to sleep one night on the surface of the soil is nearly always fatal, so deadly are the malarious emanations.

What constitutes the great charm of Georgetown is that the glorious vegetation of the country has not been excluded from it, but grows in luxuriance between the houses. Viewed from the summit of the lighthouse, Georgetown presents not the appearance of a city, but of a lovely grove of tall palms and many flower-covered trees and bushes, with habitations scattered through it. The residential houses are built in the comfortable East Indian style, with verandahs surrounding them; each stands in its own garden. There are streets in Georgetown that are more like botanical gardens than streets, to which the tropical hot-houses of Kew are very deserts.

There is one very broad street at the back of government-house, the name of which I forget (the excellent Georgetown Club, of which I was an honorary member during my stay, is in it), and of it Georgetown should be proud. Along both sides of it are villas and wonderful gardens. In its centre, between shady avenues of trees, flows a sluggish canal, entirely covered with the magnificent Victoria Regia lilies. There is a botanical garden outside Georgetown, but the skill of man cannot outdo the splendours of the vegetation that will spring up anywhere in this land, where allowed to do so.

The population of Georgetown is indeed cosmopolitan, for four continents are here abundantly represented. The Europeans are of course much in the minority. Of these, the Portuguese are the most numerous; the small tradesman and artificer class being largely made up of these frugal people. The Englishmen here are among the most agreeable and hospitable of their race. It was here I began to learn what was meant by West Indian hospitality.

After the hospitality of my countrymen in this colony, the next thing that the stranger observes is their hats. I do not think any town presents the spectacle of so varied a collection of head-gear. You could not wear anything that could be considered eccentric at Georgetown in the way of hats. Of course, first there are pith-helmets of every kind; straw hats of infinite breadth of brim; but it is, after all, in white felt-hats that the inhabitants show their ingenuity most; and high above them all towers the stupendous pyramid that graces the head of a certain popular and respected crown-officer. After the white nankeen-jacketted, much-hatted Britisher, come the representatives of Africa, the descendants of the black slaves, here a very worthless and vicious class. America is represented by nearly naked, stunted Red Indians, who come down the river in their canoes from the interior to barter bows and arrows, skins of wild beasts, and other curiosities in the capital, and get dead-drunk with the proceeds. Then we have the Asiatic coolies, who are as numerous as the blacks. First, the inscrutable Chinese, who have their own quarter, and, more frugal than even the Portuguese, are gradually cutting out the latter as small tradesmen. Then the Hindoos, nude, save for the scanty loin-cloth, slim of limb ; and, though of the lowest castes, beautiful and .with noble heads ; sad, gentle men, who, quarter-staff in hand, walk softly through the streets ; men of an antique civilization, who look with contempt on their fellow-labourers, the African and American Indians, with their heavy animal faces, who never have had, and never will have, a civilization.

So many friends did I have in Georgetown, and so agreeably did time fly, that I extended my stay to a fortnight. The town was fairly healthy while I was there, though there was some yellow fever. A frightful epidemic of this pest of South America had been till recently raging in Demerara and in the Southern Antilles, but was now dying away. In Georgetown the fever had proved most fatal to the upper-class white residents and the officers of the garrison, not, as usual, being chiefly prevalent among the shipping in the river and the low quarters of the city. In consequence of this the white troops had now been all sent home, the negro regiment alone remaining ; so great had been the mortality among the Europeans that the constant dances that so characterize Demeraran and West Indian life were now conspicuous by their absence, for all were mourning many friends, if not relations, and a gloom hung over the usually gay and lively population. As a rule, Georgetown is as healthy as any city of tropical America.

Everywhere in the neighbourhood of Georgetown the jungle is cleared, and great plantations of sugar wave in the trade-wind. The country looks as if it ought to be the most unhealthy in the world, yet it is far from being that. It is but one vast plain of mud, drained by innumerable canals and ditches, which afford passage to canoes. It is no wonder that the Dutch seized this colony that to other peoples would have appeared the most uninviting portion of all the South American coast, for it must have strongly reminded them of their native land. Demerara is a tropical Holland, as skilfully dammed, canalled, and irrigated as is the European home of its first possessors. Much of this rich land has been conquered from the ocean. Great sea-walls of faggots overlaid with stones keep out the water at high-tide, which would otherwise then overflow the plantations. At low tide the gates in this wall are opened, so that the pent

in waters from the canals and drains find exit to the sea.
Sometimes, after a spring-tide, the soft mud accumulates in
banks outside these dykes, and, being higher than the level
of the reclaimed land, prevents this out-drainage ; then very
regiments of coolies have to dig channels through the vast
slimy mass, a seemingly Herculean task, till the imprisoned
waters of the estates are released.

There is no genuine *terra firma* in this colony—that is, in
the cultivated coast-regions. The dry earth forms but a thin
crust over practically bottomless mud. Hence it has been
found very difficult to erect really heavy buildings. They
are certain to gradually sink. When the heavy machinery
for the sugar factories was first introduced, great difficulties
in this respect were experienced. As there is no stone in
the neighbourhood of Georgetown, the few roads are paved
in an ingenious manner. First brushwood is laid down on
the road and fired ; the mud that is dug out of the canals
or ditches that border every thoroughfare here is then piled
on the blazing pile. The fire bakes this into a hard red
brick-like substance, which, broken up, makes very fair
macadam.

Having obtained the necessary permission to land there, I
started one morning to visit the penal settlement on the
Mazaruni river. The little passenger-steamer that ascends
the Essequibo calls at this settlement, accomplishing the
voyage in about six hours. We steamed along the muddy
shallow water till we came to the broad mouth of the
Essequibo, and entered the river by one of the channels
between the many islands that encumber this estuary ; great
shallow islands these, formed of the alluvial matter brought
down from the interior, and all covered with a dense vegetation. One of these, the Dauntless Bank, has been but
recently formed, having grown round the wreck of a vessel
of the same name. This nucleus was sufficient to collect in
a few years an immense mass of mud and sand, and there is
now quite a large island covered with a lofty vegetation. I
visited it later on with some friends in a schooner, having
been promised considerable sport ; but, save for shooting
some scarlet ibis, and catching some small mullet with a
seine net, after wading all day up to our waists in poisonous
mud, we did nothing.

The low banks of the Essequibo are covered with a rank

vegetation, but through the openings formed by the creeks are to be seen glimpses of the plantations of sugar-cane that lie behind. After passing a small island, on which stood the ruins of an old Dutch fort, the scenery became more picturesque; the banks were higher and clothed with forest, and rocky islets rose above the water, showing that we were now so far in the interior of the country as to have reached genuine *terra firma* once again, and had passed the belt of bottomless mud.

We steamed by a long island which I observed was, unlike the others, inhabited. There were many huts on it, cattle, and cultivated patches of cassava and plantains. This was, I was informed, Cow Island, the leper-island of the colony. All who are affected with this fearful disease are sent here. There are no boats on the island, as the lepers are not allowed to leave it on any pretence.

Soon after passing this we came to where the three rivers Essequibo, Mazaruni, and Cuyuni join. It is here, on a bluff some 100 feet high, sloping down to the first named river, a most picturesque position, that the penal settlement is established.

I was well piloted over this establishment; for my friend, Captain Fortescue, the inspector of prisons for the colony, luckily happened to have come up on the steamer with me. Landing with him, I was introduced to the governor, with whom I stayed until the steamer started back for Georgetown on the morrow.

This is indeed a model penal settlement. If any fault can be found with it, it is that the most healthy, beautiful, and in every respect most desirable spot of the colonized portion of British Guiana has been selected as the residence of malefactors.

Here, at an elevation sufficient to be almost entirely free from the malaria, the buildings connected with the settlement are scattered over an undulating expanse of lawn and garden, backed behind by a primeval forest that extends to Venezuela. These buildings have a singularly cheerful and unprisonlike appearance. All have been constructed by the labour of the convicts. Indeed, this penal colony is, I believe, entirely independent of the outer world for all its necessities. The prisoners grow their own sugar-canes and make their own sugar; they cultivate an extensive provision-ground, breed cattle and sheep, work in the gneiss quarries whence comes the only stone used in muddy Demerara, and are employed in a dozen other industries at least.

The convicts are nearly all Chinese, East Indian coolies, and blacks. Of Europeans there are not many. There were but two Englishmen among them when I was there, but generally there are to be found a few Frenchmen. These are runaway convicts from the French penal colony of Cayenne. They manage to steal boats occasionally, and to escape—a dozen or so at a time—to British Guiana. As they are for the most part regular *mauvais sujets*, they generally renew their old games in Demerara, are convicted of some crime, and packed off to Mazaruni.

The Hindoo coolies give the prison authorities much trouble; for, when condemned to penal servitude for a long term of years, they are much given to committing suicide. Notwithstanding every precaution, instances of this are of frequent occurrence. They proceed to effect a happy despatch in a most deliberate manner. Being deprived of knives and any ordinary implements of destruction, they will choke themselves with their loin-girdles. Those that are suspected of this suicidal tendency are watched with unceasing vigilance.

The cemetery of the settlement is also the flower-garden, a lovely spot thickly grown with the most gorgeous plants of the tropic zone.

Behind the enclosure of the prison grounds stretches, as I have before said, the primeval forest that extends to Venezuela. The black warders entertain a wholesome dread of this unknown waste, for a fixed idea exists among them that an invading Venezuelan army will one day march out of it upon the British colony. It seems that Venezuela did, or does, lay claim to this portion of Guiana; whereas the English lay down the frontier as upwards of a hundred miles to the north-west of this. Venezuelans have been known to issue out of the depths of this forest, and make their appearance at the convict settlement; but these, far from being invaders, are unfortunate fugitives who, after the collapse of their party in one of the usual revolutionary wars that so adorn the history of all South American republics, travel through the dense jungle to seek protection on British soil. These weary tattered foreigners, speaking a strange tongue, cause a good deal of unnecessary panic among the blacks when they appear among them; but that the poor wretches should be for a moment mistaken for ferocious invaders is indeed curious.

Just as the steamer was starting the next morning, I perceived, as I stood on the bridge, a long canoe come alongside, manned by nude aborigines. These Indians were a better-looking race than I had seen in the Chaco and Pampas, and certainly of far less ferocious countenance. Their faces wore a fixed expression of apathetic content and mildness of disposition. The women were hideous, and the copper bodies of the men were ornamented with stripes of black paint. Several of them came on board to take a passage to Georgetown, carrying with them bows and arrows, cassava-crushers, skins of birds, and the logs of wood with which they poison the rivers and so secure the fish. These curiosities they would sell to the Chinese and Portuguese curiosity shopkeepers for a little silver coin, or plenty of bad rum, or, maybe, for one of those extraordinary guns that are expressly imported for their benefit—like the child's toy-gun in appearance and of scarcely more use. I believe they are known as buck-guns to the trade, not that they are intended to shoot bucks or anything else, but simply to be sold to Buck Indians, as the male aborigines are politely called by their white rulers. One of these Indians must have been a chieftain, for he owned a pair of nankeen trousers, not being girdled round the loins merely, like the others. He did not wear his trousers during the voyage, however, but kept them carefully folded under his arm till we were near Georgetown, when he deliberately, with a gravity and unconsciousness that were delicious, put them on before all the passengers on the main-deck. Then his followers clustered round him admiringly, felt the texture of the material, and expressed approval in their soft sleepy-sounding language.

I should have much liked to have undertaken an expedition into the interior of Guiana, one of the most grand of tropical countries, though but little known and explored; but the costs of such a trip are heavy, unless one has companions to share them. Mr. Barrington Brown's descriptions of the renowned Roraima Mountains and the Kaieteur Falls, which latter he himself discovered, are indeed tempting to all who love the wonders of nature,

CHAPTER XXXVI.

WITH much reluctance I tore myself away from my friends of Georgetown, and sailed for my next port, Bridgetown, in the island of Barbados, distant about four hundred miles. We reached the lightship at about daybreak, and there found a very nasty sea running. High steep rollers were coming in, that tossed us about in a very uncomfortable way.

The lightship was no less lively. As we passed her she hoisted three signals to us in succession, J. L., " Appearances are threatening;" J. P., "Heavy weather coming;" and J. S., "Get an offing." As we knew that those on board had some good reason for thus warning us, we did not disregard their advice, but made for the open sea on the port tack. At two p.m., considering that we had now got a sufficient offing, and would easily weather the outermost shoals off the Essequibo, I put the vessel about, and found that she would just lay on her course for Barbados when close-hauled on the starboard tack.

The wind N.N.E. to N.E. had now freshened; the sea was very rough, in consequence doubtlessly of the opposition of the wind and current, which was rushing with great velocity towards the Gulf of Paria. This head-sea deadened our way, and we shipped a good deal of water at times.

On the following day the weather was worse; the ship laboured a good deal and our decks were constantly full of water. We were obliged to take two reefs in our main-sail and set the third jib.

On the 17th of February the weather improved, though there was still an unpleasantly choppy sea. This day we overhauled one of the island schooners and were pleased to find that we not only sailed much faster than she did, but that she made much more leeway than ourselves. Her main-sail was a huge sliding-gunter, as is usual in West Indian schooners, and set flat as a board; indeed, the sail-makers in these islands know their trade well, and often cut sails that Lapthorne would not be ashamed of.

During the whole of this voyage I was suffering from a bad attack of remittent bilious fever, which for three days quite prostrated me, and prevented me from taking my watch. This fever, common in tropical South America, is very severe while it lasts. Nearly all the symptoms of yellow fever accompany it, including the yellowness. Indeed, it is often mistaken for yellow fever, and many deaths that occur through it on vessels at sea are put down to the more deadly and contagious disorder. My mate of course was sure that it was yellow fever from which I was suffering, and was in much dread of contagion. It may have been so, as far as I know, but I rather think it was not.

At midday, the 18th of February, we sighted the island of Barbados. As we approached it, its often-remarked likeness to the Isle of Wight, as viewed from the sea, struck me. It is about the same size as the English island, and, like it, is covered with verdure. But the verdure of Barbados, when seen nearer, proves to be that of the sugar-cane, which is planted over the whole island from the mountaintops to the seashore. We had been sailing all this time on the starboard tack, but now found that we just failed of making our destination without tacking.

At about midnight we were some four miles from the shore, under the lee of the island, between South Point lighthouse and Needham Point. Tacking off and on, we preserved this position until daylight, when we sailed into Carlisle Bay and came to an anchor off Bridgetown in the man-of-war ground.

Bridgetown, seen from the anchorage, does not look like a town at all, but more like a village of huts scattered over a pleasant grove of cabbage-palms, cotton-trees, and other tropical vegetation. No sooner had our chain run out of the hawse-pipes than we were surrounded by a very fleet of negro boats, whose garrulous occupants commenced to swarm over our decks until we drove them off forcibly.

Their importunity was fearful; there were fat bumboat women vending ginger, bananas, and what not; other damsels who wished to do our washing for us at "half a dollar de dozen piece, massa;" and others—men, women, and children —who had no ostensible trade, but were adroit beggars and thieves. I had nowhere else experienced so disagreeable an ovation. It would be well if the rigid laws about visiting vessels that prevail at Bahia and other Brazilian ports were enforced in this harbour; but the Barbadian negro is free— a great deal too free to be otherwise than exceedingly objectionable.

As I still felt very ill, and it was Sunday, I did not go on shore this day. On Monday, the 20th of February, I landed in my boat in the Carenage, or inner and artificial harbour. I was surprised to find all the shops shut, and to hear the church bells ringing; and, on inquiring the cause of this, was told that this had been proclaimed a holiday and day of thanksgiving throughout the island of Barbados for the cessation of the yellow fever. This curse of the West Indies had been raging in an epidemic form for many months in this island which is generally free from it, and is indeed considered to be by far the healthiest of all the Antilles. As at Georgetown, the white regiments had been removed.

I soon saw that my stay in Barbados would be prolonged, for I had brought several letters of introduction with me, and my friends soon became legion. The hospitality of the Barbadians is well known, and they take very good care that no stranger leaves them but with regret, and bearing away with him most agreeable memories of the delightful little island.

Barbados seemed to me utterly strange after the countries I had recently visited. I felt as if I was in Europe—in England once again; for it is not the towns merely here that show signs of civilization, but the whole country. No trackless backwoods and jungles meet the traveller; no indications of a new country and of a struggle between barbarism and civilization. The whole island is as carefully cultivated as the richest portions of Great Britain; good roads (painfully glaring, by the way, as they are macadamized with snow-white coral) are everywhere—indeed, form a closer network than anywhere in England. Pleasant country houses, too, are dotted over all the country, the habitations of planters, each surrounded with its sugar plantations, boiling-houses, and windmill; for the windmill is the great feature of a Barbadian landscape. Sugar-making is not here carried on on so large a scale as in Demerara, but by private individuals of small capital. Hence the use of wind, as a rule, instead of steam power. Happily the trade-wind blows fresh and strong during the very season of the sugar-making. Indeed, on the whole, Barbados gives one the impression of not being a colony at all, but an old settled country; it is, indeed, our most ancient settlement in this portion of the globe, having been in our undisputed possession since 1625.

24*

So many friends had I, that there was no part of the island that I did not visit at the invitation of the hospitable planters—from the petroleum wells, on the windward coast, to the quaintly-shaped hills of the districts known as Scotland at the other extremity. We had some pleasant picnics and cruises, too, in the *Falcon*, visiting in her the little ports of Holetown and Speight's-town. One day we circumnavigated the island with a party of friends, carefully avoiding of course the coral reef that entirely surrounds Barbados. This voyage we accomplished in eleven hours. We passed a vessel that had run ashore on the reefs off South Point. She was rapidly breaking up, and the timber that formed her cargo was scattered floating over the ocean. The negroes of the windward coast, famous wreckers, were hard at work collecting this, and no doubt managed to steal a good deal before a body of police was sent down to look after them.

My cook now became very ill indeed, and I was obliged to send him to the colonial hospital. His illness promised to be a very tedious one, and I was much puzzled as to what to do next. To sail away without him, the best sailor and the most trustworthy man I had—in fact, the only one of the crew worth anything—was a measure which I felt great repugnance in taking. Again, to wait at Bridgetown until he was well enough to resume his duties, which might be a question of many months, was impossible. I frequently visited the poor fellow at the hospital, as he was very lonely there, not being able to express himself in English, and finding no one who understood Spanish or Italian. That we should be obliged to sail away without him evidently preyed on his mind, for he was really attached to me and to the vessel, and nothing could compensate him for a separation.

However, other circumstances led me to decide on a course of action which certainly was the remotest from my thoughts when I sailed into Bridgetown. I was recalled to England by important business that could not well wait, and I saw that I must give up my cruise through the West Indian Islands, and sail home at once. Things standing thus, certain of my friends put it before me that it would be well to discharge my crew, lay up the *Falcon*, return to England by steamer, and in the delightful winter-season, after the hurricane months were over, come back to the West Indies.

refit the yacht, ship a native crew, and carry out my old plan. I doubt whether I should have given way, had it not been that several friends offered then to join me for a cruise right through the islands. I had now so long been alone on board that the idea of companions seemed very pleasant. Such a voyage with a merry party of West Indians who knew the islands, and would have friends everywhere, was indeed something to be looked forward to. My friend Mr. Taylor, of Fontabelle, kindly offered to store my property and look after the yacht while I was away, if I hauled her up on the beach by his garden. Thus it was that I determined to lay up the *Falcon* for a time, and suspend my cruise for some six months.

There were not wanting other reasons to help me in coming to this decision; among others, the necessity for a thorough overhauling of my vessel, and my own rather ill-condition of health. My system was soaked with malaria, which weakened me and took away much of my energy and pleasure in the voyage.

Seeing the rather unaccountable ill-health of all hands on board the yacht, continuing as it had done over a period of some months, a suspicion as to a probable cause crossed my mind, which has now been much strengthened by an article I recently read in a medical journal.

Our diet while at sea, and to a great extent also while in port, had consisted in tinned meats. Now, these preserved provisions, wholesome though they may be when fresh, do not, as many suppose, keep so for an indefinite time. Chemical changes of some kind take place in the contents of the tin, while the metal itself, dissolved as it must gradually become by the acids that some provisions contain, is itself more or less injurious. Many of our tins had been two years on board the *Falcon* and most of that time in the tropics. In my opinion this had something to do with the symptoms of blood-poisoning that were manifested by several of our company.

Had I alone been the sufferer, I should not have attributed my ill-health to the tinned meats; for malaria was sufficient to account for my condition; but here were these Italians, who had visited no very unhealthy country, had caught no malaria, drank no bad water, prostrated with disorders that decidedly indicated the presence of some poison in the system

It is a question if the old sea-diet of salt meat is not more wholesome after all than an exclusive living on these tasty, but rather treacherous, preserved meats and vegetables.

I paid off my crew, found means for them to return to Europe, and set out to lay up the *Falcon*. I anchored her off Mr. Taylor's house and took everything out of her; then with the aid of some twenty negroes, rollers, strong tackle, and screw-jacks, I gradually hauled the old vessel out of the water, up the shingle bank to a pretty berth under the shade of waving cabbage-palms, cocoas, and manchineals.

I did not return to England by the mail-steamer, but in the 500-ton barque *Augusta*, commanded by my friend, Captain Young. After a very pleasant, though rather rough voyage of thirty days, we sighted Hartland Point, a strong south-west gale blowing at the time; then hove-to under the lee of Lundy to take the pilot on board, and were towed into Bristol Docks. After a nearly two years' absence I was indeed glad to step once more on English land and walk through the streets of the dear old western town I knew so well—the fresh, rosy faces of the people seeming very pleasing after the sallow and pallid inhabitants of the tropics.

I was unable to go to Barbados in the autumn, as I proposed, to resume my cruise; for now I was laid up for many months, suffering from severe *sequelæ* of malaria. So the old vessel still lies high and dry under the waving palms, waiting till her master return to take her from isle to isle of the lovely Caribbean Sea, and across the Atlantic to her moorings off familiar old Southampton, which he is eagerly looking forward to do; but up to now, alas! the doctors insist on keeping apart the *Falcon* and her affectionate owner and captain.

THE END.

THE ABERDEEN UNIVERSITY PRESS LIMITED

A Classified Catalogue

OF WORKS IN

GENERAL LITERATURE

PUBLISHED BY

LONGMANS, GREEN, & CO.,

39 PATERNOSTER ROW, LONDON, E.C.

91 AND 93 FIFTH AVENUE, NEW YORK, AND 32 HORNBY ROAD, BOMBAY.

CONTENTS.

History, Politics, Polity, Political Memoirs, etc.

ABBOTT. — A HISTORY OF GREECE. By EVELYN ABBOTT, M.A., LL.D.

Part I.—From the Earliest Times to the Ionian Revolt. Crown 8vo, 10s. 6d.

Part II.—From the Ionian Revolt to the Thirty Years' Peace, 500-445 B.C. Crown 8vo, 10s. 6d.

Part III.—From the Peace of 445 B.C. to the Fall of the Thirty at Athens in 403 B.C. Crown 8vo, 10s. 6d.

ABBOTT. — TOMMY CORNSTALK : being some Account of the Less Notable Features of the South African War from the Point of View of the Australian Ranks. By J. H. M. ABBOTT. Crown 8vo, 5s. net.

ACLAND and RANSOME. — A HANDBOOK IN OUTLINE OF THE POLITICAL HISTORY OF ENGLAND TO 1896. Chronologically Arranged. By the Right Hon. A. H. DYKE ACLAND, and CYRIL RANSOME, M.A. Crown 8vo, 6s.

AIRY.—CHARLES II. By OSMUND AIRY, LL.D., M.A. With Photogravure Portrait. Crown 8vo.

ALLGOOD.—CHINA WAR, 1860 : LETTERS AND JOURNALS. By Major-General G. ALLGOOD, C.B., formerly Lieut. G. ALLGOOD, 1st Division China Field Force. With Maps, Plans and Illustrations. Demy 4to, 12s. 6d. net.

History, Politics, Polity, Political Memoirs, etc.—*continued*

ANNUAL REGISTER (The). A Review of Public Events at Home and Abroad, for the year 1902. 8vo, 18s.

Volumes of the ANNUAL REGIS- TER for the years 1863-1901 can still be had. 18s. each.

ARNOLD. — INTRODUCTORY LECTURES ON MODERN HISTORY. By THOMAS ARNOLD, D.D., formerly Head Master of Rugby School. 8vo, 7s. 6d.

ASHLEY (W. J.).

ENGLISH ECONOMIC HIS- TORY AND THEORY. Crown 8vo, Part I., 5s; Part II., 10s. 6d.

SURVEYS, HISTORIC AND ECONOMIC. Crown 8vo, 9s. net.

BAGWELL.—IRELAND UNDER THE TUDORS. By RICHARD BAGWELL, LL.D. (3 vols.) Vols. I. and II., from the first invasion of the Northmen to the year 1578. 8vo, 32s. Vol. III., 1578-1603. 8vo, 18s.

BAILLIE. — THE ORIENTAL CLUB AND HANOVER SQUARE. By ALEXANDER F. BAILLIE. With 6 Photo- gravure Portraits and 8 Full-page Illustra- tions. Crown 4to, 25s. net.

BELMORE.—THE HISTORY OF TWO ULSTER MANORS, AND OF THEIR OWNERS. By the EARL OF BEL- MORE, P.C., G.C.M.G. (H.M.L., County Tyrone), formerly Governor of New South Wales. Re-issue Revised and Enlarged. With Portrait. 8vo, 5s. net.

BESANT.—THE HISTORY OF LONDON. By Sir WALTER BESANT. With 74 Illustrations. Crown 8vo, 1s. 9d. Or bound as a School Prize Book, gilt edges, 2s. 6d.

BRIGHT. — A HISTORY OF ENGLAND. By the Rev. J. FRANCK BRIGHT, D.D.

Period I. MEDIÆVAL MONARCHY: A.D. 449-1485. Crown 8vo, 4s. 6d.

Period II. PERSONAL MONARCHY. 1485-1688. Crown 8vo, 5s.

Period III. CONSTITUTIONAL MON- ARCHY. 1689-1837. Crown 8vo, 7s. 6d.

Period IV. THE GROWTH OF DE- MOCRACY. 1837-1880. Crown 8vo, 6s.

Period V. IMPERIAL REACTION: Victoria, 1880-1901. Crown 8vo, 4s. 6d.

BRUCE. — THE FORWARD POLICY AND ITS RESULTS: or, Thirty Five Years' Work amongst the Tribes of our North-Western Frontier of India. By RICHARD ISAAC BRUCE, C.I.E. With Illustrations and a Map. 8vo, 15s. net.

BUCKLE.—HISTORY OF CIVILI- SATION IN ENGLAND. By HENRY THOMAS BUCKLE.

Cabinet Edition. 3 vols. Crown 8vo, 24s.

'*Silver Library*' *Edition.* 3 vols. Crown 8vo, 10s. 6d.

BURKE.—A HISTORY OF SPAIN FROM THE EARLIEST TIMES TO THE DEATH OF FERDINAND THE CATHO- LIC. By ULICK RALPH BURKE, M.A. Edited by MARTIN A. S. HUME. With Maps. 2 vols. Crown 8vo, 16s. net.

CASSERLY.—THE LAND OF THE BOXERS; or, China under the Allies. By Captain GORDON CASSERLY. With 15 Illustrations and a Plan. 8vo, 10s. 6d. net.

CHESNEY.—INDIAN POLITY: a View of the System of Administration in India. By General Sir GEORGE CHESNEY, K.C.B. With Map showing all the Adminis- trative Divisions of British India. 8vo, 21s.

CHURCHILL (WINSTON SPENCER, M.P.).

THE RIVER WAR: an Historical Account of the Reconquest of the Soudan. Edited by Colonel F. RHODES, D.S.O. With Photogravure Portrait of Viscount Kitchener of Khartoum, and 22 Maps and Plans. 8vo, 10s. 6d. net.

THE STORY OF THE MALA- KAND FIELD FORCE, 1897. With Maps and Plans. Crown 8vo, 3s. 6d.

LONDON TO LADYSMITH VIA PRETORIA. Crown 8vo, 6s.

IAN HAMILTON'S MARCH. With Portrait of Major-General Sir Ian Hamil- ton and 10 Maps and Plans. Crown 8vo, 6s.

History, Politics, Polity, Political Memoirs, etc.—*continued.*

CORBETT (JULIAN S.)

DRAKE AND THE TUDOR NAVY, with a History of the Rise of England as a Maritime Power. With Portraits, Illustrations and Maps. 2 vols. Crown 8vo, 16s.

THE SUCCESSORS OF DRAKE With 4 Portraits (2 Photogravures) and 12 Maps and Plans. 8vo, 21s.

ENGLAND IN THE MEDITERRANEAN : a Study of the Rise and Influence of British Power within the Straits, 1603-1713. 2 vols. 8vo, 24s. net.

CREIGHTON (M., D.D , late Lord Bishop of London).

A HISTORY OF THE PAPACY FROM THE GREAT SCHISM TO THE SACK OF ROME, 1378-1527. 6 vols. Cr. 8vo, 5s. net each.

QUEEN ELIZABETH. With Portrait. Crown 8vo, 5s. net.

HISTORICAL ESSAYS AND REVIEWS. Edited by LOUISE CREIGHTON. Crown 8vo, 5s. net.

HISTORICAL LECTURES AND ADDRESSES. Edited by LOUISE CREIGHTON. Crown 8vo, 5s. net.

DALE.— THE PRINCIPLES OF ENGLISH CONSTITUTIONAL HISTORY. By LUCY DALE, late Scholar of Somerville College, Oxford. Crown 8vo, 6s

DE TOCQUEVILLE. — DEMOCRACY IN AMERICA. By ALEXIS DE TOCQUEVILLE. Translated by HENRY REEVE, C.B., D.C.L. 2 vols. Crown 8vo, 16s.

FALKINER.—STUDIES IN IRISH HISTORY AND BIOGRAPHY, mainly of the Eighteenth Century. By C. LITTON FALKINER. 8vo, 12s. 6d. net.

FREEMAN.—THE HISTORICAL GEOGRAPHY OF EUROPE. By EDWARD A. FREEMAN, D.C.L., LL.D. Third Edition. Edited by J. B. BURY, M.A., D.Litt., LL.D., Regius Professor of Modern History in the University of Cambridge. 8vo, 12s. 6d.

ATLAS to the above. With 65 Maps in colour. 8vo, 6s. 6d.

FROUDE (JAMES A.).

THE HISTORY OF ENGLAND, from the Fall of Wolsey to the Defeat of the Spanish Armada. 12 vols. Crown 8vo, 3s. 6d. each.

THE DIVORCE OF CATHERINE OF ARAGON. Crown 8vo, 3s. 6d.

FROUDE (JAMES A.)—*continued.*

THE SPANI-H STORY OF THE ARMADA, and other Essays. Cr. 8vo, 3s. 6d.

THE ENGLISH IN IRELAND IN THE EIGHTEENTH CENTURY. 3 vols. Crown 8vo, 10s. 6d.

ENGLISH SEAMEN IN THE SIXTEENTH CENTURY.

Cabinet Edition. Crown 8vo, 6s.

Illustrated Edition. With 5 Photogravure Plates and 16 other Illustrations. Large Crown 8vo, gilt top, 6s. net.

'*Silver Library*' *Edition* Cr. 8vo, 3s. 6d.

THE COUNCIL OF TRENT. Crown 8vo, 3s. 6d.

SHORT STUDIES ON GREAT SUBJECTS.

Cabinet Edition 4 vols. 4s

'*Silver Library*' *Edition* 4 vols. Crown 8vo, 3s. 6d. each.

CÆSAR : a Sketch. Cr. 8vo, 3s. 6d.

SELECTIONS FROM THE WRITINGS OF JAMES ANTHONY FROUDE. Edited by P. S. ALLEN, M.A. Crown 8vo, 3s. 6d.

GARDINER (SAMUEL RAWSON, D.C.L., LL.D.).

HISTORY OF ENGLAND, from the Accession of James I. to the Outbreak of the Civil War, 1603-1642. With 7 Maps. 10 vols. Crown 8vo, 5s. net each.

A HISTORY OF THE GREAT CIVIL WAR, 1642-1649. With 54 Maps and Plans. 4 vols. Cr. 8vo, 5s. net each.

A HISTORY OF THE COMMONWEALTH AND THE PROTECTORATE. 1649-1656. 4 vols. Crown 8vo, 5s. net each.

THE STUDENT'S HISTORY OF ENGLAND. With 378 Illustrations. Crown 8vo, gilt top, 12s. *Also in Three volumes*, price 4s. each.

WHAT GUNPOWDER PLOT WAS. With 8 Illustrations. Crown 8vo, 5s.

History, Politics, Polity, Political Memoirs, etc. —*continued*

GARDINER (Samuel Rawson, D.C.L., L.L.D.)—*continued*.

CROMWELL'S PLACE IN HIS-TORY. Founded on Six Lectures delivered in the University of Oxford. Crown 8vo, 3s. 6d.

OLIVER CROMWELL. With Frontispiece. Crown 8vo, 5s. net.

GERMAN EMPEROR'S (THE) SPEECHES : being a Selection from the Speeches, Edicts, Letters and Telegrams of the Emperor William II. Translated by Louis Elkind, M.D., 8vo, 12s. 6d. net.

GERMAN EMPIRE (THE) OF TO=DAY : Outlines of its Formation and Development. By 'Veritas'. Crown 8vo, 6s. net.

GRA'HAM.—ROMAN AFRICA : An Outline of the History of the Roman Occupation of North Africa, based chiefly upon Inscriptions and Monumental Remains in that Country. By Alexander Graham, F.S.A., F.R.I.B.A. With 30 reproductions of Original Drawings by the Author, and 2 Maps. 8vo, 16s. net.

GREVILLE.—A JOURNAL OF THE REIGNS OF KING GEORGE IV., KING WILLIAM IV., AND QUEEN VICTORIA. By Charles C. F. Greville, formerly Clerk of the Council. 8 vols. Crown 8vo, 3s. 6d. each.

GROSS.—THE SOURCES AND LITERATURE OF ENGLISH HISTORY, FROM THE EARLIEST TIMES TO ABOUT 1485. By Charles Gross, Ph.D. 8vo, 18s. net.

HAMILTON.—HISTORICAL RE-CORD OF THE 14th (KING'S) HUS-SARS, from a.d. 1715 to a.d. 1900. By Colonel Henry Blackburne Hamilton, M.A., Christ Church, Oxford; late Commanding the Regiment. With 15 Coloured Plates, 35 Portraits, etc., in Photogravure, and 10 Maps and Plans. Crown 4to, gilt edges, 42s. net.

HART.—ACTUAL GOVERN-MENT, AS APPLIED UNDER AMERI-CAN CONDITIONS. By Albert Bush-nell Hart, LL.D., Professor of History in Harvard University. With 17 Maps and diagrams. Crown 8vo, 7s. 6 '. net.

HILL.—THREE FRENCHMEN IN BENGAL; or, The Commercial Ruin of the French Settlements in 1757. By S. C. Hill, B.A., B.Sc., Officer in charge of the Records of the Government of India. With 4 Maps. 8vo, 7s. 6d. net.

HARVARD HISTORICAL STUDIES.

THE SUPPRESSION OF THE AFRICAN SLAVE TRADE TO THE UNITED STATES OF AMERICA, 1638-1870. By W. E. B. Du Bois, Ph.D. 8vo 7s. 6d.

THE CONTEST OVER THE RA-TIFICATON OF THE FEDERAL CON-STITUTION IN MASSACHUSETTS By S. B. Harding, A.M. 8vo, 6s.

A CRITICAL STUDY OF NUL-LIFICATION IN SOUTH CAROLINA By D. F. Houston, A.M. 8vo, 6s.

NOMINATIONS FOR ELECTIVE OFFICE IN THE UNITED STATES By Frederick W. Dallinger, A.M. 8vo 7s. 6d.

A BIBLIOGRAPHY OF BRITISH MUNICIPAL HISTORY, INCLUDING GILDS AND PARLIAMENTARY RE-PRESENTATION. By Charles Gross Ph.D. 8vo, 12s.

THE LIBERTY AND FREE SOIL PARTIES IN THE NORTH WEST By Theodore C. Smith, Ph.D. 8vo, 7s. 6d.

THE PROVINCIAL GOVERNOR IN THE ENGLISH COLONIES OF NORTH AMERICA. By Evarts Bou-tell Greene. 8vo, 7s. 6d.

THE COUNTY PALATINE OF DURHAM : a Study in Constitutional History. By Gaillard Thomas Lapsley, Ph.D. 8vo, 10s. 6d.

THE ANGLICAN EPISCOPATE AND THE AMERICAN COLONIES. By Arthur Lyon Cross, Ph.D., Instructor in History in the University of Michigan. 8vo, 10s. 6d.

HISTORIC TOWNS. — Edited by E. A. Freeman, D.C.L., and Rev. William Hunt, M.A. With Maps and Plans. Crown 8vo, 3s. 6d. each.

Bristol. By Rev. W. Hunt.	Oxford. By Rev. C. W. Boase.
Carlisle. By Mandell Creighton, D.D.	Winchester. By G. W. Kitchin, D.D.
Cinque Ports. By Montagu Burrows.	York. By Rev. James Raine.
Colchester. By Rev. E. L. Cutts.	
Exeter. By E. A. Freeman.	New York. By Theo-dore Roosevelt.
London. By Rev. W. J. Loftie.	Boston (U.S.) By Henry Cabot Lodge.

History, Politics, Polity, Political Memoirs, etc.—*continued*.

HUNTER (Sir WILLIAM WILSON).

A HISTORY OF BRITISH INDIA.
Vol. I.—Introductory to the Overthrow of the English in the Spice Archipelago, 1623. With 4 Maps. 8vo, 18s. Vol. II.—To the Union of the Old and New Companies under the Earl of Godolphin's Award, 1708. 8vo, 16s.

THE INDIA OF THE QUEEN,
and other Essays. Edited by Lady HUNTER. With an Introduction by FRANCIS HENRY SKRINE, Indian Civil Service (Retired). 8vo, 9s. net.

INGRAM.—A CRITICAL EXAMINATION OF IRISH HISTORY. From the Elizabethan Conquest to the Legislative Union of 1800. By T. DUNBAR INGRAM, LL.D. 2 vols. 8vo, 24s.

JOYCE (P. W.).

A SHORT HISTORY OF IRELAND, from the Earliest Times to 1603. Crown 8vo, 10s. 6d.

A SOCIAL HISTORY OF ANCIENT IRELAND: Treating of the Government, Military System and Law; Religion, Learning and Art; Trades, Industries and Commerce; Manners, Customs and Domestic Life of the Ancient Irish People. With 361 Illustrations. 2 vols. 8vo, 21s. net.

KAYE and MALLESON. — HISTORY OF THE INDIAN MUTINY, 1857-1858. By Sir JOHN W. KAYE and Colonel G. B MALLESON. With Analytical Index and Maps and Plans. 6 vols. Crown 8vo, 3s. 6d. each.

LANG (ANDREW).

THE MYSTERY OF MARY STUART. With Photogravure Plate and 15 other Illustrations. Crown 8vo, 6s. 6d. net.

JAMES THE SIXTH AND THE GOWRIE MYSTERY. With Gowrie's Coat of Arms in colour, 2 Photogravure Portraits and other Illustrations. 8vo, 12s. 6d. net.

PRINCE CHARLES EDWARD STUART, THE YOUNG CHEVALIER. With Photogravure Frontispiece. Crown 8vo, 7s. 6d. net.

THE VALET'S TRAGEDY, AND OTHER STUDIES IN SECRET HISTORY. With 3 Illustrations. 8vo, 12s. 6d. net

LAURIE. — HISTORICAL SURVEY OF PRE-CHRISTIAN EDUCATION. By S. S. LAURIE, A.M., LL.D. Crown 8vo, 7s. 6d.

LECKY (WILLIAM EDWARD HARTPOLE).

HISTORY OF ENGLAND IN THE EIGHTEENTH CENTURY.

Library Edition. 8 vols. 8vo. Vols. I. and II., 1700-1760, 36s.; Vols. III. and IV., 1760-1784, 36s.; Vols. V. and VI., 1784-1793, 36s.; Vols. VII. and VIII., 1793-1800, 36s.

Cabinet Edition. ENGLAND. 7 vols. Crown 8vo, 5s. net each. IRELAND. 5 vols. Crown 8vo, 5s. net each.

LEADERS OF PUBLIC OPINION IN IRELAND. FLOOD GRATTAN O'CONNELL. 2 vols. 8vo, 25s. net.

HISTORY OF EUROPEAN MORALS FROM AUGUSTUS TO CHARLEMAGNE. 2 vols. Crown 8vo, 10s. net.

A SURVEY OF ENGLISH ETHICS: Being the First Chapter of the 'History of European Morals'. Edited with Introduction and Notes, by W. A. HIRST. Crown, 8vo, 3s. 6d.

HISTORY OF THE RISE AND INFLUENCE OF THE SPIRIT OF RATIONALISM IN EUROPE. 2 vols. Crown 8vo, 10s. net.

DEMOCRACY AND LIBERTY.

Library Edition. 2 vols. 8vo, 36s.

Cabinet Edition. 2 vols. Crown 8vo, 10s. net.

LIEVEN.— LETTERS OF DOROTHEA, PRINCESS LIEVEN, DURING HER RESIDENCE IN LONDON, 1812-1834. Edited by LIONEL G. ROBINSON. With 2 Photogravure Portraits. 8vo, 14s. net.

LOWELL. — GOVERNMENTS AND PARTIES IN CONTINENTAL EUROPE. By A. LAWRENCE LOWELL. 2 vols. 8vo, 21s.

LUMSDEN'S HORSE, RECORDS OF. — Edited by H. H. S. PEARSE. With a Map and numerous Portraits and Illustrations in the Text. 4to, 21s. net.

LYNCH.—THE WAR OF THE CIVILISATIONS: BEING A RECORD OF 'A FOREIGN DEVIL'S' EXPERIENCES WITH THE ALLIES IN CHINA. By GEORGE LYNCH, Special Correspondent of the 'Sphere,' etc. With Portrait and 21 Illustrations. Crown 8vo, 6s. net.

History, Politics, Polity, Political Memoirs, etc.—*continued.*

MACAULAY (Lord).

THE LIFE AND WORKS OF LORD MACAULAY.

'*Edinburgh*' Edition.　　0 vols. 8vo, 6s. each.

Vols. I.-IV.　HISTORY OF ENGLAND.

Vols. V.-VII. ESSAYS, BIOGRAPHIES, INDIAN PENAL CODE, CONTRIBUTIONS TO KNIGHT'S 'QUARTERLY MAGAZINE'.

Vol. VIII.　SPEECHES, LAYS OF ANCIENT ROME, MISCELLANEOUS POEMS.

Vols. IX. and X. THE LIFE AND LETTERS OF LORD MACAULAY. By Sir G. O. TREVELYAN, Bart.

Popular Edition.

ESSAYS WITH LAYS OF ANCIENT ROME, ETC. Crown 8vo, 2s. 6d.

HISTORY OF ENGLAND.　2 vols. Crown 8vo, 5s.

MISCELLANEOUS WRITINGS, SPEECHES AND POEMS. Cr. 8vo, 2s. 6d.

THE LIFE AND LETTERS OF LORD MACAULAY. By Sir G. O. TREVELYAN, Bart. Crown 8vo, 2s. 6d.

THE WORKS.

'*Albany*' Edition. With 12 Portraits. 12 vols. Large Crown 8vo, 3s. 6d. each.

Vols. I.-VI. HISTORY OF ENGLAND, FROM THE ACCESSION OF JAMES THE SECOND.

Vols. VII.-X. ESSAYS AND BIOGRAPHIES.

Vols. XI.-XII. SPEECHES, LAYS OF ANCIENT ROME, ETC., AND INDEX.

Cabinet Edition. 16 vols. Post 8vo, £4 16s.

HISTORY OF ENGLAND FROM THE ACCESSION OF JAMES THE SECOND.

Popular Edition. 2 vols. Cr. 8vo, 5s.

Student's Edition 2 vols. Cr. 8vo, 12s.

People's Edition. 4 vols. Cr. 8vo, 16s.

'*Albany*' Edition. With 6 Port aits. 6 vols. Large Crown 8vo, 3s. 6d. each.

Cabinet Edition. 8 vols. Post 8vo, 48s.

'*Edinburgh*' Edition. 4 vols. 8vo, 6s. each.

Library Edition. 5 vols. 8vo, £4.

MACAULAY (LORD)—*continued.*

CRITICAL AND HISTORICAL ESSAYS, WITH LAYS OF ANCIENT ROME, etc., in 1 Volume.

Popular Edition. Crown 8vo, 2s. 6d.

'*Silver Library*' Edition. With Portrait and 4 Illustrations to the 'Lays'. Crown 8vo, 3s. 6d.

CRITICAL AND HISTORICAL ESSAYS.

Student's Edition. 1 vol. Cr. 8vo, 6s.

'*Trevelyan*' Edition. 2 vols. Cr. 8vo, 9s.

Cabinet Edition. 4 vols. Post 8vo, 24s.

'*Edinburgh*' Edition. 3 vols. 8vo, 6s. each.

Library Edition. 3 vols. 8vo, 36s.

ESSAYS, which may be had separately. Sewed, 6d. each; cloth, 1s. each.

Addison and Walpole.
Croker's Boswell's Johnson.
Hallam's Constitutional History.
Warren Hastings.
The Earl of Chatham (Two Essays).
Frederick the Great.
Ranke and Gladstone.
Lord Bacon.
Lord Clive.
Lord Byron and The Comic Dramatists of the Restoration.

MISCELLANEOUS WRITINGS, SPEECHES AND POEMS.

Popular Edition. Crown 8vo, 2s. 6d.

Cabinet Edition. 4 vols. Post 8vo, 24s.

SELECTIONS FROM THE WRITINGS OF LORD MACAULAY. Edited, with Occasional Notes, by the Right Hon. Sir G. O. TREVELYAN, Bart. Crown 8vo, 6s.

MACKINNON (JAMES, Ph.D.).

THE HISTORY OF EDWARD THE THIRD. 8vo, 18s.

THE GROWTH AND DECLINE OF THE FRENCH MONARCHY. 8vo. 21s. net.

MALLET.—MALLET DU PAN AND THE FRENCH REVOLUTION. By BERNARD MALLET. With Photogravure Portrait. 8vo, 12s. 6d. net.

MAY.—THE CONSTITUTIONAL HISTORY OF ENGLAND since the Accession of George III. 1760-1870. By Sir THOMAS ERSKINE MAY, K.C.B. (Lord Farnborough). 3 vols. Crown 8vo, 18s.

History, Politics, Polity, Political Memoirs, etc.—continued.

MERIVALE (CHARLES, D.D.).

HISTORY OF THE ROMANS UNDER THE EMPIRE. 8 vols. Crown 8vo, 3s. 6d. each.

THE FALL OF THE ROMAN REPUBLIC: a Short History of the Last Century of the Commonwealth. 12mo, 7s. 6d.

GENERAL HISTORY OF ROME, from the Foundation of the City to the Fall of Augustulus, B.C. 753-A.D. 476. With 5 Maps. Crown 8vo, 7s. 6d.

MONTAGUE.—THE ELEMENTS OF ENGLISH CONSTITUTIONAL HISTORY. By F. C. MONTAGUE, M.A. Crown 8vo, 3s. 6d.

MORAN.—THE THEORY AND PRACTICE OF THE ENGLISH GOVERNMENT. By THOMAS FRANCIS MORAN, Ph.D., Professor of History and Economics in Purdue University, U.S. Cr. 8vo, 5s. net.

PEARS. — THE DESTRUCTION OF THE GREEK EMPIRE AND THE STORY OF THE CAPTURE OF CONSTANTINOPLE BY THE TURKS. By EDWIN PEARS, LL.B. With 3 Maps and 4 Illustrations. 8vo, 18s. net.

POWELL and TREVELYAN.— THE PEASANTS' RISING AND THE LOLLARDS: a Collection of Unpublished Documents. Edited by EDGAR POWELL and G. M. TREVELYAN. 8vo, 6s. net.

RANDOLPH. — THE LAW AND POLICY OF ANNEXATION, with special Reference to the Philippines; together with Observations on the Status of Cuba. By CARMAN F. RANDOLPH. 8vo, 9s. net.

RANKIN (REGINALD).

THE MARQUIS D'ARGENSON; AND RICHARD THE SECOND. 8vo, 10s. 6d. net.

A SUBALTERN'S LETTERS TO HIS WIFE. (The Boer War.) Crown 8vo, 3s. 6d.

RANSOME.—THE RISE OF CONSTITUTIONAL GOVERNMENT IN ENGLAND. By CYRIL RANSOME, M.A. Crown 8vo, 6s.

SCOTT.— PORTRAITURES OF JULIUS CÆSAR: a Monograph. By FRANK JESUP SCOTT. With 38 Plates and 49 Figures in the Text. Imperial 8vo, 21s. net.

SEEBOHM (FREDERIC, LL.D., F.S.A.).

THE ENGLISH VILLAGE COMMUNITY. With 13 Maps and Plates. 8vo, 16s.

SEEBOHM (FREDERIC, LL.D., F.S.A.)—continued.

TRIBAL CUSTOM IN ANGLO-SAXON LAW: being an Essay supplemental to (1) 'The English Village Community,' (2) 'The Tribal System in Wales'. 8vo, 16s.

SETON-KARR.—THE CALL TO ARMS, 1900-1901; or a Review of the Imperial Yeomanry Movement, and some subjects connected therewith. By Sir HENRY SETON-KARR, M.P. With a Frontispiece by R. CATON-WOODVILLE. Crown 8vo, 5s. net.

SHEPPARD.—THE OLD ROYAL PALACE OF WHITEHALL. By EDGAR SHEPPARD, D.D., Sub-Dean of H.M. Chapels Royal, Sub-Almoner to the King. With 6 Photogravure Plates and 33 other Illustrations. Medium 8vo, 21s. net.

SMITH.—CARTHAGE AND THE CARTHAGINIANS. By R. BOSWORTH SMITH, M.A. With Maps, Plans, etc. Crown 8vo, 3s. 6d.

STEPHENS. — A HISTORY OF THE FRENCH REVOLUTION. By H. MORSE STEPHENS. 8vo. Vols. I. and II. 18s. each.

STERNBERG.—MY EXPERIENCES OF THE BOER WAR. By ADALBERT COUNT STERNBERG. With Preface by Lieut-Col. G. F. R. HENDERSON. Crown 8vo, 5s. net.

STUBBS.—HISTORY OF THE UNIVERSITY OF DUBLIN. By J. W. STUBBS. 8vo, 12s. 6d.

STUBBS.—HISTORICAL INTRODUCTIONS TO THE 'ROLLS SERIES'. By WILLIAM STUBBS, D.D., formerly Bishop of Oxford. 8vo, 12s. 6d. net.

SUTHERLAND.—THE HISTORY OF AUSTRALIA AND NEW ZEALAND, from 1606-1900. By ALEXANDER SUTHERLAND, M.A., and GEORGE SUTHERLAND, M.A. Crown 8vo, 2s. 6d.

TAYLOR.—A STUDENT'S MANUAL OF THE HISTORY OF INDIA. By Colonel MEADOWS TAYLOR, C.S.I. Crown 8vo, 7s. 6d.

THOMSON.—CHINA AND THE POWERS: a Narrative of the Outbreak of 1900. By H. C. THOMSON. With 2 Maps and 29 Illustrations. 8vo, 10s. 6d. net.

TODD.—PARLIAMENTARY GOVERNMENT IN THE BRITISH COLONIES. By ALPHEUS TODD, LL.D. 8vo, 30s. net.

TREVELYAN.—THE AMERICAN REVOLUTION. By Sir G. O. TREVELYAN, Bart. Part I., 8vo, 13s. 6d. net. Part II., 2 vols. 8vo, 21s. net.

History, Politics, Polity, Political Memoirs, etc.—*continued*

TREVELYAN. — ENGLAND IN THE AGE OF WYCLIFFE. By GEORGE MACAULAY TREVELYAN. 8vo, 15s.

WAKEMAN AND HASSALL.—ESSAYS INTRODUCTORY TO THE STUDY OF ENGLISH CONSTITUTIONAL HISTORY. Edited by HENRY OFFLEY WAKEMAN, M.A., and ARTHUR HASSALL, M.A. Crown 8vo, 6s.

WALPOLE. — (Sir SPENCER, K.C.B.).

HISTORY OF ENGLAND FROM THE CONCLUSION OF THE GREAT WAR IN 1815 TO 1858. 6 vols. Crown 8vo, 6s. each.

THE HISTORY OF TWENTY-FIVE YEARS (1856-1881). Vols. I. and II. 8vo. [*In the Press.*]

WILLOUGHBY.—POLITICA THEORIES OF THE ANCIENT WORLI By WESTEL W. WILLOUGHBY, Ph.D. Crow 8vo, 6s. net.

WILLSON. — LEDGER AN SWORD; or, The Honourable Company (Merchants of England Trading to the Ea Indies (1599-1874). By BECKLES WILLSO. With numerous Portraits and Illustratior 2 vols. 8vo, 21s. net.

WYLIE (JAMES HAMILTON, M.A.).

HISTORY OF ENGLAND UNDE HENRY IV. 4 vols. Crown 8vo. Vol. 1399-1404, 10s. 6d. Vol. II., 1405-1406, 1! (*out of print*). Vol. III., 1407-1411, 1! Vol. IV., 1411-1413, 21s.

THE COUNCIL OF CONSTANC TO THE DEATH OF JOHN HU Crown 8vo, 6s. net.

Biography, Personal Memoirs, etc.

BACON.—THE LETTERS AND LIFE OF FRANCIS BACON, INCLUDING ALL HIS OCCASIONAL WORKS. Edited by JAMES SPEDDING. 7 vols. 8vo, £4 4s.

BAGEHOT.—BIOGRAPHICAL STUDIES. By WALTER BAGEHOT. Crown 8vo, 3s. 6d.

BAIN.—AUTOBIOGRAPHY. By ALEXANDER BAIN, LL.D., Emeritus Professor of Logic and English, University of Aberdeen. With Supplementary Chapter. 8vo. [*In the Press.*]

BLOUNT. — THE MEMOIRS OF SIR EDWARD BLOUNT, K.C.B., ETC. Edited by STUART J. REID. With 3 Photogravure Plates. 8vo, 10s. 6d. net.

BOWEN.—EDWARD BOWEN: A MEMOIR. By the Rev. the Hon. W. E. BOWEN. With Appendices, 3 Photogravure Portraits and 2 other Illustrations. 8vo, 12s. 6d. net.

CARLYLE. — THOMAS CARLYLE: A History of his Life. By JAMES ANTHONY FROUDE.

1795-1835. 2 vols. Crown 8vo, 7s.
1834-1881. 2 vols. Crown 8vo, 7s.

COLVILLE.—DUCHESS SARAH: being the Social History of the Times of Sarah Jennings, Duchess of Marlborough, Compiled and arranged by one of her descendants (Mrs. ARTHUR COLVILLE). With 10 Photogravure Plates and 2 other Illustrations. 8vo, 18s. net.

CROZIER. — MY INNER LIFE: being a Chapter in Personal Evolution and Autobiography. By JOHN BEATTIE CROZIER, LL.D. 8vo, 14s.

DANTE. — THE LIFE AN WORKS OF DANTE ALLIGHIERI : bei an Introduction to the Study of the 'Divi Commedia'. By the Rev. J. F. HOGAN, D. With Portrait. 8vo, 12s. 6d.

DANTON.—LIFE OF DANTO: By A. H. BEESLY. With Portraits. Cro 8vo, 6s.

DE BODE.—THE BARONES DE BODE, 1775-1803. By WILLIAM CHILDE-PEMBERTON. With 4 Photogravu Portraits and other Illustrations. 8vo, { top, 12s. 6d. net.

ERASMUS.

LIFE AND LETTERS C ERASMUS. By JAMES ANTHO FROUDE. Crown 8vo, 3s. 6d.

THE EPISTLES OF ERASMU From his Earliest Letters to his Fifty-fi Year, arranged in Order of Time. Engl Translations, with a Commentary. FRANCIS MORGAN NICHOLS. 8vo, 18s. n

FARADAY.—FARADAY AS DISCOVERER. By JOHN TYNDALL. Cro 8vo, 3s. 6d.

FÉNELON : his Friends and I Enemies, 1651-1715. By E. K. SANDE With Portrait. 8vo, 10s. 6d.

FOX.—THE EARLY HISTORY (CHARLES JAMES FOX. By the Ri; Hon. Sir G. O. TREVELYAN, Bart. Cro 8vo, 3s. 6d.

FROUDE. — MY RELATION WITH CARLYLE. By JAMES ANTHC FROUDE. Together with a Letter from late Sir JAMES STEPHEN, Bart., K.C.S dated December, 1886. 8vo, 2s. net.

Biography, Personal Memoirs, etc.—*continued*.

GREY. — MEMOIR OF SIR GEORGE GREY, BART., G.C.B., 1799-1882. By MANDELL CREIGHTON, D.D., late Lord Bishop of London. With 3 Portraits. Crown 8vo, 6s. net.

HAMILTON.—LIFE OF SIR WILLIAM HAMILTON. By R. P. GRAVES, 8vo. 3 vols. 15s. each. ADDENDUM. 8vo, 6d. sewed.

HARROW SCHOOL REGISTER (THE), 1801-1900. Edited by M. G. DAUGLISH, 8vo, 10s. net.

HAVELOCK.—MEMOIRS OF SIR HENRY HAVELOCK, K.C.B. By JOHN CLARK MARSHMAN. Crown 8vo, 3s. 6d.

HAWEIS.—MY MUSICAL LIFE. By the Rev. H. R. HAWEIS. With Portrait of Richard Wagner and 3 Illustrations. Crown 8vo, 6s. net.

HIGGINS.—THE BERNARDS OF ABINGTON AND NETHER WINCHENDON: A Family History. By Mrs. NAPIER HIGGINS. 2 vols. 8yo, 21s. net.

HILEY.—MEMORIES OF HALF A CENTURY. By RICHARD W. HILEY, D.D., Vicar of Wighill, near Tadcaster, Yorks. 8vo, 15s.

HUNTER.—THE LIFE OF SIR WILLIAM WILSON HUNTER, K.C.S.I., M.A., LL.D. By FRANCIS HENRY SKRINE, F.S.S. With 6 Portraits (2 Photogravures) and 4 other Illustrations. 8vo, 16s. net.

JACKSON.—STONEWALL JACK- SON AND THE AMERICAN CIVIL WAR. By Lieut.-Col. G. F. R. HENDERSON. With 2 Portraits and 33 Maps and Plans. 2 vols. Crown 8vo, 16s. net.

KIELMANSEGGE. — DIARY OF A JOURNEY TO ENGLAND IN THE YEARS 1761-1762. By Count FREDERICK KIELMANSEGGE. With 4 Illustrations. Cr. 8vo, 5s. net.

LUTHER.—LIFE OF LUTHER. By JULIUS KÖSTLIN. With 62 Illustrations and 4 Facsimiles of MSS. Cr. 8vo, 3s. 6d.

MACAULAY.—THE LIFE AND LETTERS OF LORD MACAULAY. By the Right Hon. Sir G. O. TREVELYAN, Bart.
Popular Edition. 1 vol. Cr. 8vo, 2s. 6d.
Student's Edition. 1 vol. Cr. 8vo, 6s.
Cabinet Edition. 2 vols. Post 8vo, 12s.
'Edinburgh' Edition. 2 vols. 8vo, 6s. each.
Library Edition. 2 vols. 8vo, 36s.

MARBOT.—THE MEMOIRS OF THE BARON DE MARBOT. 2 vols. Cr. 8vo, 7s.

MAX MÜLLER (F.).

THE LIFE AND LETTERS OF THE RIGHT HON. FRIEDRICH MAX MÜLLER. Edited by his Wife. With Photogravure Portraits and other Illustrations. 2 vols. 8vo, 32s. net.

MY AUTOBIOGRAPHY: a Fragment. With 6 Portraits. 8vo, 12s. 6d.

AULD LANG SYNE. Second Series. 8vo, 10s. 6d.

CHIPS FROM A GERMAN WORKSHOP. Vol. II. Biographical Essays. Crown 8vo, 5s.

MORRIS. — THE LIFE OF WILLIAM MORRIS. By J. W. MACKAIL. With 2 Portraits and 8 other Illustrations by E. H. NEW, etc. 2 vols. Large Crown 8vo, 10s. net.

ON THE BANKS OF THE SEINE. By A. M. F., Author of 'Foreign Courts and Foreign Homes'. Cr. 8vo, 6s.

PAGET.—MEMOIRS AND LETTERS OF SIR JAMES PAGET. Edited by STEPHEN PAGET, one of his sons. With Portrait. 8vo, 6s. net.

RÂMAKRISHNA : HIS LIFE AND SAYINGS. By the Right Hon. F. MAX MÜLLER. Crown 8vo, 5s.

RICH.—MARY RICH, COUNTESS OF WARWICK (1625-1678): Her Family and Friends. By C. FELL SMITH. With 7 Photogravure Portraits and 9 other Illustrations. 8vo, gilt top, 18s. net.

ROCHESTER, AND OTHER LITERARY RAKES OF THE COURT OF CHARLES II., WITH SOME ACCOUNT OF THEIR SURROUNDINGS. By the Author of 'The Life of Sir Kenelm Digby,' 'The Life of a Prig,' etc. With 15 Portraits. 8vo, 16s.

ROMANES. — THE LIFE AND LETTERS OF GEORGE JOHN ROMANES, M.A., LL.D., F.R.S. Written and Edited by his Wife. With Portrait and 2 Illustrations. Crown 8vo, 5s. net.

RUSSELL. — SWALLOWFIELD AND ITS OWNERS. By CONSTANCE LADY RUSSELL, of Swallowfield Park. With 15 Photogravure Portraits and 36 other Illustrations. 4to, gilt edges, 42s. net.

SEEBOHM.—THE OXFORD REFORMERS—JOHN COLET, ERASMUS AND THOMAS MORE: a History of their Fellow-Work. By FREDERIC SEEBOHM, 8vo, 14s.

Biography, Personal Memoirs, etc.—*continued*.

SHAKESPEARE. — OUTLINES OF THE LIFE OF SHAKESPEARE. By J. O. HALLIWELL-PHILLIPPS. With Illustrations and Facsimiles. 2 vols. Royal 8vo, 21s.

TALES OF MY FATHER.—By A. M. F. Crown 8vo, 6s.

TALLENTYRE.—THE WOMEN OF THE SALONS, and other French Portraits. By S. G. TALLENTYRE. With 11 Photogravure Portraits. 8vo, 10s. 6d. net.

THOMSON. — EIGHTY YEARS' REMINISCENCES. By Colonel J. ANSTRUTHER THOMSON. With 29 Portraits and ot' er Illustrations. 2 vols. 8vo, 21s. net.

VERNEY.—MEMOIRS OF THE VERNEY FAMILY DURING THE SEVENTEENTH CENTURY. Compiled from the Papers and Illustrated by the Portraits at Claydon House, Bucks. By FRANCES PARTHENOPE VERNEY and MARGARET M. VERNEY. Abridged and Cheaper Edition. With 24 Portraits. 2 vols. Crown 8vo.

VICTORIA, QUEEN, 1819-1901. By RICHARD R. HOLMES, M.V.O., F.S.A. With Photogravure Portrait. Crown 8vo, gilt top, 5s. net.

WALPOLE.—SOME UNPUBLISHED LETTERS OF HORACE WALPOLE. Edited by Sir SPENCER WALPOLE, K.C.B. With 2 Portraits. Cr. 8vo, 4s. 6d. net.

WELLINGTON.—LIFE OF THE DUKE OF WELLINGTON. By the Rev. G. R. GLEIG, M.A. Crown 8vo, 3s. 6d.

WILKINS (W. H.).

A QUEEN OF TEARS: Caroline Matilda, Queen of Denmark and Princess of England, Sister of George III. With 47 Portraits and other Illustrations. 2 vols. 8vo, 36s.

THE LOVE OF AN UNCROWNED QUEEN: Sophie Dorothea Consort of George I., and her Correspondence with Philip Christopher, Count Königsmarck. With 24 Portraits and Illustrations. 8vo, 12s. 6d. net.

CAROLINE THE ILLUSTRIOUS, Queen-Consort of George II. and sometime Queen-Regent: a Study of Her Life and Time. With 42 Portraits and other Illustrations. 8vo, 12s. 6d. net.

Travel and Adventure, the Colonies, etc.

ARNOLD.—SEAS AND LANDS. By Sir EDWIN ARNOLD. With 71 Illustrations. Crown 8vo, 3s. 6d.

BAKER (Sir S. W.).

EIGHT YEARS IN CEYLON. With 6 Illustrations. Crown 8vo, 3s. 6d.

THE RIFLE AND THE HOUND IN CEYLON. With 6 Illustrations. Cr. 8vo. 3s. 6d.

BALL (JOHN).

THE ALPINE GUIDE. Reconstructed and Revised on behalf of the Alpine Club by W. A. B. COOLIDGE.

Vol. I., THE WESTERN ALPS: the Alpine Region, South of the Rhone Valley, from the Col de Tenda to the Simplon Pass. With 9 New and Revised Maps. Crown 8vo, 12s. net.

HINTS AND NOTES, PRACTICAL AND SCIENTIFIC, FOR TRAVELLERS IN THE ALPS: being a Revision of the General Introduction to the 'Alpine Guide'. Crown 8vo, 3s. net.

BENT.—THE RUINED CITIES OF MASHONALAND: being a Record of Excavation and Exploration in 1891. By J. THEODORE BENT. With 117 Illustrations. Crown 8vo, 3s. 6d.

BRASSEY (The Late Lady).

A VOYAGE IN THE 'SUNBEAM'; OUR HOME ON THE OCEAN FOR ELEVEN MONTHS.

Cabinet Edition. With Map and 66 Illustrations. Crown 8vo, gilt edges, 7s. 6d.

'*Silver Library' Edition.* With 66 Illustrations. Crown 8vo, 3s. 6d.

Popular Edition. With 60 Illustrations. 4to, 6d. sewed; 1s. cloth.

School Edition. With 37 Illustrations. Fcp., 2s. cloth, or 3s. white parchment.

SUNSHINE AND STORM IN THE EAST.

Popular Edition. With 103 Illustrations. 4to, 6d. sewed; 1s. cloth.

IN THE TRADES, THE TROPICS AND THE 'ROARING FORTIES'.

Cabinet Edition. With Map and 220 Illustrations. Cr. 8vo, gilt edges, 7s. 6d.

COCKERELL. — TRAVELS IN SOUTHERN EUROPE AND THE LEVANT, 1810-1817. By C. R. COCKERELL, Architect, R.A. Edited by his Son, SAMUEL PEPYS COCKERELL. With Portrait. 8vo, 10s. 6d. net.

Travel and Adventure, the Colonies, etc.—*continued*.

FOUNTAIN (PAUL).

THE GREAT DESERTS AND FORESTS OF NORTH AMERICA. 8vo, 9s. 6d. net.

THE GREAT MOUNTAINS AND FORESTS OF SOUTH AMERICA. With Portrait and 7 Illustrations. 8vo, 10s. 6d. net.

THE GREAT NORTH-WEST AND THE GREAT LAKE REGION OF NORTH AMERICA. 8vo, 10s. 6d. net.

FROUDE (JAMES A.).

OCEANA: or England and her Colonies. With 9 Illustrations. Crown 8vo, 3s. 6d.

THE ENGLISH IN THE WEST INDIES: or, the Bow of Ulysses. With 9 Illustrations. Crown 8vo, 2s. boards; 2s. 6d. cloth.

GROVE.—SEVENTY-ONE DAYS' CAMPING IN MOROCCO. By LADY GROVE. With Photogravure Portrait and 32 Illustrations from Photographs. 8vo, 7s. 6d. net.

HAGGARD.—A WINTER PILGRIMAGE: Being an Account of Travels through Palestine, Italy and the Island of Cyprus, undertaken in the year 1900. By H. RIDER HAGGARD. With 31 Illustrations from Photographs.

HARDWICK.— AN IVORY TRADER IN NORTH KENIA: the Record of an Expedition to the Country North of Mount Kenia in East Equatorial Africa, with an account of the Nomads of Galla-Land. By A. ARKELL-HARDWICK, F.R.G.S. With 23 Illustrations from Photographs, and a Map. 8vo, 12s. 6d. net.

HOWITT.—VISITS TO REMARKABLE PLACES. Old Halls, Battle-Fields, Scenes, Illustrative of Striking Passages in English History and Poetry. By WILLIAM HOWITT. With 80 Illustrations. Crown 8vo, 3s. 6d.

KNIGHT (E. F.).

SOUTH AFRICA AFTER THE WAR. With 17 Illustrations. 8vo, 10s. 6d. net.

WITH THE ROYAL TOUR: a Narrative of the Recent Tour of the Duke and Duchess of Cornwall and York through Greater Britain. With 16 Illustrations and a Map. Crown 8vo, 5s. net.

THE CRUISE OF THE 'ALERTE': the Narrative of a Search for Treasure on the Desert Island of Trinidad. With 2 Maps and 23 Illustrations. Crown 8vo, 3s. 6d.

WHERE THREE EMPIRES MEET: a Narrative of Recent Travel in Kashmir, Western Tibet, Baltistan, Ladak, Gilgit, and the adjoining Countries. With a Map and 54 Illustrations. Crown 8vo, 3s. 6d.

KNIGHT (E. F.)—*continued.*

THE 'FALCON' ON THE BALTIC: a Voyage from London to Copenhagen in a Three Tonner. With 10 Full-page Illustrations. Cr. 8vo, 3s. 6d.

LEES AND CLUTTERBUCK.—B.C. 1887: A RAMBLE IN BRITISH COLUMBIA. By J. A. LEES and W. J. CLUTTERBUCK. With Map and 75 Illustrations. Crown 8vo, 3s. 6d.

LYNCH.—ARMENIA: Travels and Studies. By H. F. B. LYNCH. With 197 Illustrations (some in tints) reproduced from Photographs and Sketches by the Author, 16 Maps and Plans, a Bibliography, and a Map of Armenia and adjacent countries. 2 vols. Medium 8vo, gilt top, 42s. net.

NANSEN.—THE FIRST CROSSING OF GREENLAND. By FRIDTJOF NANSEN. With 143 Illustrations and a Map. Crown 8vo, 3s. 6d.

RICE.—OCCASIONAL ESSAYS ON NATIVE SOUTH INDIAN LIFE. By STANLEY P. RICE, Indian Civil Service. 8vo, 10s. 6d.

SMITH. — CLIMBING IN THE BRITISH ISLES. By W. P. HASKETT, SMITH. With Illustrations and Numerous Plans.

Part I. ENGLAND. 16mo. 3s. net.

Part II. WALES AND IRELAND. 16mo, 3s. net.

SPENDER.—TWO WINTERS IN NORWAY: being an Account of Two Holidays spent on Snow-shoes and in Sleigh Driving, and including an Expedition to the Lapps. By A. EDMUND SPENDER. With 40 Illustrations from Photographs. 8vo, 10s. 6d. net.

STEPHEN. — THE PLAYGROUND OF EUROPE (The Alps). By Sir LESLIE STEPHEN, K.C.B. With 4 Illustrations. Crown 8vo, 3s. 6d.

STUTFIELD AND COLLIE.—CLIMBS AND EXPLORATIONS IN THE CANADIAN ROCKIES. By HUGH E. M. STUTFIELD and J. NORMAN COLLIE, F.R.S. With 2 Maps, 24 Full-page Illustrations, and 56 Half-page Illustrations. 8vo, 12s. 6d. net.

SVERDRUP. — NEW LAND: being a Record of the Voyage of the *Fram* to the Arctic Regions, 1898-1902. By Captain OTTO SVERDRUP. With Maps and Illustrations. 8vo.

THREE IN NORWAY. By Two of Them. With a Map and 59 Illustrations. Crown 8vo, 2s. boards, 2s. 6d. cloth.

TYNDALL (JOHN).

THE GLACIERS OF THE ALPS. With 61 Illustrations. Cr. 8vo, 6s. 6d. net.

HOURS OF EXERCISE IN THE ALPS. With 7 Illustrations. Crown 8vo, 6s. 6d. net.

Sport and Pastime.

THE BADMINTON LIBRARY.

Edited by HIS GRACE THE (EIGHTH) DUKE OF BEAUFORT, K.G.,
and A. E. T. WATSON.

ARCHERY. By C. J. LONGMAN and Col. H. WALROND. With Contributions by Miss LEGH, Viscount DILLON, etc. With 2 Maps, 23 Plates and 172 Illustrations in the Text. Crown 8vo, cloth, 6s. net; half-bound, with gilt top, 9s. net.

ATHLETICS. By MONTAGUE SHEARMAN. With Chapters on Athletics at School by W. BEACHER THOMAS; Athletic Sports in America by C. H. SHERRILL; a Contribution on Paper-chasing by W. RYE, and an Introduction by Sir Richard WEBSTER (Lord ALVERSTONE). With 12 Plates and 37 Illustrations in the Text. Cr. 8vo, cloth, 6s. net; half bound, with gilt top, 9s. net.

BIG GAME SHOOTING. By CLIVE PHILLIPPS-WOLLEY.

Vol. I. AFRICA AND AMERICA. With Contributions by Sir SAMUEL W. BAKER, W. C. OSWELL, F. C. SELOUS, etc. With 20 Plates and 57 Illustrations in the Text. Crown 8vo, cloth, 6s. net; half-bound, with gilt top, 9s. net.

Vol. II. EUROPE, ASIA, AND THE ARCTIC REGIONS. With Contributions by Lieut.-Colonel R. HEBER PERCY, Major ALGERNON C. HEBER PERCY, etc. With 17 Plates and 56 Illustrations in the Text. Crown 8vo, cloth 6s. net; half-bound, with gilt top, 9s. net.

BILLIARDS. By Major W. BROAD-FOOT, R.E. With Contributions by A. H. BOYD, SYDENHAM DIXON, W. J. FORD, etc. With 11 Plates, 19 Illustrations in the Text, and numerous Diagrams. Crown 8vo, cloth, 6s. net; half-bound, with gilt top, 9s. net.

COURSING AND FALCONRY. By HARDING COX, CHARLES RICHARDSON, and the Hon. GERALD LASCELLES. With 20 Plates and 55 Illustrations in the Text. Crown 8vo, cloth 6s. net; half-bound, with gilt top, 9s. net.

CRICKET. By A. G. STEEL and the Hon R. H. LYTTELTON. With Contributions by ANDREW LANG, W. G. GRACE, F. GALE, etc. With 13 Plates and 52 Illustrations in the Text. Crown 8vo, cloth, 6s. net; half-bound, with gilt top, 9s. net.

CYCLING. By the EARL OF ALBE-MARLE and G. LACY HILLIER. With 19 Plates and 44 Illustrations in the Text. Crown 8vo, cloth, 6s. net; half-bound, with gilt top, 9s. net.

DANCING. By Mrs. LILLY GROVE. With Contributions by Miss MIDDLETON. The Hon. Mrs. ARMYTAGE, etc. With Musical Examples, and 38 Full-page Plates and 93 Illustrations in the Text. Crown 8vo, cloth, 6s. net; half-bound, with gilt top, 9s. net.

DRIVING. By His Grace the (Eighth) DUKE OF BEAUFORT, K.G. With Contributions by A. E. T. WATSON, the EARL OF ONSLOW, etc. With 12 Plates and 54 Illustrations in the Text. Crown 8vo, cloth, 6s. net; half-bound, with gilt top, 9s. net.

FENCING, BOXING, AND WRESTLING. By WALTER H. POLLO K, F. C. GROVE, C. PREVOST, E. B. MITCHELL, and WALTER ARMSTRONG. With 18 Plates and 24 Illustrations in the Text. Crown 8vo, cloth, 6s. net; half-bound, with gilt top, 9s. net.

FISHING. By H. CHOLMONDELEY-PENNELL.

Vol. I. SALMON AND TROUT. With Contributions by H. R. FRANCIS, Major JOHN P. TRAHERNE, etc. With 9 Plates and numerous Illustrations of Tackle, etc. Crown 8vo, cloth, 6s. net; half-bound, with gilt top, 9s. net.

Vol. II. PIKE AND OTHER COARSE FISH. With Contributions by the MAR-QUIS OF EXETER, WILLIAM SENIOR. G. CHRISTOPHER DAVIS, etc. With 7 Plates and numerous Illustrations of Tackle, etc. Crown 8vo, cloth, 6s. net; half-bound, with gilt top, 9s. net.

FOOTBALL. HISTORY, by MON-TAGUE SHEARMAN; THE ASSOCIATION GAME, by W. J. OAKLEY and G. O. SMITH; THE RUGBY UNION GAME, by FRANK MITCHELL. With other Contributions by R. E. MAC-NAGHTEN, M. C. KEMP, J. E. VINCENT, WALTER CAMP and A. SUTHERLAND. With 19 Plates and 35 Illustrations in the Text. Crown 8vo, cloth, 6s. net; half-bound, with gilt top, 9s. net.

GOLF. By HORACE G. HUTCHINSON. With Contributions by the Rt. Hon. A. J. BALFOUR, M.P., Sir WALTER SIMPSON, Bart., ANDREW LANG, etc. With 34 Plates and 56 Illustrations in the Text. Crown 8vo, cloth, 6s. net; half-bound, with gilt top, 9s. net.

Sport and Pastime—*continued.*

THE BADMINTON LIBRARY—*continued.*

Edited by HIS GRACE THE (EIGHTH) DUKE OF BEAUFORT, K.G., and A. E. T. WATSON.

HUNTING. By His Grace the (Eighth) DUKE OF BEAUFORT, K.G., and MOWBRAY MORRIS. With Contributions by the EARL OF SUFFOLK AND BERKSHIRE, Rev. E. W. L. DAVIES, G. H. LONGMAN, etc. With 5 Plates and 54 Illustrations in the Text. Crown 8vo, cloth, 6s. net ; half-bound, with gilt top, 9s. net.

MOTORS AND MOTOR-DRIVING. By ALFRED C. HARMSWORTH, the MARQUIS DE CHASSELOUP - LAUBAT, the Hon. JOHN SCOTT-MONTAGU, R. J. MECREDY, the Hon. C. S. ROLLS, Sir DAVID SALOMONS, Bart., etc. With 13 Plates and 136 Illustrations in the Text. Crown 8vo, cloth, 9s. net ; half-bound, 12s. net.
A Cloth Box for use when Motoring, 2s. net.

MOUNTAINEERING. By C. T. DENT. With Contributions by the Right Hon. J. BRYCE, M.P., Sir MARTIN CONWAY, D. W. FRESHFIELD, C. E. MATTHEWS, etc. With 13 Plates and 91 Illustrations in the Text. Crown 8vo, cloth, 6s. net ; half-bound, with gilt top, 9s. net.

POETRY OF SPORT (THE).— Selected by HEDLEY PEEK. With a Chapter on Classical Allusions to Sport by ANDREW LANG, and a Special Preface to the BADMINTON LIBRARY by A. E. T. WATSON. With 32 Plates and 74 Illustrations in the Text. Crown 8vo, cloth, 6s. net ; half-bound, with gilt top, 9s. net.

RACING AND STEEPLE-CHASING. By the EARL OF SUFFOLK AND BERKSHIRE, W. G. CRAVEN, the Hon. F. LAWLEY, ARTHUR COVENTRY, and A. E. T. WATSON. With Frontispiece and 56 Illustrations in the Text. Crown 8vo, cloth, 6s. net ; half-bound, with gilt top, 9s. net.

RIDING AND POLO. By Captain ROBERT WEIR, J. MORAY BROWN, T. F. DALE, THE LATE DUKE OF BEAUFORT, THE EARL OF SUFFOLK AND BERKSHIRE, etc. With 18 Plates and 41 Illustrations in the Text. Crown 8vo, cloth, 6s. net ; half-bound, with gilt top, 9s. net.

ROWING. By R. P. P. ROWE and C. M. PITMAN. With Chapters on Steering by C. P. SEROCOLD and F. C. BEGG ; Metropolitan Rowing by S. LE BLANC SMITH ; and on PUNTING by P. W. SQUIRE. With 75 Illustrations. Crown 8vo, cloth, 6s. net ; half-bound, with gilt top, 9s. net.

SEA FISHING. By JOHN BICKERDYKE, Sir H. W. GORE-BOOTH, ALFRED C. HARMSWORTH, and W. SENIOR. With 22 Full-page Plates and 175 Illustrations in the Text. Crown 8vo, cloth, 6s. net ; half-bound, with gilt top, 9s. net.

SHOOTING.

Vol. I. FIELD AND COVERT. By LORD WALSINGHAM and SIR RALPH PAYNE-GALLWEY, Bart. With Contributions by the Hon GERALD LASCELLES and A. J. STUART-WORTLEY. With 11 Plates and 95 Illustrations in the Text. Crown 8vo, cloth, 6s. net ; half-bound, with gilt top, 9s. net.

Vol. II. MOOR AND MARSH. By LORD WALSINGHAM and Sir RALPH PAYNE-GALLWEY, Bart. With Contributions by LORD LOVAT and LORD CHARLES LENNOX KERR. With 8 Plates and 57 Illustrations in the text. Crown 8vo, cloth, 6s. net ; half-bound, with gilt top, 9s. net.

SKATING, CURLING, TOBOGANING. By J. M. HEATHCOTE, C. G. TEBBUTT, T. MAXWELL WITHAM, Rev. JOHN KERR, ORMOND HAKE, HENRY A. BUCK, etc. With 12 Plates and 272 Illustrations in the Text. Crown 8vo, cloth, 6s. net ; half-bound, with gilt top, 9s. net.

SWIMMING. By ARCHIBALD SINCLAIR and WILLIAM HENRY, Hon. Secs. of the Life-Saving Society. With 13 Plates and 112 Illustrations in the Text. Cr. 8vo, cloth, 6s. net ; half-bound, with gilt top, 9s. net.

TENNIS, LAWN TENNIS, RACKETS AND FIVES. By J. M. and C. G. HEATHCOTE, E. O. PLEYDELL-BOUVERIE, and A. C. AINGER. With Contributions by the Hon. A. LYTTELTON, W. C. MARSHALL, Miss L. DOD, etc. With 14 Plates and 65 Illustrations in the Text. Crown 8vo, cloth, 6s. net ; half-bound, with gilt top, 9s. net.

YACHTING.

Vol. I. CRUISING, CONSTRUCTION OF YACHTS, YACHT RACING RULES, FITTING-OUT, etc. By Sir EDWARD SULLIVAN, Bart., THE EARL OF PEMBROKE, LORD BRASSEY, K.C.B., C. E. SETH-SMITH, C.B., G. L. WATSON, R. T. PRITCHETT, E. F. KNIGHT, etc. With 21 Plates and 93 Illustrations in the Text. Crown 8vo, cloth, 6s. net ; half-bound, with gilt top, 9s. net.

Vol. II. YACHT CLUBS, YACHTING IN AMERICA AND THE COLONIES, YACHT RACING, etc. By R. T. PRITCHETT, THE MARQUIS OF DUFFERIN AND AVA, K.P., THE EARL OF ONSLOW, JAMES MCFERRAN, etc. With 35 Plates and 160 Illustrations in the Text. Crown 8vo, cloth, 9s. net ; half-bound, with gilt top, 9s. net.

Sport and Pastime—*continued*.

FUR, FEATHER, AND FIN SERIES.

Edited by A. E. T. WATSON.

Crown 8vo, price 5s. each Volume, cloth.

** *The Volumes are also issued half-bound in Leather, with gilt top.*
Price 7s. 6d. net each.

THE PARTRIDGE. Natural History, by the Rev. H. A. MACPHERSON; Shooting, by A. J. STUART - WORTLEY; Cookery, by GEORGE SAINTSBURY. With 11 Illustrations and various Diagrams. Crown 8vo, 5s.

THE GROUSE. Natural History, by the Rev. H. A. MACPHERSON; Shooting, by A. J. STUART-WORTLEY; Cookery, by GEORGE SAINTSBURY. With 13 Illustrations and various Diagrams. Crown 8vo, 5s.

THE PHEASANT. Natural History, by the Rev. H. A. MACPHERSON; Shooting, by A. J. STUART-WORTLEY; Cookery, by ALEXANDER INNES SHAND. With 10 Illustrations and various Diagrams. Crown 8vo, 5s.

THE HARE. Natural History, by the REV. H. A. MACPHERSON; Shooting, by the Hon. GERALD LASCELLES; Coursing, by CHARLES RICHARDSON; Hunting, by J. S. GIBBONS and G. H. LONGMAN; Cookery, by Col. KENNEY HERBERT. With 9 Illustrations. Crown 8vo, 5s.

THE RABBIT. By JAMES EDMUND HARTING. Cookery, by ALEXANDER INNES SHAND. With 10 Illustrations. Crown 8vo, 5s.

SNIPE AND WOODCOCK. By L. H. DE VISME SHAW. With Chapters on Snipe and Woodcock in Ireland by RICHARD J. USSHER. Cookery, by ALEXANDER INNES SHAND. With 8 Illustrations. Crown 8vo, 5s.

RED DEER. Natural History, by the Rev. H. A. MACPHERSON; Deer Stalking, by CAMERON OF LOCHIEL; Stag Hunting, by Viscount EBRINGTON; Cookery, by ALEXANDER INNES SHAND. With 10 Illustrations. Crown 8vo, 5s.

THE SALMON. By the Hon. A. E. GATHORNE-HARDY. With Chapters on the Law of Salmon Fishing by CLAUD DOUGLAS PENNANT; Cookery, by ALEXANDER INNES SHAND. With 8 Illustrations. Crown 8vo, 5s.

THE TROUT. By the MARQUESS OF GRANBY. With Chapters on the Breeding of Trout by Col. H. CUSTANCE; and Cookery, by ALEXANDER INNES SHAND. With 12 Illustrations. Crown 8vo, 5s.

PIKE AND PERCH. By WILLIAM SENIOR ('Redspinner,' Editor of the 'Field'). With Chapters by JOHN BICKERDYKE and W. H. POPE; Cookery, by ALEXANDER INNES SHAND. With 12 Illustrations. Crown 8vo, 5s.

ALVERSTONE AND ALCOCK. SURREY CRICKET: its History and Associations. Edited by the Right Hon. LORD ALVERSTONE, L.C.J., President, and C. W. ALCOCK, Secretary, of the Surrey County Cricket Club. With 48 Illustrations. 8vo, 5s. net.

BICKERDYKE.—DAYS OF MY LIFE ON WATER, FRESH AND SALT; and other Papers. By JOHN BICKERDYKE. With Photo-etching Frontispiece and 8 Full-page Illustrations. Crown 8vo, 3s. 6d.

BLACKBURNE. — MR. BLACKBURNE'S GAMES AT CHESS. Selected, Annotated and Arranged by Himself. Edited, with a Biographical Sketch and a brief History of Blindfold Chess, by P. ANDERSON GRAHAM. With Portrait of Mr. Blackburne. 8vo, 7s. 6d. net.

ELLIS.—CHESS SPARKS; or, Short and Bright Games of Chess. Collected and Arranged by J. H. ELLIS, M.A. 8vo, 4s. 6d.

Sport and Pastime—*continued.*

FORD.—THE THEORY AND PRACTICE OF ARCHERY. By HORACE FORD. New Edition, thoroughly Revised and Re-written by W. BUTT, M.A. With a Preface by C. J. LONGMAN, M.A. 8vo, 14s.

FRANCIS.—A BOOK ON ANGLING: or, Treatise on the Art of Fishing in every Branch; including full Illustrated List of Salmon Flies. By FRANCIS FRANCIS. With Portrait and Coloured Plates. Crown 8vo, 15s.

FREMANTLE.—THE BOOK OF THE RIFLE. By the Hon. T. F. FREMANTLE, V.D., Major, 1st Bucks V.R.C. With 54 Plates and 107 Diagrams in the Text. 8vo, 12s. 6d. net.

GATHORNE-HARDY.— AUTUMNS IN ARGYLESHIRE WITH ROD AND GUN. By the Hon. A. E. GATHORNE-HARDY. With 8 Illustrations by ARCHIBALD THORBURN. 8vo, 6s. net.

GRAHAM.—COUNTRY PAS- TIMES FOR BOYS. By P. ANDERSON GRAHAM. With 252 Illustrations from Drawings and Photographs. Crown 8vo, gilt edges, 3s. net.

HUTCHINSON.—THE BOOK OF GOLF AND GOLFERS. By HORACE G. HUTCHINSON. With 71 Portraits from Photographs. Large crown 8vo, gilt top, 7s. 6d. net.

LANG.—ANGLING SKETCHES.— By ANDREW LANG. With 20 Illustrations. Crown 8vo, 3s. 6d.

LILLIE.—CROQUET UP TO DATE. Containing the Ideas and Teachings of the Leading Players and Champions. By ARTHUR LILLIE. With 19 Illustrations (15 Portraits), and numerous Diagrams. 8vo, 10s. 6d. net.

LONGMAN.—CHESS OPEN- INGS. By FREDERICK W. LONGMAN. Fcp. 8vo, 2s. 6d.

MACKENZIE.—NOTES FOR HUNTING MEN. By Captain CORTLANDT GORDON MACKENZIE. Crown 8vo, 2s. 6d. net.

MADDEN.—THE DIARY OF MASTER WILLIAM SILENCE: a Study of Shakespeare and of Elizabethan Sport. By the Right Hon. D. H. MADDEN, Vice-Chancellor of the University of Dublin. 8vo, gilt top, 16s.

MASKELYNE.—SHARPS AND FLATS: a Complete Revelation of the Secrets of Cheating at Games of Chance and Skill. By JOHN NEVIL MASKELYNE. of the Egyptian Hall. With 62 Illustrations. Crown 8vo, 6s.

MILLAIS (JOHN GUILLE).

THE WILD-FOWLER IN SCOTLAND. With a Frontispiece in Photogravure by Sir J. E. MILLAIS, Bart., P.R.A., 8 Photogravure Plates, 2 Coloured Plates and 50 Illustrations from the Author's Drawings and from Photographs. Royal 4to, gilt top, 30s. net.

THE NATURAL HISTORY OF THE BRITISH SURFACE-FEEDING DUCKS. With 6 Photogravures and 66 Plates (41 in Colours) from Drawings by the Author, ARCHIBALD THORBURN, and from Photographs. Royal 4to, cloth, gilt top, £6 6s. net.

MODERN BRIDGE. By 'Slam'. With a Reprint of the Laws of Bridge, as adopted by the Portland and Turf Clubs. 18mo, gilt edges, 3s. 6d. net.

PARK.—THE GAME OF GOLF. By WILLIAM PARK, Jun., Champion Golfer, 1887-89. With 17 Plates and 26 Illustrations in the Text. Crown 8vo, 7s. 6d.

PAYNE-GALLWEY (Sir RALPH, Bart.).

THE CROSSBOW: Mediæval and Modern; Military and Sporting; its Construction, History and Management, with a Treatise on the Balista and Catapult of the Ancients. With 220 Illustrations. Royal 4to, £3 3s. net.

LETTERS TO YOUNG SHOOTERS (First Series). On the Choice and use of a Gun. With 41 Illustrations. Crown 8vo, 7s. 6d.

LETTERS TO YOUNG SHOOTERS (Second Series). On the Production, Preservation and Killing of Game. With Directions in Shooting Wood-Pigeons and Breaking-in Retrievers. With Portrait and 103 Illustrations. Crown 8vo, 12s. 6d.

LETTERS TO YOUNG SHOOTERS (Third Series). Comprising a Short Natural History of the Wildfowl that are Rare or Common to the British Islands, with complete directions in Shooting Wild owl on the Coast and Inland. With 200 Illustrations. Crown 8vo, 18s

Sport and Pastime—*continued.*

POLE.—THE THEORY OF THE MODERN SCIENTIFIC GAME OF WHIST. By WILLIAM POLE, F.R.S. Fcp. 8vo, gilt edges, 2s. net.

PROCTOR.—HOW TO PLAY WHIST: WITH THE LAWS AND ETIQUETTE OF WHIST. By RICHARD A. PROCTOR. Crown 8vo, gilt edges, 3s. net.

RONALDS.— THE FLY-FISHER'S ENTOMOLOGY. By ALFRED RONALDS. With 20 coloured Plates. 8vo. 14s.

SOMERVILLE.— SLIPPER'S A B C OF FOX-HUNTING. By E. Œ. SOMERVILLE, M.F.H., Joint Author of 'Some Experiences of an Irish R.M.,' etc. With Illustrations in Colour by the Author. 4to, boards, 10s. 6d. net.

THOMAS-STANFORD.—A RIVER OF NORWAY: being the Notes and Reflections of an Angler. By CHARLES THOMAS-STANFORD. With 10 Photogravure Plates, 1 Map and 1 Plan. 8vo, 9s. net.

THOMPSON, CANNAN AND DONERAILE.—COMBINED HAND-IN-HAND FIGURE SKATING. By NOR-CLIFFE G. THOMPSON, F. LAURA CANNAN and VISCOUNT DONERAILE, Members of the Skating Club. 16mo.

WARNER.—CRICKET ACROSS THE SEAS : being an Account of the Tour of Lord Hawke's Team in New Zealand and Australia. By P. F. WARNER. With 32 Illustrations from Photographs. Crown 8vo, 5s. net.

Mental, Moral and Political Philosophy.

LOGIC, RHETORIC, PSYCHOLOGY, ETHICS, ETC.

ABBOTT.—THE ELEMENTS OF LOGIC. By T. K. ABBOTT, B.D. 12mo, 3s.

ARISTOTLE.

THE ETHICS: Greek Text, Illustrated with Essay and Notes. By Sir ALEXANDER GRANT, Bart. 2 vols. 8vo, 32s.

AN INTRODUCTION TO ARISTOTLE'S ETHICS. Books I.-IV. (Book X. c. vi.-ix. in an Appendix). With a continuous Analysis and Notes. By the Rev. E. MOORE, D.D. Crown 8vo, 10s. 6d.

BACON (FRANCIS).

COMPLETE WORKS. Edited by R. L. ELLIS, JAMES SPEDDING and D. D. HEATH. 7 vols. 8vo, £3 13s. 6d.

LETTERS AND LIFE, including all his occasional Works. Edited by JAMES SPEDDING. 7 vols. 8vo, £4 4s.

THE ESSAYS : with Annotations. By RICHARD WHATELY D.D. 8vo, 10s. 6d.

BACON (FRANCIS)—*continued.*

THE ESSAYS: with Notes. By F. STORR and C. H. GIBSON. Cr. 8vo, 3s. 6d.

THE ESSAYS : with Introduction, Notes, and Index. By E. A. ABBOTT, D.D. 2 vols. Fcp. 8vo, 6s. The Text and Index only, without Introduction and Notes, in One Volume. Fcp. 8vo, 2s. 6d.

BAIN (ALEXANDER).

MENTAL AND MORAL SCIENCE : a Compendium of Psychology and Ethics. Crown 8vo, 10s. 6d.

Or separately,

Part I. PSYCHOLOGY AND HISTORY OF PHILOSOPHY. Crown 8vo, 6s. 6d.

Part II. THEORY OF ETHICS AND ETHICAL SYSTEMS. Crown 8vo, 4s. 6d.

LOGIC. Part I. DEDUCTION. Cr. 8vo, 4s. Part II. INDUCTION. Cr. 8vo, 6s. 6d,

Mental, Moral and Political Philosophy—*continued*.

BAIN (ALEXANDER)—*continued*.

THE SENSES AND THE IN-
TELLECT. 8vo, 15s.

THE EMOTIONS AND THE
WILL. 8vo, 15s.

PRACTICAL ESSAYS. Cr. 8vo, 2s.

DISSERTATIONS ON LEADING
PHILOSOPHICAL TOPICS. 8vo,
7s. 6d. net.

BALDWIN.—A COLLEGE MAN-
UAL OF RHETORIC. By CHARLES SEARS
BALDWIN, A.M., Ph.D. Crown 8vo, 4s. 6d.

BROOKS.—THE ELEMENTS OF
MIND : being an Examination into the
Nature of the First Division of the Ele-
mentary Substances of Life. By H. JAMYN
BROOKS. 8vo, 10s. 6d. net.

BROUGH.—THE STUDY OF
MENTAL SCIENCE : Five Lectures on
the Uses and Characteristics of Logic and
Psychology. By J. BROUGH, LL.D. Crown
8vo, 2s. net.

CROZIER (JOHN BEATTIE).

CIVILISATION AND PRO-
GRESS : being the Outlines of a New
System of Political, Religious and Social
Philosophy. 8vo, 14s.

HISTORY OF INTELLECTUAL
DEVELOPMENT : on the Lines of
Modern Evolution.

Vol. I. 8vo, 14s.

Vol. II. (*In preparation*.)

Vol. III. 8vo, 10s. 6d.

FITE. — AN INTRODUCTORY
STUDY OF ETHICS. By WARNER FITE.
Crown 8vo, 6s. 6d.

GREEN (THOMAS HILL).—THE
WORKS OF. Edited by R. L. NETTLESHIP.

Vols. I. and II. Philosophical
Works. 8vo, 16s. each.

Vol. III. Miscellanies. With Index
to the three Volumes, and Memoir. 8vo,
21s.

LECTURES ON THE PRIN-
CIPLES OF POLITICAL OBLIGA-
TION. With Preface by BERNARD
BOSANQUET. 8vo, 5s.

GURNHILL.—THE MORALS OF
SUICIDE. By the Rev. J. GURNHILL, B.A.
Vol. I., Crown 8vo, 5s. net. Vol. II., Crown
8vo, 5s. net.

HODGSON (SHADWORTH H.).

TIME AND SPACE : a Metaphysical Essay. 8vo, 16s.

THE THEORY OF PRACTICE :
an Ethical Inquiry. 2 vols. 8vo, 24s.

THE PHILOSOPHY OF RE-
FLECTION. 2 vols. 8vo, 21s.

THE METAPHYSIC OF EX-
PERIENCE. Book I. General Analysis
of Experience ; Book II. Positive Science ;
Book III. Analysis of Conscious Action ;
Book IV. The Real Universe. 4 vols. 8vo,
36s. net.

HUME.—THE PHILOSOPHICAL
WORKS OF DAVID HUME. Edited by
T. H. GREEN and T. H. GROSE. 4 vols. 8vo,
28s. Or separately, Essays. 2 vols. 14s.
Treatise of Human Nature. 2 vols. 14s.

JAMES (WILLIAM, M.D., LL.D.).

THE WILL TO BELIEVE, and
Other Essays in Popular Philosophy.
Crown 8vo, 7s. 6d.

THE VARIETIES OF RELI-
GIOUS EXPERIENCE : a Study in
Human Nature. Being the Gifford Lectures
on Natural Religion delivered at Edinburgh
in 1901-1902. 8vo, 12s. net.

TALKS TO TEACHERS ON PSY-
CHOLOGY, AND TO STUDENTS ON
SOME OF LIFE'S IDEALS. Crown
8vo, 4s. 6d.

JUSTINIAN.—THE INSTITUTES
OF JUSTINIAN : Latin Text, chiefly that
of Huschke, with English Introduction,
Translation, Notes and Summary. By
THOMAS C. SANDARS, M.A. 8vo, 18s.

KANT (IMMANUEL).

CRITIQUE OF PRACTICAL
REASON, AND OTHER WORKS ON
THE THEORY OF ETHICS. Trans-
lated by T. K. ABBOTT, B.D. With
Memoir. 8vo, 12s. 6d.

FUNDAMENTAL PRINCIPLES
OF THE METAPHYSIC OF ETHICS.
Translated by T. K. ABBOTT, B.D. Crown
8vo, 3s.

INTRODUCTION TO LOGIC,
AND HIS ESSAY ON THE MIS-
TAKEN SUBTILTY OF THE FOUR
FIGURES. Translated by T. K. ABBOTT.
8vo, 6s.

Mental, Moral and Political Philosophy—*continued.*

KELLY.—GOVERNMENT OR HUMAN EVOLUTION. By EDMOND KELLY, M.A., F.G.S. Vol. I. Justice. Cr. 8vo, 7s. 6d. net. Vol. II. Collectivism and Individualism. Crown 8vo, 10s. 6d. net.

KILLICK.—HANDBOOK TO MILL'S SYSTEM OF LOGIC. By Rev. A. H. KILLICK, M.A. Crown 8vo, 3s. 6d.

LADD (GEORGE TRUMBULL).

PHILOSOPHY OF CONDUCT: a Treatise of the Facts, Principles and Ideals of Ethics. 8vo, 21s.

ELEMENTS OF PHYSIOLOGICAL PSYCHOLOGY. 8vo, 21s.

OUTLINES OF DESCRIPTIVE PSYCHOLOGY: a Text-Book of Mental Science for Colleges and Normal Schools. 8vo, 12s.

OUTLINES OF PHYSIOLOGICAL PSYCHOLOGY. 8vo, 12s.

PRIMER OF PSYCHOLOGY. Cr. 8vo, 5s 6d.

LECKY (WILLIAM EDWARD HARTPOLE).

THE MAP OF LIFE: Conduct and Character. Crown 8vo, 5s. net.

HISTORY OF EUROPEAN MORALS FROM AUGUSTUS TO CHARLEMAGNE. 2 vols. Crown 8vo, 10s. net.

A SURVEY OF ENGLISH ETHICS: being the first chapter of W. E. H. Lecky's ' History of European Morals'. Edited, with Introduction and Notes, by W. A. HIRST. Crown 8vo, 3s. 6d.

HISTORY OF THE RISE AND INFLUENCE OF THE SPIRIT OF RATIONALISM IN EUROPE. 2 vols. Crown 8vo, 10s. net.

DEMOCRACY AND LIBERTY.
Library Edition. 2 vols. 8vo, 36s.
Cabinet Edition. 2 vols. Cr. 8vo, 10s. net.

LUTOSLAWSKI.—THE ORIGIN AND GROWTH OF PLATO'S LOGIC. With an Account of Plato's Style and of the Chronology of his Writings. By WINCENTY LUTOSLAWSKI. 8vo, 21s.

MAX MÜLLER (F.).

THE SCIENCE OF THOUGHT. 8vo, 21s.

THE SIX SYSTEMS OF INDIAN PHILOSOPHY. Crown 8vo, 7s. 6d. net.

THREE LECTURES ON THE VEDANTA PHILOSOPHY. Cr. 8vo, 5s.

MILL (JOHN STUART).

A SYSTEM OF LOGIC. Cr. 8vo, 3s. 6d.

ON LIBERTY. Cr. 8vo, 1s. 4d.

CONSIDERATIONS ON REPRESENTATIVE GOVERNMENT. Crown 8vo, 2s.

UTILITARIANISM. 8vo, 2s. 6d.

EXAMINATION OF SIR WILLIAM HAMILTON'S PHILOSOPHY 8vo, 16s.

NATURE, THE UTILITY OF RELIGION AND THEISM. Three Essays. 8vo, 5s.

MONCK.—AN INTRODUCTION TO LOGIC. By WILLIAM HENRY S. MONCK M.A. Crown 8vo, 5s.

MYERS.—HUMAN PERSONALITY AND ITS SURVIVAL OF BODILY DEATH. By FREDERIC W. H. MYERS. 2 vols. 8vo, 42s. net.

PIERCE.—STUDIES IN AUDITORY AND VISUAL SPACE PERCEPTION: Essays on Experimental Psychology. By A. H. PIERCE. Crown 8vo, 6s. 6d. net.

RICHMOND.—THE MIND OF A CHILD. By ENNIS RICHMOND. Cr. 8vo, 3s. 6d. net.

ROMANES.—MIND AND MOTION AND MONISM. By GEORGE JOHN ROMANES. Crown 8vo, 4s. 6d.

SULLY (JAMES).

AN ESSAY ON LAUGHTER: its Forms, its Cause, its Development and its Value. 8vo, 12s. 6d. net.

THE HUMAN MIND; a Textbook of Psychology. 2 vols. 8vo, 21s.

OUTLINES OF PSYCHOLOGY. Crown 8vo, 9s.

THE TEACHER'S HANDBOOK OF PSYCHOLOGY. Crown 8vo, 6s. 6d.

STUDIES OF CHILDHOOD. 8vo, 12s. 6d. net.

CHILDREN'S WAYS: being Selections from the Author's 'Studies of Childhood'. With 25 Illustrations. Crown 8vo, 4s. 6d.

SUTHERLAND.—THE ORIGIN AND GROWTH OF THE MORAL INSTINCT. By ALEXANDER SUTHERLAND, M.A. 2 vols. 8vo, 28s.

SWINBURNE.—PICTURE LOGIC: an Attempt to Popularise the Science of Reasoning. By ALFRED JAMES SWINBURNE, M.A. With 23 Woodcuts. Crown 8vo, 2s. 6d.

Mental, Moral and Political Philosophy—*continued*.

THOMAS.—INTUITIVE SUG-GESTION. By J. W. Thomas, Author of 'Spiritual Law in the Natural World,' etc. Crown 8vo, 3s. 6d. net.

WEBB.—THE VEIL OF ISIS: a Series of Essays on Idealism. By Thomas E. Webb, LL.D., Q.C. 8vo, 10s. 6d.

WEBER.—HISTORY OF PHIL-OSOPHY. By Alfred Weber, Professor in the University of Strasburg. Translated by Frank Thilly, Ph.D. 8vo, 16s.

WHATELY (Archbishop).

BACON'S ESSAYS. With Anno-tations. 8vo, 10s. 6d.

ELEMENTS OF LOGIC. Crown 8vo, 4s. 6d.

ELEMENTS OF RHETORIC. Cr. 8vo, 4s. 6d.

ZELLER (Dr. Edward).

THE STOICS, EPICUREANS, AND SCEPTICS. Translated by the Rev. O. J. Reichel, M.A. Crown 8vo, 15s.

OUTLINES OF THE HISTORY OF GREEK PHILOSOPHY. Translated by Sarah F. Alleyne and Evelyn Ab-bott, M.A., LL.D. Crown 8vo, 10s. 6d.

PLATO AND THE OLDER ACADEMY. Translated by Sarah F. Alleyne and Alfred Goodwin, B.A. Crown 8vo, 18s.

SOCRATES AND THE SO-CRATIC SCHOOLS. Translated by the Rev. O. J. Reichel, M.A. Crown 8vo 10s. 6d.

ARISTOTLE AND THE EARLIER PERIPATETICS. Translated by B. F. C. Costelloe, M.A., and J. H. Muirhead, M.A. 2 vols. Crown 8vo, 24s.

STONYHURST PHILOSOPHICAL SERIES.

A MANUAL OF POLITICAL ECONOMY. By C. S. Devas, M.A. Crown 8vo, 7s. 6d.

FIRST PRINCIPLES OF KNOW-LEDGE. By John Rickaby, S.J. Crown 8vo, 5s.

GENERAL METAPHYSICS. By John Rickaby, S.J. Crown 8vo, 5s.

LOGIC. By Richard F. Clarke, S.J. Crown 8vo, 5s.

MORAL PHILOSOPHY (ETHICS AND NATURAL LAW). By Joseph Rickaby, S.J. Crown 8vo, 5s.

NATURAL THEOLOGY. By Ber-nard Boedder, S.J. Crown 8vo, 6s. 6d.

PSYCHOLOGY. By Michael Maher, S.J., D.Litt., M.A. (Lond.). Crown 8vo, 6s. 6d.

History and Science of Language, etc.

DAVIDSON.—LEADING AND IMPORTANT ENGLISH WORDS: Ex-plained and Exemplified. By William L. Davidson, M.A. Fcp. 8vo, 3s. 6d.

GRAHAM. — ENGLISH SYNO-NYMS, Classified and Explained: with Practical Exercises. By G. F. Graham. Fcp. 8vo, 6s.

MAX MÜLLER (F.).

THE SCIENCE OF LANGUAGE. 2 vols. Crown 8vo. 10s.

BIOGRAPHIES OF WORDS, AND THE HOME OF THE ARYAS. Crown 8vo, 5s.

MAX MÜLLER (F.)—*continued*.

CHIPS FROM A GERMAN WORKSHOP. Vol. III. ESSAYS ON LANGUAGE AND LITERATURE. Crown 8vo, 5s.

LAST ESSAYS. First Series. Essays on Language, Folk-lore and other Subjects. Crown 8vo, 5s.

ROGET.—THESAURUS OF ENG-LISH WORDS AND PHRASES. Clas-sified and Arranged so as to Facilitate the Expression of Ideas and assist in Literary Composition. By Peter Mark Roget, M.D., F.R.S. With full Index. Crown 8vo, 9s. net.

Political Economy, Economics, etc.

ASHLEY (W. J.).

ENGLISH ECONOMIC HISTORY AND THEORY. Crown 8vo, Part I., 5s. Part II., 10s. 6d.

SURVEYS, HISTORIC AND ECONOMIC. Crown 8vo, 9s. net.

THE ADJUSTMENT OF WAGES: a Study on the Coal and Iron Industries of Great Britain and the United States. With 4 Maps. 8vo, 12s. 6d. net.

BRITISH INDUSTRIES: a Series of General Reviews for Business Men and Students. By various Authors. Edited by W. J. ASHLEY. Crown 8vo, 5s. 6d. net.

BAGEHOT. — ECONOMIC STUDIES. By WALTER BAGEHOT. Crown 8vo, 3s. 6d.

BARNETT.—PRACTICABLE SOCIALISM: Essays on Social Reform. By SAMUEL A. and HENRIETTA BARNETT. Crown 8vo, 6s.

DEVAS.—A MANUAL OF POLITICAL ECONOMY. By C. S. DEVAS, M.A. Crown 8vo, 7s. 6d. (Stonyhurst Philosophical Series.)

DEWEY.—FINANCIAL HISTORY OF THE UNITED STATES. By DAVIS RICH DEWEY. Crown 8vo, 7s. 6d. net.

LESLIE.—ESSAYS ON POLITICAL ECONOMY. By T. E. CLIFFE LESLIE, Hon. LL.D., Dubl. 8vo, 10s. 6d.

MACLEOD (HENRY DUNNING).

BIMETALLISM. 8vo, 5s. net.

THE ELEMENTS OF BANKING. Crown 8vo, 3s. 6d.

THE THEORY AND PRACTICE OF BANKING. Vol. I. 8vo, 12s. Vol. II. 14s.

MACLEOD (HENRY DUNNING)—continued.

THE THEORY OF CREDIT. 8vo. In 1 Vol. 30s. net; or separately, Vol. I., 10s. net. Vol. II., Part I., 10s. net. Vol. II., Part II. 10s. net.

INDIAN CURRENCY. 8vo, 2s. 6d. net.

MILL.—POLITICAL ECONOMY. By JOHN STUART MILL. Popular Edition. Crown 8vo, 3s. 6d. Library Edition. 2 vols. 8vo, 30s.

MULHALL.—INDUSTRIES AND WEALTH OF NATIONS. By MICHAEL G. MULHALL, F.S.S. With 32 Diagrams. Crown 8vo, 8s. 6d.

SYMES.—POLITICAL ECONOMY: a Short Text-book of Political Economy. By J. E. SYMES, M.A. Cr. 8vo, 2s. 6d.

TOYNBEE.—LECTURES ON THE INDUSTRIAL REVOLUTION OF OF THE 18TH CENTURY IN ENGLAND. By ARNOLD TOYNBEE. 8vo, 10s. 6d.

WEBB.—LONDON EDUCATION. By SIDNEY WEBB. Crown 8vo, 2s. 6d. net.

WEBB (SIDNEY and BEATRICE).

THE HISTORY OF TRADE UNIONISM. With Map and Bibliography. 8vo, 7s. 6d. net.

INDUSTRIAL DEMOCRACY: a Study in Trade Unionism. 2 vols. 8vo, 12s. net.

PROBLEMS OF MODERN INDUSTRY. 8vo, 5s. net.

THE HISTORY OF LIQUOR LICENSING IN ENGLAND PRINCIPALLY FROM 1700 TO 1830. Crown 8vo, 2s. 6d. net.

Evolution, Anthropology, etc.

ANNANDALE AND ROBINSON.— FASCICULI MALAYENSES: Anthropological and Zoological Results of an Expedition to Perak and the Siamese Malay States, 1901-2. Undertaken by NELSON ANNANDALE and HERBERT C. ROBINSON. With Plates and Illustrations in the Text. ANTHROPOLOGY, Part I., 4to, 15s. net. ZOOLOGY, Part I., 4to, 30s. net; Part II. 4to, 20s. net.

AVEBURY.—THE ORIGIN OF CIVILISATION, and the Primitive Condition of Man. By the Right Hon. LORD AVEBURY. With 6 Plates and 20 Illustrations. 8vo, 18s.

CLODD (EDWARD).

THE STORY OF CREATION: a Plain Account of Evolution. With 77 Illustrations. Crown 8vo, 3s. 6d.

A PRIMER OF EVOLUTION: being a Popular Abridged Edition of 'The Story of Creation'. With Illustrations. Fcp. 8vo, 1s. 6d.

DOUBTS ABOUT DARWINISM. By a SEMI-DARWINIAN. Cr. 8vo, 3s. 6d.

KELLER.—QUERIES IN ETHNOGRAPHY. By ALBERT GALLOWAY KELLER, Ph.D. Fcp. 8vo, 2s. net.

Evolution, Anthropology, etc.—*continued.*

LANG AND ATKINSON.— SOCIAL ORIGINS. By ANDREW LANG, M.A., LL.D.; and PRIMAL LAW. By J. J. ATKINSON. 8vo, 10s. 6d. net.

PACKARD.—LAMARCK, THE FOUNDER OF EVOLUTION: his Life and Work, with Translations of his Writings on Organic Evolution. By ALPHEUS S. PACKARD, M.D., LL.D. With 10 Portrait and other Illustrations. Large Crown 8vo, 9s. net.

ROMANES (GEORGE JOHN). ESSAYS. Edited by C. LLOYD MORGAN. Crown 8vo, 5s. net.

AN EXAMINATION OF WEIS- MANNISM. Crown 8vo, 6s.

ROMANES (GEORGE JOHN)—*cont.*

DARWIN, AND AFTER DAR- WIN: an Exposition of the Darwinian Theory, and a Discussion on Post-Dar- winian Questions.

Part I. THE DARWINIAN THEORY. With Portrait of Darwin and 125 Illustra- tions. Crown 8vo, 10s. 6d.

Part II. POST-DARWINIAN QUES- TIONS: Heredity and Utility. With Por- trait of the Author and 5 Illustrations. Crown 8vo, 10s. 6d.

Part III. POST-DARWINIAN QUES- TIONS: Isolation and Physiological Selection. Crown 8vo, 5s.

The Science of Religion, etc.

BALFOUR.—THE FOUNDA- TIONS OF BELIEF: being Notes Intro- ductory to the Study of Theology. By the Right Hon. ARTHUR JAMES BALFOUR. Crown 8vo, 6s. net.

BARING-GOULD.—THE ORIGIN AND DEVELOPMENT OF RELIGIOUS BELIEF. By the Rev. S. BARING-GOULD. 2 vols. Crown 8vo, 3s. 6d. each.

CAMPBELL.—RELIGION IN GREEK LITERATURE. By the Rev. LEWIS CAMPBELL, M.A., LL.D. 8vo, 15s.

JAMES.—THE VARIETIES OF RELIGIOUS EXPERIENCE: a Study in Human Nature. Being the Gifford Lectures on Natural Religion delivered at Edinburgh in 1901-1902. By WILLIAM JAMES, LL.D., etc. 8vo, 12s. net.

LANG (ANDREW).

MAGIC AND RELIGION. 8vo, 10s. 6d.

CUSTOM AND MYTH: Studies of Early Usage and Belief. With 15 Illus- trations. Crown 8vo, 3s. 6d.

MYTH, RITUAL, AND RE- LIGION. 2 vols. Crown 8vo, 7s.

MODERN MYTHOLOGY: a Reply to Professor Max Müller. 8vo, 9s.

THE MAKING OF RELIGION. Crown 8vo, 5s. net.

MAX MÜLLER (The Right Hon. F.).

THE SILESIAN HORSEHERD ('DAS PFERDEBÜRLA'): Questions of the Hour answered by F. MAX MÜLLER. With a Preface by J. ESTLIN CARPENTER. Crown 8vo, 5s.

CHIPS FROM A GERMAN WORKSHOP. Vol. IV., Essays on Mythology and Folklore. Crown 8vo, 5s.

THE SIX SYSTEMS OF INDIAN PHILOSOPHY. Crown 8vo, 7s. 6d. net.

CONTRIBUTIONS TO THE SCIENCE OF MYTHOLOGY. 2 vols. 8vo, 32s.

THE ORIGIN AND GROWTH OF RELIGION, as illustrated by the Religions of India. The Hibbert Lectures, delivered at the Chapter House, West- minster Abbey, in 1878. Crown 8vo, 5s.

INTRODUCTION TO THE SCIENCE OF RELIGION: Four Lec- tures delivered at the Royal Institution. Crown 8vo, 5s.

NATURAL RELIGION. The Gifford Lectures, delivered before the University of Glasgow in 1888. Crown 8vo, 5s.

The Science of Religion, etc.—*continued.*

MAX MÜLLER (The Right Hon. F.)—*continued.*

PHYSICAL RELIGION. The Gifford Lectures, delivered before the University of Glasgow in 1890. Crown 8vo, 5s.

ANTHROPOLOGICAL RELIGION. The Gifford Lectures, delivered before the University of Glasgow in 1891. Crown 8vo, 5s.

THEOSOPHY, OR PSYCHOLOGICAL RELIGION. The Gifford Lectures, delivered before the University of Glasgow in 1892. Crown 8vo, 5s.

THREE LECTURES ON THE VEDANTA PHILOSOPHY, delivered at the Royal Institution in March, 1894. Crown 8vo, 5s.

LAST ESSAYS. Second Series— Essays on the Science of Religion. Crown 8vo, 5s.

OAKESMITH.—THE RELIGION OF PLUTARCH: a Pagan Creed of Apostolic Times. An Essay. By JOHN OAKESMITH, D.Litt., M.A. Crown 8vo, 5s. net.

WOOD-MARTIN (W. G.).

TRACES OF THE ELDER FAITHS OF IRELAND: a Folk-lore Sketch. A Hand-book of Irish Pre-Christian Traditions. With 192 Illustrations. 2 vols. 8vo, 30s. net.

PAGAN IRELAND: an Archæological Sketch. A Handbook of Irish Pre-Christian Antiquities. With 512 Illustrations. 8vo, 15s.

Classical Literature, Translations, etc.

ABBOTT.—HELLENICA. A Collection of Essays on Greek Poetry, Philosophy, History, and Religion. Edited by EVELYN ABBOTT, M.A., LL.D. Crown 8vo, 7s. 6d.

ÆSCHYLUS.—EUMENIDES OF ÆSCHYLUS. With Metrical English Translation. By J. F. DAVIES. 8vo, 7s.

ARISTOPHANES. — THE ACHARNIANS OF ARISTOPHANES, translated into English Verse. By R. Y. TYRRELL. Crown 8vo, 1s.

BECKER (W. A.). Translated by the Rev. F. METCALFE, B.D.

GALLUS: or, Roman Scenes in the Time of Augustus. With Notes and Excursuses. With 26 Illustrations. Cr. 8vo, 3s. 6d.

CHARICLES: or, Illustrations of the Private Life of the Ancient Greeks. With Notes and Excursuses. With 26 Illustrations. Crown 8vo, 3s. 6d.

CAMPBELL.—RELIGION IN GREEK LITERATURE. By the Rev. LEWIS CAMPBELL, M.A., LL.D., Emeritus Professor of Greek, University of St. Andrews. 8vo, 15s.

CICERO.—CICERO'S CORRESPONDENCE. By R. Y. TYRRELL. Vols. I., II., III., 8vo, each 12s. Vol. IV., 15s. Vol. V., 14s. Vol. VI., 12s. Vol. VII. Index, 7s. 6d.

HARVARD STUDIES IN CLASSICAL PHILOLOGY. Edited by a Committee of the Classical Instructors of Harvard University. Vols. XI., 1900; XII., 1901; XIII., 1902; XIV., 1903. 8vo, 6s. 6d. net each.

HIME.—LUCIAN, THE SYRIAN Satirist. By Lieut.-Col. HENRY W. L. HIME, (late) Royal Artillery. 8vo, 5s. net.

HOMER.—THE ODYSSEY OF HOMER. Done into English Verse. By WILLIAM MORRIS. Crown 8vo, 5s. net.

HORACE.—THE WORKS OF HORACE, RENDERED INTO ENGLISH PROSE. With Life, Introduction and Notes. By WILLIAM COUTTS, M.A. Crown 8vo, 5s. net.

LANG.—HOMER AND THE EPIC. By ANDREW LANG. Crown 8vo, 9s. net.

LUCIAN. — TRANSLATIONS FROM LUCIAN. By AUGUSTA M. CAMPBELL DAVIDSON, M.A., Edin. Crown 8vo, 5s. net.

Classical Literature, Translations, etc.—*continued*.

OGILVIE.—HORAE LATINAE: Studies in Synonyms and Syntax. By the late ROBERT OGILVIE, M.A., LL.D., H.M. Chief Inspector of Schools for Scotland. Edited by ALEXANDER SOUTER, M.A. With a Memoir by JOSEPH OGILVIE, M.A., LL.D. 8vo, 12s. 6d. net.

RICH.—A DICTIONARY OF ROMAN AND GREEK ANTIQUITIES. By A. RICH, B.A. With 2,000 Woodcuts. Crown 8vo, 6s. net.

SOPHOCLES.—Translated into English Verse. By ROBERT WHITELAW, M.A., Assistant Master in Rugby School. Crown 8vo, 8s. 6d.

THEOPHRASTUS. — THE CHARACTERS OF THEOPHRASTUS : a Translation, with Introduction. By CHAS. E. BENNETT and WILLIAM A. HAMMOND, Professors in Cornell University. Fcp. 8vo, 2s. 6d. net.

TYRRELL. DUBLIN TRANS-LATIONS INTO GREEK AND LATIN VERSE. Edited by R. Y. TYRRELL. 8vo, 6s.

VIRGIL.

THE POEMS OF VIRGIL. Translated into English Prose by JOHN CONINGTON. Crown 8vo, 6s.

THE ÆNEID OF VIRGIL. Translated into English Verse by JOHN CONINGTON. Crown 8vo, 6s.

THE ÆNEIDS OF VIRGIL. Done into English Verse. By WILLIAM MORRIS. Crown 8vo, 5s. net.

THE ÆNEID OF VIRGIL, freely translated into English Blank Verse. By W. J. THORNHILL. Crown 8vo, 6s. net.

THE ÆNEID OF VIRGIL. Translated into English Verse by JAMES RHOADES.

Books I.-VI. Crown 8vo, 5s.

Books VII.-XII. Crown 8vo, 5s.

THE ECLOGUES AND GEOR-GICS OF VIRGIL. Translated into English Prose by J. W. MACKAIL, Fellow of Balliol College, Oxford. 16mo, 5s.

WILKINS.—THE GROWTH OF THE HOMERIC POEMS. By G. WIL-KINS. 8vo, 6s.

Poetry and the Drama.

ARNOLD.—THE LIGHT OF THE WORLD : or, The Great Consummation. By Sir EDWIN ARNOLD. With 14 Illustrations after HOLMAN HUNT. Crown 8vo, 5s. net.

BELL (MRS. HUGH).

CHAMBER COMEDIES : a Col-lection of Plays and Monologues for the Drawing Room. Crown 8vo, 5s. net.

FAIRY TALE PLAYS, AND HOW TO ACT THEM. With 91 Diagrams and 52 Illustrations. Crown 8vo, 3s. net.

NURSERY COMEDIES : Twelve Tiny Plays for Children. Fcp. 8vo, 1s. 6d.

RUMPELSTILTZKIN : a Fairy Play in Five Scenes (Characters, 7 Male : 1 Female). From 'Fairy Tale Plays and How to Act Them'. With Illustrations, Diagrams and Music. Cr. 8vo, sewed, 6d.

COCHRANE. — COLLECTED VERSES. By ALFRED COCHRANE, Author of 'The Kestrel's Nest, and other Verses,' 'Leviore Plectro,' etc. With a Frontispiece by H. J. Ford. Fcp. 8vo, 5s. net.

DABNEY. — THE MUSICAL BASIS OF VERSE : a Scientific Study of the Principles of Poetic Composition. By J. P. DABNEY. Crown 8vo, 6s. 6d. net.

GRAVES.—CLYTÆMNESTRA : A TRAGEDY. By ARNOLD F. GRAVES. With a Preface by ROBERT Y. TYRRELL, Litt.D. Crown 8vo, 5s. net.

HITHER AND THITHER : Songs and Verses. By the Author of 'Times and Days,' etc. Fcp. 8vo, 5s.

INGELOW (JEAN).

POETICAL WORKS. Complete in One Volume. Crown 8vo, gilt top, 6s. net.

LYRICAL AND OTHER POEMS. Selected from the Writings of JEAN INGELOW. Fcp. 8vo, 2s, 6d. cloth plain, 3s. cloth gilt.

Poetry and the Drama—*continued*.

KENDALL.—POEMS OF HENRY CLARENCE KENDALL. With Memoir by FREDERICK C. KENDALL. Crown 8vo, 6s.

LANG (ANDREW).

GRASS OF PARNASSUS. Fcp. 8vo, 2s. 6d. net.

THE BLUE POETRY BOOK. Edited by ANDREW LANG. With 100 Illustrations. Crown 8vo, gilt edges, 6s.

LECKY.—POEMS. By WILLIAM EDWARD HARTPOLE LECKY. Fcp. 8vo, 5s.

LYTTON (The Earl of), (OWEN MEREDITH).

THE WANDERER. Crown 8vo, 10s. 6d.

LUCILE. Crown 8vo, 10s. 6d.

SELECTED POEMS. Crown 8vo, 10s. 6d.

MACAULAY.—LAYS OF ANCIENT ROME, WITH 'IVRY' AND 'THE ARMADA'. By LORD MACAULAY.

Illustrated by G. SCHARF. Fcp. 4to, 10s. 6d.

——————— Bijou Edition. 18mo, 2s. 6d. gilt top.

——————— Popular Edition. Fcp. 4to, 6d. sewed, 1s cloth.

Illustrated by J. R. WEGUELIN. Crown 8vo, 3s. net.

Annotated Edition. Fcp. 8vo, 1s. sewed, 1s. 6d. cloth.

MacDONALD.—A BOOK OF STRIFE, IN THE FORM OF THE DIARY OF AN OLD SOUL : Poems. By GEORGE MacDONALD, LL.D. 18mo, 6s.

MORRIS (WILLIAM).

POETICAL WORKS. LIBRARY EDITION. Complete in 11 volumes. Crown 8vo, price 5s. net each.

THE EARTHLY PARADISE. 4 vols. Crown 8vo, 5s. net each.

THE LIFE AND DEATH OF JASON. Crown 8vo, 5s. net.

THE DEFENCE OF GUENE-VERE, and other Poems. Crown 8vo, 5s. net.

THE STORY OF SIGURD THE VOLSUNG, AND THE FALL OF THE NIBLUNGS. Crown 8vo, 5s. net.

POEMS BY THE WAY, AND LOVE IS ENOUGH. Crown 8vo, 5s. net.

MORRIS (WILLIAM).—*continued*.

THE ODYSSEY OF HOMER. Done into English Verse. Crown 8vo, 5s. net.

THE ÆNEIDS OF VIRGIL. Done into English Verse. Crown 8vo, 5s. net.

THE TALE OF BEOWULF, SOMETIME KING OF THE FOLK OF THE WEDERGEATS. Translated by WILLIAM MORRIS and A. J. WYATT. Cr. 8vo, 5s. net.

Certain of the POETICAL WORKS may also be had in the following Editions :—

THE EARTHLY PARADISE.

Popular Edition. 5 vols. 12mo, 25s.; or 5s. each, sold separately.

The Same in Ten Parts, 25s.; or 2s. 6d. each sold separately.

Cheap Edition, in 1 vol. Crown 8vo, 6s. net.

POEMS BY THE WAY. Square Crown 8vo, 6s.

THE DEFENCE OF GUENE-VERE AND OTHER POEMS. Cheaper Impression. Fcp. 8vo, 1s. 6d. net.

** For Mr. William Morris's other Works see pp. 27, 28, 37 and 40.

MORS ET VICTORIA. Cr. 8vo, 5s. net.

** This is a drama in three acts, the scene of which is laid in France shortly after the massacre of St. Bartholomew.

MORTE ARTHUR.—An Alliterative Poem of the Fourteenth Century. Edited from the Thornton MS., with Introduction, Notes and Glossary. By MARY MACLEOD BANKS. Fcp. 8vo, 3s. 6d.

NESBIT.—LAYS AND LEGENDS. By E. NESBIT (Mrs. HUBERT BLAND). First Series. Crown 8vo. 3s. 6d. Second Series. With Portrait. Cr. 8vo, 5s.

RILEY.—OLD FASHIONED ROSES : Poems. By JAMES WHITCOMB RILEY. 12mo, gilt top, 5s.

ROMANES.—A SELECTION FROM THE POEMS OF GEORGE JOHN ROMANES, M.A., LL.D., F.R.S. With an Introduction by T. HERBERT WARREN, President of Magdalen College, Oxford. Crown 8vo, 4s. 6d.

Poetry and the Drama—*continued.*

SAVAGE-ARMSTRONG.— BAL-LADS OF DOWN. By G. F. SAVAGE-ARMSTRONG, M.A., D.Litt. Crown 8vo, 7s. 6d.

SHAKESPEARE.

BOWDLER'S FAMILY SHAKE-SPEARE. With 36 Woodcuts. 1 vol. 8vo, 14s. Or in 6 vols. Fcp. 8vo, 21s.

THE SHAKESPEARE BIRTH-DAY BOOK. By MARY F. DUNBAR. 32mo, 1s. 6d.

STEVENSON.—A CHILD'S GAR-DEN OF VERSES. By ROBERT LOUIS STEVENSON. Fcp. 8vo, gilt top, 5s.

TREVELYAN.—CECILIA GON-ZAGA : a Drama. By R. C. TREVELYAN. Fcp. 8vo, 2s. 6d. net.

WAGNER.—THE NIBELUNGEN RING. Done into English Verse by REGINALD RANKIN, B.A., of the Inner Temple, Barrister-at-Law.

Vol. I. Rhine Gold, The Valkyrie. Fcp. 8vo, gilt top, 4s. 6d.

Vol. II. Siegfried, The Twilight of the Gods. Fcp. 8vo, gilt top, 4s. 6d.

Fiction, Humour, etc.

ANSTEY (F.).

VOCES POPULI. (Reprinted from ' Punch '.)

First Series. With 20 Illustrations by J. BERNARD PARTRIDGE. Crown 8vo, gilt top, 3s. net.

Second Series. With 25 Illustrations by J. BERNARD PARTRIDGE. Crown 8vo, gilt top, 3s. net.

THE MAN FROM BLANKLEY'S, and other Sketches. (Reprinted from ' Punch '.) With 25 Illustrations by J. BERNARD PARTRIDGE. Crown 8vo, gilt top, 3s. net.

BAILEY (H. C.).

MY LADY OF ORANGE : a Romance of the Netherlands in the Days of Alva. With 8 Illustrations. Crown 8vo, 6s.

KARL OF ERBACH : a Tale of the Thirty Years' War. Crown 8vo, 6s.

THE MASTER OF GRAY : a Tale of the Days of Mary Queen of Scots. Crown 8vo, 6s.

BEACONSFIELD (The Earl of).

NOVELS AND TALES. Complete in 11 vols Crown 8vo, 1s. 6d. each, or in sets, 11 vols., gilt top, 15s. net.

Vivian Grey.
The Young Duke; Count Alarcos: a Tragedy.
Alroy; Ixion in Heaven; The Infernal Marriage; Popanilla.
Tancred.
Contarini Fleming; The Rise of Iskander.
Sybil.
Henrietta Temple.
Venetia.
Coningsby.
Lothair.
Endymion.

NOVELS AND TALES. THE HUGHENDEN EDITION. With 2 Portraits and 11 Vignettes. 11 vols. Crown 8vo, 42s.

BOTTOME.—LIFE, THE INTER-PRETER. By PHYLLIS BOTTOME. Crown 8vo, 6s.

CHURCHILL.—SAVROLA : a Tale of the Revolution in Laurania. By WINSTON SPENCER CHURCHILL, M.P. Cr. 8vo, 6s.

CONVERSE.—LONG WILL : a Tale of Wat Tyler and the Peasant Rising in the Reign of Richard II. By FLORENCE CONVERSE. With 6 Illustrations by GARTH JONES. Crown 8vo, 6s.

DAVENPORT.—BY THE RAM-PARTS OF JEZREEL: a Romance of Jehu, King of Israel. By ARNOLD DAVENPORT. With Frontispiece by LANCELOT SPEED. Crown 8vo, 6s.

DOUGALL.—BEGGARS ALL. By L. DOUGALL. Crown 8vo, 3s. 6d.

DOYLE (Sir A. CONAN).

MICAH CLARKE : a Tale of Monmouth's Rebellion. With 10 Illustrations. Crown 8vo, 3s. 6d.

THE REFUGEES : a Tale of the Huguenots. With 25 Illustrations. Cr. 8vo, 3s. 6d.

THE STARK MUNRO LETTERS. Crown 8vo, 3s. 6d.

THE CAPTAIN OF THE POLE-STAR, and other Tales. Cr. 8vo, 3s. 6d.

Fiction. Humour, etc.—*continued.*

DUNBAR.—THE SONS O' COR-
MAC : Irish Legends. By ALDIS DUNBAR.
With 8 Illustrations by Miss LUXMORE. Cr.
8vo.

FARRAR (F. W., late DEAN OF
CANTERBURY).

DARKNESS AND DAWN : or.
Scenes in the Days of Nero. An Historic
Tale. Crown 8vo, gilt top, 6s. net.

GATHERING CLOUDS : a Tale
of the Days of St. Chrysostom. Crown
8vo, gilt top, 6s. net.

FOWLER (EDITH H.).

THE YOUNG PRETENDERS.
A Story of Child Life. With 12 Illustra-
tions by Sir PHILIP BURNE-JONES, Bart.
Crown 8vo, 6s.

THE PROFESSOR'S CHIL-
DREN. With 24 Illustrations by ETHEL
KATE BURGESS. Crown 8vo, 6s.

FRANCIS (M. E.)

CHRISTIAN THAL : a Story of
Musical Life. Crown 8vo, 6s.

FIANDER'S WIDOW. Crown
8vo, 6s.

YEOMAN FLEETWOOD. With
Frontispiece. Crown 8vo, 3s. net.

PASTORALS OF DORSET. With
8 Illustrations. Crown 8vo, 6s.

THE MANOR FARM. With
Frontispiece by CLAUD C. DU PRÉ COOPER.
Crown 8vo, 6s.

FROUDE.—THE TWO CHIEFS
OF DUNBOY : an Irish Romance of the
Last Century. By JAMES A. FROUDE. Crown
8vo, 3s. 6d.

HAGGARD SIDE, THE : being
Essays in Fiction. By the Author of 'Times
and Days,' 'Auto da Fé,' &c. Crown 8vo,
5s.

HAGGARD (H. RIDER).

ALLAN QUATERMAIN. With 31
Illustrations. Crown 8vo, 3s. 6d.

ALLAN'S WIFE. With 34 Illustrations. Crown 8vo, 3s. 6d.

BEATRICE. With Frontispiece
and Vignette. Crown 8vo, 3s. 6d.

HAGGARD (H. RIDER)—*continued.*

BLACK HEART AND WHITE
HEART, AND OTHER STORIES. With
33 Illustrations. Crown 8vo, 3s. 6d.

CLEOPATRA. With 29 Illustrations. Crown 8vo, 3s. 6d.

COLONEL QUARITCH, V.C.
With Frontispiece and Vignette. Crown
8vo, 3s. 6d.

DAWN. With 16 Illustrations.
Crown 8vo, 3s. 6d.

DR. THERNE. Cr. 8vo, 3s. 6d.

ERIC BRIGHTEYES. With 51
Illustrations. Crown 8vo, 3s. 6d.

HEART OF THE WORLD. With
15 Illustrations. Crown 8vo, 3s. 6d.

JOAN HASTE. With 20 Illustrations. Crown 8vo, 3s. 6d.

LYSBETH. With 26 Illustrations.
Crown 8vo, 6s.

MAIWA'S REVENGE. Crown 8vo,
1s. 6d.

MONTEZUMA'S DAUGHTER.
With 24 Illustrations. Crown 8vo, 3s. 6d.

MR. MEESON'S WILL. With
16 Illustrations. Crown 8vo, 3s. 6d.

NADA THE LILY. With 23 Illustrations. Crown 8vo, 3s. 6d.

PEARL-MAIDEN : a Tale of the
Fall of Jerusalem. With 16 Illustrations.
Crown 8vo, 6s.

SHE. With 32 Illustrations. Cr.
8vo, 3s. 6d.

STELLA FREGELIUS : a Tale of
Three Destinies. Crown 8vo, 6s.

SWALLOW : a Tale of the Great
Trek. With 8 Illustrations. Crown 8vo,
3s. 6d.

THE PEOPLE OF THE MIST.
With 16 Illustrations. Crown 8vo, 3s. 6d.

THE WITCH'S HEAD. With 16
Illustrations. Crown 8vo, 3s. 6d.

HAGGARD AND LANG.—THE
WORLD'S DESIRE. By H. RIDER HAG-
GARD and ANDREW LANG. With 27 Illus-
trations. Crown 8vo, 3s. 6d.

Fiction, Humour, etc.—*continued.*

HARTE.—IN THE CARQUINEZ WOODS. By BRET HARTE. Crown 8vo, 3s. 6d.

HOPE.—THE HEART OF PRINCESS OSRA. By ANTHONY HOPE. With 9 Illustrations. Crown 8vo, 3s. 6d.

HOWARD.—THE FAILURE OF SUCCESS. By LADY MABEL HOWARD. Crown 8vo, 6s.

HUTCHINSON.—A FRIEND OF NELSON. By HORACE G. HUTCHINSON. Crown 8vo, 6s.

JEROME.—SKETCHES IN LAVENDER: BLUE AND GREEN. By JEROME K. JEROME, Author of 'Three Men in a Boat,' etc. Crown 8vo, 3s. 6d.

JOYCE.—OLD CELTIC ROMANCES. Twelve of the most beautiful of the Ancient Irish Romantic Tales. Translated from the Gaelic. By P. W. JOYCE, LL.D. Crown 8vo, 3s. 6d.

LANG (ANDREW).

A MONK OF FIFE: a Story of the Days of Joan of Arc. With 13 Illustrations by SELWYN IMAGE. Crown 8vo, 3s. 6d.

THE DISENTANGLERS. With 7 Full-page Illustrations by H. J. FORD. Crown 8vo, 6s.

LYALL (EDNA).

THE HINDERERS. Crown 8vo, 2s. 6d.

THE AUTOBIOGRAPHY OF A SLANDER. Fcp. 8vo, 1s. sewed.

Presentation Edition. With 20 Illustrations by LANCELOT SPEED. Crown 8vo, 2s. 6d. net.

DOREEN. The Story of a Singer. Crown 8vo, 6s.

WAYFARING MEN. Cr. 8vo, 6s.

HOPE THE HERMIT: a Romance of Borrowdale. Crown 8vo, 6s.

MARCHMONT.—IN THE NAME OF A WOMAN: a Romance. By ARTHUR W. MARCHMONT. With 8 Illustrations. Crown 8vo, 6s.

MASON AND LANG.—PARSON KELLY. By A. E. W. MASON and ANDREW LANG. Crown 8vo, 3s. 6d.

MAX MÜLLER. — DEUTSCHE LIEBE (GERMAN LOVE): Fragments from the Papers of an Alien. Collected by F. MAX MÜLLER. Translated from the German by G. A. M. Cr. 8vo, gilt top, 5s.

MELVILLE (G. J. WHYTE).

The Gladiators.	Holmby House.
The Interpreter.	Kate Coventry.
Good for Nothing.	Digby Grand.
The Queen's Maries.	General Bounce.

Crown 8vo, 1s. 6d. each.

MERRIMAN. — FLOTSAM: a Story of the Indian Mutiny. By HENRY SETON MERRIMAN. With Frontispiece and Vignette by H. G. MASSEY. Crown 8vo, 3s. 6d.

MORRIS (WILLIAM).

THE SUNDERING FLOOD. Cr. 8vo, 7s. 6d.

THE WATER OF THE WONDROUS ISLES. Crown 8vo, 7s. 6d.

THE WELL AT THE WORLD'S END. 2 vols. 8vo, 28s.

THE WOOD BEYOND THE WORLD. Crown 8vo, 6s. net.

THE STORY OF THE GLITTERING PLAIN, which has also been called The Land of the Living Men, or the Acre of the Undying. Square post 8vo, 5s. net.

THE ROOTS OF THE MOUNTAINS, wherein is told somewhat of the Lives of the Men of Burgdale, their Friends, their Neighbours, their Foemen, and their Fellows-in-Arms. Written in Prose and Verse. Square crown 8vo, 8s.

A TALE OF THE HOUSE OF THE WOLFINGS, and all the Kindreds of the Mark. Written in Prose and Verse. Square crown 8vo, 6s.

A DREAM OF JOHN BALL, AND A KING'S LESSON. 16mo, 2s. net.

Fiction, Humour, etc.—*continued.*

MORRIS (William)—*continued.*

NEWS FROM NOWHERE: or, An Epoch of Rest. Being some Chapters from an Utopian Romance. Post 8vo, 1s. 6d.

THE STORY OF GRETTIR THE STRONG. Translated from the Icelandic by Eiríkr Magnússon and William Morris. Crown 8vo, 5s. net.

THREE NORTHERN LOVE STORIES, AND OTHER TALES. Translated from the Icelandic by Eiríkr Magnússon and William Morris. Cr. 8vo, 6s. net.

** For Mr. William Morris's other Works, see pp. 24, 37 and 48.

NEWMAN (Cardinal).

LOSS AND GAIN: the Story of a Convert. Crown 8vo, 3s. 6d.

CALLISTA: a Tale of the Third Century. Crown 8vo, 3s. 6d.

PHILLIPPS-WOLLEY. SNAP: a Legend of the Lone Mountain. By C. Phillipps-Wolley. With 13 Illustrations. Crown 8vo, 3s. 6d.

PORTMAN. — STATION STUDIES: being the Jottings of an African Official. By Lionel Portman. Crown 8vo, 5s. net.

SEWELL (Elizabeth M.).

A Glimpse of the World.	Amy Herbert.
Laneton Parsonage.	Cleve Hall.
Margaret Percival.	Gertrude.
Katharine Ashton.	Home Life.
The Earl's Daughter.	After Life.
The Experience of Life.	Ursula. Ivors.

Crown 8vo, cloth plain, 1s. 6d. each. Cloth extra, gilt edges. 2s. 6d. each.

SHEEHAN.—LUKE DELMEGE. By the Rev. P. A. Sheehan, D.D., Author of ' My New Curate '. Crown 8vo, 6s.

SOMERVILLE (E. Œ.) **AND** ROSS (Martin).

SOME EXPERIENCES OF AN IRISH R.M. With 31 Illustrations by E. Œ. Somerville. Crown 8vo, 6s.

ALL ON THE IRISH SHORE: Irish Sketches. With 10 Illustrations by E. Œ. Somerville. Crown 8vo, 6s.

THE REAL CHARLOTTE. Cr. 8vo, 3s. 6d.

THE SILVER FOX. Crown 8vo, 3s. 6d.

AN IRISH COUSIN. Cr. 8vo, 6s.

STEVENSON (Robert Louis).

THE STRANGE CASE OF DR. JEKYLL AND MR. HYDE. Fcp. 8vo, 1s. sewed, 1s. 6d. cloth.

THE STRANGE CASE OF DR. JEKYLL AND MR. HYDE: WITH OTHER FABLES. Crown 8vo, bound in buckram, with gilt top, 5s. net.

' *Silver Library* ' Edition. Cr. 8vo, 3s. 6d.

MORE NEW ARABIAN NIGHTS —THE DYNAMITER. By Robert Louis Stevenson and Fanny van de Grift Stevenson. Crown 8vo, 3s. 6d.

THE WRONG BOX. By Robert Louis Stevenson and Lloyd Osbourne. Crown 8vo, 3s. 6d.

SUTTNER.—LAY DOWN YOUR ARMS (*Die Waffen Nieder*): The Autobiography of Martha von Tilling. By Bertha von Suttner. Translated by T. Holmes. Crown 8vo, 1s. 6d.

TROLLOPE (Anthony).

THE WARDEN. Crown 8vo, 1s. 6d.

BARCHESTER TOWERS. Crown 8vo, 1s. 6d.

VAUGHAN.— OLD HENDRIK'S TALES. By Captain Arthur O. Vaughan, With 12 Full-page Illustrations by J. A. Shepherd. Crown 8vo.

WALFORD (L. B.).

STAY-AT-HOMES. Cr. 8vo, 6s.

CHARLOTTE. Crown 8vo, 6s.

ONE OF OURSELVES. Crown 8vo, 6s.

THE INTRUDERS. Cr. 8vo, 2s. 6d.

LEDDY MARGET. Cr. 8vo, 2s. 6d.

IVA KILDARE: a Matrimonial Problem. Crown 8vo, 2s. 6d.

MR. SMITH: a Part of his Life. Crown 8vo, 2s. 6d.

THE BABY'S GRANDMOTHER. Crown 8vo, 2s. 6d.

Fiction, Humour, etc.—*continued*.

WALFORD (L. B.)—*continued*.

COUSINS. Crown 8vo, 2s. 6d.

TROUBLESOME DAUGHTERS. Crown 8vo, 2s. 6d.

PAULINE. Crown 8vo, 2s. 6d.

DICK NETHERBY. Crown 8vo, 2s. 6d.

THE HISTORY OF A WEEK. Crown 8vo, 2s. 6d.

A STIFF-NECKED GENERA- TION. Crown 8vo, 2s. 6d.

NAN, and other Stories. Cr. 8vo, 2s. 6d.

THE MISCHIEF OF MONICA. Crown 8vo, 2s. 6d.

THE ONE GOOD GUEST. Cr. 8vo, 2s. 6d.

'PLOUGHED' and other Stories. Crown 8vo, 2s. 6d.

THE MATCHMAKER. Cr. 8vo, 2s. 6d.

WARD.—ONE POOR SCRUPLE. By Mrs. WILFRID WARD. Crown 8vo, 6s.

WEYMAN (STANLEY).

THE HOUSE OF THE WOLF. With Frontispiece and Vignette. Crown 8vo, 3s. 6d.

A GENTLEMAN OF FRANCE. With Frontispiece and Vignette. Crown 8vo, 6s.

THE RED COCKADE. With Frontispiece and Vignette. Crown 8vo, 6s.

SHREWSBURY. With 24 Illus- trations by CLAUDE A. SHEPPERSON. Crown 8vo, 6s.

SOPHIA. With Frontispiece. Cr. 8vo, 6s.

THE LONG NIGHT. A Story of Geneva in 1602. Crown 8vo, 6s.

YEATS (S. LEVETT).

THE CHEVALIER D'AURIAC· Crown 8vo, 3s. 6d.

THE TRAITOR'S WAY. Crown 8vo, 6s.

YOXALL.—THE ROMMANY STONE. By J. H. YOXALL, M.P. Crown 8vo, 6s.

Popular Science (Natural History, etc.).

FURNEAUX (W.).

THE OUTDOOR WORLD: or, The Young Collector's Handbook. With 18 Plates (16 of which are coloured), and 549 Illustrations in the Text. Crown 8vo, gilt edges, 6s. net.

BUTTERFLIES AND MOTHS (British). With 12 Coloured Plates and 241 Illustrations in the Text. Crown 8vo, gilt edges, 6s. net.

LIFE IN PONDS AND STREAMS. With 8 Coloured Plates and 331 Illustrations in the Text. Crown 8vo, gilt edges, 6s. net.

THE SEA SHORE. With 8 Coloured Plates and 300 Illustrations in the Text. Crown 8vo, 6s. net.

HARTWIG (GEORGE).

THE SEA AND ITS LIVING WONDERS. With 12 Plates and 303 Woodcuts. 8vo, gilt top, 7s. net.

THE TROPICAL WORLD. With 8 Plates and 172 Woodcuts. 8vo, gilt top, 7s. net.

THE POLAR WORLD. With 3 Maps, 8 Plates and 85 Woodcuts. 8vo, gilt top, 7s. net.

THE SUBTERRANEAN WORLD. With 3 Maps and 80 Woodcuts. 8vo, gilt top, 7s. net.

Popular Science (Natural History, etc.)—*continued.*

HELMHOLTZ.—POPULAR LEC-
TURES ON SCIENTIFIC SUBJECTS.
By HERMANN VON HELMHOLTZ. With
68 Woodcuts. 2 vols. Crown 8vo, 3s. 6d.
each.

HOFFMANN.—ALPINE FLORA:
For Tourists and Amateur Botanists. With
Text descriptive of the most widely distri-
buted and attractive Alpine Plants. By
JULIUS HOFFMANN. Translated by E. S.
BARTON (Mrs. A. GEPP). With 40 Plates
containing 250 Coloured Figures from Water-
Colour Sketches by HERMANN FRIESE. 8vo,
7s. 6d. net.

HUDSON (W. H.).

HAMPSHIRE DAYS. With 11
Plates and 36 Illustrations in the Text
from Drawings by BRYAN HOOK, etc. 8vo,
10s. 6d. net.

BIRDS AND MAN. Large crown
8vo, 6s. net.

NATURE IN DOWNLAND. With
12 Plates and 14 Illustrations in the Text
by A. D. McCORMICK. 8vo, 10s. 6d. net.

BRITISH BIRDS. With a Chap-
ter on Structure and Classification by
FRANK E. BEDDARD, F.R.S. With 16
Plates (8 of which are Coloured), and over
100 Illustrations in the Text. Crown 8vo,
gilt edges, 6s. net.

MILLAIS.—THE NATURAL HIS-
TORY OF THE BRITISH SURFACE
FEEDING-DUCKS. By JOHN GUILLE
MILLAIS, F.Z.S., etc. With 6 Photogravures
and 66 Plates (41 in Colours) from Drawings
by the Author, ARCHIBALD THORBURN, and
from Photographs. Royal 4to, £6 6s.

PROCTOR (RICHARD A.).

LIGHT SCIENCE FOR LEISURE
HOURS. Familiar Essays on Scientific
Subjects. Crown 8vo, 3s. 6d.

ROUGH WAYS MADE SMOOTH.
Familiar Essays on Scientific Subjects.
Crown 8vo, 3s. 6d.

PROCTOR(RICHARD A.)—*continued*

PLEASANT WAYS IN SCIENCE
Crown 8vo, 3s. 6d.

NATURE STUDIES. By R. A
PROCTOR, GRANT ALLEN, A. WILSON, T
FOSTER and E. CLODD. Crown 8vo, 3s. 6d

LEISURE READINGS. By R. A
PROCTOR, E. CLODD, A. WILSON, T
FOSTER and A. C. RANYARD. Crown 8vo
3s. 6d.

*** For Mr. Proctor's other books see pp. 1
and 35, and Messrs. Longmans & Co.'s Catalogu
of Scientific Works.*

STANLEY.—A FAMILIAR HIS
TORY OF BIRDS. By E. STANLEY, D.D.
formerly Bishop of Norwich. With 16
Illustrations. Cr. 8vo, 3s. 6d.

WOOD (Rev. J. G.).

HOMES WITHOUT HANDS: a
Description of the Habitations of Animals
classed according to their Principle o
Construction. With 140 Illustrations
8vo, gilt top, 7s. net.

INSECTS AT HOME: a Popular
Account of British Insects, their Structure
Habits and Transformations. With 700
Illustrations. 8vo, gilt top, 7s. net.

INSECTS ABROAD: a Popular
Account of Foreign Insects, their Structure, Habits and Transformations. With
600 Illustrations. 8vo, 7s. net.

OUT OF DOORS: a Selection of
Original Articles on Practical Natural
History. With 11 Illustrations. Crown
8vo, 3s. 6d.

PETLAND REVISITED. With 33
Illustrations. Crown 8vo, 3s. 6d.

STRANGE DWELLINGS: a De-
scription of the Habitations of Animals,
abridged from 'Homes without Hands'.
With 60 Illustrations. Crown 8vo, 3s. 6d.

Works of Reference.

ANNUAL REGISTER (THE). A Review of Public Events at Home and Abroad, for the year 1902. 8vo, 18s.

Volumes of the Annual Register for the years 1863-1901 can still be had. 18s. each.

CHARITIES REGISTER. THE ANNUAL, AND DIGEST: being a Classified Register of Charities in or available in the Metropolis. 8vo, 5s. net.

CHISHOLM.—HANDBOOK OF COMMERCIAL GEOGRAPHY. By GEORGE G. CHISHOLM, M.A., B.Sc., Fellow of the Royal Geographical and Statistical Societies. With 19 Folding-out Maps and numerous Maps in the Text. 8vo, 15s. net.

GWILT.—AN ENCYCLOPÆDIA OF ARCHITECTURE. By JOSEPH GWILT, F.S.A. With 1,700 Engravings. Revised (1888), with Alterations and Considerable Additions by WYATT PAPWORTH. 8vo, 21s. net.

LONGMANS' GAZETTEER OF THE WORLD. Edited by GEORGE G. CHISHOLM, M.A., B.Sc. Imperial 8vo, 18s. net cloth; 21s. half-morocco.

MAUNDER (SAMUEL).

BIOGRAPHICAL TREASURY. With Supplement brought down to 1889. By REV. JAMES WOOD. Fcp. 8vo, 6s.

MAUNDER (SAMUEL)—*continued.*

THE TREASURY OF BIBLE KNOWLEDGE. By the REV. J. AYRE, M.A. With 5 Maps, 15 Plates, and 300 Woodcuts. Fcp. 8vo, 6s.

TREASURY OF KNOWLEDGE AND LIBRARY OF REFERENCE. Fcp. 8vo, 6s.

THE TREASURY OF BOTANY. Edited by J. LINDLEY, F.R.S., and T. MOORE, F.L.S. With 274 Woodcuts and 20 Steel Plates. 2 vols. Fcp. 8vo, 12s.

RICH—A Dictionary of Roman and Greek Antiquities. By A RICH, B.A. With 2,000 Woodcuts. Crown 8vo, 6s. net.

ROGET.—THESAURUS OF ENGLISH WORDS AND PHRASES. Classified and Arranged so as to Facilitate the Expression of Ideas and assist in Literary Composition. By PETER MARK ROGET, M.D., F.R.S. Recomposed throughout, enlarged and improved, partly from the Author's Notes, and with a full Index, by the Author's Son, JOHN LEWIS ROGET. Crown 8vo, 9s. net.

WILLICH.—POPULAR TABLES for giving information for ascertaining the value of Lifehold, Leasehold, and Church Property, the Public Funds, etc. By CHARLES M. WILLICH. Edited by H. BENCE JONES. Crown 8vo, 10s. 6d.

Children's Books.

ADELBORG.—CLEAN PETER AND THE CHILDREN OF GRUBBYLEA. By OTTILIA ADELBORG. Translated from the Swedish by Mrs. GRAHAM WALLAS. With 23 Coloured Plates. Oblong 4to, boards, 3s. 6d. net.

ALICK'S ADVENTURES.— By G. R. With 8 Illustrations by JOHN HASSALL. Crown 8vo, 3s. 6d.

BOLD TURPIN: a Romance, as Sung by Sam Weller. With 16 Illustrations in Colour by L. D. L. Oblong 4to, boards, 6s.

BROWN.—THE BOOK OF SAINTS AND FRIENDLY BEASTS. By ABBIE FARWELL BROWN. With 8 Illustrations by FANNY Y. CORY. Crown 8vo, 4s. 6d. net.

CRAKE (Rev. A. D.).

EDWY THE FAIR: or, The First Chronicle of Æscendune. Crown 8vo, silver top, 2s. net.

ALFGAR THE DANE: or, The Second Chronicle of Æscendune. Crown 8vo, silver top, 2s. net.

THE RIVAL HEIRS: being the Third and Last Chronicle of Æscendune. Crown 8vo, silver top, 2s. net.

THE HOUSE OF WALDERNE. A Tale of the Cloister and the Forest in the Days of the Barons' Wars. Crown 8vo, silver top, 2s. net.

BRIAN FITZ-COUNT. A Story of Wallingford Castle and Dorchester Abbey. Crown 8vo, silver top, 2s. net.

Children's Books—*continued*.

DENT.—IN SEARCH OF HOME:
a Story of East-End Waifs and Strays. By
PHYLLIS O. DENT. With a Frontispiece in
Colour by HAMEL LISTER. Crown 8vo, 3s. 6d.
net.

HENTY (G. A.).—EDITED BY.

YULE LOGS: A Story-Book for
Boys. By VARIOUS AUTHORS. With 61
Illustrations. Crown 8vo, gilt edges, 3s.
net.

YULE TIDE YARNS: a Story-
Book for Boys. By VARIOUS AUTHORS.
With 45 Illustrations. Crown 8vo, gilt
edges, 3s. net.

LANG (ANDREW).—EDITED BY.

THE BLUE FAIRY BOOK. With
138 Illustrations. Crown 8vo, gilt edges,
6s.

THE RED FAIRY BOOK. With
100 Illustrations. Crown 8vo, gilt edges, 6s.

THE GREEN FAIRY BOOK.
With 99 Illustrations. Crown 8vo, gilt
edges, 6s.

THE GREY FAIRY BOOK. With
65 Illustrations. Crown 8vo, gilt edges, 6s.

THE YELLOW FAIRY BOOK.
With 104 Illustrations. Crown 8vo, gilt
edges, 6s.

THE PINK FAIRY BOOK. With
67 Illustrations. Crown 8vo, gilt edges, 6s.

THE VIOLET FAIRY BOOK.
With 8 Coloured Plates and 54 other Illustrations. Crown 8vo, gilt edges, 6s.

THE CRIMSON FAIRY BOOK.
With 8 Coloured Plates and 43 other Illustrations. Crown 8vo, gilt edges, 6s.

THE BLUE POETRY BOOK.
With 100 Illustrations. Crown 8vo, gilt
edges, 6s.

THE TRUE STO Y BOOK. With
66 Illustrations. Crown 8vo, gilt edges, 6s.

THE RED TRUE STORY BOOK.
With 100 Illustrations. Crown 8vo, gilt
edges, 6s.

THE ANIMAL STORY BOOK.
With 67 Illustrations. Crown 8vo, gilt
edges, 6s.

THE RED BOOK OF ANIMAL
STORIES. With 65 Illustrations. Crown
8vo, gilt edges, 6s.

LANG (ANDREW) EDITED BY—*cont.*

THE ARABIAN NIGHTS EN-
TERTAINMENTS. With 66 Illustrations. Crown 8vo, gilt edges, 6s.

THE BOOK OF ROMANCE. With
8 Coloured Plates and 44 other Illustrations.
Crown 8vo, gilt edges, 6s.

LYALL.— THE BURGES
LETTERS: a Record of Child Life in the
Sixties. By EDNA LYALL. With Coloured
Frontispiece and 8 other Full-page Illustra-
tions by WALTER S. STACEY. Crown 8vo,
2s. 6d.

MEADE (L. T.).

DADDY'S BOY. With 8 Illustrations. Crown 8vo, gilt edges, 3s. net.

DEB AND THE DUCHESS. With
7 Illustrations. Cr. 8vo, gilt edges, 3s. net.

THE BERESFORD PRIZE. With
7 Illustrations. Cr. 8vo, gilt edges, 3s. net.

THE HOUSE OF SURPRISES.
With 6 Illustrations. Crown 8vo, gilt
edges, 3s. net.

PACKARD.—THE YOUNG ICE
WHALERS: a Tale for Boys. By WIN-
THROP PACKARD. With 16 Illustrations.
Crown 8vo, 6s.

PENROSE.—CHUBBY: A NUI-
SANCE. By Mrs. PENROSE. With 8 Illustrations by G. G. MANTON. Crown 8vo,
3s. 6d.

PRAEGER (ROSAMOND).

THE ADVENTURES OF THE
THREE BOLD BABES: HECTOR,
HONORIA AND ALISANDER A Story
in Pictures. With 24 Coloured Plates and
24 Outline Pictures. Oblong 4to, 3s. 6d.

THE FURTHER DOINGS OF
THE THREE BOLD BABES. With
24 Coloured Pictures and 24 Outline
Pictures. Oblong 4to, 3s. 6d.

ROBERTS.—THE ADVENTURES
OF CAPTAIN JOHN SMITH: Captain of
Two Hundred and Fifty Horse, and some-
time President of Virginia. By E. P.
ROBERTS. With 17 Illustrations and 3 Maps.
Crown 8vo, 5s. net.

STEVENSON.—A CHILD'S
GARDEN OF VERSES. By ROBERT
LOUIS STEVENSON. Fcp. 8vo, gilt top, 5s.

Children's Books—*continued.*

UPTON (FLORENCE K. AND BERTHA).

THE ADVENTURES OF TWO DUTCH DOLLS AND A 'GOLLI-WOGG'. With 31 Coloured Plates and numerous Illustrations in the Text. Oblong 4to, 6s.

THE GOLLIWOGG'S BICYCLE CLUB. With 31 Coloured Plates and numerous Illustrations in the Text. Oblong 4to, 6s.

THE GOLLIWOGG AT THE SEASIDE. With 31 Coloured Plates and numerous Illustrations in the Text. Oblong 4to, 6s.

THE GOLLIWOGG IN WAR. With 31 Coloured Plates. Oblong 4to, 6s.

UPTON (FLORENCE K. AND BERTHA) —*continued.*

THE GOLLIWOGG'S POLAR ADVENTURES. With 31 Coloured Plates. Oblong 4to, 6s.

THE GOLLIWOGG'S AUTO-GO-CART. With 31 Coloured Plates and numerous Illustrations in the Text. Oblong 4to, 6s.

THE GOLLIWOGG'S AIR-SHIP. With 30 Coloured Pictures and numerous Illustrations in the Text. Oblong 4to, 6s.

THE GOLLIWOGG'S CIRCUS. With 31 Coloured Pictures. Oblong 4to, boards, 6s.

THE VEGE-MEN'S REVENGE. With 31 Coloured Plates and numerous Illustrations in the Text. Oblong 4to, 6s.

THE SILVER LIBRARY.

Crown 8vo, 3s. 6d. EACH VOLUME.

Arnold's (Sir Edwin) Seas and Lands. With 71 Illustrations. 3s. 6d.

Bagehot's (W.) Biographical Studies. 3s. 6d.

Bagehot's (W.) Economic Studies. 3s. 6d.

Bagehot's (W.) Literary Studies. With Portrait. 3 vols., 3s. 6d. each.

Baker's (Sir S. W.) Eight Years in Ceylon. With 6 Illustrations. 3s. 6d.

Baker's (Sir S. W.) Rifle and Hound in Ceylon. With 6 Illustrations. 3s. 6d.

Baring=Gould's (Rev. S.) Curious Myths of the Middle Ages. 3s. 6d.

Baring=Gould's (Rev. S.) Origin and Development of Religious Belief. 2 vols. 3s. 6d. each.

Becker's (W. A.) Gallus : or, Roman Scenes in the Time of Augustus. With 26 Illustrations. 3s. 6d.

Becker's (W. A.) Charicles : or, Illustrations of the Private Life of the Ancient Greeks. With 26 Illustrations. 3s. 6d.

Bent's (J. T.) The Ruined Cities of Mashonaland. With 117 Illustrations. 3s. 6d.

Brassey's (Lady) A Voyage in the 'Sunbeam'. With 66 Illustrations. 3s. 6d.

Buckle's (H. T.) History of Civilisation in England. 3 vols. 10s. 6d.

Churchill's (Winston S.) The Story of the Malakand Field Force, 1897. With 6 Maps and Plans. 3s. 6d.

Clodd's (E.) Story of Creation : a Plain Account of Evolution. With 77 Illustrations. 3s. 6d.

Conybeare (Rev. W. J.) and Howson's (Very Rev. J. S.) Life and Epistles of St. Paul. With 46 Illustrations. 3s. 6d.

Dougall's (L.) Beggars All : a Novel. 3s. 6d.

Doyle's (Sir A. Conan) Micah Clarke. A Tale of Monmouth's Rebellion. With 10 Illustrations, 3s. 6d.

Doyle's (Sir A. Conan) The Captain of the Polestar, and other Tales. 3s. 6d.

Doyle's (Sir A. Conan) The Refugees : A Tale of the Huguenots. With 25 Illustrations. 3s. 6d.

Doyle's (Sir A. Conan) The Stark Munro Letters. 3s. 6d.

Froude's (J. A.) The History of England, from the Fall of Wolsey to the Defeat of the Spanish Armada. 12 vols. 3s. 6d. each.

THE SILVER LIBRARY—*continued.*

Froude's (J. A.) The English in Ireland. 3 vols. 10s. 6d.

Froude's (J. A.) The Divorce of Catherine of Aragon. 3s. 6d.

Froude's (J. A.) The Spanish Story of the Armada, and other Essays. 3s. 6d.

Froude's (J. A.) English Seamen in the Sixteenth Century. 3s. 6d.

Froude's (J. A.) Short Studies on Great Subjects. 4 vols. 3s. 6d. each.

Froude's (J. A.) Oceana, or England and Her Colonies. With 9 Illustrations. 3s. 6d.

Froude's (J. A.) The Council of Trent. 3s. 6d.

Froude's (J. A.) The Life and Letters of Erasmus. 3s. 6d.

Froude's (J. A.) Thomas Carlyle : a History of his Life. 1795-1835. 2 vols. 7s. 1834-1881. 2 vols. 7s.

Froude's (J. A.) Cæsar : a Sketch. 3s. 6d.

Froude's (J. A.) The Two Chiefs of Dun= boy : an Irish Romance of the Last Century. 3s. 6d.

Froude's (J. A.) Writings, Selections from. 3s 6d.

Gleig's (Rev. G. R.) Life of the Duke of Wellington. With Portrait. 3s. 6d.

Greville's (C. C. F.) Journal of the Reigns of King George IV., King William IV., and Queen Victoria. 8 vols. 3s. 6d. each.

Haggard's (H. R.) She : A History of Adventure. With 32 Illustrations. 3s. 6d.

Haggard's (H. R.) Allan Quatermain. With 20 Illustrations. 3s. 6d.

Haggard's (H. R.) Colonel Quaritch, V.C.; a Tale of Country Life. With Frontispiece and Vignette. 3s. 6d.

Haggard's (H. R.) Cleopatra. With 29 Illustrations. 3s. 6d.

Haggard's (H. R.) Eric Brighteyes. With 51 Illustrations. 3s. 6d.

Haggard's (H. R.) Beatrice. With Frontispiece and Vignette. 3s. 6d.

Haggard's (H. R.) Black Heart and White Heart. With 33 Illustrations. 3s. 6d.

Haggard's (H. R.) Allan's Wife. With 34 Illustrations. 3s. 6d.

Haggard (H. R.) Heart of the World. With 15 Illustrations. 3s. 6d.

Haggard's (H. R.) Montezuma's Daughter. With 25 Illustrations. 3s. 6d.

Haggard's (H. R.) Swallow : a Tale of the Great Trek. With 8 Illustrations. 3s. 6d.

Haggard's (H. R.) The Witch's Head. With 16 Illustrations. 3s. 6d.

Haggard's (H. R.) Mr. Meeson's Will. With 16 Illustrations. 3s. 6d.

Haggard's (H. R.) Nada the Lily. With 23 Illustrations. 3s. 6d.

Haggard's (H. R.) Dawn. With 16 Illustrations. 3s. 6d.

Haggard's (H. R.) The People of the Mist. With 16 Illustrations. 3s. 6d.

Haggard's (H. R.) Joan Haste. With 20 Illustrations 3s. 6d.

Haggard (H. R.) and Lang's (A.) The World's Desire. With 27 Illustrations. 3s. 6d.

Harte's (Bret) In the Carquinez Woods and other Stories. 3s. 6d.

Helmholtz's (Hermann von) Popular Lectures on Scientific Subjects. With 68 Illustrations. 2 vols. 3s. 6d. each.

Hope's (Anthony) The Heart of Princess Osra. With 9 Illustrations. 3s. 6d.

Howitt's (W.) Visits to Remarkable Places. With 80 Illustrations. 3s. 6d.

Jefferies' (R.) The Story of My Heart : My Autobiography. With Portrait. 3s. 6d.

Jefferies' (R.) Field and Hedgerow. With Portrait. 3s. 6d.

Jefferies' (R.) Red Deer. With 17 Illustrations. 3s. 6d.

Jefferies' (R.) Wood Magic : a Fable. With Frontispiece and Vignette by E. V. B. 3s. 6d.

Jefferies' (R.) The Toilers of the Field. With Portrait from the Bust in Salisbury Cathedral. 3s. 6d.

Kaye (Sir J.) and Malleson's (Colonel) History of the Indian Mutiny of 1857=8. 6 vols. 3s. 6d. each.

Knight's (E. F.) The Cruise of the 'Alerte' : the Narrative of a Search for Treasure on the Desert Island of Trinidad. With 2 Maps and 23 Illustrations. 3s. 6d.

Knight's (E. F.) Where Three Empires Meet : a Narrative of Recent Travel in Kashmir, Western Tibet, Baltistan, Gilgit. With a Map and 54 Illustrations. 3s. 6d.

THE SILVER LIBRARY—*continued.*

Knight's (E. F.) The 'Falcon' on the Baltic: a Coasting Voyage from Hammersmith to Copenhagen in a Three-Ton Yacht. With Map and 11 Illustrations. 3s. 6d.

Kostlin's (J.) Life of Luther. With 62 Illustrations and 4 Facsimiles of MSS. 3s. 6d.

Lang's (A.) Angling Sketches. With 20 Illustrations. 3s. 6d.

Lang's (A.) Custom and Myth: Studies of Early Usage and Belief. 3s. 6d.

Lang's (A.) Cock Lane and Common-Sense. 3s. 6d.

Lang's (A.) The Book of Dreams and Ghosts. 3s. 6d.

Lang's (A.) A Monk of Fife: a Story of the Days of Joan of Arc. With 13 Illustrations. 3s. 6d.

Lang's (A.) Myth, Ritual, and Religion. 2 vols. 7s.

Lees (J. A.) and Clutterbuck's (W. J.) B.C. 1887, A Ramble in British Columbia. With Maps and 75 Illustrations. 3s. 6d.

Levett=Yeats' (S.) The Chevalier D'Auriac. 3s. 6d.

Macaulay's (Lord) Complete Works. 'Albany' Edition. With 12 Portraits. 12 vols. 3s. 6d. each.

Macaulay's (Lord) Essays and Lays of Ancient Rome. etc. With Portrait and 4 Illustrations to the 'Lays'. 3s. 6d.

Macleod's (H. D.) Elements of Banking. 3s. 6d.

Marshman's (J. C.) Memoirs of Sir Henry Havelock. 3s. 6d.

Mason (A. E. W.) and Lang's (A.) Parson Kelly. 3s. 6d.

Merivale's (Dean) History of the Romans under the Empire. 8 vols. 3s. 6d. each.

Merriman's (H. S.) Flotsam: a Tale of the Indian Mutiny. 3s. 6d.

Mill's (J. S.) Political Economy. 3s. 6d.

Mill's (J. S.) System of Logic. 3s. 6d.

Milner's (Geo.) Country Pleasures: the Chronicle of a Year chiefly in a Garden. 3s. 6d.

Nansen's (F.) The First Crossing of Greenland. With 142 Illustrations and a Map. 3s. 6d.

Phillipps=Wolley's (C.) Snap: a Legend of the Lone Mountain. With 13 Illustrations. 3s. 6d.

Proctor's (R. A.) The Orbs Around Us. 3s. 6d.

Proctor's (R. A.) The Expanse of Heaven. 3s. 6d.

Proctor's (R. A.) Light Science for Leisure Hours. 3s. 6d.

Proctor's (R. A.) The Moon. 3s. 6d.

Proctor's (R. A.) Other Worlds than Ours. 3s. 6d.

Proctor's (R. A.) Our Place among Infinities: a Series of Essays contrasting our Little Abode in Space and Time with the Infinities around us. 3s. 6d.

Proctor's (R. A.) Other Suns than Ours. 3s. 6d.

Proctor's (R. A.) Rough Ways made Smooth. 3s. 6d.

Proctor's (R. A.) Pleasant Ways in Science. 3s. 6d.

Proctor's (R. A.) Myths and Marvels of Astronomy. 3s. 6d.

Proctor's (R. A.) Nature Studies. 3s. 6d.

Proctor's (R. A.) Leisure Readings. By R. A. Proctor, Edward Clodd, Andrew Wilson, Thomas Foster, and A. C. Ranyard. With Illustrations. 3s. 6d.

Rossetti's (Maria F.) A Shadow of Dante. 3s. 6d.

Smith's (R. Bosworth) Carthage and the Carthaginians. With Maps, Plans, etc. 3s. 6d.

Stanley's (Bishop) Familiar History of Birds. With 160 Illustrations. 3s. 6d.

Stephen's (Sir Leslie) The Playground of Europe (The Alps). With 4 Illustrations. 3s. 6d.

Stevenson's (R. L.) The Strange Case of Dr. Jekyll and Mr. Hyde; with other Fables. 3s. 6d.

Stevenson (R. L.) and Osbourne's (Ll.) The Wrong Box. 3s. 6d.

Stevenson (Robert Louis) and Stevenson's (Fanny van de Grift) More New Arabian Nights.—The Dynamiter. 3s. 6d.

Trevelyan's (Sir G. O.) The Early History of Charles James Fox. 3s. 6d.

Weyman's (Stanley J.) The House of the Wolf: a Romance. 3s. 6d.

Wood's (Rev. J. G.) Petland Revisited. With 33 Illustrations. 3s. 6d.

Wood's (Rev. J. G.) Strange Dwellings. With 60 Illustrations. 3s. 6d.

Wood's (Rev. J. G.) Out of Doors. With 11 Illustrations. 3s. 6d.

Cookery, Domestic Management, etc.

ACTON. — MODERN COOKERY. By Eliza Acton. With 150 Woodcuts. Fcp. 8vo, 4s. 6d.

ANGWIN.—SIMPLE HINTS ON CHOICE OF FOOD, with Tested and Economical Recipes. For Schools, Homes, and Classes for Technical Instruction. By M. C. Angwin, Diplomate (First Class) of the National Union for the Technical Training of Women, etc. Crown 8vo, 1s.

ASHBY.—HEALTH IN THE NURSERY. By Henry Ashby, M.D., F.R.C.P., Physician to the Manchester Children's Hospital. With 25 Illustrations. Crown 8vo, 3s. net.

BULL (Thomas, M.D.).

HINTS TO MOTHERS ON THE MANAGEMENT OF THEIR HEALTH DURING THE PERIOD OF PREGNANCY. Fcp. 8vo, sewed, 1s. 6d.; cloth, gilt edges, 2s. net.

THE MATERNAL MANAGEMENT OF CHILDREN IN HEALTH AND DISEASE. Fcp. 8vo, sewed, 1s. 6d.; cloth, gilt edges, 2s. net.

DE SALIS (Mrs.).

À LA MODE COOKERY: Up-to-date Recipes. With 24 Plates (16 in Colour). Crown 8vo, 5s. net.

CAKES AND CONFECTIONS À LA MODE. Fcp. 8vo, 1s. 6d.

DOGS: A Manual for Amateurs. Fcp. 8vo, 1s. 6d.

DRESSED GAME AND POULTRY À LA MODE. Fcp. 8vo, 1s. 6d.

DRESSED VEGETABLES À LA MODE. Fcp. 8vo, 1s. 6d.

DRINKS À LA MODE Fcp. 8vo, 1s. 6d.

DE SALIS (Mrs.)—*continued.*

ENTRÉES À LA MODE. Fcp 8vo, 1s. 6d.

FLORAL DECORATIONS. Fcp 8vo, 1s. 6d.

GARDENING À LA MODE. Fcp 8vo, Part I., Vegetables, 1s. 6d. Part II. Fruits, 1s. 6d.

NATIONAL VIANDS À LA MODE Fcp. 8vo, 1s. 6d.

NEW-LAID EGGS. Fcp. 8vo 1s. 6d.

OYSTERS À LA MODE. Fcp 8vo, 1s. 6d.

PUDDINGS AND PASTRY À LA MODE. Fcp. 8vo, 1s. 6d.

SAVOURIES À LA MODE. Fcp. 8vo, 1s. 6d.

SOUPS AND DRESSED FISH À LA MODE. Fcp. 8vo, 1s. 6d.

SWEETS AND SUPPER DISHES À LA MODE. Fcp. 8vo, 1s. 6d.

TEMPTING DISHES FOR SMALL INCOMES. Fcp. 8vo, 1s. 6d.

WRINKLES AND NOTIONS FOR EVERY HOUSEHOLD. Crown 8vo, 1s. 6d.

LEAR.—MAIGRE COOKERY. By H. L. Sidney Lear. 16mo, 2s.

POOLE. — COOKERY FOR THE DIABETIC. By W. H. and Mrs. Poole. With Preface by Dr. Pavy. Fcp. 8vo, 2s. 6d.

ROTHERAM. — HOUSEHOLD COOKERY RECIPES. By M. A. Rotheram, First Class Diplomée, National Training School of Cookery, London ; Instructress to the Bedfordshire County Council. Crown 8vo, 2s.

The Fine Arts and Music.

BURNE-JONES. — THE BEGINNING OF THE WORLD: Twenty-five Pictures by Sir Edward Burne-Jones, Bart. Medium 4to, Boards, 7s. 6d. net.

BURNS AND COLENSO.—LIVING ANATOMY. By Cecil L. Burns, R.B.A., and Robert J. Colenso, M.A., M.D. 40 Plates, 11¼ by 8¾ ins., each Plate containing Two Figures—(a) A Natural Male or Female Figure ; (b) The same Figure Anatomatised. In a Portfolio, 7s. 6d. net.

HAMLIN.—A TEXT-BOOK OF THE HISTORY OF ARCHITECTURE. By A. D. F. Hamlin, A.M. With 229 Illustrations. Crown 8vo, 7s. 6d.

HAWEIS (Rev. H. R.).

MUSIC AND MORALS. With Portrait of the Author. Crown 8vo, 6s. net.

MY MUSICAL LIFE. With Portrait of Richard Wagner and 3 Illustrations. Crown 8vo, 6s. net.

The Fine Arts and Music—continued.

HUISH, HEAD AND LONGMAN. SAMPLERS AND TAPESTRY EMBROIDERIES. By MARCUS B. HUISH, LL.B.: also 'The Stitchery of the same,' by Mrs. HEAD; and 'Foreign Samplers,' by Mrs. C. J. LONGMAN. With 30 Reproductions in Colour, and 40 Illustrations in Monochrome. 4to, £2 2s. net.

HULLAH.—THE HISTORY OF MODERN MUSIC. By JOHN HULLAH. 8vo, 8s. 6d.

JAMESON (Mrs. ANNA).

SACRED AND LEGENDARY ART, containing Legends of the Angels and Archangels, the Evangelists, the Apostles, the Doctors of the Church, St. Mary Magdalene, the Patron Saints, the Martyrs, the Early Bishops, the Hermits, and the Warrior Saints of Christendom, as represented in the Fine Arts. With 19 Etchings and 187 Woodcuts. 2 vols. 8vo, 20s. net.

LEGENDS OF THE MONASTIC ORDERS, as represented in the Fine Arts, comprising the Benedictines and Augustines, and Orders derived from their Rules, the Mendicant Orders, the Jesuits, and the Order of the Visitation of St. Mary. With 11 Etchings and 88 Woodcuts. 1 vol. 8vo, 10s. net.

LEGENDS OF THE MADONNA, OR BLESSED VIRGIN MARY. Devotional with and without the Infant Jesus, Historical from the Annunciation to the Assumption, as represented in Sacred and Legendary Christian Art. With 27 Etchings and 165 Woodcuts. 1 vol. 8vo, 10s. net.

THE HISTORY OF OUR LORD, as exemplified in Works of Art, with that of His Types, St. John the Baptist, and other persons of the Old and New Testament. Commenced by the late Mrs. JAMESON; continued and completed by LADY EASTLAKE. With 31 Etchings and 281 Woodcuts. 2 vols. 8vo, 20s. net.

KRISTELLER.—ANDREA MANTEGNA. By PAUL KRISTELLER. English Edition by S. ARTHUR STRONG, M.A., Librarian to the House of Lords, and at Chatsworth. With 26 Photogravure Plates and 162 Illustrations in the Text. 4to, gilt top, £3 10s. net.

MACFARREN.—LECTURES ON HARMONY. By Sir GEORGE A. MACFARREN. 8vo, 12s.

MATTHAY. — THE ACT OF TOUCH IN ALL ITS DIVERSITY. An Analysis and Synthesis of Pianoforte Tone Production. By TOBIAS MATTHAY, Fellow and Professor of the Royal Academy of Music, London, etc. With 22 Illustrations. 8vo, 7s. 6d.

MORRIS (WILLIAM).

ARCHITECTURE, INDUSTRY AND WEALTH. Collected Papers. Cr. 8vo, 6s. net.

HOPES AND FEARS FOR ART. Five Lectures delivered in Birmingham, London, etc., in 1878-1881. Cr. 8vo, 4s. 6d.

AN ADDRESS DELIVERED AT THE DISTRIBUTION OF PRIZES TO STUDENTS OF THE BIRMINGHAM MUNICIPAL SCHOOL OF ART ON 21ST FEBRUARY, 1894. 8vo, 2s. 0d. net. (Printed in 'Golden' Type.)

SOME HINTS ON PATTERN-DESIGNING: a Lecture delivered at the Working Men's College, London, on 10th December, 1881. 8vo, 2s. 6d. net. (Printed in 'Golden' Type.)

ARTS AND ITS PRODUCERS (1888) AND THE ARTS AND CRAFTS OF TO-DAY (1889). 8vo, 2s. 6d. net. (Printed in 'Golden' Type.)

ARTS AND CRAFTS ESSAYS. By Members of the Arts and Crafts Exhibition Society. With a Preface by WILLIAM MORRIS. Crown 8vo, 2s. 6d. net.

⁎ For Mr. William Morris's other Works, see pp. 24, 27, 28 and 40.

ROBERTSON.—OLD ENGLISH SONGS AND DANCES. Decorated in Colour by W. GRAHAM ROBERTSON. Royal 4to, 42s. net.

SCOTT.—PORTRAITURES OF JULIUS CÆSAR: a Monograph. By FRANK JESUP SCOTT. With 38 Plates and 49 Figures in the Text. Imperial 8vo, 21s. net.

The Fine Arts and Music—*continued*.

VANDERPOEL.—COLOUR PRO-
BLEMS: a Practical Manual for the Lay
Student of Colour. By EMILY NOYES
VANDERPOEL. With 117 Plates in Colour.
Sq. 8vo, 21s. net.

VAN DYKE.—A TEXT-BOOK ON
THE HISTORY OF PAINTING. By
JOHN C. VAN DYKE. With 110 Illustrations.
Crown 8vo, 6s.

WOTTON.—THE ELEMENTS
OF ARCHITECTURE. Collected by
HENRY WOTTON, Kt., from the best Authors
and Examples. Royal 16mo. boards, 10s. 6d.
net.

WELLINGTON.—A DESCRIP-
TIVE AND HISTORICAL CATALOGUE
OF THE COLLECTIONS OF PICTURES
AND SCULPTURE AT APSLEY HOUSE
LONDON. By EVELYN, Duchess of Wel-
lington. Illustrated by 52 Photo-Engravings
specially executed by BRAUN, CLEMENT &
Co., of Paris. 2 vols. Royal 4to, £6 6s. net

WILLARD.—HISTORY OF
MODERN ITALIAN ART. By ASHTON
ROLLINS WILLARD. Part I. Sculpture
Part II. Painting. Part III. Architecture
With Photogravure Front spiece and
numerous full-page Illustrations. 8vo, 21s
net.

Miscellaneous and Critical Works.

AUTO DA FÉ AND OTHER
Essays: some being Essays in Fiction.
By the Author of 'Essays in Paradox' and
'Exploded Ideas'. Crown 8vo, 5s.

BAGEHOT.—LITERARY
STUDIES. By WALTER BAGEHOT. With
Portrait. 3 vols. Crown 8vo, 3s. 6d. each.

BARING-GOULD.—CURIOUS
MYTHS OF THE MIDDLE AGES. By
Rev. S. BARING-GOULD. Crown 8vo, 3s. 6d.

BAYNES.—SHAKESPEARE
STUDIES, and other Essays. By the late
THOMAS SPENCER BAYNES, LL.B., LL.D.
With a Biographical Preface by Professor
LEWIS CAMPBELL. Crown 8vo, 7s. 6d.

BONNELL.—CHARLOTTE
BRONTÉ, GEORGE ELIOT, JANE
AUSTEN: Studies in their Works. By
HENRY H. BONNELL. Crown 8vo, 7s. 6d.
net.

BOOTH.—THE DISCOVERY AND
DECIPHERMENT OF THE TRILING-
UAL CUNEIFORM INSCRIPTIONS. By
ARTHUR JOHN BOOTH, M.A. With a Plan
of Persepolis. 8vo, 14s. net.

CHARITIES REGISTER, THE
ANNUAL, AND DIGEST: being a Classified Register of Charities in or available
in the Metropolis. 8vo, 5s. net.

CHRISTIE.—SELECTED
ESSAYS. By RICHARD COPLEY CHRISTIE,
M.A., Oxon. Hon. LL.D., Vict. With 2 Portraits and 3 other Illustrations. 8vo, 12s.
net.

DICKINSON.—KING ARTHUR
IN CORNWALL. By W. Howship DICKIN-
SON, M.D. With 5 Illustrations. Crown
8vo, 4s. 6d.

ESSAYS IN PARADOX. By the
Author of 'Exploded Ideas' and 'Times and
Days'. Crown 8vo, 5s.

EVANS.—THE ANCIENT STONE
IMPLEMENTS, WEAPONS AND
ORNAMENTS OF GREAT BRITAIN
By Sir JOHN EVANS, K.C.B. With 537 Illus-
trations. 8vo, 10s. 6d. net.

FITZWYGRAM.—HORSES AND
STABLES. By Lieut.-General Sir F. FITZ-
WYGRAM, Bart. With 56 pages of Illustra-
tions. 8vo, 3s. net.

FROST.—A MEDLEY BOOK. By
GEORGE FROST. Crown 8vo, 3s. 6d. net

GEIKIE.—THE VICAR AND HIS
FRIENDS. Reported by CUNNINGHAM
GEIKIE, D.D , LL.D. Crown 8vo, 5s. net.

GILKES.—THE NEW REVOLU-
TION. By A. H. GILKES, Master of Dulwich
College. Fcp. 8vo, 1s. net.

HAGGARD (H. RIDER).

A FARMER'S YEAR: being his
Commonplace Book for 1898. With 36
Illustrations. Crown 8vo, 7s. 6d. net.

RURAL ENGLAND. With 23
Agricultural Maps and 56 Illustrations from
Photographs. 2 vols., 8vo, 36s. net.

HARVEY-BROOKS.—MAR-
RIAGE AND MARRIAGES: Before and
After, for Young and Old. By E. C. HARVEY-
BROOKS. Crown 8vo, 4s. net.

HODGSON.—OUTCAST ESSAYS
AND VERSE TRANSLATIONS. By
SHADWORTH H. HODGSON. Crown 8vo,
8s. 6d.

HOENIG.—INQUIRIES CON-
CERNING THE TACTICS OF THE
FUTURE. By FRITZ HOENIG. With 1
Sketch in the Text and 5 Maps. Translated
by Captain H. M. BOWER. 8vo, 15s. net.

HUTCHINSON.—DREAMS AND
THEIR MEANINGS. By HORACE G.
HUTCHINSON. 8vo, gilt top, 9s. 6d. net.

Miscellaneous and Critical Works—*continued*.

JEFFERIES (RICHARD).

FIELD AND HEDGEROW : With Portrait. Crown 8vo, 3s. 6d.

THE STORY OF MY HEART ; my Autobiography. Crown 8vo, 3s. 6d.

RED DEER. With 17 Illustrations. Crown 8vo, 3s. 6d.

THE TOILERS OF THE FIELD. Crown 8vo, 3s. 6d.

WOOD MAGIC : a Fable. Crown 8vo, 3s. 6d.

JEKYLL (GERTRUDE).

HOME AND GARDEN : Notes and Thoughts, Practical and Critical, of a Worker in both. With 53 Illustrations from Photographs. 8vo, 10s. 6d. net.

WOOD AND GARDEN : Notes and Thoughts, Practical and Critical, of a Working Amateur. With 71 Photographs. 8vo, 10s. 6d. net.

OLD WEST SURREY : Some Recollections. With numerous Illustrations from Photographs by the Author. 8vo.

JOHNSON (J. & J. H.).

THE PATENTEE'S MANUAL : a Treatise on the Law and Practice of Letters Patent. 8vo, 10s. 6d.

AN EPITOME OF THE LAW AND PRACTICE CONNECTED WITH PATENTS FOR INVENTIONS, with a reprint of the Patents Acts of 1883, 1885, 1886 and 1888. Crown 8vo, 2s. 6d.

JOYCE. — THE ORIGIN AND HISTORY OF IRISH NAMES OF PLACES. By P. W. JOYCE, LL.D. 2 vols. Crown 8vo, 5s. each.

LANG (ANDREW).

LETTERS TO DEAD AUTHORS. Fcp. 8vo, 2s. 6d. net.

BOOKS AND BOOKMEN. With 2 Coloured Plates and 17 Illustrations. Fcp. 8vo, 2s. 6d. net.

OLD FRIENDS. Fcp. 8vo, 2s. 6d. net.

LETTERS ON LITERATURE. Fcp. 8vo, 2s. 6d. net.

ESSAYS IN LITTLE. With Portrait of the Author. Crown 8vo, 2s. 6d.

COCK LANE AND COMMON-SENSE. Crown 8vo, 3s. 6d.

THE BOOK OF DREAMS AND GHOSTS. Crown 8vo, 3s. 6d.

MATTHEWS. — NOTES ON SPEECH-MAKING. By BRANDER MATTHEWS Fcp. 8vo, 1s. 6d. net.

MAX MÜLLER (The Right Hon. F.)

COLLECTED WORKS. 20 vols. Vols. I.-XIX. Crown 8vo, 5s. each. Vol. XX., 7s. 6d. net.

Vol. I. NATURAL RELIGION : the Gifford Lectures, 1888.

Vol. II. PHYSICAL RELIGION : the Gifford Lectures, 1890.

Vol. III. ANTHROPOLOGICAL RELIGION : the Gifford Lectures, 1891.

Vol. IV. THEOSOPHY ; or, Psychological Religion : the Gifford Lectures, 1892.

CHIPS FROM A GERMAN WORKSHOP.

Vol. V. Recent Essays and Addresses.

Vol. VI. Biographical Essays.

Vol. VII. Essays on Language and Literature.

Vol. VIII. Essays on Mythology and Folk-lore.

Vol. IX. THE ORIGIN AND GROWTH OF RELIGION, as Illustrated by the Religions of India : the Hibbert Lectures, 1878.

Vol. X. BIOGRAPHIES OF WORDS, AND THE HOME OF THE ARYAS.

Vols. XI., XII. THE SCIENCE OF LANGUAGE : Founded on Lectures delivered at the Royal Institution in 1861 and 1863. 2 vols. 10s.

Vol. XIII. INDIA : What can it Teach Us ?

Vol. XIV. INTRODUCTION TO THE SCIENCE OF RELIGION. Four Lectures, 1870.

Vol. XV. RÂMAKRISHNA : his Life and Sayings.

Vol. XVI. THREE LECTURES ON THE VEDANTA PHILOSOPHY, 1894.

Vol. XVII. LAST ESSAYS. First Series. Essays on Language, Folk-lore, etc.

Vol. XVIII. LAST ESSAYS. Second Series. Essays on the Science of Religion.

Vol. XIX. THE SILESIAN HORSE-HERD (' Das Pferdebürla ') : Questions of the Hour answered by F. MAX MÜLLER. Translated by OSCAR A. FECHTER, Mayor of North Jakima, U.S.A. With a Preface by J. ESTLIN CARPENTER.

*** *This is a translation of a work which was published some years back in Germany, but which is now for the first time translated into English. It consists of a controversy on religion carried on between Professor Max Müller and an unknown correspondent in America.*

Vol. XX. THE SIX SYSTEMS OF INDIAN PHILOSOPHY. Crown 8vo, 7s. 6d. net.

Miscellaneous and Critical Works—*continued.*

MILNER.—COUNTRY PLEAS-URES: the Chronicle of a Year chiefly in a Garden. By GEORGE MILNER. Crown 8vo, 3s. 6d.

MORRIS.—SIGNS OF CHANGE. Seven Lectures delivered on various Occasions. By WILLIAM MORRIS. Post 8vo, 4s. 6d.

PARKER AND UNWIN.—THE ART OF BUILDING A HOME: a Collection of Lectures and Illustrations. By BARRY PARKER and RAYMOND UNWIN. With 68 Full-page Plates. 8vo, 10s. 6d. net.

POLLOCK.—JANE AUSTEN: her Contemporaries and Herself. By WALTER HERRIES POLLOCK. Crown 8vo, 3s. 6d. net.

POORE (GEORGE VIVIAN, M.D.).

ESSAYS ON RURAL HYGIENE. With 13 Illustrations. Crown 8vo, 6s. 6d.

THE DWELLING HOUSE. With 36 Illustrations. Crown 8vo, 3s. 6d.

THE EARTH IN RELATION TO THE PRESERVATION AND DESTRUCTION OF CONTAGIA: being the Milroy Lectures delivered at the Royal College of Physicians in 1899, together with other Papers on Sanitation. With 13 Illustrations. Crown 8vo, 5s.

COLONIAL AND CAMP SANITATION. With 11 Illustrations. Crown 8vo, 2s. net.

ROSSETTI.—A SHADOW OF DANTE: being an Essay towards studying Himself, his World and his Pilgrimage. By MARIA FRANCESCA ROSSETTI. Crown 8vo, 3s. 6d.

SERIA LUDO. By a DILETTANTE. Post 4to, 5s. net.

*** *Sketches and Verses, mainly reprinted from the St. James's Gazette.*

SHADWELL. DRINK: TEMPERANCE AND LEGISLATION. By ARTHUR SHADWELL, M.A., M.D. Crown 8vo, 5s. net.

SOULSBY (LUCY H. M.).

STRAY THOUGHTS ON READING. Fcp. 8vo, cloth, 2s. 6d. net; limp leather, gilt edges, 3s. 6d. net.

STRAY THOUGHTS FOR GIRLS. Fcp. 8vo, cloth, 2s. 6d. net.; limp leather, gilt edges, 3s. 6d. net.

*** *Copies of the Original Edition can still be had.* 16mo, 1s. 6d. net.

STRAY THOUGHTS FOR MOTHERS AND TEACHERS. Fcp. 8vo, cloth, 2s. 6d. net.; limp leather, gilt edges, 3s. 6d. net.

SOULSBY (LUCY H. M.)—*continue*

STRAY THOUGHTS ON CHARACTER. Fcp. 8vo, cloth, 2s. 6d. net. limp leather, gilt edges, 3s. 6d. net.

STRAY THOUGHTS FOR INVALIDS. 16mo, 2s. net.

SOUTHEY.—THE CORRESPONDENCE OF ROBERT SOUTHEY WITH CAROLINE BOWLES. Edited by EDWARD DOWDEN. 8vo, 14s.

STEVENS.—ON THE STOWAGE OF SHIPS AND THEIR CARGOES. With Information regarding Freights, Charter-Parties, etc. By ROBERT WHITE STEVENS. 8vo, 21s.

THUILLIER.—THE PRINCIPLES OF LAND DEFENCE, AND THEIR APPLICATION TO THE CONDITIONS OF TO-DAY. By Captain H. F. THUILLIER, R.E. With Maps and Plans. 8vo, 12s. 6d. net.

TURNER AND SUTHERLAND.—THE DEVELOPMENT OF AUSTRALIAN LITERATURE. By HENRY GYLES TURNER and ALEXANDER SUTHERLAND. With Portraits and Illustrations. Crown 8vo, 5s.

WARD. PROBLEMS AND PERSONS. By WILFRID WARD, Author of 'The Life and Times of Cardinal Wiseman,' &c. 8vo, 14s. net.

CONTENTS.—The Time-Spirit of the Nineteenth Century—The Rigidity of Rome—Unchanging Dogma and Changeful Man—Balfour' 'The Foundations of Belief'—Candour in Biography—Tennyson—Thomas Henry Huxley—Two Mottoes of Cardinal Newman—Newman and Rnéan—Some Aspects of the Life-work of Cardinal Wiseman—The Life of Mrs. Augustus Craven.

WEATHERS.—A PRACTICAL GUIDE TO GARDEN PLANTS. By JOHN WEATHERS, F.R.H.S. With 159 Diagrams. 8vo, 21s. net.

WINSTON.—MEMOIRS OF A CHILD. By ANNIE STEGER WINSTON. Fcp. 8vo, 2s. 6d. net.

Contents.—I. The Child and the Child's Earth—II. People.—III. The Garden and a few Related Things.—IV. Divers Delights.—V. The Child and 'The Creatures'.—VI. Playthings.—VII. Portable Property.—VIII. Pomps and Vanities.—IX. Social Divertisements.—X. Conduct and Kindred Matters.—XI. Dreams and Reveries.—XII. Bugbears.—XIII. Handicraft—XIV. School, Slightly Considered.—XV. Books.—XVI. Language.—XVII. Random Reflections.—Conclusion.

25,000—2/04.